LEFT or RIGH

Impressions of Sussex on Foot

By
Graham Pollard

All the best
from
Graham
Pollard

Published by LR Publishing

This edition published in 2007
By LR Publishing

ISBN 978-0-9555919-0-7

A CIP catalogue record for this title
is available from the British Library

Paperback ISBN 978-0-9555919-0-7

Typeset Times New Roman 11 by author
Printed and Bound by www.printondemand-worldwide.com, Peterborough
Published by LR Publishing, 4 Rockall Drive Hailsham East Sussex BN27 3BG

PREFACE

Many, many years ago, whilst still a pupil of Hailsham Senior School, later called Comprehensive School, and when we got really posh it was later called Community College, I was forced to read a book called 'Tarka the Otter', written by 'Somebody or other' Williamson. I hated it with a vengeance. It was about, yes; you've guessed an Otter called Tarka. We were made to read extracts from it in front of the class, we were asked questions about it and we were asked to interpret, in writing, whole chapters, in our own words, what it would be like to have been that otter. For a year I lived and breathed that damned otter. The whole experience could have maimed me for life or, at the very least, made me never to want to read a book again.

And I didn't, for ages until... a friend, Phil, brought me a book called 'The Ragged Trousered Philanthropist' by Robert Tressell which is a fascinating story based in a place called Mugsborough, (thought now to be Hastings, East Sussex) in the early 1900's. I have now read that book twice and found a new fascination with the written word. Now I buy mainly macabre crime books, by authors such as Cornwell, Kellerman, Reichs etc. but am always open to suggestions of new authors. Again it was Phil who first introduced me to Hilaire Belloc, a prolific author from Sussex who became a legend with his writings. The book that Phil suggested I read was 'The Four Men' which was about; you have got it again, four men. Three were fictitious, but 'they' meet in a pub and decided, for some reason, to walk across Sussex and jot down the route and what was discussed. It is another insight into country life in the early 1900's.

This got me thinking. I know very little about my local surroundings. I have lived in Hailsham, East Sussex, most of my life, apart from a brief spell in Eastbourne shortly after my marriage to Emelia. I pass 'Public Footpath' signs whilst driving my car every day but have never walked one. I am ignorant of country matters. Yet I live in a county which has some the most beautiful countryside in England. I am now semi retired. I am now over weight. I now have time to go for a walk, and to see, and to learn. I also have a very good friend, Ron, who is a real Sussex countryman, himself semi retired. He is a very keen walker and we have agreed to do what Hilaire Belloc did all those years ago. Not to walk across Sussex but to walk around the County, both east and west, following planned walks, and putting pen to paper. We have completed one walk, every week, for a year, sampling the atmosphere, finding out facts, meeting new people and enjoying the scenery and the hospitality of various towns and villages on our routes. We hope that the following pages give you a glimpse of what Sussex is all about. Hilaire wrote his words in the early 1900's. I hope my words; written in these pages over 100 years later will encourage others to realise that all books don't have to be like 'Tarka the Otter'.

G. Pollard

ACKNOWLEDGEMENTS

Throughout the year of walking for this book both Ron and I have met, discussed with, argued with and been fascinated as well as frustrated by, many people. Should we forget anyone person then we humbly apologise and can honestly say that it is an oversight on my part and nothing else? I have not put the names in any order.

So, thanks must go to Sophie (but it's my job!) and Lyn for all there suggestions on punctuation and grammar. Beverley, the now ex-landlady of The Kings Head, for keeping us under control, to Des (he who knows everything about everything) whose stories and anecdotes about country life and people were both fascinating and enlightening, to Sean (who sadly passed away before the book was completed), Tim and Gordon for the books, maps and suggestions, Wibbs for advice on what to look for, Mogs and Debbie for being themselves and seeing the funny side of most things. To Derek for his wisdom on the area and its characters, and Arthur, for all his encouragement, and insistence, that he wouldn't read a single page until completion. Without all of your advice, reasoning, argument and patience, during some periods, these jottings would not have been completed.

Should any one go into the Kings Head, South Road, Hailsham during any evening it will be possible that at least one of these people will be at the bar having a well earned drink and served by our new innkeepers, Helen and Darren. But without all of them this book would not be the same. I must also mention Ellen and Halle, two of the girls I transport to and from school who, on my Birthday, very thoughtfully gave me a book on Ghost walks in Sussex which has been used on a couple of the walks in the following pages.

I, personally, would like to thank Ron. His sense of humour, wit and, above all his knowledge of all things country has been an inspiration to me. Also in need of our thanks are the people that Ron and I have met, whilst on our walks, whose names we do not know, but who have added that certain something to the tales that follow within these pages.

Finally, our thanks must also go to the writers of the books we have consulted, which have, on most occasions directed us on our walks, and are noted, in the respective chapters. But please be aware that changes can happen overnight and whilst these writings and observations of our beautiful county are correct at the time of writing, both Ron and I can take no responsibility or blame for any alterations to routes or enforced diversions that are put, or have been put, in place since the publication of the book.

This work is dedicated to my family,
whose help and support throughout
the year made the completion possible.
To my children, Michelle and Anthony,
thank you for pushing
To my wife Emelia,
thank you for not pulling.
I love you all dearly.

CONTENTS

WALK 1- Arlington Reservoir

Wednesday 25th January 2006

My memory isn't so good. I'm sure my old friend and walking partner Ron is expecting me to pick him up, in my car, from his house when it suddenly occurs to me that I should be collecting him from The Kings Head Inn, Cacklebury. Our local drinking establishment, for far more years than I can remember. Yes, that's where I find him, downing his favourite pint of Harvey's Best Bitter as he slips his coat on and we're soon on our way for my first walk in many years. This is a start of a fitter me!

We arrive at the car park of Arlington Reservoir in good time to find out that we have to pay (£2) and it closes in one hour forty-five minutes. The leaflet[1] advises us that this walk is three miles and will take one hour thirty minutes to complete. I suggested to Ron that as we were not professionals this walk could take longer than that and we would not get back in time. But Ron insists that this walk would be no trouble – 'put the money in the dam machine and lets get started.'

The Reservoir is a manmade area covering 120 acres of land. Construction started in 1971 and thirty years later (2001) Bill Oddie, the television wildlife 'expert', opened part of a new pathway called 'The Osprey Nature Trail' which is now very popular with bird watchers. The Reservoir has been designated as a Site of Specific Scientific Interest and a Local Nature Reserve[2].

The leaflet tells us to head for the information boards in the Reservoir grounds and to turn right were we would find the bridleway. We then have to go between some trees and look for a lane. This was easy. If all the instructions in the guidebook were this accurate this walk would be a piece of cake. The lane appeared to be no wider than a wide footpath and to the left was another track with a sign which said 'Fishermen only' on the post. Ron thought that we had to walk along the wide path as our leaflet advised us that the lane was tarmac and the Reservoir would soon come into view. After about 100 yards doubt started to overcome us and we both decided to walk back to the start, as no Reservoir was coming into view. Just as we reached the line of trees a vehicle turned into the lane. On the side of the Land Rover was the legend 'Polhills Farm'. Looking at our map in the guidebook the lane we were standing on leads to Polhills Farm. We were heading in the right direction initially so we started off again.

Kissing Gate

At the entrance to Polhills Farm we are instructed to turn right and traverse the farm buildings by following the signs along the path. Polhills Farm is a large whitewashed building and appears very old, lots of small lead light windows. Ron said that he wouldn't like to live there – too expensive to keep warm in winter but more importantly for Ron not a pub in sight. The path was well used and had become very muddy and slippery after many weeks of damp, dull weather. What appeared to be empty chicken runs are on the right of us but conversation is very limited as we struggle to keep our balance. Ron insists that he is going to purchase proper walking boots before we go out next week.

St Pancras Church

We eventually arrive at a 'kissing gate'. I had some ideas what this could be but my ideas were dashed when Ron explained that it was called a Kissing

[1] *Arlington Reservoir Walk* Route 26 – www.eastsussex.gov.uk - downloaded from site 08/01/2006
[2] South East Water (*Arlington Reservoir*) viewed 23/01/2006
www.southeastwater.co.uk/arlington

Gate because the gate kisses both posts when someone passes through. He believes a Sussex man, whose wife had problems getting over stiles, invented the gate. When I got home I looked up kissing gate on the Internet[3] and I have found evidence that this type of gate is used on land to prevent animals from wandering from one field to the next and take many different guises.

Interested onlookers

The walk now takes us over a number of fields that are much used by the farm animals. Sheep and cattle wander across the pastures and don't appear bothered that we are walking past them. The guidebook advises us to keep the Reservoir bank to our left and cross pastures until we reach the main road. The instructions are very concise and we eventually reach a small road. The road is very narrow and sees very little traffic. We turn left onto the road and head towards a metal bridge that carries this road over the River Cuckmere. If you stand on this bridge 'and rest awhile' the Reservoir water can be heard in the distance. The feeling is quite eerie. To continue we have to turn left after the bridge and we are now on part of the Weald Way and we must follow a sign for Arlington. As we walk along the drive the reservoir is on our left. Shortly before some houses we veer left over yet another stile. The ground underfoot is very muddy and waterlogged. Ron, still in his best brogues (now smothered in dirt) swears he's going to buy some walking boots before our next outing. The reason for the poor conditions underfoot is made evident when we cross the next field. Some young cattle are grazing and wallowing in mud up to their knees, their coats are matted and it looks as if they've been lying in the mud. In the far corner of this field is a small wooden bridge that leads us into another field as we head towards the church. The spire of Arlington church can be easily seen from here. I explained to Ron that some time ago I was doing some research for an Australian family that involved a visit to the church at Arlington[4] (The Church of St Pancras). I was very disappointed at the condition of the grounds. The churchyard was very unkempt and overgrown with nettles and thistles. Some of the monuments were impossible to get too, let alone read, due to this overgrowth. I remember visiting the church once with my daughter, who didn't know Arlington was a village; she thought it was just a Speedway Track. On entering the church building we found it to be incredibly cold. In every spare space you looked there was a portable gas heater that was presumably used to warm the place up for Sunday Services. On the Notice Board there was a list of parishioners whose turn it was to make refreshments for the Services and a rota for maintenance. All the names were female. Ron suggested that one reason could be that all the Sussex women were a lot hardier than the men-folk, or of course, it could be a sign of the times when a small local church such as Arlington are having difficulty in finding a following in this modern day society. Who knows? But as I say, on my last visit to the church I was not impressed with the maintenance but have to admit that being inside it certainly made me feel humble. Or is humble the wrong word?

My first memory of Arlington was a man named Mr Keylock. Many years ago I used to repair televisions and Mr Keylock was one of my customers. I'm going back to the 'good old days' when valves were used in televisions. Mr Keylock lived in a place called Gamekeepers Cottage. He originally came from Somerset where, I'm told by Des, back at the Kings Head, he was a 'chip chaser'. This meant he drove a steamroller. His accent was strange to me and I was told that as he lived on his own he was not used to company so he sometimes mumbled or made words up, which never made it easy to understand what he was saying. But whenever his television broke down it was always the same thing – 'the lights had gone out'. He was always at home when you called, always had a glass of home-made ginger beer for you,

[3] *Kissing Gates* - www.handbooks.btcv.org.uk/kissinggate - viewed 26/01/2006
[4] '*A Visit to Arlington Church*' conducted by Col. F H Foster – Leaflet from church – price 30p

2

which tasted vile, but there was always a home made mint to suck on which took the taste of the ginger beer away. It took longer to get away from Mr Keylock than it did to repair his television but he is always fondly remembered. Again, as stories go, when he brought Gamekeepers Cottage there was a large wood backing on to his garden and Mr Keylock, being a keen gardener, used to cut down some of these trees and extend his garden every year. Just round the corner from his cottage was Bates Green Farm. We always got our fresh Christmas Turkey from there, but back to our walk.

River Cuckmere

Once through the gate, by the church, the guidebook tells us that the building on the right used to be the Old School. We could see very little evidence of a school. The houses led us up the lane to the Yew Tree Inn, famous for its food, as are most pubs of today. Unfortunately I am conscious of the time and practically had to drag Ron from the door to make sure we got back to the car park on time.

We called in to the churchyard and I was very surprised at the improvements made since my last visit. The nettles and thistles had been removed and the place looked so much better for the work carried out. The first monument I find is that of Mr. George Walter Keylock. He died on 4th February 1984 aged 86 years and was buried with his wife, Dorothy Mabel[5], who died on 9th July 1962 aged 62. Until this day I never knew that he was married. It took me some time to drag myself away from the monument. Such were my memories of this lovely old man. When we eventually left the church we exit through the gate at the other end of the churchyard and retrace our way a few yards back to the small wooden bridge when the book advises us to turn right. We then walk across a pasture to a footbridge, which crosses the River Cuckmere again. The view from this bridge, with the sunlight streaming through the clouds is something else. Both Ron and I just stood for a few moments taking it all in. The fact that it was so still, so unpolluted and quiet made it feel that we were miles away from civilisation. Ron thought that the reason it was clean and tidy and not polluted was that it was too far away from civilisation for the '….bastards to come out here and drop litter'. He could be right. In the distance Ron can see some joggers. I vaguely make out some movement on the horizon but my eyes are about as good as my memory.

We are instructed to walk along a vague path and head towards a line of trees where we go through a galvanised gate and turn right towards another kissing gate. At the kissing gate are the joggers that Ron had already seen. As they were young and female it is obvious why Ron saw them. The girls are from St. Bedes School and are out on a Cross Country run. We

Arlington Reservoir

walk along the track to be overtaken by the joggers who all, very politely shouted 'excuse me' before going past. Ron suggested that the young ladies were 'a different breed of female to what we were used to'; the youngsters from town wouldn't be half as polite. These girls were obviously 'brought up proper'. I must say they looked good too. It must be my age.

All along this track we can see work being carried out on the hedgerows. Ron explained that it was layering when the branches of the hedge are entwined with each other and is a living hedge. The strength of the hedge is astonishing and, of course, allows the wild birds to nest in during the mating season. The actual 'hedge' was extremely neat and tidy and is obviously the work of a craftsman. Unfortunately I was so impressed with the workmanship I didn't get any photos.

---

[5] Mr Keylock always referred to his wife as Dot – from memory of Des

As we continue the walk, on the left is a bird hide. This is the area that was opened by Bill Oddie in 2001. As time was against us we decided that on a return visit it will be possible to have a closer look. But what greeted me next was the expanse of the reservoir. I really had no idea how large this place was. I had to take photos and, as you can see, the light was poor with the sun setting in front of us, which has made the pictures a little dark, but I think the reader can see how large the area is. We are told that the water level is low and we must expect water shortages during the coming summer of 2006 but to look at this vast expanse of water it is difficult to imagine why. But, as Ron pointed out, the high water level is three feet above the current water level and with little to no rain throughout January that three feet over the whole area must be thousands of gallons of water. Information boards advise us that from readings of water levels taken the week before our walk the reservoir is only 82% full. But it was the overall size of the area that made my chin hit the floor. The area is so well-kept. The birds that frequent the reservoir are in abundance and, during the summer months fishing and water sports go hand in hand with each other. I must come again, during the warmer weather and see the reservoir in its full glory.

We managed to get back to the car with ten minutes to spare before the car park closure time and the whole experience of the walk was a joy. Ron was great company and, in his own way made the walk more enjoyable with his comments, tales and explanations. I considered myself a country boy, but today has opened my eyes to what the countryside is about.

It's our first walk of, hopefully, many and I look forward to the next. Now it is time to get home, to a hot bath and a rub down with the Sporting Life. My legs are aching like mad.

Some things to remember for the next walk are – go with plenty of time, make sure photographs are taken and, most of all, take notes. It's surprising the things you see and forget about as well as the things that are said. Just to write this chapter I have had to return to the area and perform research on things that I saw and witnessed at the time but didn't take notes. A valuable lesson learnt I think.

Night time approaches

WALK 2-Snake River

Wednesday 1ˢᵗ February 2006

& Completed Wed 7ᵗʰ February 2006

Today is the first anniversary of my mother's sudden death[6]. I am determined that it will not affect me. My wife and I placed flowers at the crematorium yesterday, and tears have been shed. My mother is always in my thoughts, but I must come to terms with our loss, and need to progress.

A nice brisk walk along Snake River[7] and back will blow the cobwebs away. The car park fee is again £2.00 for the day and we start at the entrance to the walk. It was decided on the way to the car park that we would attempt the smaller of the two walks, being only 3 miles. The longer walk is attractive[8] (5¾ miles) but time is not on our side and getting home in daylight is one of our objectives. Perhaps on another occasion we will do the 5¾-mile walk. Within the car park there is a school bus laden with youngsters. A couple of teachers are outside counting Wellington boots to make sure all the children were on board. It must be

Man-made stream

great fun, as well as a learning objective, to permit small children to be in such areas. The view, as soon as you leave the car park is beautiful. Along the left are mounds that are dotted with rabbit holes. While to our right meanders Snake River, which is basically the overflow of the River Cuckmere. Ron explains that consideration was being given to flood the area we are now walking on. The object is to reduce the possibility of flooding further up river, around Lewes[9]. Unfortunately this would mean a considerable loss of wildlife habitat as well as some historical buildings further along the walk. [10]Local opposition to the plan is overwhelming and for the moment plans to flood have been blocked. Only time will tell if the planners get their own way.

Water erosion

I must admit that for the amount of years that I have passed this area heading toward Eastbourne and looking down on the river I had thought, all this time, that what I was looking at was the River Cuckmere. Little did I know that what I was looking at was a man-made waterway to help with the flow of the Cuckmere? In this area the man-made Cuckmere runs in a straight line from the bridge near the Golden Galleon Pub to the sea. Ron explains that at high tide water overflows into the old Cuckmere and the water is directed back to the man-made Cuckmere, at low tide, and then flows back towards the sea. Due to the movement of the water and the construction of the waterway (in the shape of a snake) the outer walls of the 'river' are being eroded all the time. If you stand close to one of these bends in the river the erosion is very obvious. As we are walking along the riverbank the water is very still and I'm amazed at how clear it is. The bottom can be seen very clearly but Ron says that although it doesn't look very deep at the outer edge it is considerably deeper towards the middle. The water is commonly used for

---

[6] My mum, Joan Rosemary Pollard (nee Churcher) died 1ˢᵗ February 2005
[7] A local name given to the overflow of the River Cuckmere at an area called Seven Sisters
[8] '50 Walks in Sussex' – AA Publishing – Reprint 2003- ISBN 0749528761 – Page 38
[9] Torrential rain caused flooding in 2000
[10] www.eastsussex.gov.uk/Lewes visited 1st February 2006

canoeists during the summer months. It is at this moment that I am aware of someone behind us and I turn round to see, on the path in the distance, a fellow male walker, dressed in customary fashion complete with walking boots and walking stick and he is not on his own. But a young lady accompanies him with mini skirt, black fur coat and knee length black high-heeled boots. "Not the sort of fashion you expect to find on a ramble" I suggest to Ron who practically fell over himself when he saw what I was looking at. Ron thought that, in the interest of being friendly, we should slow down and say hello. But before we could do or say anything the couple must have got a spurt on because they were suddenly past us and heading off in the distance. I tried to get a photo but as luck would have it the camera packed up.

Is it a joke?

It is now that our instructions advise us to pass a sign for Foxhole Campsite and head through a gate towards the beach. It is very noticeable here that the amount of sheep droppings has increased dramatically. I suggested to Ron that this might be due to the sheep sheltering from the vicious east wind. To my surprise Ron thought I was correct and told me that I had started

Pill Box

to think like a country boy at last. Further along the trail we arrive at another gate with a sign that could only be placed by a council official. The steps were practically vertical and we are advised not to cycle. Going up or down those steps on a cycle could be painful. Ron was glad we hadn't brought cycles because he thought we would have to try it out?

We follow the sign towards the beach and approach a couple of WW II pillboxes that remind us of less peaceful times. The area used to house other buildings and we can only guess that they may have been storehouses, toilets or billets for the men who used to man these pillboxes. The whole area is so open to the elements. Whilst I could appreciate the fear of invasion from enemy forces the thought of having to be out here in the middle of nowhere, at night, in all weathers, fearing what might come over the hill was impossible for me to comprehend. But as Ron said, in his matter of fact way, "I'd rather be in one o' them boxes than on the Somme". The boxes are easily accessible and I had to get inside one to find out what sort of view could be had. The impression, from the outside is that your view is restricted but that is so far from the truth. The view is really panoramic. The reason you cannot see anything to the left is simply that the Severn Sisters are located there. But you can see from the pictures that anything coming over the beach as well as up the river would be seen (and presumably shot at?) But while I was in the box the claustrophobic feeling was overwhelming. The boxes are so small, cold and uncomfortably damp. I couldn't imagine having to remain in one for too long during the night, not knowing what to expect, but they are part of our history and heritage. Ron explains that more sea defences can be seen further

Panoramic view

round on our walk. So we leave the boxes and head towards the beach.

White Chalky Cliffs

Through a gate we come across a life belt station. This is positioned some way from the beach and Ron wonders how long the little piece of blue string attached to the life belt is. It only measures a few feet. We wonder if anyone has had the misfortune to need to use it. But just further onto the beach the views are astounding. To the left of us are the chalk cliffs with the chalk looking so clean against the blue sky. Apart from some workers to the right of us we are the only people on this beach and apart from the wash of the sea the calmness of the area takes your breath away. The constant battle to keep the flow of the River Cuckmere alive by dragging the beach from the waters edge to the top of the beach again is a full time job employing the digger and three lorries who are always working with the tide. Unfortunately the beach is a little untidy with rubbish, tin cans and, regrettably, signs of drug use scattered about. As soon as I spotted the litter I knew that it wouldn't be long before Ron would have to say something.

Unspoilt beach?

As he rightly points out "we have over a million people sitting on their arses, not working, and getting paid for the privilege. Why can't they clean up our countryside? All they need is to be told they've got 10 square feet of land to keep clean and they don't get a penny in dole money until it's done. Not only does our countryside get tidy but gives the lazy ones something to do". Since returning from the walk and discussing the subject with other people it is surprising how many agree with his feelings. In fact not one person disagreed. One person thought that it wouldn't happen because it would be against the 'human rights' of the unemployed. Where have we heard that excuse before? Anyway Ron is now thinking of bringing a metal detector down to the beach with him next time. Apparently he's not against people dropping litter if he can find it and its worth something. Is that what you call double standards?

More Sea Defences

At the end of the beach we approach the Cuckmere Haven and are instructed to look for an emergency point sign. This sign also houses a life belt with the required small length of blue string (?) Just beyond this sign can be seen the next line of sea defences to stop any enemy tanks landing on this part of the coastline. Large concrete pointed pillars are placed in the ground from the Cuckmere to Snake River. We now follow the River Cuckmere, to our left, and head towards a kissing gate on the 'Habitat Trail'. From here the path is practically a straight line following the River towards the A259 and the pub called the Golden Galleon.

Along the narrow walk we come across a post[11] and Ron has no idea why or what it depicts. Various ideas have been suggested what the post represents, ranging from high water level, distance to waters edge, distance to outfall, amongst others but we are unable to find out

---

[11] Many thoughts have been put to us but nothing conclusive – possibly length marker?

the exact reason for the post. As you can see it is a fair way from the water's edge so can anyone explain the reason for this post (there are no others along this stretch of the water)?

Unfortunately, along this small trail we also start to talk about the current trend for political and religious sections of our country that make statements against the country that has welcomed them and given them shelter. Needless to say now is not the place to air our views but it must be said that our views are echoed by a number of our friends who cannot understand how our Government can permit these things to happen. Again 'human rights' was mentioned. But both Ron and I realise that as the years go by we are becoming increasingly more pro-British and wonder in what direction our country is heading?

What is it for?

Meanwhile, towards the end of our walk we come to the area where the overflow of water is returned back to the Cuckmere at low tide and where the country walk meets the road. As we head along the road, back towards the car park it is noticeable how close you are to, not only the traffic heading towards you on our left but also how steep the bank down to the river is on our right. "Not the place to be walking at night after a few jars in the pub" say Ron. I wonder how many people have fallen, if any. There seems to be a number of gaps in the flimsy hedge and no warning signs of danger.

On the way round our walk Ron has collected some rubbish and, back at the car park, we can't find a rubbish bin. "They probably remove them to ensure that undesirable elements can't 'plant' things in them," suggests Ron.

I enjoyed this walk very much. A combination of nature mixed with some history. I enjoyed it so much that I brought my wife here at the weekend and it was packed. We couldn't find a parking space so didn't stop. But it does prove what a popular area this is at weekends. So if you enjoy a quiet walk don't go on a Saturday or Sunday.

WALK 3 – Pevensey

Wednesday 14th February 2006

During the past week, since our last walk, it was decided that Ron and me would like to attempt a slightly longer walk. The days are getting a little longer but not only that the only walk left to do close to Hailsham is 5 miles long. The starting place for the walk is the Car Park at Pevensey Castle. Again I pick Ron up at our favourite watering establishment. Throughout the previous night the rain did not stop. At times it woke me up as it hit the windows at home. I noticed that Ron was still wearing his best brogues. I asked if he had managed to get some walking boots. "I've tried all over Hailsham to get a pair of size nines", says Ron. "Would you believe it 'They're too popular' say's the girl in the shop. If they were that popular why didn't they get more in?" asks Ron. "I can get size seven or size eight, lots of size tens and elevens; I can even get size twelve but not a single size nine in Hailsham. The girl even asked me if I was sure I was a size nine. I said to her 'I'm 61 years old I should know what bloody size boot I take! Damn cheek". To prove his point Ron has carried out a detailed survey within our favourite watering establishment and of all the locals at the bar that evening they both wore size nines. Apparently this proves Ron's point! Anyway the previous night's rainfall hasn't dampened our enthusiasm.

Whilst driving to Pevensey we discuss the latest political suggestion to come from our esteemed government, which is to ban smoking in all public places. Being a smoker Ron can picture his local pub closing down and being that I'm a non-smoker I really have no comment other than to wonder how it can be enforced. Since packing up smoking I have tried to be unbiased about the subject. Both my children do not smoke but my wife does. I'm pleased that my children do not smoke but I also do not complain about my wife's habit. After all it is a habit that <u>can</u> kill and is very difficult to break, I know. But taking drugs is also a habit that

Dredged River Bank

does kill but we supply drug takers, who inject their lethal doses, with free needles so that the addict can continue with the habit and not share needles? Does this make sense to you?

Let's return to the walk. We arrive at Pevensey Castle to find, strategically parked in the car park are some who prefer to be called 'travellers'. This starts Ron off on a completely new area of moaning. "Just count the wheels when we get back to the car" I say to Ron as I try to find the pay and display machine. Our luck is in today. The car park is free until Easter. At last we have a result. Our guidebook[12] tells us to walk on the pavement between the castle walls and the Priory Court Hotel heading towards the 1066 walk. This is where we must turn right, into a narrow lane between houses and head into the open countryside. Because of the heavy rain the ground is very stodgy and slippery as we head towards the main Eastbourne to Hastings Road (A27). The noise of traffic is very evident here as the road is constantly used by fast moving vehicles. When you get to the road it's a case of look left and right, head down and go for it! The road is straight for about a mile and a half and cars, as well as lorries, get a fair speed up along this stretch. Once over the other side we go through a gate and continue along a path keeping what is known as 'Martins Ditch' to our left. We believe that this ditch is named after the digger Martin Holmes and not Martin McGinty who we first joked about. Anyone who used our local pub over the past years will recognise the name, Martin McGinty, as the affable Irishman who always had a new

---

[12] '50 Walks in Sussex' Walk 11 Page 32 – AA Publishing

invention for something or other everyday. But we think that this ditch was named after a local farmer who dug across the Pevensey levels to ensure that the birdlife in the area were being looked after.

Once we leave the ditch we head for the area where Chilley Stream and the Pevensey Haven meet. The whole area is currently being dredged and the mud piled on the left-hand riverbank. We're not sure of the exact reason for depositing the soil so far away from the river but it is the same the whole length of our walk. We head towards a wooden bridge that takes us over the Pevensey Haven and we now head across open countryside towards Chilley Farm. As we walk across these very muddy fields Ron suddenly stops and says "you could have the

biggest most beautiful diamond in your hand right now and it could be priceless. Just look at this view. Priceless. And so would be a pair of bloody boots right now!" His shoes were caked with mud. But we battled on. We reached Chilley Farm and I remembered, when I worked for Royal Mail, we needed to make savings (nothing changes) and we needed to change the large van used by the regular postie (Snowy Ruffell) to a smaller more compact model. Snowy refused saying that with a large van he can see over the fences to see what's heading towards him and other drivers can see him coming. To prove his point he invited me to be

Wooden Footbridge

with him on his delivery. One of his breakfast stops was Chilley Farm. The then owners, Mr & Mrs Plumley, used to give Snowy his breakfast. He had warned them that I would be with him on this particular morning and they had laid out a breakfast for me. It was enormous. Served on a platter it consisted of sausages, bacon, eggs, mushrooms, fried bread and baked beans. That was the first course. After this I was expected to have cereal. When my hosts' sons arrived for their breakfast they were enormous too. Big strapping lads, over six feet tall, who persuaded me to let Snowy keep his large van. The farm has changed somewhat. The farmhouse is the same but some of the barns have been converted into a farm shop selling home grown produce.

On leaving Chilley Farm we turn left onto the road. We walk a short distance, cleaning our shoes as we go, until the

Dog friendly stile

road bears right as we bear left back into fields and we now head towards Rickney. Ron has decided that enough is enough and insists on putting on his Sussex Wellingtons, which consist

of two supermarket carrier bags. He's actually brought three bags with him because, being a conservationist, when the two he's wearing get dirty he needs the third to put them in and take home. Always prepared?? One of the simple things that I noticed on this particular walk was the stile we go over to get to the next field. They all seem to have this extra width to them with a handle at the top. Again, Ron comes to the rescue. "If your out for a walk with your dog, rather than lift it over the stile you pull the handle up, which raises the sides of the stile, the dog walks through and you release the handle which closes the stile". A very simple yet very effective devise. All the stiles on this walk look as if they have been replaced recently or have been very well maintained. Of course it could be that they are not used too much.

Back on a road towards Rickney I recognise an area of the Pevensey Haven that, when I was a young boy, I used to fish. I

Sussex Wellies

Inlet to the overflow

used to ride my bike down to this river, slide down the edge of the road onto the bank and fish for many wonderful hours. Due to the high rainfall the river level is very high and I was surprised to see that there was no bank to sit on and although the water looked relatively still you could hear running water from upstream. Ron says that he has caught some really good pike from this river. As we turn a corner onto Rickney Bridge he explains that he once caught a pike from this bridge that was so large the tail dragged along the ground as he carried it on his bike. Is that a fisherman's story??

We turn left again here and head back towards the castle. Now we have to keep the Pevensey Haven on our left and simply follow it all the way back to the A27. Ron sees some Plovers on the wing and becomes very excited. Apparently he hasn't seen some of these birds for ages and wished he had some binoculars that had been promised from a previous walk so that he could see them more clearly. I make a note for next time.

As we again approach Martins Ditch we notice a distinct gurgle sound and find that, as with Snake River (previous Walk) there is a need to release any overflow of water to ensure the levels don't flood. To do this a pipe is inserted vertically in the ground and cut off at just below the high water level. The other end of the pipe is then directed, underground, towards the river. When the water rises above the high level it disappears into the pipe and is fed to the river. Martin McGinty would have been proud of an invention like that!! Again it's the simple ideas that are so effective.

Outlet from overflow to river

From here we again head for the A27, risk life and limb to get to the other side and make our way back to the car. All in all, the entire walk is a long 5 miles. Not made particularly easy with the abundance of mud. I have to say that it was a little boring. Yes, some memories came flooding back but it is called a Norman Walk in the book and as Ron said "Didn't see a single Norman, Edward or Fred", in fact we saw no one at all apart from one fisherman in the distance. The scenery, as ever, was stunning, but...........

Still, the car was still in one piece, wheels and tyres all present and accounted for. Here's to next week

WALK 4 - Berwick

Wednesday 22nd February 2006

For the general information of the reader it must be said that Ron and I do not make the walks up but, in fact, have a guidebook. Over the past four walks this guidebook, titled '50 Walks in Sussex'[13], has been invaluable. Up to now the book has been extremely accurate and both Ron and I cannot sing its praises enough. The maps are spot on and the directions given are precise. Our next walk was an exception to that guidebook.

When I picked Ron up from… you all know by now, it had been raining persistently for hours. Not always heavy, but nevertheless you'd get pretty wet. But Ron, as always, assured me that it doesn't rain on Wednesday afternoons in Sussex. He has been right so far but by God it has certainly got cold.

Heading towards Alfriston, for this is where our next jaunt starts, Ron explains that he still hasn't got his boots but expects to pick them up on Thursday. A pair of size nines have, apparently, been tracked down and ambushed and are being transported, as we speak, towards Hailsham ready for collection first thing in the morning. Until then his good old Sussex Wellingtons (carrier bags) will have to suffice. As it had been raining for some time Ron admitted that he had not only brought two pairs of wellies with him but also a pair of leggings. I think he's going soft.

We parked at the Willows Car Park in Alfriston. (Another £2.00 'pay and display'). Have you had one of those feelings where you go to do something but, in the back of your mind something tells you it's not right? Well, on consulting the guidebook this walk is called

15th Century Cross

'Lasting Impressions of Berwick'[14]. There should have been a clue here but I didn't see it. If it was an impression of Berwick what the hell are we doing in Alfriston? All will be revealed. The first thing I remember saying to Ron was that I hoped the instructions are accurate because we had no map to assist us should, and it was a big should, we get lost. And did we get lost!

After leaving the Car Park we are instructed to make for the centre of Alfriston, which is a really beautiful village dating back to about the 14th Century. In the centre of the village, in Waterloo Square, is a 15th century stone cross that marks the centre of what was a thriving market village. According to the literature obtained at the Car Park[15] this stone cross is only one of two that still remain in Sussex. It certainly is a formidable structure which we pass as we head towards the Star Inn situated in the High Street. The Star describes itself as the hotel that likes to say 'yes' to locals and visitors. Ron was hoping to try out the description but I reminded him that walking and not drinking was the object of today. But I have to say the place did look very inviting. Opposite the Star is a road called Kings Ride.

We are advised, in the guidebook, to follow Kings Ride, go straight over the junction and continue on the South Downs Way. The guidebook isn't wrong. Good. I read on… the road climbs, but not steeply, it says and how very wrong it is. By the time we are halfway up this hill I am gasping for air. I'm not fit, I believe I mentioned this at the start of Walk One but the guidebook is lying to me. We should pass a bridleway, it says. We never saw one. We follow the little track up the <u>steep</u> hill, which was a drovers' route for sheep being driven to market and are advised to look for a gate on our right-hand side. We never saw one. I kept stopping on the pretence of looking for directions from the book. I was really trying to breathe. I was hoping to take a photograph of the hill but because of the cold and the exhaustion of the climb

---

[13] '50 Walks in Sussex' – AA Publishing
[14] Ibid –Walk 15, Pge. 42
[15] 'Alfriston – a brief history' free leaflet available at the kiosk at the car park

it was impossible. Once we reached the top of the South Downs, in the distance, Ron spots a sign that instructs us to bear right down the hill. Now I was feeling like the Duke who

marched to the top of the hill just to march back down again. I just needed the other 10,000 men to carry me. There is no way that we have followed the instructions in the guidebook. Somehow we've missed our turning. But it's no use complaining now, in the middle of nowhere, high up, freezing cold and not sure where you are or which way to go. We head down. The guidebook advises us that we can see Arlington Reservoir in the distance. It looked like a dot on the horizon. We must be miles out of our way. We soldier on regardless. The guidebook tells us to head for the spire of Berwick Church. I can't see a spire. Ron says we have to follow the blue signs on the posts. I haven't seen a blue sign let alone a post. We are lost. We are lost and Ron has started giggling. "What's so funny?" asks I. "Tell yer in a minute" chortles Ron. He's practically falling over himself with his fit of the giggles.

Open countryside heading for?

"What is there to laugh at Ron? We've been walking for over an hour and we're lost and all you can do is laugh!" All Ron said was "See that road we're about to come to? If you turn right there, about ten minutes along that road you'll come to the car park we left over an hour ago!" Ron couldn't go on. He had to stop to get the fit of giggles out of his system. After crossing this road and walking across another field we eventually arrive at a post which advises us that if we turn left we will reach Firle in 4 miles but if we bear right, Berwick is just ¼ of a mile away. This sign for ¼ of a mile was in the hollow on the approach to yet another field. Ron insists that there is no way that Berwick church was ¼ of a mile away from that sign. Ron is convinced that we are heading for Firle church and, again, can't stop laughing. To get to the church means that we have to walk across a field. Now being a bit of a Townie I

The church spire can just be seen

thought that we should follow the country code i.e. close all gates and walk around the outside of fields. But I had suddenly realised that since walking through the fields to get to Berwick (or Firle?) we had both walked straight through the middle of every field. When I mentioned this to Ron he explained that all the paths we had followed were public footpaths. As the paths run through the middle of fields it simply means that the farmer has not requested that the path be diverted. In fact the very path we were now on could have been walked centuries ago by parishioners on their way to Sunday Service.

We eventually arrived at the door of the church with the sign pinned to the door 'Welcome to Berwick Church'. I was so pleased to see that sign and to realise that we were now back on route I forgot how cold I was. It was such a relief.

It is surprising how churches, although similar in design, are so different. I noticed straight away that the windows of the church were not stained glass but ordinary plain glass. From a leaflet[16] picked up at the church we discovered that during the Second World War many of the windows were destroyed and the Bishop of Chichester decided that it would be more appropriate for artists to decorate church walls rather than design windows. Inside, over the chancel arch, a soldier and

Berwick Church entrance

---

[16] 'Berwick Church' - a visitors guide

airman from Firle and a sailor from Berwick are seen kneeling. It is a wonderful church and the grounds are well looked after. Now I'm not sure if the reader is familiar with Berwick. But of all the people I have spoken to about the village of Berwick have, practically to a man said, 'I didn't realise that Berwick had a church'. And neither did I. The Berwick I know has a Petrol Station, a Railway Station, whose gates seem to take for ever to open once they've closed, a pub (used to do great food?) with a large garden for kiddies to play in, a village stores come Post Office and a few houses. That's it. Until today. I've found the Church! It's past what I know as the village and across the other side of the A27 (Polegate to Brighton road)

The Cricketers Arms

Our guidebook says that prior to arriving at the church we should have walked along Vanguard Way and passed the Cricketers Inn. It is obvious that we must have taken a wrong turning somewhere near the beginning of the walk. We now retrace what should have been our original steps and arrive at The Cricketers Arms. A really, lovely, 'olde worlde' place, well worth a visit during summer when we can sit out in the garden and have a few glasses of…………. a lovely dream. But we must get back to the car!

Our guidebook now advises us that, to get back to Alfriston we need to retrace our steps back to the Church along Vanguards Way. No problem with that. We then need to climb the stile at the end of Vanguard Way and head for and go straight ahead at a right-hand bend. Our problems started again. There was no bend. We could see another stile in the distance that looked, to Ron, to be heading in the right direction but I wasn't sure. Ron convinced me that it was the right direction by leaving me and heading for the stile in the distance. "Climb over these next four stiles", says Ron as he's walking away from me "and we'll be back at the car park in Alfriston in no time". I run to catch up. We climb over the fourth stile to find ourselves, not at the car park in Alfriston, but at Drusilla's Zoo Park. Alfriston is a further mile up the road. We turn right and start walking. I had noticed in the last field we crossed what looked like half eaten cabbage/broccoli plants in the

Large dung pile, nice?

ground and asked Ron why they would be there. Apparently they are Swede plants used by the farmer as feed for his cattle. Because of the poor soil condition it is very rare to grow Swedes in this part of the country. All planted seeds will grow, forming green leaves but the plants will not produce Swedes. Another interesting fact?

I have driven along our current route many, many times and have noticed an abundance of manure on the side of the road. During the summer months this dung pile can be seen steaming in the mid-day sun. The farmer collects all the manure from his farm animals, piles it up on the side of the road and gives it away by the bag load. When we pass it today the farmer has put a wooden fence up to stop the dung from falling into the road. Very thoughtful. Another thing

The Clergy House

I've noticed, whilst out walking, is how friendly other walkers are. On each of our walks, apart from Pevensey, we have met other walkers who, without prompting, seem to want to talk. This one was no exception. As we near the car park a couple, walking a large overweight boxer dog, insist on informing us that it's a cold but bright day and just the kind of day for a brisk walk in the countryside and no they hadn't walked far because their poor old boxer has been under the weather recently and only able to take short walks. Ron takes great enjoyment in telling this couple where we had walked from and the sort of problems we had encountered. They must have thought we'd been let out for the day because they soon made their excuses and walked on?

Just before the car park, at Alfriston, on the left, is a little narrow road with a wooden finger post advising passing motorist what is in which direction and by how many miles. The finger post has been pointing downwards for a number of months. Both Ron and I know a man who used to spend everyday making or repairing these posts. Sussex is one of the only Counties to still have these wooden finger posts on their roads. Unfortunately our friend became seriously ill and, for some time, wasn't able to continue with his work. To help out I made some posts for him and was surprised to find out that they are actually made of solid oak with a metal cap and are concreted three feet into the ground. They weigh a ton and take two or three people to install. The finger arms are made out of white wood so are easily broken and need replacing but the posts usually remain in place. The letters are black plastic screwed onto the finger. He had done an enormous amount of work to ensure that he kept the contracts for East Sussex Parish Councils, which included routine maintenance, and was soon getting requests from West Sussex, but he couldn't seem to get motivated enough to progress. His friends often told him that if he was organised he could be a wealthy man. But, slowly, he seemed to become less and less motivated and eventually this type of work dried up. He is such a nice guy and has many, many friends who have tried to help out but we are starting to seriously worry about him. He has become a very independent man and now gives us the impression that he no longer needs our help. It's a real shame but there it is.

Could this be the start of our next walk?

Alfriston Stores

We eventually arrive back at the Car Park and I am so pleased. Let's get home to a hot bath thought I but Ron has other ideas. 'I'll show yer the church' says Ron as he disappears through the wall of the car park. He takes me behind some buildings that look a bit run down and, possibly, dwelt in by Ron's 'traveller friends'. I have the picture in my mind of some traveller wielding a shotgun screaming at us to 'get off my land!!!' but as we climb a stile and turn a slight bend what comes into view is a beautiful sight. The river Cuckmere is on our left and in front of us is Alfriston Church, known as 'The Cathedral of The Downs' in a secluded setting by a spacious green hidden away from the main street. It is idyllic. I have stepped back in time. The churchyard is covered in white snowdrops. The whole scene takes my breath away. Ron says that after the 'hurricane' of 1987 he was working for the Council and he had to make the area safe when some trees had been uprooted.

Right next to the church is the Clergy House with its thatched roof. The National Trust now owns the property and, in fact, was the first house they purchased in 1896 for the princely sum of £10[17]. The floor inside the house is unusual in that it is made of chalk and sour milk. The house is open to the public from March to the middle of December each year. This area of Alfriston is called The Tye. When I got home I tried looking up the word in the Dictionary without luck. I eventually found the word's meaning in a book titled, 'The Local Historians Encyclopaedia'[18] which has two definitions of the word. 1. Ref A251 Tye. 'A small enclosure, often where three roads meet, and 2. Ref A369 Tye. A southern term for a large common. I suspect that the large common reference is the one that describes 'The Tye' at Alfriston.

Just to the left of the church is a sign for a walk, which, according to the sign, should take us just over an hour and thirty minutes to complete. The walk is called Kissing Gate Walk and takes us into a village called Litlington and back. Just the job for next Wednesday. Both Ron and I agree that this is our next walk and the result of that walk will fill our next chapter.

Back to The Tye and from here Ron takes me through a small passageway that leads us to the High Street. The feeling is really Dickensian. You expect some little urchin to pick your pocket as you walk through this passage. I am reliably informed by many people since completing this walk that Alfriston, every Christmas, have a Dickensian evening when the village dress in period costume and literally go back in time. It has become very popular with the local people and is a very busy time for what is a very quiet, very, very old and pretty village.

Ron has decided that he needs food and has disappeared into the local village shop. He's gone for ages. On his exit he's loaded with little white paper bags. "Come and look," says Ron "It's like going back in time". I've not seen Ron so excited. "It's just like it used to be when I was ten years old. What a fantastic place". The lady who served Ron commented that '..he was broad'. Ron thought that he was being chatted up and she meant he was a well-built specimen until he realised she actually meant his broad Sussex accent. He's told the assistant that we would be back next week to take photographs of the shop. I think he likes the chat up line.

Anyway, the chicken pie he brought me was very edible on the way back to the car and the afternoon, although very tiring had, again, been an education and, I'm sure it will definitely be 'a lasting impression'. I'm really looking forward to next week's walk.

---

[17] Leaflet obtained from The Clergy House
[18] John Richardson *The Local Historians Encyclopedia* (Historical Publication, 2003) Pages 17 & 21

WALK 5 - Alfriston

Wednesday 1st March 2006

I've been looking forward to this walk since last week. After 'The Lasting Impressions of Berwick' I needed a more tranquil, leisurely walk in the countryside to make me feel better with myself and to relieve the stresses of today's modern rush and tear. In fact there is more than one reason to look forward to this particular walk. There are lots of reasons. We were about to visit a really beautiful church with its churchyard full of snowdrops. The walk is on the level, no hills to climb. At the end of the walk is the Village Stores, where we had been invited back, or did Ron invite us (?) to sample some more of their homemade pies. But, above all this, the one most important fact of the day was that Ron was now in receipt of, not one, but two pairs of size nine walking boots. "Can't believe it", says Ron, "walk in ter the shoe shop and pay fer me boots then, I walks onto 'ailsham Market, and would yer credit it, but a lady was selling size nine walking boots there as well. Must have been one o'them omens, so's I 'ad to buy another pair. Been wearin' 'em out so's I can wear 'em in" says Ron. "And just so's you don't feels left out", he says to me, "I bought you a 'at". He supplies me with a black thermal hat. "Keeps yer warm that will" states Ron. As today is one of the warmest days this year I'm hoping I won't need the hat.

Before I explain the walk there is one thing I have to say regarding my personal feelings about churches. Not just churches, but cathedrals affect me the same way. I have always loved church buildings. There is something inertly peaceful and I am not biased with my beliefs.

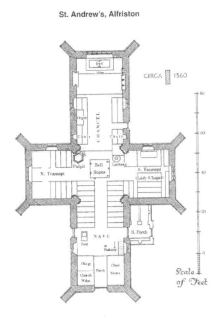

St. Andrew's, Alfriston

The effect on me can, and has, happened in many churches, but for some reason, only recently. Friends who know me are aware of the outcome. I can walk round a church and be totally ok until someone starts playing the organ. I honestly don't know why it affects me in the way it does but at the point of the organ starting I must sit down and I cry. Not simple tears and a sniffle but I sob my heart out. It can be very embarrassing. When this happens to me on holiday my wife has to explain to curious onlookers that I am emotionally affected by the beautiful music. But it's not that. They could be playing badly. It's something else that I cannot explain. Anyway, thankfully, there is no organ playing as we enter St Andrews Church at Alfriston. The church is built on a mound and dates to around the 1360's and it is more than just beautiful. From the small plan[19] it is obvious that the church is built in the shape of a crucifix. What is unusual is that the bell ringers are actually in full view of the congregation. Must be a bit off putting while you're heaving on a bell rope, to have people walking past you. The oldest bell currently in the bell tower is bell no. 6, which dates from around the 1400s'. This book isn't intended to be a history lesson but jottings of two Sussex men in need of exercise. But when Ron was here, just after the hurricane in 1987, he remembers a stone monument in the graveyard, which will always remain in his thoughts. We found the stone, exactly where Ron remembered it to be, some 20 years ago. The words are a little difficult to make out due to

---

[19] *A Guide to St Andrews Church, Alfriston* the work of Walter Godfrey and Cecil Piper obtained from the church priced 50p

weathering but the monument is in remembrance to five sisters who all died at a young age. The inscription reads:

TO THE SACRED MEMORY OF
THE BELOVED CHILDREN OF
THOMAS AND AUGUSTA RUSSELL
ELLEN
WHO DEPARTED THIS LIFE
JULY 7TH 1864 AGED 16 YEARS
EMMA
WHO DEPARTED THIS LIFE
SEPT 18TH 1853 AGED 4 YEARS
FANNY
WHO DEPARTED THIS LIFE
JAN 11TH 1857 AGED 2 YEARS
AND
KATE AND ELIZABETH TWINS
JAN 29TH AND FEB 14TH 1865
AGED 4 MONTHS[20]

View of Alfriston Church

Beware - Toads Crossing

Whatever could have happened to that poor family to warrant the deaths of these children between 1853 and 1865? What agonies did the parents go through? Reading something like that always makes me feel very humble.

Let us return to the walk. From the church we need to go left and head towards the White Bridge that crosses the Cuckmere. Our intention is to walk the Kissing Gate Walk, which should take us one hour thirty minutes. It is now two fifteen so we have plenty of time. Except Ron has decided that we would not do the Kissing Gate Walk but head towards the village of Litlington by following the little yellow arrows, strategically placed on posts along our way. As we cross the White Bridge I notice how quickly the water is moving. On one of these walks I am hoping to bring my sons two Labradors but they are not used to staying on leads. One look at the river and they would both be in for a swim. Whilst one, called Tess, is a very good swimmer, her daughter, Pip is a little small and would probably struggle with the current. I'm glad they're not with us today.

The first path we walk on is tarmac and is very smooth but best of all, clean. Perhaps we won't need to clean our boots tonight?? At the end of the path we come to a road, which, presumably, heads for Litlington village but Ron isn't happy with walking along the road. "I didn't come out 'ear to be run over by some toff with a mobile phone glued to 'is ear" says Ron as he heads for a small path between some trees. The path runs parallel with the road for a while before veering off to the right over a stile. It is very noticeable to both of us that the amount of snowdrops along this path is incredible. Where do they all come from? There must be thousands, all in clumps and both sides of the path. When we climb over the first stile we now have to perform what I believed to be the country code. And that is to walk around the outside of the field to

---

[20] Transcribed from headstone found at St Andrew's Church, Alfriston

the next stile. We now traverse the Farm Buildings until we reach another stile. We are still following the 'Yellow route' when we appear, back on the road by a very nice house called North Ham. "Bet you don't get many canvassers for the Labour Party in these parts" suggests Ron. I must admit that I have a job to visualise a local worker being able to afford this type of house. The path we are now on runs parallel, but above, the road so we are looking down on any passing traffic, until just as we reach a house called Bauhinia the path stops and we have to walk on the road.

The Church of St Michael, Litlington

A few yards along this road, in the middle of nowhere, is an abandoned car. 'Police aware' sign on the windscreen. "Yer see, even in beautiful surroundings like this there 'as to be some moron 'oo just can't wait ter clutter up the countryside" says Ron who then leads off about the youths of today, probably pinched the car, more likely on drugs and booze, no consideration, should be made to pay etc. etc.

Just past the abandoned car is a sign that advises everyone to slow down due to 'Toad Migration'. Apparently, at this time of year, this particular road is used by lots of toads who cross it to get to their breeding grounds and the locals warn unsuspecting people that they might come across a hop-a-long creature as they head towards the village. Just to the right of the sign is Church Farm. Next to the Farm is a church and before I realise this Ron said to me "Could 'ave a problem here" I hadn't a clue what he meant until he said "Can't you 'ear the organ?" "It's Wednesday afternoon," says I "who would be playing an organ at this time of day?" "Don't know," says Ron "p'rhaps it's practice day?" As we approach Litlington Church, dedicated to St Michael the Archangel, it is obvious that either a service was in progress or, as Ron suggested, someone was practising on the organ. Either way I had absolutely no intention of going inside. Thankfully Ron understood but as we stood back at this small church Ron thought he could see mistletoe growing up the large elm tree in the churchyard. Ron had a closer look to find out it was nothing more than ivy. But he thought that someone would have a thought and cut it back so that the tree would survive. The bell tower of the church had some work done to it recently and the finish certainly isn't in keeping with the building but looked to be plastic cladding. Not in keeping at all. I wasn't sorry when Ron suggested we head further into the village and "....go and see the local pub 'The Plough and Arrow". What a strange name for a pub thought I. But still, onward we continued. Just as we approach the pub I can see a sign that says that Ramblers are welcome. It has been warm today and Ron has set off towards the pub with a big grin and a light step. Throughout our walks we have passed a few pubs and not been tempted, but today, it was too much for both Ron and I. A sign in the pub car park advertises 'Fish and Chip takeaways' every Friday 6 'til 9. As we got to the front of the pub Ron explains to me that the large object out the front of the pub with handles attached was the plough. "But where is the bow and arrow?" asks I. "What bow and arrow?" asks Ron. "You said the pub was called the Plough and arrow" it is now that I realise my stupid mistake. "You meant the Plough and Harrow didn't you Ron?" "That's what I said," says Ron, "The Plough and Arrow". Just as we approach the door a customer comes out. We let him pass. The door shuts and is audibly bolted, from the inside. It is obvious that these particular ramblers are certainly not welcome. No refreshments for us. "We'll get something back at Alfriston village shop" says Ron as we head towards the yellow arrow which directs us down a little lane called Plough Lane. From here we follow the signs over a footbridge and onto an area called Burnt House Brooks, which is owned by The National Trust and covers 13 acres of land[21].

We can see Alfriston church spire from here so we are obviously on the right track. The river, running to our right is fast moving but not very deep, according to Ron. The ground underfoot is very boggy and damp. I get the impression we're not walking along a track but in fact, we're on the high water level of the river. When I point this out to Ron he responds with his little giggle and advises me that we are on the wrong side of the river anyway, but not to worry as we're heading in the right direction. It's 3.30 in the afternoon and it's started to snow. The 'path' we are on is getting narrower as we walk and I can see no stiles or gates to get us into the next field. At a bend in the river the next gate/stile is under water. It's 3.32 in the afternoon and the snow has stopped. We traverse the water and make our way onto a clear path. To our left the road from Alfriston to Seaford can be seen, and heard but to our right nothing but beautiful views of the countryside. In the distance Ron tells me two Reed Buntings are flirting in the tall long grass. The male has beautiful colourings as he flits from grass to grass showing off in front of his lady. We seem to be able to get very close to the birds before they become worried and fly on and the traffic is only a few yards away.

As with all the walks we have completed, there is always someone who passes and speaks to us. Today is no exception. We have spoken to a number of passing walkers who have answered our 'good afternoons' with cheery comments and words. Every now and again you meet someone and something's not quite right. Like walk two and the lady with high-heeled boots. Today was one of those days. As we approach the last stile at Alfriston a couple are heading towards us, we say our usual 'good afternoon' and the couple stop and the gentleman, in an accent that could possibly be American or, as Ron thought, Danish?, and asked us if they could reach The Golden Galleon, a well-known bar and restaurant (see walk 2) at Exceat if they followed this track. We suggested they could although the track was a little muddy and it seemed a long way to walk, about 5 miles, especially if you had to walk back to Alfriston. The gentleman looked at our boots, said that we had made it reasonably cleanly and they would give it a go. This was nothing really out of the ordinary, except they appeared to have a Chinese takeaway with them. Not our problem thought Ron and me. Let's get to the Village Shop.

As we walk through the High Street towards the shop it is surprising how many people are wandering through the village. We pass a group of tourists who Ron thinks 'Looks like they could be pie eaters. Better get to the shop before they do'. Entering the Village Shop at Alfriston really is like stepping back in time. We are greeted with a very pleasant 'Good afternoon' and 'where have you been walking today' as they recognise old Ron who explains to our shopkeepers that we had walked to Litlington and back and that he was, again, hungry. We are led to the Deli counter where Ron proceeds to order a number of different pies. "What are you doing Ron?" I ask as the lady behind the counter puts the pies in bags. "I've got me orders," says Ron "got to get some pies for Sean back at The Kings Head for his lunch box. Told 'im about these last week and he asked me to get 'im some and I'll 'ave a large slice of Steak and Stilton pie to eat now" he says as he returns his attention back to the lady behind the counter.

Back at the car and it has, again been a good afternoon. We have to decide on next week's walk but Ron is suggesting that we actually complete the Kissing Gate Walk. This would mean coming back to Alfriston again. I'm not so sure. We'll have a think and decide before next Wednesday.

---

[21] Information gathered from detailed signposts at entrance to Brooks

WALK 6 - Lullington

Wednesday 8ᵗʰ March 2006

Our Local - The Kings Head

Before we start on our next walk I need to let readers know the pressures that these walks are having on Ron and me. Before we started our weekly excursions the conversation at The Kings Head was normal, day-to-day discussions, what's in the newspapers, what's on television, how work went today. You know what I mean? Our writings have been handed out by Ron to a number of the regulars of our favourite hostelry and the reaction from these people has been both favourable and encouraging. Now people are starting to suggest walks that we should go on. Both Ron and I appreciate everyone's thoughts, explanations, offers and suggestions but every week now more walks are suggested and unless both Ron and I live to be a hundred, or we walk every day, there is no way that we could cover all the walks suggested by all our friends. Also, at the time of writing it is still late winter and whilst a brisk walk through a local wood, as suggested by one of our drinking partners, would be both invigorating and beneficial I would find it difficult to fill pages of the written word to keep the readers turning pages. You may have noticed that all our walks, without exception, are circular. I see no possible reason why, as has been suggested, we should walk 5 or 6 miles in a straight line only to have to get back by bus or taxi, and then write about how nice the bus/taxi driver was. But, yes our Sussex countryside is beautiful and yes, we can see different things during different seasons, everyone we've spoken to has agreed this, but what we are trying to achieve here, with these written words, is an interesting and enjoyable account of what I, as a townie, and Ron, as a country boy can see, do and learn about on a Wednesday afternoon's walk. Both Ron and I are very sorry if the walk that you have suggested to us has not been completed in this book but the truth is we can't please everyone. We also appreciate that someone's idea of going back over the same ground during another season will allow us to get a different perspective on that area but I will then have to write about it and I've already done that. We want to be able to see and share, with others, lots of different places, not the same places over and over again. During the winter, spring, summer, and autumn of 2006/07 our walks will reflect the seasons. But for now, it's cold, frosty with the threat of snow on a daily basis, crocus and snowdrops have just started to poke their heads through the crusty earth's surface, which proves that spring is actually on its way and, I hope, our current excursions are a reflection on that.

For me, today it's raining. It started yesterday and hasn't stopped. To Ron it's a sea fret, whatever that is. "A sea-fret," explains Ron "is a sea mist blown inland by the wind. In the distance it looks like a fog." To me it's rain and his assurance that it doesn't rain in Sussex on a Wednesday afternoon has been blown apart, sea fret or not.

One of the places we missed last week on our walk was Lullington Church. Ron remembers this place from when he visited some twenty years ago and would like to revisit. The Church is one of the smallest churches in the country, only seating 23 parishioners. It is also in the middle of nowhere so, for once, rather than walk to it we decided to visit by car. Also the sea fret is getting heavier.

Confusion reigns

To convince Ron that we are, in fact moving into the 21st century I have brought along some computer technology, Satellite Navigation. "This will direct us to anywhere" I tell Ron as I am telling the machine to find a route to Lullington. Would you believe it? It doesn't understand 'Lullington'. "Never mind," says I, "I'll ask it the way to Polegate." "I knows the way to Polegate," says Ron, "don't need no machine to tell me". "It'll demonstrate how it works," I say as the machine now speaks to me and tells me that I am now facing the wrong direction and need to turn around. "Cor'," says Ron, "she sounds sexy. Who is she?" I explain to Ron that it is a computer-generated voice and her name is Jane. "There must be thousands of people with one o'them contraptions, how can she speak to them all at the same time (?) Mind, 'tis a wonderful thing."

As we approach Lullington the sea fret is throwing it down. "Are you sure you want to do this Ron?" I ask. "Don't you fuss? The sea fret won't last long." We approach Lullington and see a signpost directing me to turn right for the church. This I do and to my surprise end up in someone's driveway. "That's odd," says Ron "this wasn't 'ear fifty years ago, where the 'ells the church gone?" "It can't be far away," says I, "perhaps we need to go down the road a bit further. I'll just back out and go down the road." Further down the road we find a turning to Alfriston and nothing else. "Must be where we were in the first place," says Ron "but whereabouts the church is I 'ave no idea." We head back towards the signpost and as we approach I notice more writing on this side than the other. It is now obvious to us that there must be a path to the church. If you look at the middle of the three pictures, to the left of the car, is a small path leading through the trees. This is the path we take just as the sea-fret stops. "See," says Ron "the winds dropped, no sea-fret. We'll be o.k. now." The path leading to the church is narrow and slippery but it is well worth the effort. At the end of the pathway is a wooden gate that leads you into the churchyard. The Church, called The Church of Our Shepherd, is indeed very small. It can currently seat twenty-three people and, as Ron said, "bit of a squeeze for a funeral" but, looking around the very few monuments in the grounds it looks as if the last funeral took place in 1906. Ron insists on signing the 'visitors' book' where he writes 'Just as beautiful as 50 years ago'. The place has an obvious memory for Ron. "Worth the journey just to come out 'ear to this ol' church" he says. I must admit it was really quaint and reminded me so much of some of the smaller village churches

Church of the Good Shepherd, Lullington

in Devon that I had seen on holidays. I really didn't expect to find such a peaceful place, literally just down the road from where I live.

Back at the car it is decided that as we didn't walk along the Kissing Gate Walk at Alfriston and as it was just round the corner we could complete the walk so that, at least, we could say that we had done it. Whilst saying that, I wasn't fussed on going to the same place twice. I did point out to Ron that this was the third, and last time, we would be in Alfriston for a while.

To be honest this walk was basically Walk six in reverse. We started at the white bridge, turned right, through a Kissing Gate and walked along the river bank until we reached Burnt House Brooks. The only thing that was noticeably different along this stretch was the number of breeding ducks we saw, the six Kissing Gates we passed through and the amount of mud and water lying because of the sea fret. We walked back up Plough Lane, didn't bother with The Plough and Harrow but continued along the road back towards Alfriston.

Again we met someone. As we are walking along the road a horse and rider are approaching us. Just as they pass Ron gives the young lady rider his usual cheery greeting. She pulls over to our side of the road and, looking down at us, asks if we know the direction to Jevington. Now I don't like horses. They're big and don't appear to like me. I stand back and this horse is looking at me like he's about to kill. Ron is now trying to explain to the lady that there is a bridleway further along the road that will lead her to Jevington Car Park and asks me to confirm his directions. Personally, I have no idea where we are let alone where Jevington is. And the horse hasn't taken his eyes off me. The horse reminded me of my sister-in-law's pony who, although small had a nasty streak in it and would take off without warning. This particular horse was big, but the girl riding it seemed to have good control. She said that she would find her way and if she did have a problem she would use her mobile phone. She then trotted off in a completely different direction to what Ron had said. "Do you think it's true what they say about girls riding horses," Ron asks. "I don't know Ron, why didn't you ask her?" "I'm too much of a gentleman to ask such things but 'tis a lovely thought."

The abandoned car is still abandoned in the same place and as we walk past the farmhouse I wonder if the farmer remembers us from last week and thinks it's taken us a week to walk back? That's the one thing I've tended to do since starting to walk the countryside, my mind wanders and stupid thoughts come into play. Just in front of us is the white bridge and Ron has decided that another visit to the village shop is required as we won't be back for a while. More pies for us, more pies for Sean's lunch box. We decide to stop for a cup of tea for Ron and a cup of coffee for me to warm us through after our walk. "We won't be back for a while ladies," says Ron "but rest assured your in the book." I'm not sure what they will miss most, Ron's friendly chat or the amount of money we've spent in their shop over the last three weeks.

It's time to get back home. As we walk back to the car it's started to rain again. "See," says Ron, "winds got up, and that damn sea fret's started again".

WALK 7 - Firle

Wednesday 15th March 2006

Today I went for my first job interview in 25 years and it's aged me by as many years. I was absolutely terrified. What I needed after this was a relaxing walk with Ron. No cares in the world just the elements and us. The sun had been shining all day so there was no fear of last week's sea fret. We had decided to complete a walk[22] of 4½ miles starting at Firle Car Park (there's only one car park?). The whole circular walk should take us about 2 hours to complete and our guide book has supplied us with a map so we should have no difficulty in finding our way about. Not only that, but since the start of our little expeditions, I had been promising Ron the use of some binoculars. Today, eight weeks after my original promise I have actually found the binoculars and remembered to bring them with me. We had also invited another friend to walk with us.

At Ron's usual pick up point, The Kings Head, we are to be joined by Peter. Peter informs us that he has carried out numerous walks in the area as well as many cycle rides. He is well

Firle Stores

prepared for today, all dressed up in a thermal top, waterproof leggings, and, we are advised a little later, he is also wearing thermal underwear. He hasn't worn his walking shoes for some time and he's worried about blisters? Never mind, he has a rucksack that holds one of the most expensive cameras I've ever seen, and is full of enthusiasm. Heading towards our starting point Peter does say that he hasn't completed today's walk before.

Ron tells us that the area is well known for the Gage family who have owned Firle Place for over 500 years. "One o'them Gage people was the last Sheriff of Sussex", says Ron "then they lost the lot when they turned cath'lic. Another 'ovem took charge of the burning of the Martyrs in Lewes. 'Tis in all them 'istory books." The whole area of the village was a popular place for Ron who used to work the area with his father. Ron's dad used to be the local rat catcher and he has spent some great times in Firle. Ron was a sportsman in his younger days and his one claim to fame at Firle was at a cricket match when he scored 49 runs. "How come you didn't score the magic 50?" I ask. "Some bugger caught me on the very next ball," he explains, "should have gone for six," he says, "but I didn't get it right and it went straight into the swine's 'ands."

Abandoned??

When we arrive at the car park, it's free. No machine to feed, no £2 to find. I'm beginning to like Firle already. Our guidebook advises us to leave the car park and turn left, heading towards the village centre and the church. "Why are all the front doors painted the same horrible green colour?" I ask. "Well," says Ron "All the doors within the village are painted green to denote that the property was part of the feudal lord's estate." The only shop in the village is really tiny. Ron needs his weekly pie allowance and as I didn't think we come past this way on the way back to the car he pops inside to taste Firle's cuisine only to be bitterly disappointed because the foreign owner could not supply him with any home-made fare, only 'massed produced sh**' as Ron calls it. "I could 'ave gone to a supermarket and brought this rubbish. Not a patch on Alfriston!" says Ron who managed to devour his plastic wrapped pork pie within seconds. As we leave the shop we notice, chained to plastic buckets full of concrete, a couple of rusty motor scooters that don't

---

[22] '50 Walks in Sussex' AA Publishers – Walk 18 - Page 50

look as if they've moved for months. Why they should be left there is any ones guess but they were taxed so they must belong to and be used by someone.

Again snowdrops line the path to the door of the Church of St. Peter. A sign on the door says that it's open from dawn to dusk and will not be put off by the occasional theft. The inside, as with all churches, is magnificent and one of the stain glass windows is called the John Piper Window and was installed in 1985[23]. This window is in the oldest part of the church that houses the tomb of the late Sir John Gage, K.C and his wife Philippa. Sir John is wearing his armour and Philippa is in a long gown. The brasses within the church are said to be among the finest in Sussex. But it is not known when the first church was built. Most of

Interior, Firle Church

the current building can be dated to around the 14th and 15th centuries so in any one's language, it's old. There has been a vicar at Firle since 1197 and all the names are listed in a frame hung on the Vestry wall.

Our walk now takes us out of the village and onto some concrete tracks. We turn right and head for a road that will lead us to Firle Beacon. Along this track have been planted

View from Firle Beacon

hawthorn bushes and they have obviously been left without any attention. It seems strange to me that so much time, effort and money can be put into planting the hawthorn just to let them die. What is the point? The only ones who seem to get enjoyment out of the area we are now in are the horses. These aren't so big so when Peter encourages them to come over to us I'm not so worried. When we get to the road we turn left. The book advises us that we now 'begin the long climb, steep in places.' Remembering what the book described as a 'slight slope' in one of our previous walks I still wasn't prepared for how steep this next part was going to be. It was really hard work and covered, according to Peter, about 2 miles. Within these 2 miles we were amazed at the litter that could be seen on the side of the road. Someone must have had a party. We counted 7 empty Vodka bottles, 4 empty wine bottles and we lost count of the amount of empty larger cans littering the roadway. On our climb towards the top, where we should find a car park, we needed to stop for a breather and the view is stunning. It was about now that Peter informed us that he was wearing thermal underwear and was beginning to feel the heat in certain areas of his person. How he was going to feel at the end of the walk we weren't sure but he really looked warm.

---

[23] A Guide to the Church of St Peter, Firle, by Rev FBR Browne obtained at the church priced 50p

Directly behind us is a Southern Water Treatment Plant. It's fenced off and padlocked to deter intruders, but someone's obviously gained entry somehow because, hanging from a tree is a bag containing empty bottles. After our walk Ron spoke to someone from The Water Authority who simply said that they were aware of the problem but they didn't seem that bothered.[24] Ron, now with binoculars in hand, is panning the

Red Kite

landscape, "I don't bloody believe it," shouts he, "just you look up there." Both Peter and I turn to look, expecting to find some rarely seen animal, or perhaps a bird of prey floating in the blue sky above. But we can't see anything. "Up there," shouts Ron, pointing to a green tree lined slope, "someone's left another bloody carrier bag and it's blown up the slope and attached itself to a tree, bloody disgusting." Both Peter and I didn't know what to say so we left Ron, muttering and swearing in his own Sussex way, as we stride out for the top. Again the slog to the top is well worth the effort. The views from up here are unbelievable. Peter notices what looks like a watchtower in the distance and believes it's a 'folly' (?). Ron thinks it could be "one o'them Gages churches since 'e turned cath'lic", and I have no idea. We'll get a closer look as we go down the hill. When we get to the car park it is obvious that part of it has been taken over by travellers with the inevitable results but both Peter and I manage to steer Ron away from the subject of what they should do with these people.

We now find a gate that leads us along South Downs Way. Suddenly Ron stops and says "Listen, skylarks. I haven't heard that bird song for years." Although I couldn't actually see the birds you could definitely hear their song. It was beautiful. But the inevitable was

about to happen. In the distance I see, heading towards us, what I think is a golf buggy. But we are miles from a golf course? As the 'buggy' gets closer it becomes obvious to all that it is, in fact, an invalid buggy. Not just an ordinary buggy but a 4 by 4 rough terrain, invalid buggy. "I haven't got treads like that on my car tyres" say Peter. It was one mean, green machine and the rider has been everywhere on it. He explained that he came from Hailsham and rather than stay indoors on days like today he liked nothing better than to charge the battery and go for it. We never did ask how he got up to the top of Firle beacon but he would certainly have no trouble getting down as he was heading for the road that we had just come up. To our right is a very large flock of sheep. Peter is a proud Welshman so some banter was caused about Welshmen and sheep. Peter denies any knowledge regarding his kin and sheep but did think a couple of the sheep winked at him. Who knows?

Ron and me at Firle

Our next instruction is to head for a large gateway with a kissing gate attached. Here we are to turn sharp left and head down the steep 'escarpment'. The gate we came across was

The gate with no fence?

large, but there was no kissing gate. "This must be it," say I. "We'll turn left here and head down that hill". Peter pointed out that there was no kissing gate, so did Ron. Undeterred, we turned left and the steep escarpment turned out to be practically vertical. "Told you we turned left too soon", said Peter. "There's no way you can get down this way". The guidebook says that we should head for a grassy slope. This is a sheer drop. But to our right, Peter points out a definite pathway. To get to it we have to walk across and down the side of the hill. No easy feat for Peter whose shoes are starting to cause blisters. Just

---

[24] Since been removed by Mr Hearns, Southern Water employee and Hailsham Club Member

as we hit the bottom of the slope Ron shouts, "I don't believe it!" again. "If it's another bloody plastic bag" Peter says "I'm going to take those binoculars away from him". But this time Ron is looking straight up and I could just make out two birds relaxing on the thermals. "What are they?" asks I. "They look like kites" says Ron. "If they're kites where's the string?" I ask. "Silly sod" replies Ron, "they're Red Kites, and there being harassed by a rook. They won't put up with that for too long." Peter thought that Red Kites were pretty rare but Ron said that they were starting to make a bit of a comeback. As we watch, the rook starts to chase after one of the kites. Both kites got lower and lower in the sky then, all of a sudden, one of the kites heads straight for the rook and chases him off. "There you go, see, those rooks and kites don't get on at all, always fighting they are but usually the kite gets the better o' the rook." They truly are stunning to watch. They hardly flap their wings at all but soar on the thermals created by the warm air and the hills. Since returning from our walk we have discussed these birds with Mogs who tells us that a number of them had been released into the wild along the Downs recently and that they mate for life and when out hunting for food one of the pair flies high whilst the other forages out small wildlife. When the other bird sees its prey it falls out of the sky to catch it. The speed as the bird drops from the sky has been recorded at over 200-mph., which is a phenomenal speed.

As we pass through the gate in front of us we must keep Firle Plantation to our left and follow the fence into the corner of the field. From here the 'Tower' is clearly visible but we still have no real idea what the purpose of the building is. All I can see of 'the plantation' is an unkempt piece of land where someone has planted a huge number of trees and then left them to fend for themselves. A lot of the trees look dead. Why spend all that money and time? I can see no reason for leaving this land the way it is. Peter believes that after the hurricane, trees had to be replaced and the Government of the day paid people grants to plant new trees.

Beautifully built wall complete with tree stump

Unfortunately they didn't pay for their upkeep so many haven't survived.

At the end of 'the Plantation' we came to another gate. We pass through and need to turn left. As we pass through the gate I notice, cycling down the hill towards us are two gentlemen. One has a very noticeable baldhead. It glistens with his sweat. It is now that Ron starts his giggle. He's found another gate. There is no fence either side of the gate, left or right; you can walk round the gate on either side. But the gate has a padlock on it. Why? Again I don't understand. Just as we are getting Ron to calm down the two cyclists shoot past with a cheery hello and head down the hill. The guidebook tells us to walk down the hill, back towards the church, keeping the flint wall to our right. This wall is a work of art and must have taken a very long time to build. The craftsmanship is amazing. But as we approach a bend in the track there is what looks like a gateway built into the wall. I have no real problem with this except, on closer inspection, in the middle of this gateway had, at some time, been a large tree. The stump is still visible up against the wall end. Why would anyone, build a wall, and then make an entrance/exit right where there was a tree that would stop anyone from using that exit/entrance?

We move on and are now approaching the church again. We are coming to the end of this week's walk. As we turn the bend, the two cyclists are heading back towards us. "You'll not believe it," says bald headed one, "they've shut the bloody pub!" and they both disappeared up the lane. "Well that's all we need", says Ron "somebody giving us some more good news".

Still, the walk was energetic. Peter said something about getting his endomorphines moving up the hill to Firle Beacon, or it sounded like endomorphines. Possibly something to do with his thermals, I'm not sure. But he said it was enjoyable anyway. The one thing that gets me about this particular walk was the number of questions I've come back with. Hopefully, before next week's little saunter I will have some answers.

WALK 8 - Herstmonceux

Wednesday 22nd March 2006

Is it really Wednesday again? This week has flown by. The trauma caused by last week's interview has paid off. I am now gainfully employed again. Luckily it shouldn't interfere too much with our Wednesday walks. We may have to start out earlier but Ron is ok with that.

As usual I pick Ron up in the car. Peter, who is still dressed in his thermals, has asked if he could join us again. Today is a bit cold so we may be jealous of his warm clothing.

On our way home from last week's walk around Firle, Peter asked if he could choose this

Ron gives a lesson on water creatures

week's little stroll. His request was discussed at our usual Monday evening meeting over pints of nectar and it was agreed that Peter's suggestion to walk around the Herstmonceux Castle area would be enjoyable. As it was only three miles I was more than happy.

I park the car, as suggested by our guidebook[25], in a lay-by close to the Science Centre. Again there is no parking fee. The one thing that worried me about this short walk was that there was no map supplied in our book. The same problem was encountered with our walk to Berwick. We got lost then but this time I am prepared. I have purchased an Ordinance Survey Map of the area. I just hope at least one of us can understand it, should it be needed. Our instructions tell us to look for a stile across the road from the lay-by. No problem finding this, so off we go. The path is well signed and clear. A small lake is just the other side of the stile and Ron points out different reeds and plants to me. Although the weather is cold it is dry so we have no problems underfoot.

The path takes us through a wooded area that is sparse in places but the effects of the hurricane are still very evident. Really large trees have been uprooted and lay where they fell. It is surprising how some large trees are down but smaller ones have remained standing. Ron suggests that this may be due to the old trees being weak as well as shallow rooted. Some of the

Always prepared?

trees have just broken at the trunk, snapped like twigs, yet are still alive because some new shoots are visible. Ron tells us that this is natures was of coppicing a tree. Men are actually employed to cut down trees but they leave the stump and roots in the ground and the tree eventually grows new shoots. I am amazed at not only the size of the felled trees but also how many there are that appear to be dead. Peter then says that there doesn't appear to be any wildlife about. We realise that there are no bird sounds. No chirpy songs, nothing. It is deathly quiet. You can actually hear Peter's camera focusing on his next subject. It's eerie.

Peter, dressed for the part?

---

25 '50 Walks in Sussex' AA Publishers – Walk 10 – Page 30

To bring us back from our reverie, Ron, complete with wide grin is holding a meat pie. "Knew there'd be no shops out 'ere so went ter 'omely Maid in 'ailsham and brought a steak an' kidney pie, special for this walk". Both Peter and I just look on. What can you say apart from "where's ours?"

Hurricane damage

Unisex Loo!

A little further into our walk Ron points out catkins and rhododendron bushes growing wild. Peter is suggesting we come back in the summer to see everything in bloom. I must admit that the thought is appealing and could be included as a later chapter in our weekly meanderings. Before we reach the end of this particular trail we come across a huge tree that has blown over. Peter's artistic talents are promptly brought to bear as he describes the dynamics of the particular picture he wishes to take. He describes, at length, the force that can be displayed as well as the overall dramatic effect that can be achieved using one particular filter compared to another so that he captures that perfect picture which will reflect the visible characteristics and power of the destruction of this life form. Both Ron and I think it's not a bad snap, but can't really understand the fuss. But each to his own. We also meet our inevitable two horses in a paddock that seem to take great pride in trying to kick the hell out of each other as we look on in amusement. The stile that leads us to Wood Lane is now in view and, once over it, we need to turn left. Peter usually found climbing stiles with camera and thermals and waterproof leggings something of a challenge. But he stuck with it.

Opposite the stile is a large galvanised gate with a 'Beware of the Bull' sign attached to a 'Public Footpath' sign. To me, that can't be right, can it? Peter wants to go down the footpath to find the bull, but our instructions tell us to walk down Wood Lane and as far as I am concerned, bull or no bull, that is the way we are heading. Our instructions advise to walk towards a road junction and join a bridleway that should take us towards Herstmonceux Church.

Halfway along Wood Lane Peter notices, high above the road and to our left, what every walker must need at one stage – a loo. Not just any loo but one of the unisex varieties. We weren't sure how you got to it but we're sure it must have been handy for someone at sometime. Although, looking at the state of it, I'm not sure that I would use it, even if I was desperate. At the junction, we cross the road, and head for the clearly marked bridleway. We must say, again, that the instructions for this walk are accurate and the signs are clearly displayed on the posts. I haven't had to consult the Survey Map at all. What a waste of money. We now wander into another wooded area. Here there are lots of pine trees growing high into the sky. The coverage on the ground from these trees makes the ground very dark and sinister. Yet, in complete contrast to earlier, there are bird sounds all around us. Workmen have been busy along this stretch of path. Trees have been felled and a large amount of logs are piled on the side. "I wonder how this type of wood would turn on a lathe." I ask Ron. "You'll need 'eck of a long 'lectric lead for out 'ere" is the reply from Ron. "I turned some apple on my lathe once and made some really nice mushrooms. When I was turning it the fragrance was really nice". "Must have been soft then, if yer turned apple," says Ron. "No, I soaked them in varnish and they looked really good" I said before I realised that Ron was taking the Mickey. His grin was from ear to ear. He got me this week. Just because I couldn't

see the string attached to last week's kites he's been trying to get his own back. Now he's succeeded, he's happy.

It's now that the path widens and we pass a reed clogged stream. But it is beyond this stream that you get close to some really huge trees. When you see the actual size of the trees it takes your breath away. They are gnarled, twisted and enormous. They must be years old.

At the end of this path we go through a gate and head across a field to a slight rise and head for a gap in the trees. Again it is well sign-posted and apart from a little apprehension with what Ron advised was an electric fence that Peter failed to see, we managed to get to the top of the rise and are now in a small wooded pathway heading towards the road.

As with every walk we have been on, this one was to prove no exception. We always meet someone. This time it was, at first, a something. A dog, an old Welsh collie came walking towards us. At first we thought, being Welsh, it was heading for Peter to say 'yaki dah', or whatever. But it became a little nervous, as it got closer. Its owner followed shortly. An elderly man, wearing green wellies approached us. He seemed more nervous of us than the dog. Peter and I move on but Ron, in typical Ron fashion insists that he speak, not only to the dog, but also to the elderly gentleman. Peter and I wait. "Always something strange about a man who wears

How old are these trees?

green wellies" I say to Peter. "I've never noticed" he replies. It isn't until I get home and am relating the story to my wife that she reminds me that I've got a pair of green wellies in the back

Concrete marker post

of the car. Perhaps they're not so strange after all. Ron catches up with us just as we reach a strange concrete pillar, in the ground. It is approximately two feet high and a foot square. At the top, front, is engraved a ships anchor. Below the anchor is the word 'No' (number) and below this is a 5. What is it? Why is it there? What does it mean? Why is a ships anchor cut into it? We do not know. Ron thinks it may be a boundary marker for the Castle grounds but is unsure. Ron's idea may be correct because as we reach the road leading to the Church we find another one with the same anchor but with the number 3 on it.

Approaching the church along the road Peter notices some very old stone steps against the

Post with number 3?

church wall. "This must have been where the Gentry dismounted their horses to go to church" says Peter and he is obviously fascinated with the age of these steps. "I've got an aunt and uncle buried here" I say to no one in particular. "We'll 'ave to see if we can finds 'em" say Ron. I've noticed that Ron, when getting to a church, seems to come alive, in a strange sort of way. He is really enthusiastic about wandering around gravestones and finding names that he recognises. Today is no different. "Use ter play cricket against 'im", and "went ter school with their son", "knew im", are all things that Ron says as he wanders around this churchyard. And I must admit, after finding the stone of my relations, I recognised some of the names on the stones, Dr Moynihan, whose TV I had repaired. I also found my grandmother's doctor, Dr Robson, who was the Herstmonceux doctor for 30 years. Other names I recognised, Relf, Penfold, Fairall. These are all names and memories from my past.

Very well preserved tomb

Stained glass at it's best

The castle

The church itself is, as they all are, a wonderful, peaceful place. And to our surprise it is open. Part of the church is dedicated to the Fiennes and Dacre households whose names are infamous from this area. The best money you could spend here is to purchase the little booklet titled 'All Saints Church Herstmonceux'. It is full to the brim of information, not only of the church and its patrons but also about the area itself. I have no intention to repeat its contents here but be assured that I have learnt so much about Herstmonceux, just from this small publication, than I have over my many years of living in the area. From the church we are advised to turn left and follow the path around to the left where we will join a public footpath that now takes us past the castle itself. Peter has been looking forward to seeing the castle from this vantage point but is disappointed to see not only the castle but also cars parked in front of it. "This is a poor photographic opportunity," according to Peter. But he still clicked away like a man demented.

When I was a Postie I used to deliver the mail to the Castle and have always found this building particularly beautiful but have never wondered why it was made of brick. In the early mornings, with the mist over the moat, it looked like something from a fairy tale. There is a moat, a drawbridge and, after all, it's a castle. But I never realised that it was a 'folly'. Not built to protect the King's country, but permission had to be sought from Parliament to build the castle purely to entertain friends and impress people. A truly wonderful structure, nevertheless. A medieval tournament is held within the grounds every summer. The entry price is a little high and Peter and I think it's to keep the troublemakers away and only true interested people will attend. "All them others go ter Festival 'o Transport" say Ron "'tis on the same weekend as them medieval days". He could be right.

From here we stroll past what used to be The Royal Greenwich Observatory[26] with its large domes. One of which held the Isaac Newton Telescope until the atmosphere in the area got so bad that you couldn't see anything. It's now been relocated in the Canary Isles, somewhere.

Again, we come across a huge tree felled by the hurricane and left. It's so large that Ron could climb into the hollowed trunk. "If I were 'omeless I could live in there, no problem. Luv'ly an warm 'tis" says Ron. From here it's just a few yards back to the car. This was a very pleasant walk, with some good company. The book tells us that the walk is only three miles but it did seem longer than that. Ron gave it as "least four if not four 'an 'alf" but who knows?

Ron's new tree house

Peter cannot be with us for a while due to work commitments. We have enjoyed his company and hope he has enjoyed the two walks with us. He hopes to join us again soon and will be welcome.

Where we go next week is a bit of a surprise for me. Ron is suggesting that as this was a short walk we should do a longer one next week. We'll discuss it next Monday over a jar.

---

[26] Derek (Kings Head) pumped the concrete for the construction of the Observatory in 1952/3. A brickyard had to be re-opened to supply the bricks to match the castle. The bricks cost 2/6d for three.

WALK 9 – Wilmington

Wednesday 29th March 2006

I didn't take much persuasion in agreeing to a 6½-mile stroll during our Monday evening discussion or perhaps Ron waited until I was sufficiently oiled with amber nectar before the subject was approached. Whatever the reason, we have agreed to do the Wilmington Man Walk from our guidebook[27]. As this walk is further than any of our previous walks it was decided to leave an hour earlier, just in case.

The walk towards The Long Man

The weather today is cold and overcast. My dearly beloved wife has insisted that I wear a 'proper' coat and take a hat and scarf with me 'just in case'? My insistence that 'It doesn't rain in Sussex on a Wednesday afternoon' fell on deaf ears. So, with coat, hat and scarf I pick up Ron and we head for Wilmington Priory and another free car park.

The car park is relatively small. Only holding ten to fifteen cars but we were amazed at how much litter had been strewn over the area. I counted six circular concrete rubbish bins within the car park grounds yet beer cans, cardboard drink containers, and other public debris were just left over the ground. The place looked awful. Ron couldn't stand it, and had to clear the place up before we left for our walk muttering things about 'yobs, unemployed layabouts and midnight parties' in Ron's usual fashion. On leaving the car park I mentioned to Ron that a large plaque explaining the Long Man used to be on the edge of the picnic area but it didn't seem to be there now. All that was left was the stand, smashed and lying on the ground. What has become of people of today who can walk away and leave such a beautiful area in this state? Ron is gutted. "I used to come 'ere and mow that grass," he says, "used to get a cup 'o tea an' a biscuit from the posh lady in the 'ouse every time we came. It never used 'ter look like this. 'Twas a picture. I planted that 'edge nearly thirty years ago. Look at it now." Ron was not happy and went quiet. We walked towards the start of the walk in relative silence. I didn't know what to say.

The first part of the walk takes us up to the feet of The Long Man. There is some doubt as to who this figure depicts, how old he is and why he came to be on the South Downs[28]. Some records go back to 1710, from a drawing made by John Rowley, but his real origins are shrouded by mystery. Experts have been trying to solve the puzzle for centuries but no one has been able to prove conclusively who he is or what he symbolises. During World War II the site was camouflaged to prevent enemy aircraft using it as a landmark and restoration work is regularly carried out to ensure that he can be seen to his best advantage.

As we approach The Long Man I attempt to take a photograph. The camera will not work. "I don't understand. It was ok before I left home. I checked it." But it is now telling me that the battery is low! "We can always go to Alfriston Village Shop an get some new batteries," says Ron. "No," I say, "We're here now. If we go to the shop we'll have to buy pies as well.

---

[27] '50 Walks in Sussex' AA Publishing - Walk 16 – Page 44
[28] Ibid

We can do the walk without pictures, but if I need some, I'll have to come back again, another day." (Any pictures found on this chapter have been collected since the walk was completed). Where are Peter and that expensive camera when you need them? But words alone cannot describe the views that we are about to see.

From the foot of The Long Man we head along Weald Way towards the Windover Reservoir, which is on our right. Just as we pass the building we can hear a skylark singing. The sound is very loud yet we can't see the bird. Suddenly, out of the sky, the bird drops straight to the ground. How the bird managed to stop before it hit the ground I will never know. The speed the bird fell was amazing. "He'll drop to the ground an' walk along to 'is nest," says Ron. "They never fall straight to the nest. I used to chase after them birds for ages with me dad. See 'em drop and go, we did. Never found one 'ov 'em. Run along the ground to their nests they do. Puts people off finding the nest and takin' the eggs. My dad used to say – see the bird drop and walk in a circle of twenty feet and slowly go to the centre. You may find the nest – you may not." But Ron never did find one. At the end of the track we reach a road, Chapel Hill. Here we have to turn left and head towards Seaford.

I didn't see the people by the car, but Ron did. "They're scattering someone's ashes," says Ron, in a whisper. "Who is?" I whisper back. "Couple over by car, opposite track" whispers Ron, and there was a couple with what looked like an urn and light coloured ashes coming out as the lady looked on. I was just pleased that Ron didn't go over and ask the couple anything as we walked past; like it was something you see every day. Further down the road I recognised the finger post to Lullington Church. (Previous chapter) and as we passed, an elderly gentleman was unloading his car with carrier bags of shopping. This time, Ron couldn't resist. "Been shopping then?" asks Ron. "Yes," replies the startled man. "Looks like you spent some money at Tesco's" remarks Ron as the man is now hurriedly trying to get as many Tesco carrier bags as he can into one hand, shut the boot, lock his car and get inside his house all at the same time. "Spent a bit," replies the man. "Got any money left?" asks Ron. With this, the man escapes along his drive and is up his path like a rabbit. "I don't believe you asked him that," I said to Ron. "Poor bloke probably thought he was about to be mugged." "Jus' tryin' to be friendly," says Ron as we both head off down the hill.

As we pass the turning to Alfriston Ron says "We've no need to go to Alfriston for some pies. I went to Hailsham this mornin' and got a couple for us. Knew there'd be no shops out 'ere. I got you a chicken an' mushroom. 'ope that's ok." And out of his pocket comes two pies. Mine was delicious; the taste was enriched by the very strong smell of silage coming from the farm we were passing.

Our guidebook advises us to look for a pillar-box and swing left and to head towards Jevington. This was easily found, and as you walk up the track and look back, you get this remarkable view of Alfriston village. Whenever we walk up country tracks or pathways Ron is forever looking at hedgerows. This track was no different. "Look at this," he says, pointing to the top of a hedge that contained a large, tree trunk. "Woodpecker did that," he says. "Did what?" I ask as he is now climbing up the hedgerow. "This small 'ole," he says and I can just make out a perfect circle cut into the bark of the tree. "It's probably done for food. It's not lived in although there are some feathers and moss just below the 'ole. Will be used by a blue tit or robin I expect. Could be a nut 'atch, but they usually fill the entrance 'ole with mud to stop predators from gettin' in." Just as he was climbing down from the hedge a Land Rover passed by with two Labrador dogs running behind. "That's the way to take your dogs for a walk," I said "but I bet there pretty tired when they get back".

Wonderful view as we approach the top of the Downs

33

The track has started to rise quite steeply now and preservation of energy is high on my mind. I keep stopping for a rest, but the views from this track are astounding. You can literally see for miles. When you eventually reach the top of the hill, nothing in any book will prepare you for the scenery at this height. The number of different shades of green is astonishing. "Couldn't paint a picture that good," says Ron, and he is so right. Sussex never stops amazing me.

The beauty to be found on our own doorstep is something to behold. I have no idea how high we are but the book says the climb is just less than five hundred feet and we are not at the very top yet. But from where we are now standing, you can clearly see Arlington Reservoir, Berwick Church, Alfriston and Lullington, all places that we have both walked around over the past few weeks.

After a short climb up the track we arrive at the start of Lullington Heath National Nature Reserve. This is a conservation area that looks after the wildlife and plants that thrive on this part of the South Downs. Just by the sign for the Heath is a very large flint moneybox to put donations in. Ron says it was empty. Sheep and goats wander freely among the grasses and gorse and the whole scene is one of peace and tranquillity. None of the sheep have had their tails removed and it gives them an odd look. "Can see what Peter sees in 'em though can't you?" says Ron. "I'm beginning to get worried about you." I replied crossing over to the other side of the track. Another walking couple head towards us as we stroll through the heath. Ron, as always, can't resist a chat "Been walking long?" he asks. "We're heading towards Alfriston," says the young lady. "You've got the easy part now then," says Ron, "all down 'ill from 'ere. 'Ave you seen the

Looking towards Berwick

moneybox at the entrance?" asks Ron. "No we haven't" the man says and now Ron describes the box at the entrance to the heath. It's obvious that the couple want to get on and we wish them well on their walk. "Go into the village shop, at Alfriston. Mention that you've seen us and you may get a free pie".

Our guidebook advises us to now pass a bridleway to Charleston Bottom. We found a post that advises us of the bridleways but there was no mention of Charleston Bottom? "'ere it is," says Ron, pointing to the ground. He picks up the arm that has fallen off and it was now Ron's job to put the sign back on the post, using any available material. This included twigs, dead wood and willpower. We walked on with the knowledge that the next person heading towards Charleston Bottom will be aware of that turning. As we approach some gorse a distant memory flashes into mind. The thought involves fire paddles. In my younger days my parents used to take me to East Grinstead to visit my grandparents. Passing through Ashdown Forest, by bus, on the way to East Grinstead I used to see these sticks with pieces of rubber attached. I asked my father what they were for and he told me that should a fire start in the forest you could put it out with one of these paddles. I remember thinking, one paddle, big forest, some chance, and here we are, on top of the South Downs, miles from anywhere, no phone, lots of trees, even more grass and not one but two fire paddles in a wooden frame. Does this make any sense whatsoever? "I'll just try to put out this raging forest fire with my trusty 6 by 6 inch piece of rubber, whilst you run the four miles back to a telephone Ron, but please hurry." It's strange how memories come back.

As we approach the exit of the Reserve I notice that although the track starts to descend into a gradual slope as we veer left, it also rises twice as steeply around the next bend. From here you notice that the farmer has ploughed an 'arrowed his fields and the soil breaks up like sand. It really is a dark colour and the fields are enormous. It must take days to prepare the land for crops. Ron wants to get his metal detector and scour the area but it would take weeks.

As we exit the Reserve we meet up with the South Downs Way and follow the path through two gates. The directions, again, are very reliable.

As we walk across the top of the Downs the views are outstanding. You really can see for miles in every single direction. I am totally in awe. I have not seen views like it before and am now confident that another visit is called for, just to get photographs of these stunning surroundings. We pass a dry valley known as Tenantry Ground and apart from a small wire fence there is nothing to stop you from falling down into the steep valley. The feeling of going over the edge is quite chilling. Ron grabs at the binoculars to see some hares playing in the grass way below us. Jokes about hair come to mind but this isn't the time. From where we are now standing you can see Exceat and we watched the Newhaven Ferry heading out towards France.

We now head back over the top of The Long Man. This is the first time that I, personally, have ventured to the top of this monument, normally happy with being by his feet. The path takes us over and to the right of the monument, leading us back to the path, just by the Reservoir, where we started our walk two and a half hours ago.

As we head back towards the car, heading down a small narrow track Ron says, "Look, dunnocks, are nesting in the 'edge". Now, I'm not sure but when we last spoke to Des in our local I'm sure he told me that a dummock was a bull. When I said this to Ron he replied, " I didn't say dummock, I said dunnock. The word dunnock is Sussex for Hedge Sparrow". Of course, obvious, isn't it?

Another walk completed. Although it was over six miles I enjoyed it. I ache all over, but the experience and sights were well worth the pain I am now in. Whether I feel it was worth the pain in the morning, well, that's something else. Let's hope next week is just as good.

Another wonderful view

WALK 10 – Horsted Keynes

Wednesday 5th April 2006

It's nostalgia time. It was decided on Monday that we would go for something different this Wednesday. A little bit of reminiscing, for both of us. A step back in time to the 1950's for Ron, the 1960's for me. (I was born in September 1951 so have very little memory of the 50's but I can remember the 60's). So much has changed since my early years living in Hailsham. I can remember the High Street when Vicarage Field was actually a field and one-way traffic was never heard of. We often talk about the good old days yet wonder if they really were that good? Some things have improved there's no doubt about that. But some

Horsted Keynes Railway Station

things just bring you back to the early days of your life. Memories can be jogged by the simplest of events. Thoughts, sights and smells can trigger something deep inside and you start a sentence with "Do you remember when?" Today is going to be one of those days because we have decided to complete a 5 mile walk around Horsted Keynes, part of The Bluebell Railway Line, which has been restored and worked by volunteers at this station since 1963, although the Bluebell Line commenced in 1959 and is now in daily operation during April to October. There is also a service, run especially for children, in the run up to Christmas when the children can meet Santa and be given a present on one of the steam trains.

When I pick Ron up in the car I explain that I have set the Satellite Navigation up and that we will have no problem getting to Horsted Keynes. "Will that sexy lady be talking to us again?" asks Ron. "Yes she will," I reply. Immediately Ron stretches across to the Satellite

View along the railway line

Navigation screen, taps it with his finger and says "I'm Ron by the way. Pleased to meet yer."

The trip to Horsted Keynes is uneventful. We pass through some beautiful places. One being a village called Fletching. "Used to mow the grass 'ere," says Ron "an' played cricket on the green, for Hailsham. Been to the pub 'ere that used to be owned by Jimmy Edwards (well known comedian in the 50's and 60's with a big handlebar moustache). "'Tis really lovely ere", and I must agree the village is beautiful but the road is very narrow and people park cars on both sides which causes problems with traffic passing through the village.

Finding the village of Horsted Keynes was no problem, finding the station was. Ron noticed a sign that indicated a free car park. We went for it, but no joy. We had to ask a local person. The station is about 2 miles outside the village and not well signposted. But we got there in the end.

As soon as you step out of the car you can smell steam engine. It's fantastic! My children think they're dirty, smelly things, but you have to admire the size and strength that is generated by these monsters out of just coal and water. I noticed an advertisement on the station wall offering a stay in a seaside resort for 11/9d per week (less than our current 60p). The good old days?

Even the bins are numbered

Our guidebook[29] tells us to walk away from the station, keeping the railway line on our left. We must bear left at the end of the car park and then cross a footbridge over the railway line into a fenced walkway. The line is now on our right-hand side and should a train come past we could touch it. We are that close to the track. But our walk takes us, briefly, away from the railway line and circle round a wooded area that has been recently fenced off. Within this area we notice a number of bird boxes placed in the trees. When we get closer to the boxes we can see that they're numbered. I wonder why?

We rejoin the line after climbing over some stiles and are, again, very close to the track. "Would be great if we could see a train," says Ron handing me a steak pie.

Just as I start devouring the pie I notice a walker heading towards us. "Goin' out fer a walk?" asks Ron in typical fashion. "No!" is the reply "I'm on my way back" and the man was gone in a flash. Ron mutters something about stuck-up and West Sussex foreigners. "If a train does come along it will be pretty close to us Ron." I say, hoping to get Ron back from moaning. "And it looks as if we might be in luck. The signal up ahead has changed to 'go'."

Blackmore Vale

Sometime ago I fancied building a model train layout in 'n' gauge, which is still in the construction process. During the planning stage of this layout I learnt a little bit about railway signals. They appear to be different from one region to the other and, in some cases vary from one route to another within the same region. Apparently, any new driver of trains doesn't learn signals but has to learn the route, which will then teach him the signals for that route. Some signals are called 'home' and some are called 'away' depending on which way the signal is facing. Complicated isn't it? So much so that my model layout has signals that are constantly on go from either direction.

Back to the steam train, that is about to approach. We can hear the rhythmic puff-puff sound of the train in the distance. As it appeared round the bend, heading towards us, I, personally, felt a mixture of excitement and dismay. Heading towards us wasn't one of those enormous great black metal workhorses but a gleaming, newish green monster called 'Blackmore Vale'. There was very little, if any, steam coming from the funnel and, all in all, I felt a little let down. Ron said he felt the same way about the actual train but was just very pleased to have been able to see a steam train, up close, working for a living, and not left in a scrapheap to rust. I had to agree. The sight as it went passed us with the passengers all waving to us is a little memory to cherish.

Train heads for Horsted Keynes

---

[29] *50 Walks in Sussex* – AA Publishing Page 54

Newly fenced woodland

There is a wooden walkway which takes us over the track to the other side. This is the way our guidebook tells us to go next. So, after listening and looking carefully for any further activity on the line, we ran like hell, across the line and over the stile into the opposite field. We now join the West Sussex Border Path that was opened in 1989 and takes us away from the railway line towards some woodland. The new fencing that has been erected around this woodland is very noticeable. A large number of fences have been renewed along this walk and a vast amount of work has been carried out to clear the areas by coppicing etc. It looks really nice. Another thing that is very evident is the number of pheasants that wander this area. Ron believes they are some exotic breed but, whatever breed they are, they surely scare the hell out of you if they come out of their hiding places screeching when you least expect it.

Our direction now takes us down a slope and we have to head towards a break in the trees. Here we walk over a stream by a narrow path to the other side. No mean achievement when you're terrified of water but I managed to get over to the other side in time to take the picture of Ron following behind. Although the water looks still it is constantly on the move and at the end of the little walkway the water drops by about six feet before it meanders on its way.

Walking the plank, Ron style

As we cross one of the many fields we meet the inevitable sheep with lambs. Lovely, woolly things are sheep but I much prefer them with mint sauce. However, these sheep got a little upset with Ron and me wandering across there pasture and are bleating for their young ones to keep up with mum, whilst some lambs didn't care if we were there or not and carried on suckling. Ron said that one of the sheep had a crotel bell attached to it and you could hear this bell keep clanging. "P'robly the oldest sheep in the flock" explains Ron, "all the other sheep will foller' 'er if they get a problem". Again, the setting here is very peaceful, apart from the bleating, the clanging of that bell and the constant sound of Gatwick Hawks, as Ron called them. When he

Mum keeps an eye on us

first mentioned Gatwick Hawks I had no idea what he meant until he looked straight up and pointed out the aeroplane.

From this field of sheep we climb over a stile and turn right onto a road. We are now to head for Broadhurst Manor Road. "'We haven't seen many people on this walk have we?" I ask Ron. "Thems' we 'ave seen don't talk!" points out Ron. "We've got a little while to go yet before the end of the walk. Perhaps you'll get lucky." "P'rhaps" he replies. We pick up the Sussex Border Path again that leads us now into Broadhurst Manor. We are instructed to head towards the Manor gates and then veer right by these gates and head towards a lake. How the other half live. The Manor is enormous with massive double gates and a gravel, circular drive up to the front door. Carla Lane, the person who wrote the TV series 'Bread', amongst others, owns it. "She's supposed to have used a lot of 'er money on wildlife sanctuaries" says Ron.

Yes, I can see she must be down to her last shilling. The place must be worth millions", I can't get over the actual size of the place.

The lake we are looking for soon comes into view on our right. "That's no lake," says Ron, "no more 'an a puddle". When you walk round it there are six fishing pegs. That is a

Reflections in water are my favourite subjects for photography

small lake. But, as we walk down the lane, heading back towards Horsted Keynes, there is another lake, fed by the first, and this one is bigger, after about ¾'s of a mile, we had counted 5 lakes, all getting bigger than the previous one. The last lake, at the bottom of the hill, was huge. We discovered that the lakes on the right of the lane are fished by Horsted Keynes Angling Club whilst the largest lake was fished by Isfield and District Angling Club and was equipped with landing stages for boats as well as areas to fish from. The wildlife here must cherish this area. It is so naturally beautiful and must take many people lots of free time to ensure that it stays this way. As we get ready to leave the area and head for the village another walker, this time with dog, approaches us. "Hello," Ron says to the dog as he bends down to give it a stroke, "been in the water 'ave we?" he asks. "Yes," replies the owner who immediately drags the poor thing away from Ron and walks up the lane away from us. "Must think we're foreigners" says Ron as he walks past me and heads for the end of the lane.

At the lane's end we turn right and head towards the church. On our right are a number of beehives. "I haven't seen hives being used for years", I say to Ron. "Not many people keep 'em these days. Too much trouble I s'pose. Still, they are lovely little things to watch." There was 15 hives and they all looked as if they had inhabitants. The faint buzzing sound was a little soothing, I must say.

From here we go to the church. As you know by now both Ron and I have a thing about churches. But this one was different. Ron didn't get excited as he normally does, walking

Working hives

through a graveyard. Perhaps it was the fact that, being in Horsted Keynes, he wouldn't know anyone. It was a strange feeling. Inside the church was cold and uninviting. It didn't have a welcoming feel about it. We wandered around, found the memorial to Harold MacMillan M.P. and his wife on the wall of the church but that was it, nothing remarkable, just nothing. A pure coincidence, for both Ron and me, was that the vicar's name was Moggs. When we returned home I read that the church[30] was built differently from most churches in England in that it was not laid out East to West but North East to South West. Perhaps that was why it looked so dull. I really don't know. But Ron says that he felt the same way. When I told him that the French might have built it he now believes it was their fault all along for building a miserable church. "Typical 'o them 'Frenchies'" he says, "miserable so an so's".

Our guidebook is a little misleading from here. We are advised to turn onto a path past a house called 'Timbers'. We can't find the house. We find a path, but no 'Timbers'. "Go down this path and you'll get to the Railway Station", advises a local lady. Ron has now seen two young ladies putting green wellies on from a Range Rover car. "Goin' for a walk then ladies?" asks Ron, "We certainly are" is the reply. "We'd invite you to join us but you'd prob'ly leave us be'ind. You could always give us a 2-mile start," suggests Ron. "I'm sure you're going in a totally different direction to us" says one of the young ladies. To which Ron explains where our walk has taken us and where we are now headed. "No, we're not going

---

[30] St Giles Church, Horsted Keynes – A church guide obtained from the church

Horsted Keynes Church

that way" they said and we parted with a pleasant wave. "Could 'ave done me some good there" whispered Ron. "Not your type," I replied, "they're wearing green wellies."

While walking down the pathway we can hear children playing in the woodland to our left. We follow the path round a bend and we meet three ladies, complete with chairs, thermos flasks and cups sitting in the middle of the pathway. "Can you good young ladies tell us if this is the way to Horsted Keynes station?" asks Ron in his best Sussex. "Yes it is," replies one of the ladies, "but it's not the right way," says another laughing at us as we walk away. "Nice to find a woman with a sense of humour for a change" whispers Ron as we round the bend. At the end of the path, which we completed twice because I thought we were going in the wrong direction at first, we come to a road. We are instructed to turn right, walk over a bridge, and pick up the public footpath on the left. Walk across the field towards another stile and we should be back at the Railway Station. Wrong. We end up in a farmyard. The farmer is friendly and explains to me why he needs to harrow his pasture, to get all the dead grass and mole hills out, before his father goes over it all again with a roller. We also discover that the ground is wetter now than it was during the winter and that the strange looking pine tree in yonder pasture is not, in fact, a disguised mobile phone mast but a strange looking pine tree but, no doubt, a mast will be built at some time. It's half past four in the afternoon and he's about to start harrowing this giant field. Surely, it's time for tea? A female farmyard employee (?) explains to us that the public footpath runs right through the middle of the farm and "we always get people wandering through" and to get to the station we need to turn right at the end of the cow shed and follow the path straight to the station.

And that was it. A very nostalgic walk completed in near perfect weather. The sight of the steam train is something to remember and I'm sure Ron enjoyed it.

One of the many comments I've had, when discussing this walk back at the Kings Head, is the way that I pronounce the name Horsted Keynes. I pronounce the Keynes as canes, like the sticks you use to tie up plants in the garden. Many have told me that it should be pronounced 'keens'. They are wrong. I have a book about Horsted Keynes that tells us that the name is produced from the family name Ralph de Cahaignes who originated from Normandy in France and whose family lived in the village for generations. And from this book 'A guide to the History of St Giles Church, Horsted Keynes[31]: - '. The name of the village has been spelled in many different ways over the years but always pronounced CANES'. (Researched by Robert Sellens.)

Next week's walk will be my last before I go on an early holiday with my wife to the Cotswolds. While I'm away I will have a walk round on the Wednesday and write my findings in chapter twelve. Perhaps I'll compare the scenery in Sussex with that of Gloucester. I'm told it is very pretty up there. I'll let you know.

Until then both Ron and I meet again, Monday, in the pub (life can be hell) and we'll discuss what will, eventually, turn into chapter eleven.

---

[31] *A Guide to the history of St Giles Church Horsted Keynes* by Robert Sellens - booklet obtained from the church

WALK 11 - Hellingly

Wednesday 12th April 2006

This walk was agreed, after much discussion on the Monday. It is 7 miles long. It's a local circular walk, starting and returning to Hellingly and incorporates part of the Cuckoo Walk and can be found in 'Wealden Walks' – '20 Walks Exploring the Heritage of The Rich and Diverse Wealden Landscape'[32]. This is Walk 5 from the book, it is a category 3 that

includes hills and stiles, and it looks a lot longer than 7 miles to Ron and me.

My son, Anthony, has agreed that we can take his two Labradors with us. Please, God, don't let there be too much water. I know that both Tess and Pip will head straight for it and we could have all sorts of problems getting them out. As the walk is 7 miles, or over, we again start out earlier than our usual two p.m. I collect the dogs, complete with towels (in case they get wet??), covers (for the car, in case they get wet??), chocolate and biscuits (to entice them from water??) and leads. As you can

Tess and Pip, my son's Labradors

tell I am a little paranoid about them getting into water. Ron is ready and waiting, as usual, and is greeted with lots of licking and frenzied excitement. But I tell Ron to calm down or he wouldn't be going.

Parking in the car park opposite the now derelict Golden Martlet Inn is no problem and we set off with dogs towards Hellingly Parish Church. "Where's the map Ron?" I ask hastily checking every pocket I've got. "Must be back in car," says Ron, but no. I can't find it. "I don't believe this. Twice I've had problems with the camera and now I don't bring the map with me." My apologies to Ron go unheard, as he insists that the walk is on the Wealden Way and we will have no problem following the signposts on route. Famous last words!

We continue along the road towards the Church. Surrounding this church is what is regarded as the finest Saxon raised churchyard in Sussex. It stands up to seven feet above the circling houses and is held in place by tall brick walls and criss-crossed by brick paths laid by unemployed labourers in 1824.

Ron had already explained that he has seen a stone in the graveyard that marks the grave of a person who was shot in a gunfight in America in the 1800's. My daughter is fascinated with all things Western (especially outlaws) so I was hoping to get a photo and a name and date to take home and see what could be found out about the person who was shot. Unfortunately we are unable to find the stone. The

Hellingly Parish Church

gravestones in the area, that Ron thinks the stone was, are very badly worn and it is impossible to read most of them. Should I have more time, one day, I'll return and try again.

As you can see from the photo of the church some very tall trees are in the graveyard. But not as many as prior to the hurricane. Ron was sent to the churchyard to assist in the clearing of fallen trees and was met by the children who had erected a wooden seat in the churchyard in memory of their parents. The inscription reads 'In Loving Memory of Joyce & Winston Evenden'. A large tree had fallen across the seat. Ron and his workmates carefully cut away

---

[32] Part of a series of pamphlets obtainable from the offices of Wealden District Council, Crowborough

at the tree expecting to find the seat a smashed pulp, level with the ground, only to find the seat intact with just one broken slat. One of the large stone monuments had also been

Seat dedicated to Mr & Mrs Evenden

dislodged and had to be put back in place. It took Ron and his gang ages to lever the stone onto its plinth using logs of wood as levers. Ron says that you could still see the pencil line, drawn by the mason, where he had to cut the stone when it was being prepared.

We leave the churchyard and head along the road towards the Wealden Way. The Way is clearly marked and directs us across a field and heads towards the main road that runs from The Boship Roundabout to Horam. We let the dogs off the lead as soon as we establish that no farm animals are about and they shoot off sniffing and doing what animals do. We eventually arrive at a stile close to the road. We put the dogs back on the lead and climb over. The dogs seem confused. They're not sure if they should go over, under or through. With encouragement from Ron both dogs get under the stile. We wonder why they haven't got round to installing the stiles seen at Pevensey (Walk 3) which were so dog friendly. It would have made getting the dogs through a stile so much easier as we had a number of stiles to get over in this walk. Once over the stile Ron says, "Stopped 'ere once when I was metal detectin'. Stopped for a pee, up that tree there. I'd left the detector switched on, laying on the ground, an' when I picked it up, I 'ad a faint signal. Started to dig an' found 2 George III shillings. Must be loads 'o coins an' things in these fields." I asked Ron why he didn't do more metal detecting and he explained that you now had to get permission from the landowners and there were so many

Wealden Way sign

rules and regulations he sometimes couldn't be bothered. But there were a few fields in this area that he would love to scour.

We cross the main road and head for the Wealden Way sign on the righthand side of the road. This is the first mistake. We head towards Lealands. Looking on our map, when we get home, it is obvious that this was a big mistake. We should have turned left at the road and found the path, through Broad Farm. We are now walking the wrong way along the Wealden Way. The fact that I have left the directions at home only add to my stupidity as I write this. The signs on these walks instruct you in both directions. Unless you have a map you have no idea which way you are going. Please forgive me Ron, but because of this mistake, we walked miles out of our way. The

Low Tide?

instructions on the post tell us to walk towards Lealands. So, unknowing, this is what we do.

"Used to be a post box up this lane," I explain to Ron, "the postman that used to empty it, in the afternoons, used to drive all the way from Chalvington Village just for this one small pillar box. There's only a handfull of houses up this lane and you would only find the odd letter in the box. I tried to have the box removed but the locals created hell because, during the Spring, birds nest in the box. So it had to stay. The postman told me that during the Spring anyone wanting to use the box used to put their letter in a bag and attach it to the outside of

Tess enjoys a swim

the box so they didn't disturb the nesting birds. We also had problems with slugs in that particular box. They seem to be attracted to the glue used on postage stamps and you would find a big tasty slug feasting on the stamps on the letters. It's strange but very true. I've witnessed it myself when I was a Postman at Bodle Street.

We find a stile, complete with Wealden Way sign and head for, what I now know is, West Street Farm. The dogs are let off the lead and they run about. Ron notices an old boat hull laying in the field. "Tide must o' come in a damned long way to wash that up 'ere," he says. It must have been there a few years, the hull was green with mould. "It always amazes me" I say, "all these poor hard up farmers bleating about they can't make a livin' and they leave tractors, machines and the like in their fields to rot and rust."

As we approach West Street Farm we put the dogs back on leads. Pip smells a bit strange. "Think she's been rollin' in foxes sh$*," says Ron, "saw 'er rollin' on the ground a ways back." It was awful. "We'll have to find a pond for her to swim in. Hopefully it'll wash off." I said. "Thought you didn't want 'em in water." "I didn't but I can't put up with that smell." Pip didn't seem to mind but, luckily, a pond was in sight and we managed to get her in. Getting both out wasn't any trouble either. A biscuit for each of them, as a mark of my relief, was in order. Now that Pip smelt better we continued on our way.

As we make our way around the farm we notice an old Fire Engine parked by a barn, rotting away. "Just like you said," say Ron "poor 'ard up farmer 'an 'e leaves a contraption like that to rot." As I'm about to take a photo a large dog, something like a wolf crossed with an alsation

Abandoned Fire Engine

comes running towards us barking and teeth showing and glaring at us with his one blue eye. As you know, I don't particularly like dogs. Wolfie ones are no exception. "Just keep walkin'," says Ron "'e wont 'urt yer." The only one whose worried about this monster is me. Both Tess and Pip walk on like nothing's happening, as good as gold. Ron said that he would hold the two dogs if I wanted to go back and take a photo. I told him I'd take one from here. There was no way I was going back on my own. Also, in the middle of this field we found another stile. No fence either side of it. Just a stile. "Per'aps it's used for getting

Stile with no fence?

on an' off horses," suggests Ron. "But why would they put a Wealden Way sign on it?" I asked "when you can see, from here, that the next stile is clearly marked as well". One little mystery. Perhaps they moved the hedge and decided to leave the stile? A talking point over the amber nectar at The Kings Head later on.

From the farm we are now on a lane. The Wealden Way signs are still in sight but for some reason, I know not why, I direct Ron towards a public footpath. Another mistake. We end up walking round a field that appears to have only one exit. The way we came in. Why we went into that field is a complete mystery. We go back to the lane to find that the Wealden Way sign tell us to continue up the lane towards Gun Hill.

As with all the walks we have completed the scenery and peacelfulness is stunning. Trees and hedge shrubs are just starting to bud and wild flowers are popping their heads above the surface. Some flowers, primroses, anenomes and daffodils are in full bloom. We realise now that we haven't met anyone since leaving Hellingly Church and Ron thought now would be a good time to produce the inevitable pies. As we walk along the road the field, to our left,

contains a number of old vehicles. Again they appear to be left to rot. They are not covered, but left to the elements and must, in good condition, be worth something. They must have been brought by someone, so why leave them to rot. What a waste of money. I can't see the point. We now see our first sign of human life. A man is putting his dog into his car. He spins round and says "Oh, there's two of you!" "What did you think,"says Ron with his big grin. "'twas one talkin' to 'is self?" "You never know out here," is the reply. "There's nothing strange 'bout us two an' the dogs," says Ron as we head up the road. "You never know out here," says the old man again, as we turn the bend.

Now here is when it definitely went wrong. We approach a road junction. The Wealden Way arrows are clearly on the pole. One tells us to turn left, the other is pointing, sort of, the way we had just come. But, for some reason, I ignored the left arrow and assumed that the other told us to turn right. The wooden finger post, also at this road junction, indicated that turning right would

Vintage car collection?

take us to Gun Hill and I knew that Gun Hill was on the map I had left at home. If I had realised, at the time, that we were walking this walk backwards it would have been obvious that turning left was the correct way. So we turned right and, merrily, headed for Gun Hill. "If we walk along here we should see another Wealden Way sign telling us to turn right again." I explain to Ron. "But Chiddingly Church is on our left," says Ron "an' that's were we should be 'eadin'". For some reason even this blunt statement from Ron didn't ring alarm bells from within. He was correct. But we still headed for Gun Hill. We started to complain to each other that we hadn't seen any signs for Wealden Way at

all. How bad this was and someone should complain. But it's not really surprising when we now realise we were nowhere near the Wealden Way walk. We plodded on. The dogs were now looking decidedly tired. They, and we, had been walking for two hours. "Don't worry," says Ron, "We'll meet up with the Cuckoo Trail at Horam and walk back that way". "But Ron," says I, "Horam's two miles away. That signpost back there said Hailsham 6 miles. This walk is supposed to be 7 miles long. We've walked 7 miles already and are still over 5 miles from the car." To which Ron replied, "Don't worry, we'll meet up with the Cuckoo Trail at Horam and walk back that way", and that's exactly what we did.

The road to Horam is narrow and winding. Traffic hurtles down this road without any thought for pedestrians. There is no footpath. We arrive at the 15th century Gun Inn. A formidable building which can

Cuckoo Trail marker post

supply a welcome drink and meal. We are strong and resist the temptation. The Inn's name commemorates the Wealden iron industry and nearby is an old disused furnace at Stream Farm. Just past the Inn is Gun Cottage which looks considerably older than the Inn with its oak beams and thatched roof. Many a story to be heard from here no doubt.

We eventually reach Horam. My son has phoned because he's worried about his dogs. "What do you mean your at Horam. You're supposed to be going to Chiddingly," he says. "It's a long story," I say "but the route isn't well signposted. We should be back by five o'clock." I get the impression that he's not pleased. Never mind, the Cuckoo Trail is just ahead, we will soon be on our way home.

As we descend onto the Trail we meet up with an old work colleague of mine, Steve, who used to be a postman at Hailsham. "What are you doing out here?" he asks. "The Wealden Way walk," I reply. "God, your miles off course," is his reply. "Yes, we gathered that. So we thought we'd head for the Cuckoo Trail and head back this way". As he rode off on his bike we let the dogs off the leads and they seemed to spring back into life. As you can see from the sign post, Hailsham is 5 miles away. We start off, following the dogs who are now darting from one side to the other.

Gradient sign on disused railway line

If you haven't walked along this Trail, please, take time to discover the beauty of this area. The actual Trail runs from Heathfield to Polegate and follows what was once, the old steam railway line. The "Cuckoo" line was first opened in 1880 and originally, trains ran from Polegate to Redgate Mill junction. The line was named after the tradition that the first cuckoo of spring was heard at Heathfield Fair. The line was eventually closed between 1965 and 1968 and converted into a walkway. Some signs of its original use can still be seen. Obsolete signs indication gradients have been left, and most of the tunnels are intact. The peaceful surroundings are complemented with numerous places to stop and picnic with wooden tables and chairs placed at regular intervals along the Trail. Surprisngly, today, we don't see that

Watermill at Hellingly

many people and those we do see are out walking dogs or riding push bikes. It really is a paradise for dogs. They have no traffic to worry about and can, basically, roam wherever they wish. Pip, again, has found something foxy to roll in and desperately needs a wash down. Even the very sweet smelling wood anemones, which blanket both sides of the Trail, cannot disguise the awful aroma of this dog. Relief is at hand again, when yet another little river is found and she's let loose in the water.

Towards the end of the Trail for us we need to turn right, onto a road which leads us back to Hellingly church. With the dogs back on leads we head towards Watermill House. There is a plaque on the wall that states that there has been a watermill on this site since around 1255 when it was owned by Battle Abbey. The plaque also tells us that an agreement has been found, produced in 1255, which limits the sluice height to '2 feet and a half and 3 inches' to give sufficient flow to other, downstream, mills. The current building dates from the mid 1700's. In 1924 the mill was no longer used but a new wheel was installed during 1984/5 and the current owner is hoping to restore the machinery to working order.

From here it is just a short walk, past the church, along the road and back to the car. I am in agony. My feet hurt like hell and my legs ache like I've never felt them before. "We must a done 'bout 12 miles. Not bad for a 7 mile stroll," giggles Ron. I want the world to open up and devour me. Not only because of my own stupidity in leaving the map behind but also because of the agony I now find myself in. But the dogs loved it. And Ron says that he enjoyed it and if I'm really, really honest with you all, in a strange way, aches and pains aside, I have to admit, this was a bloody long walk.

WALK 12 - Cirencester

Wednesday 19th April 2006

Monday wasn't usual. I had travelled to Gloucestershire during the day with both my wife and mother-in-law. If you haven't travelled with, what is now, Wallace Arnold Shearings, give it a try. Get on the coach, sit back, relax and let the driver take the stress. You can't beat it. The hotel we're in is, would you believe, The Kings Head. But this one is in Market Street,

A Caquettoire

The Church of St John The Baptist

Cirencester. It was, originally, a home for the Augustinian monks in the early 1100's and converted to a hotel when the abbey was abolished around the 15th and 16th century. Around the hotel are various artefacts that were found in the area. Most are instruments of torture but one, a large wooden chair, called a Caquettoire and dates from the 1600s[33]. It was used by women to sit whilst working on their needlework in the parlour and to gossip. The word is derived from the French verb Caquetter – to chat, and is a wonderful, ornately carved piece of furniture. We had to pass this seat every time we went to and from our room, which was a long way from the reception, to the side of the building. There are also many pictures including past royalty, scattered about the walls with various historical facts printed with the picture. One depicts a burning carriage right outside the hotel when on the 15th August 1642 a Lord Chandos arrived at Cirencester to enlist men for King Charles I. But as Cirencester was mainly Parliamentarian and not Royalist they smashed and burnt his carriage and killed some of the Lord's Company. Lord Chandos managed to escape but it is said that this was the first bloodshed of the Civil War.

Anyway, one of the things I had promised Ron was that I would carry out our tradition of going for a walk on Wednesday afternoon. The problem I had, was finding a walk. After a visit to the Information Centre and the purchase of a couple of guide books, I settled down at the bar, amber nectar in one hand, and scanned the available walks with both wife and mum-in-law. One of the books, Cotswold Walkabout, had various walks including 'Knibly Knoll', 'Crickley Hill' and 'Stumps Cross'. Unfortunately though most were not circular and I needed to catch public transport to get to the start. The walk I settled on was the Town Walk[34]. It started right outside the hotel, covered about 3 miles and returned, via the abbey, to the hotel.

Brass way mark on pavement

One of the things I didn't expect was that both my wife and mother-in-law expected to come with me. With guidebook in hand we decided that I would give a guided walk of the town, at 2 o'clock

---

[33] From information gathered at the Hotel
[34] *Cirencester a town walk* – 2003 edition – Published by Cirencester Civic Society

we set off.

As you are aware it never rains in Sussex on a Wednesday afternoon (according to Ron). Unfortunately, it does in Gloucestershire. Not hard, just wet. But, being true British we were not deterred.

Opposite the hotel is the Parish Church of St John the Baptist. This has to be one of the largest parish churches I have seen. It is Cathedral size, and dominates the Market Square in Cirencester. Luckily for us there is no organ playing so I was able to walk round comfortably. The building inside is impressive and the decorations are formidable. But, probably due to its size, there seemed to be something ugly about it.

Admiring the hedge

Broad Drive

7 Cecily Hill with one floor missing

Back outside our guidebook advises that the walk is marked out by brass waymarks set into the pavements and footpaths at various points along our route. These were put in place to commemorate Marjorie Burn (1914-1992) who initiated the tradition in this area of regular town walks. A brilliant idea, very handy, I thought. Not only got a map but clear signs as well. We found the one outside the church and headed across the road towards Castle Street. It isn't until you visit another town that you realise how boring our street names are in Hailsham. North Street, South Road and the like are not very inspiring, yet Black Jack Street and Spitalgate Lane in Cirencester conjure various pictures in the mind.

From Castle Street we turn right into Silver Street where we find Abberley House that dates back to the 1750s' and was given to the Council in 1936 by the Bathurst and Cripps family. This property, and its Victorian neighbours, now houses the Corinium Museum with some remarkable Roman mosaics. (Cirencester now sits on the site of a Roman town called Corinium).

We now bear left into Park Street where buildings date, again from the 1700s'. A number of these houses have windows blocked off, probably to avoid the 1697 window tax, a rating device that lasted until 1850. At the end of this street and the junction of Park Lane is said to be the tallest yew hedge in the world. Behind this hedge and rustic gateway is the mansion of Earl Bathurst that has strict 'no entry' signs. The estate wall runs the complete length of Park Street with some estate cottages on our right. At the end of the wall we turn left and walk up the lefthand side of Cecily Hill.

There used to be an old chapel here dedicated to St Cecilia that disappeared centuries ago. This road used to be the main thoroughfare to Bisley and Stroud but is now a cul-de-sac. The buildings along here vary in date from 1702 to 1909. The buildings have the dates of construction carved on them. Number 7 Cecily Hill has a design problem in that the original house had three storeys when built but a later extension only has two that gives the large house an odd outward appearance.

At the top of the Cecily Hill are some enormous metal gates, which cross the road and leads you into Broad Drive, a large avenue some five miles long. Earl Bathurst has given permission that visitors on foot or horseback can use this part of Cirencester Park. The cottages on either side of the gates date from the 17th century on the left and the 19th century on the right. But looking at them they look as if they are from the same era.

It was about now that we met our first local. My wife and mother-in-law were looking for the brass plate on the pavement which would direct us back along the other side of Cecily Hill when a lady asked "Have you lost something?" "No," replies mum-in-law, "we're looking for a sign." Now I can only assume that the lady thought that we were some religious fanatics, it being around Easter and all, and we were looking for some spiritual sign to guide us. My wife came to the rescue of the lady's strange looks when she explained about the Town Walk waymark. "Oh," says the lady, "I'm sorry to interrupt your guided tour but I thought you'd lost something. How long have tours been given and when were the waymarks put into the pavement?" I spent the next few minutes telling the lady about her own town. We eventually found the way marker by The Barracks. This was built in 1857 and was the

Tontine houses

headquarters and armoury for the Royal North Gloucester Militia and is now used for offices.

As we walk back down Cecily Hill we pass what used to be The Old Dolphin. The tavern sign no longer exists but the iron brackets still remain in place. Lower down Cecily Hill are a range of dwellings with the inscription 'Tontine' over the archway. The word Tontine is given to a financial scheme, now illegal, whereby the last surviving subscriber to a joint enterprise finished by owning the lot. Again, the bricked up windows can be clearly seen.

We bear left here and Park Street becomes Thomas Street. The street name is fixed to Monmouth House. The original house dates back to the 14th century around the time of Chaucer. Opposite is the former wool warehouse with a prominent cart way arch. There are many blocked windows here. The top row of blocked windows are purely dummies, as the wall into which they are set is only a screen to a steep roof, with no rooms behind it.

Turning right into Coxwell Street is the 17th century Woolgatherers, built as the residence of the owner of the adjoining warehouse in Thomas Street. Next door is the counting house with its own little flight of stone steps to the raised door. Other places to note are the Old Court, formerly a rich clothiers house and the large Baptist Chapel built around 1857.

Number 10 Coxwell Street has the date and initials of the builder, lawyer John Plot on the doorjamb. Though John Plot was a Royalist, King Charles's men pillaged his house in 1642

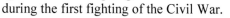

Dry-stone wall

during the first fighting of the Civil War.

We now turn left into Dollar Street, named after the charitable Dole Hall of the Abbey. A few feet along this road is a bakery with its yard entry. Immediately beyond this is a second opening. The way-marker advises us to head along this passage into St Clements Walk. One of the things that have surprised me in Gloucestershire is the number of dry stone-walls. Whist I have seen them in Yorkshire I didn't, for some reason expect to see them here. Yet

everywhere you look, there are dry-stone walls. St Clements Walk was no exception. The area used to be gardens and small, very old properties, that could not be modernised. In 1967 architects were asked to provide flats, small houses and garages in a style, which 'should be modern but appropriate within the traditional setting'. They did really well, and although fairly new the buildings fit in well with their surroundings. We pass through an iron gate and are back onto Thomas Street.

The Friends Meeting House

We turn right and pass the Friends Meeting House that is dated 1673. Just opposite is the Temperance Hall, built in 1846 by philanthropists, to combat the demon drink. It has been restored and is now used by the Salvation Army. Next is St Thomas's Hospital, now known as Weavers Hall. This building is the most ancient non-ecclesiastical building in the town. It was founded by Sir William Nottingham (d1483) who would be glad to know that the almshouse has been lived in, continuously, since then. At the end of Thomas Street we cross Dollar Street. We are now in Spitalgate Lane where they are carrying out restoration work on what was St Johns Hospital and Chantry, which was founded by Henry II. I am now confronted by a holidaymaker, who has been following us for a while, and thought I was being paid to conduct one-on-one tours of the town. My wife muttered something about me not being for hire and we moved on by turning left into Dugdale Road.

On our left is 'modern housing whose names Hakeburn and Estcote commemorate two Abbots of St. Marys. We now turn left and follow a grassy path to the right, round a car park. We are now in what used to be the old Abbey grounds. The main path leads you straight past the modern Abbey House towards the Parish Church but if you bear left you can walk around this beautiful area and take in the stunning surroundings. One pathway to our left takes you towards the Norman Arch and gatehouse, which is the only remnant, above ground, of the once extensive St Mary's Abbey, built in the 1100's for the Canons Regular of St Augustine. The whole area is so wonderfully peaceful. Just past the Norman Arch is a fenced off play area for children. "You couldn't have anything like that round where we live. Be vandalised within days," says mum-in-law, who is starting to sound so much like Ron? But it

Original Norman Arch

could be true. I have noticed that everywhere we have been this week, not just Cirencester, but everywhere in Gloucester is so clean. No rubbish, not a sign of graffiti on walls. It has been a real pleasure to be here.

The walk now takes us past a lake, complete with ducks and swans before veering off to the left where the last remaining parts of the Roman wall can be seen. The original Abbey was demolished many years ago but as recently as 1965 its foundations have been excavated and indicated by paving stones in the grass. The guidebook says that the original abbey was considerably larger than the present parish church. So it must have been a considerable structure.

The lake within the Abbey grounds

From here it is just a short walk, through the gates and we are back at the Parish Church and opposite our hotel. To finish the walk, as no pies were consumed, it was decided to find an olde worlde coffee shop and sit down, dry out and have a nice, hot coffee before returning to the hotel. Throughout the walk it has rained on and off but both wife and mother-in-law say that they were pleasantly surprised at how nice the walk was. They had found out a lot about the town and, hopefully, I have managed to pass the information on, with some interest. The walk wasn't the same without Ron, and the type of walk was a little different. I have learnt many things about observation since starting the country walks and I hope that what Ron has taught me to observe in the country, can also work in a town.

WALK 13 – Hailsham/Polegate

Wednesday 25th April 2006

I am back in good Old Sussex by the Sea. Monday evening's decision over the amber nectar was to walk 6 miles. Even though I am now gainfully employed and this is my first week at the new job, ferrying schoolgirls from Hastings into Eastbourne in the morning and home in the evening, and I have to be in Eastbourne by 10 to 5, Ron thinks that 6 miles is a doddle. I'm not so sure. So I suggest an earlier start. Just in case.

For the avid reader of this journal, you will remember that I forgot the map to Walk 11. I do not propose to do the same this week. The map hasn't left my side since Monday evening. This walk is number 7 in the Wealden Walk[35] pamphlets and is titled 'A Tale of Two Towns'. It should start in Polegate, and head us along the Cuckoo Trail to Hailsham and then take us back, through countryside, to Polegate. I say should, because we didn't. We actually started at The Old Loom Mill (by Mulbrooks Farm) and did the whole walk in the opposite direction to that shown on the guide. Why did we do this? The theory was that should we get round in plenty of time we could stop at the very pleasant coffee house at The Old Loom Mill for a well-earned cuppa.

Again, those who have followed our travels will be aware that one of the reasons I am carrying out these walks is to lose weight. At the thirteen-week period I have to say I have not lost a pound. There are various reasons, I am told, why this could be. One is that we are taking a stroll, and not walking at pace. This is true. But, anyone who knows Ron will be

aware, that he doesn't rush anywhere. Ron is always telling me that 'to rush is to miss things'. Ron's reputation for finding 'things' is becoming infamous. He can see a coin, lying in mud, from fifty paces.

Of course another reason could be the delicious pies Ron has started to bring with him on the walk. My wife advises me that should I return from one of these walks and fail to eat my dinner again, she will not be a happy lady. On this advice, I have asked Ron not to supply me with pastries. I will let you know if any weight loss occurs in a future chapter.

Picnic tables along Cuckoo Walk

I collected Ron at ¼ past 12 from our regular hostelry. A nice early start, just in case. We park the car in the car park at The Old Loom Mill. It is a warm, sunny day without a rain cloud in the sky. I have attached one of those step things to my trouser belt. This will count how many steps I have taken and convert it to mileage. I'm curious. We leave the car park at The Old Loom and enter the Cuckoo Trail turning left.

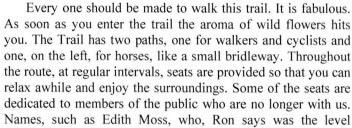

Every one should be made to walk this trail. It is fabulous. As soon as you enter the trail the aroma of wild flowers hits you. The Trail has two paths, one for walkers and cyclists and one, on the left, for horses, like a small bridleway. Throughout the route, at regular intervals, seats are provided so that you can relax awhile and enjoy the surroundings. Some of the seats are dedicated to members of the public who are no longer with us. Names, such as Edith Moss, who, Ron says was the level

Peaceful views

crossing keeper. "Used to 'ave to knock the door so that she could open the gates to let you

---

[35] Part of a series of pamphlets obtainable from the offices of Wealden District Council, Crowborough

cross the road," says Ron, "lovely lady, she was". Margaret Springett, "Used to 'ave an allotment at Cophall Farm, she did". Pamella Terry, "Used 'ter live at the big crossing gate house in Ersham Road, 'ad a lovely daughter. 'Er 'usband used to make model traction engines and always wore bib an' brace". Ron seemed to know them all. "I was on the last train that came along this track to Polegate in September 1968", reminisces Ron, "I think it was the 9:44. Loads o' people on it there were. Most o' them never used a train from one week to the next but this one was packed. Got all the way to Polegate, we did, then 'ad to find our own way 'ome, 'cause there were no train back. Some took bus. I walked. Never forget that." Heading towards us is a lady, with pushchair and dog off the lead. "'Ello," says Ron, to the dog, bending down to give it a stroke. The dog had other ideas and skirted round Ron. "Don't want ter stop fer a chat, then," says Ron, "He's probably got better things to do" says the lady, and walks off pushing her pram.

Some very pretty white hawthorn trees edge the Trail and the sound of birds is very prominent. Ron sees two Goldfinches and practically goes orgasmic. We are only a short distance from Hailsham yet the surroundings are very much all country. Primroses grow abundantly along this Trail and the sweet smell is evident most of the time. As we head towards Polegate you can hear traffic noise but you must try to tune this traffic noise out, then the sounds of the country become very loud. Birds singing and the bleating of sheep can be clearly heard. It really is very peaceful. One of the differences I have noticed on this side of the Cuckoo Trail is the modern art pieces at most of the road junctions. These may have been on the other walk (Walk 11) but I can't remember them being so prominent. The one in this picture represents what? It is an open wire-framed, three-legged archway and strategically placed on each leg are rocks. At first we thought they

Modern Art Forms?

were to hold the structure down but then we noticed that the three legs are bolted to metal posts. Another of the modern art structures is of a tunnel and is easily recognisable, but this one has us baffled.

Shortly after passing this we hear cyclists coming up behind us. When I turned to see what was coming I was surprised to see what could be described as a contingent of the geriatric 'Tour de France'. Six cyclists complete with day glow bright yellow jerseys, lycra black shorts and bums in the air are heading in our direction. "Thank you," shouts the leader, the youngest lad aged about sixty. We let them pass. "You're a long way from France," Ron shouts at the trailing bum, "but

Polegate by-pass

'yer 'eading in the right direction." Why do some cyclists dress in this way? Some have all the colourful gear, even shoes that are the same colour as their shirts. Some of them look ridiculous. Yet they go out, in public. On the open road I assume it is so they can be seen and in a race the colours of your team are something to be proud of - but on The Cuckoo Trail? Another cyclist we saw on the trail had a black crash hat, bright pink jersey and purple shorts. He looked like a Liquorice Allsort.

It's here that old meets new. The new A27 bypass goes under the walk. We cross over this road by a

Linseed Rape plants

bridge. The traffic is oblivious to us as it speeds towards Hastings or Eastbourne. The developers have planted trees along the route so, hopefully, this should reduce the noise level when they are fully-grown. It will also make the area look a little more attractive as well as improving the environment.

Polegate is at the end of this part of the Trail and is described as a Victorian 'new town' in our guidebook. The decision to drive the railway from Brighton straight through to Hastings in 1846 led to the establishment of a junction at Polegate. Around this junction a settlement grew up, its origins visible in the terraces of Victorian houses such as Brook Street and in road names such as Victoria Road and Albert Terrace.

It is back on the Trail that our map becomes a little unhelpful. Whilst the map is good, it has no written directions. Which is unlike our '50 Walks in Sussex' book used on other walks. We eventually pick up what we believe is the walk, on the other side of the A27, and now walk parallel to the road, heading towards Hastings. I wonder how many people are aware, as they speed along this road, that a public footpath is only a few feet away and the only thing to stop a vehicle hurtling towards us is a small wire mesh fence. To our right is a field full of rape plants (used for making linseed). The smell is a little overpowering after a while. I can't write what Ron thought it smelt like. It was now, with a small glint in his eye, that Ron opens his binocular case and withdraws a paper bag. "I hope you haven't got a pie," I say, as my wife's threatening voice appears in my mind. "I 'avn't got you a pie but I got this," he says and he puts his hand in the bag and produces a dainty sausage roll. "Couldn't eat me pie and you 'ave nothing'. It didn't seem right." It was delicious. Full of herbs and it was very tasty. I wouldn't be getting home from work till ½ past 7 this evening so the effects should have worn off by then and I'll be able to eat my dinner. Wife will be none the wiser. I hope.

Man-made lake in the area of the old Otham Abbey

We have to cross back over the A27 now and head towards Shepham Lane. When we get to the other side there is an 'Official' diversion of the public footpath and we are pointed across a field. I think this will just cut off the corner, on the map, and will make us miss Shepham Lane. The route we now take passes close to Otteham Court, where, in the year 1180 an Abbey was founded and, at the time, was the only building in what is now Polegate parish. The area was chosen for its seclusion. Unfortunately for the monks, other people soon followed and within 40 years the monks had relocated to Bayham Abbey on the Kent border. Some of the old ruins of the original Otteham abbey can still be seen. Again, the views along this stretch of the walk are stunning. We pass a man-made lake that has become the home of a large number of

Quiet inland waters

swans and the location of this lake is simply beautiful. The whole area has been fenced off and new trees planted around the perimeter. The whole area, in the middle of nowhere, is going to be a safe haven for so much wildlife. Yet only a few yards away is the very busy A27. It's incredible.

We now walk along a hedgerow towards the estate called Priesthawes, which is situated on the B2104, the road from Hailsham to Stones Cross. Part of the hedge encloses some very large and old pine trees that have rooks nesting high in the top. "Build a nest high means we'll 'ave a fine summer," says Ron, "an' you can't get no 'igher than them rooks." All along this hedgerow Ron is looking for something. When I asked him what he was looking for all I got was "tell yer when I find it! But the farmer's taken pride in cuttin' this 'edge. Look 'ow neat 'tis". It was very neat, not a twig out of place and all the same height. A lovely hedge. Ron, again, went orgasmic. He had, obviously, found what he was looking for. "Look at this," he whispers, beckoning me to look in the hedge. "See that?" he asks. "It's a bird's nest," I reply. "That 'ant no ordin'ry birds nest but 'tis the nest of a Dunnock. Look, she's laid eggs, four of 'em. Bright blue they are." I could just make out something at the bottom of a nest but couldn't get as excited about it as Ron obviously was. "Made my day, just to see that nest," he exclaims, as excited as if someone had given him the winner of the Grand National.

We cross the B2104 and enter Priesthawes. Our guidebook describes the mansion house as 'fair and sumptuous, and newly built in 1620.' It is a massive building and I'm beginning to feel as if we a trespassing as we walk around the perimeter of the building and head towards the farm buildings at the back of the property. It is now I hear the dog. It sounds big. It sounds angry. It's in the Range Rover, with the drivers' door open. I don't like

A strange barrel?

dogs that sound big and angry. A man stands by a barn talking on his mobile. Ron tries to ask the man if we were on the right track for the Wealden Walk. He shrugs his shoulders, points to his mobile and turns his back on us. The angry, brown dog is now out of the Range Rover, and is big. He is barking, his lips are rolled back, his hackles are up and he is heading towards us. The man totally ignores what happens next. This snarling dog runs around us and takes a lunge at Ron. I didn't think he made contact but when we get round the bend and the dog has gone Ron says, "I think that bastard bit me." Sure enough, Ron has a mark on the back of his leg and blood has been drawn. Just as we are thinking of heading back to confront the owner, the dog comes at us again. This time, with much waving and Sussex cursing the dog backs off. What we should have done now

was to go back and confront the man. But all of a sudden our bravery seemed to evaporate and, I'm ashamed to admit, we just walked out of the drive. In retrospect we should have complained. The path we were on was a public footpath and anyone could walk along it. The man or owner didn't say or do anything to prevent this from happening. We will be taking a stick on our next walk.

From here we now cross the marsh road and head for the fields behind Glyndley Manor. Again our map is less than helpful and the Wealden Way signs have become non-existent. We cross a small river, which, Ron tells me he used to fish when he was a young man. It is edged with hawthorn trees and is one of the most tranquil spots I have seen on our walks. We also pass a strange object hanging from one of the trees in the corner of a field. It is a barrel, with a number 22 painted on it. Under the barrel is what looks like a spring. The barrel has a screw on top and there is nothing inside it? There is no indication what it could be for but a number of what look like

More of the dreaded animals

footprints of sheep (according to Ron) can be seen around the barrel. I think it may be used as a substitute mum for feeding lambs?? But any ideas would be appreciated.

We now cross over another stile, still no markings for Wealden Walk, and enter a field full of sheep. All with lambs. To get to the other stile, across the field we have to go, through the centre of this flock of sheep. Now perhaps it's because I am a Townie that most animals worry me. I do not profess to be an animal lover. In fact I don't like pets of any sort. Even my own sons' dogs worry me. But I do believe that animals can sense this. These sheep were going to be no exception. As soon as we started to walk towards them they looked at me. Every single one of them. They didn't look at Ron. It was me they had their eyes on. All the sheep, as we walked towards them, moved to let us through. As soon as we passed them they followed me. Not me and Ron, just me. The sound from these animals was deafening, as they appeared to chase me the last few yards to the stile, which I cleared, in Olympic fashion. Ron was in hysterics.

Moving on, we come to the outskirts of Little Downash Farm, and are, again, within farm buildings and hastily checking for sounds of dogs. Nothing heard, we head straight for the stile at the end of the drive. It is obvious that this path is not walked on often, as the area is not cleared. But is an overgrown shambles. Some signs stating that the area is sponsored by a Rambling Association leads you to suspect that someone is not maintaining the area as best as it could be, compared with other walks.

We now come to Saltmarsh Lane, where we turn left and head towards the Mushroom Farm. On our right Ron explains that, during World War II, a South African pilot from the R.A.F. was involved in a dogfight with a German plane. The R.A.F. pilots name, he believes, was Percy Burton. The story goes that Percy had run out of ammunition and to ensure that the Germans didn't get away he flew his plane at the enemy plane and hit it. This caused his plane and the Germans to crash. Percy's plane hit the top of an old oak tree in the field to our right and he was killed instantly. The seven German airmen were also killed and buried at Hailsham, later to be exhumed and returned to Germany. The name of a street in Hailsham, Burton Walk, is named in his memory and a plaque has been placed at the base of the tree. To this day, the tree has not grown from where the plane hit it.

From the Mushroom Farm it is just a short walk across a field to get back onto the Cuckoo Trail, where we turn left and head back towards The Old Loom Mill. We are instructed to turn right into Hailsham but time, I'm afraid, is now my enemy. But should anyone be unaware, Hailsham is an established Market Town that used to have a thriving rope making industry. The town was nicknamed String Town. Unfortunately, the rope industry is no longer with us but the town thrives on smaller industries within the Industrial Estates in and around Hailsham. Another of the big

Pathway back to the Cuckoo Trail

employers in the Town was Hellingly Hospital but, again, that is no longer here and the beautiful hospital grounds are awaiting the attention of the property developers.

Back onto the Cuckoo Trail bird songs fill the air and Ron is trying to identify them for me. "That's a Robin, … and that's a Song Thrush. Nothin' lovelier than to hear a Song Thrush," says Ron. Just then I look down to see two elderly, large proportioned ladies, possibly mother and daughter, walking towards us. Still looking up to the skies Ron says "an' that's the tit family." "My god Ron, you do know everybody." But Ron didn't see the funny side.

Back at the car my step machine says that I had completed 12, 942 steps and that it was equal to about six miles. Not bad timing, getting back at just turned 3 o'clock. So I had plenty of time to get home, showered, shaved and changed for work by 10 to 5.

I must say that this was a lovely walk, spoilt by being a bit unkempt in places, and, should you decide to complete the walk yourselves, watch out for angry dogs, ignorant dog owners and sheep that chase you. Also remember to take a stick with you on walks, just in case.

Hopefully our next walk will be just as pleasant, visually, as this one.

WALK 14 – Westdean

Wednesday 3rd May 2006

We meet, as usual, at The Kings Head, South Road, for our usual Monday evening debate. It has become common practice now that both Ron and I take it in turns to suggest a walk, and the reason why the walk should be completed. This Monday it is my turn to suggest the walk.

I remember a comment from one of our many followers that it may be a good idea to return to one of our previous walks, at a later time of the year, to see if there was any

West Dean signs clearly seen from the start

difference in what could be seen. At first I didn't like the idea, but on reflection, what you don't try, you don't experience. Whilst I, particularly, don't fancy completing the same walk again I have found a walk, titled '_Et non plures_', in our borrowed Wealden Walk[36] pamphlets which may fit the bill. The walk starts at Exceat (Walk 2) but continues over the Seven Sisters Country Park and returns us, to Exceat, via the River Cuckmere. We, therefore, get the best of both worlds. We will see some new areas and we are also able to compare differences, if any, with the areas seen in Walk 2.

It must be obvious to all that read this that we have actually completed the walk before I put pen to paper. I have to say that my impressions of the Wealden Walks pamphlet are not good. This walk was to be no exception. Suffice to say we will not, and Ron agrees; be entertaining any of these walks in the future. Don't get us wrong. The actual walks are, probably, very nice walks. But the directions on the pamphlets are non-existent, the markers on the walks are few and far between and, all in all, I'm afraid to say, I can have no confidence in any of the walks supplied. All will unfold.

Wealden Walk signs

Again, due to work, we set off early and arrive at Exceat car park at 12:30. The first thing I notice, compared to Walk 2, is the car park fee has risen to £3 if you intend to stay for over 2 hours. Our guide pamphlet shows us that we need to leave the car park and cross the road opposite the gates to the Seven Sisters Country Park. The actual directions are non-existent, but the map appears to direct us up the side of the visitors centre. Please bear in mind that the writers of the Wealden Walk pamphlets list this walk as Grade 2. Which means that it is '…a easy walk with some gentle hills'. The path leading up the side of the Visitors Centre, through the kissing gate, to a flint wall has to be a gradient of 1 in 3. Both Ron and I had to stop twice to get our breath back before we got to the top. At this point we have not seen a Wealden Walk sign and can only assume we are on the correct path. We clamber over the flint wall that used to mark

Steep steps

---

[36] Part of a series of pamphlets obtainable from the offices of Wealden District Council, Crowborough

Westdean Church

the parish boundary between Westdean and Exceat and head towards a pathway that, at last bears the Wealden Way sign. This path will lead us to the village of Westdean. Before reaching the village we have to go down 216 steps that have been cut into the ground. ('Gentle hill??'). The sound of rooks overhead is deafening. At the bottom is a road and we now find another Wealden Way sign that leads us past a pond and some very nice old houses towards the church. Our pamphlet tells us that King Alfred visited West Dean (note spelling) in the year 880 when it was a royal manor with its own settlement of slaves or churls at 'churlston', now Charleston. Ships would sail up a creek, now represented by the pond, to reach this point. The church here may date back to King Alfred's time. It is certainly a beautiful structure with a unique tower and spire, which is said to represent a monk's cowl, possibly in tribute to its owner, Battle Abbey. Inside the church has that cold feel and the lovely old smell that is

Not a pretty churchyard!

Friston Forest

characteristic of these buildings. If you visit the church, pick up the guidebook and carry it round with you to find out all the facts about this wonderful place. I must say at this point that it appears that everyone is unsure on how to spell the village name. On the front page of our Wealden Way pamphlet it is spelt 'Westdean' but over the page the spelling is 'West Dean'. The booklet 'A History of West Dean Church and Parish' has the two word spelling yet on my maps West Dean is near Chichester???? I will now throw caution to the wind and probably upset some people. The graveyard and surrounding church grounds are a big disappointment for visitors to this church and a reflection on the people of the village. How they could allow their churchyard to get into this terrible condition is beyond both Ron and me. We were prepared to go straight home, get tools, and clear the place up ourselves.

From the church we continue along a track until we reach another sign, which instructs us to turn right. We now head into Friston Forest. What a joy this place is. The forest was planted in 1927 and covers 2,000 acres. Unfortunately, when the original beech trees were first planted the salt in the air affected their growth. It was decided to plant pine trees along the 'front' of the forest to protect the much slower growing beech. Today, 80 years after the initial planting, they are in the final stages of removing the pine trees to leave an almost pure beech forest. You can immediately see the difference in this woodland to one with nothing but pine trees. Firstly the ground, under the trees, is covered in plants as opposed to dead everything under pine trees. The forest boasts over 350 species of plant and is a fantastic, quiet and oh so peaceful area to just sit and let the time go by.

'Hot path' through the forest

The temperature today is pretty high, at least in the high teens to low twenties. Beads of sweat had started to appear long ago on both Ron and me. "'Ang on," says Ron as he opens his binocular box and produces two bottles of iced, still water. "Bought this 'duck wine' for us. Thought it would be 'ot today." "Ron, this is water, where did 'duck wine' come from?" I ask. "Wouldn't drink water when I was a lad," says Ron "me dad used to run the cold tap till it was really cold, put a bottle under the tap an' fill it to the top with tap water. Screw lid on an' tell me it was duck wine. Used to drink it then. Somethin' you just don't ferget." It was lovely and cool and very refreshing, even if we did have a problem with the lids. Along come two fellow walkers who pass us as if they were on a mission. The lady gave us a very cheery "Good afternoon", dressed in a skimpy tee shirt, short trousers with her jumper tied round her waist. Her partner, husband or boyfriend? (they were holding hands) wore a heavy coat, jeans and a hat. He must be baking under that lot. "Takes all sorts," giggles Ron.

It is now, about the furthest distance from the car, that our Wealden Way signs totally disappear. We are in a forest, our map, for what its worth, indicates that we turn right and then bear left heading towards a place called New Barn. We find the building, which is described as 18th or 19th century and built of flint walls. Apart from the fact that it was built in some beautiful countryside I, personally, could find nothing remarkable about the place. I don't think Ron even saw it. We are now on a made track. Remember that this is a walk with slight hills. As you can see we have come up another 'slight hill' and working on the theory that what goes up etc. somewhere along this walk we will have to go down again. Somewhere along this 'road' we have to turn right. If you take a wander around Friston Forest you will encounter hundreds of little tracks that disappear into the woodland and go who knows where? We are looking for a right-hand turn. We pass eight right-hand turns. All without signs. We see a sign. It's a post with a purple arrow on it. "What does a purple arrow mean Ron?" I ask the expert. "Yellers footpath and blues bridleway," says Ron. "No idea what purple is." "Shall we turn right down this path then?" I ask. "No idea, but it looks like it goes downhill an' we want to head uphill to main road," suggests Ron. We walk on a little further and decide to take the next turning on the right anyway. We seemed to be walking for ages when I turn to Ron and say, "Can you hear those rooks?" "I

What do purple arrows mean?

surely can," says Ron "an' if you look through them trees you can see Westdean church." We had done a complete circle and ended up practically where we started. "If we turn left here and climb the hill we should be back on the main road," suggest Ron "then we cross road an' 'ead fer Cuckmere." Sure enough at the top is the main road; heading for Exceat, and across the road is a stile directing us across fields.

People who know Ron will understand when I say that he can get excited and words don't seem to come out right. He gets there in the end but when he needs to tell you things his brain seems to be working faster than his mouth. Whilst walking across this field I noticed some very pretty little flowers growing on the sheltered side. "What are those?" I ask. Poor Ron went into spasm. Apparently they are cowslips. Used to be in abundance at one time but now not often seen. They are making a comeback, in the wild, and Ron thinks they are a protected flower. At least, I think that's what he said. When we reached the top of this field the view is astonishing.

At the very top of this field was the original church and village of Exceat. The Normans landed in England, by sailing up this estuary. Their village, initially, thrived with a population

Views towards Snake River (see Walk 1)

of over 100 people living in small houses, next to a church, overlooking the river. However, in the 14th century, poor harvests, French raids and the Black Death decimated the village. In 1428 the same village comprised 'Henry Chesman et non plures (and no others). The rough, nettled-covered ground shows the site of the village. The church was left to fall down - a memorial stone marks its former site. The inscription reads: 'here formerly stood the Parish Church of Excete. Built probably in the XIth century and abandoned in the XVth century [the parish being incorporated with West Dene in 1528] The foundations were uncovered under the supervision of the Rev GWA Lawrance rector of West Dene and the Sussex Archaeological Society by the ....' The stone is dated 1913. George W. A. Lawrance was rector from 1891 to 1930.

From here it is just a short walk, down the hill to the car park and home.

Unfortunately, due to the inaccuracies in the signs for the Wealden Way we did not complete the walk as expected. None the less, a very pretty, and in places, informative stroll. The graveyard was a bitter disappointment to me personally although the church itself was very well-kept. One of my new work colleagues walks the forest often and commented that in the many years he has walked Friston Forest this is the first year that he hadn't seen foxes. He also confirmed the many paths and trails within the forest, and as yet, has not been able to find an accurate map of the area. So how do you spell the village name?

At the start of this chapter I stated that the walk is completed and then pen is put to paper. On this particular walk, as the signs were so bad, I decided to go back on my own and do it all again on Thursday morning just to see if we had missed something. I will stop telling fibs and own up. To be honest, when I got home, my wife asked if she could look at the photos on the digital camera for this walk, and to my horror, I had no photos. They'd gone, disappeared, vanished and I was bloody livid. "You must have pressed the wrong button" and "what have you done?" are all comments from family members that are useless and infuriating at a time like this. I had nothing on the camera so; the pictures on this chapter were, in fact, taken after the walk. By the way, on the second walk round I got hopelessly lost and ended up heading towards East Dean. I passed the same wooden seat three times and was getting worried that I wouldn't see my family again. I had been in the Forest for over two hours and not seen a soul. World War III could have broken out and I would not have known. But, luckily for me, an old couple, out for a morning stroll, pointed me in the right direction. My deepest gratitude goes to that couple. Whoever they were.

Next week I think Ron has something a little different in store. I look forward to Monday's discussion.

WALK 15 – Pluckley, Kent

Wednesday 10th May 2006

Many weeks ago, shortly after starting our weekly walks, a friend let us borrow a book that contains pub walks around Kent. Originally, I thought Kent, not interested because we are only walking Sussex. But something happened to change that thought. One evening Bev, our landlady at The Kings Head, happened to pick the book up and randomly opened it to a walk in Pluckley. "I'll be damned," exclaims Ron "if that ain't the very pub where me old mum an' dad met 65 years ago."

I think, if truth be known, I was hoping that Ron would agree to carry out the Pluckley walk there and then, but it has taken just a little encouragement to persuade him that a little trip down memory lane may do some good. Ron lost his father some time ago. His mum

passed away a couple of years ago and he doesn't stop talking about her. Everyone knows that he misses both his parents terribly, especially his mum. I just hope that the memories brought back on this walk are not too upsetting for him.

With satellite navigation running in the car, because I have absolutely no idea how to get to Pluckley, we set off at 10 o'clock on, what I hope, is not going to be too traumatic a trip for Ron. As Pluckley is in Kent, Ron has brought his passport with him. "Expired last year," he explains, "but they should let us back into Sussex if they don't look too close." The drive takes us just over the hour and Ron starts to reminisce before we leave Hailsham. "Mum's name was Annie Winifred Jennings. She was in the Land Army during the war. Never seen a cow till she came to Kent," he says. "What part of the country was she from?" I ask. "Bradford. Used ter be on stage at The Lamberer 'til she was fifteen. Joined the Land Army an' came to Kent. Used ter work a farm owned by a Mr Gilbert, or Gilby can't remember the name. But 'e was an old man when me mum was there. Everyone used ter say she 'ad a lovely smile an' was always polite. Everyone loved me mum."

I must admit to not knowing a lot about the Land Army but have found out[37] that it was formed, obviously, because of the lack of young men who could work the land and help with the war effort. Each applicant for the WLA (Women's Land Army) was interviewed and given a medical. Once accepted into the WLA they were sent to farms around the country to work the land. The wage was £1 2s 6d per week (£1.12p) after deductions had been made for lodgings and food. There was an agreed maximum working week – 50 hours in the summer and 48 hours in the winter. A normal week consisted of 5½ days work with Saturday afternoon and Sunday off. All members of the WLA who were posted more than 20 miles from home

Pictures from Ron's family album

would receive a free rail warrant for a visit home every six months. The farmers themselves paid the women and there is evidence that some farmers paid less than the accepted rate. The

---

[37] www.wartimememories.co.uk/womanslandarmy.html visited 12/05/2006

WLA came under the control of the Ministry of Agriculture and Fisheries. It was given an honorary head, Lady Denham and her home, Balcombe Place, became its headquarters.

"So your parents actually met in Pluckley?" I ask. "They certainly did an' I 'ave to thank 'itler fer invading Poland. If 'e 'adn't done that me, mum 'an dad would never 'ave met," states Ron. "So what was your dad doing in Pluckley?" I ask. "He was a Regular soldier in the Sussex Regiment," explains Ron, proudly, "His name was Ronald an 'e was a sergeant. I think 'e was guarding prisoners in the area. I'm not sure. One evening he decided to go to the Black Horse fer a drink. Whilst he was walking to the pub, 'e 'eard something coming towards 'im, 'Stop, who goes there, friend or foe?' 'e asks. Me mum says 'foe' so 'e arrests 'er. They both end up at the pub for the evening an' that was the start. Best mum an' dad anyone could ask for," he says. (The photo of Ron's dad is dated 1934)

Ron's father

We reach Pluckley in exactly an hour. The drive was very comfortable with very little traffic on the road. My first impressions of the village are small, but with character. We park in the car park of the Black Horse and Ron is obviously excited and wants to go into the pub. "Lets leave the pub until after the walk," I suggest, "or there could be a possibility that we might not get round." Thankfully, Ron agrees and we consult our book to find out which direction to proceed.

Should you not be aware, the village of Pluckley has one or two other reasons to be popular, apart from Ron's mum and dad meeting? One is that the area was filmed and

The Black Horse, Pluckley

used for the entertaining television series, The Darling Buds of May, starring Sir David Jason and Catherine Zeta-Jones. Another is that it is reported to be the most haunted village in Kent claiming at least 12 ghosts.

Our guidebook is titled 'Pub Walks in Kent'[38] and contains 40 circular walks. The walk we are about to start is walk 27.

On leaving the pub car park, we turn right and head along the road a short distance and turn right at the T-junction. We walk up the hill a short distance and pick up the waymarker for Greensand

The very large orchard

---

[38] *Pub Walks in Kent* by David Hancock (Dorset: Power Publications) Page 66

Way, which takes us across the playing fields towards an orchard. We pass the old wooden cricket pavilion, and a grounds man marking out a running track, and head for a hole in the hedge into the orchard. I have to say I've never seen so many apple trees in one field. Looking ahead of us there has to be more than five fields full of apple trees. Line after line after line of apple trees. "Just think of the poor bumble bee having to pollinate this lot," says Ron. "Must 'ave wings like 'elicopter blades." As far as you can see are apple trees. We notice that the tops have been lopped and the bare wood painted in different colours. "Why do you think that is?" I ask. "Probably different types of tree," suggests Ron. "Surely they wouldn't put different types of apple tree in the same orchard." I say, "I know that you have to have more than one variety so that they pollinate but there are red, blue, yellow, green, white and orange coloured paints in this one area. I think it's to show what month the tree was lopped" It is now that help arrives. A man and lady are walking their dogs in the orchard. "Can I help?" asks the lady. "We were discussing the reason for the paint on the apple trees," I explain. "That's to stop the trees getting infected when we lop the tops out," is the answer. "Yes, we understand that," say Ron, "but why the different colours. Does it mean a different apple or, as Graham thinks, to show what month it was cut?" "Neither," says the lady, smiling, "it's just the only paint we had at the time" Simple isn't it? We were looking for a technical reason and all along they were just getting rid of leftover paint. Apparently, every ninth tree in a single row of trees is the pollinator and has a large metal rod placed in the ground by the tree. Ron asks the lady if she knew the name Gilbert or Gilby in the area and explained to her that his parents met at the local pub in 1940 and that his mum worked on a farm around the area. She explained that she had owned the orchard for a number of years and thought the name was familiar but suggested we ask in the village stores. We walked for a whole hour before coming to the other end of the orchard. It really was enormous.

My fascination for water

Tree lined path

When was this gate last used?

Crossing over a couple of stiles led us to a tree-lined path then on to, not another orchard, but a vineyard. The vines are planted in rows of fifteen by twenty five deep. It must have been early in the season because they didn't look too good. Across more stiles and tracks and we are, yet again, in a large orchard. This time some of the trees look like cherry or plum trees. The blossom has disappeared from the trees already so they are about to produce fruit. Our guidebook advises us to cross an open field keeping left of the church. We couldn't see a church and the open field was now an orchard. We did find the steps down to a lane in a village called Little Chart so we must be on the correct path.

We turn left and walk along the road a short distance before turning right between Rockhurst Bungalow and Little Chart Mill. Our book advises us to ignore the footbridge on our right but I can hear running water and have to investigate. A small stream is falling into a little river and the whole area is such a pretty scene I thought it couldn't be ignored. Further along the walk we see a gate with a warning sign about dogs. It looks as if the warning has worked, as the gate didn't look as if it had been used in years.

Our next instruction from our guidebook is to enter Chart Court Farm. Regular readers will be aware of what happened the last time we walked into a farm area, a dog bit Ron and we are desperately hoping that we will not have a repeat performance. A notice asking for dogs to be kept on leads is reassuring and we passed through the farm area without problems and now head towards a ruined church.

This is St Mary's Church, Little Chart, and the board, placed by the remains, tells us that the nave and chancel were built in local rag stone around 1250. Sir Peter de Bending built the North aisle in about 1350 with the west tower and porch added by Sir John Darell in 1500. I gathered this information from a sign by the church. But, to date, I have no factual reason as to why it is now in this state. Some of the headstones, although not new, are dated early 1930's so the church was in use, presumably, at that time.

It is now that our walk became a little surreal for me. I am standing in front of a church that is 760 years old and my mobile phone rings. It was a really strange feeling, looking at something so old, and sadly in ruins, whilst talking to my wife on a mobile phone.

We head out of the churchyard and turn left onto a road. We now need to cross the road and turn right onto a way marked path. Our guidebook advises us to walk along the edge of an orchard and turn right into another orchard. This area is now planted with runner beans. Thousands of them. "'ow come slugs don't get 'is runner beans like they do mine?" asks Ron "It must be something to do with insecticides," I offer as a reason. "Or they're too busy eatin' mine to bother with 'is," giggles Ron. "But 'tis a lovely area though, can you smell bluebells?" Sure enough as we get to

The remains of St Mary's Church

the end of the field and climb a small hill we are greeted by a wonderful show of bluebells in the woodland. The smell is overpowering and the sight of the vivid blue flowers is exceptional. "What a beautiful county Kent has become," says Ron. Anyone knowing Ron will be aware that he is a Sussex man, through and through. "Changing your mind about Kent then Ron?" I ask. "Don't be daft!" he replies. "Tis pretty, yes, but they don't have the downs or the marshland. And they can't play cricket like us".

Before we cross a field of corn and head for another stile some fellow walkers appear to be floundering over their map. Would you believe, they actually asked us for advice on which way to head. As soon as Ron told them where we were from and why we were walking this area they made there excuses and walked on in a different direction. Once across this field we are in another field containing, what looked to me like, bullocks. We have to cross this field to get to the road by a farm called Pivington Farm. "Why are those bullocks looking at me Ron?" I ask. "Ignore 'em," says Ron, "they won't touch yer." The herd moves to the left of us. I speed up. You all know my feelings about animals. "Don't run," says Ron. "Why not, they are," I say as the bullocks are now veering round towards us. They are heading, full run, towards me. I speed up again - I'm practically running. "Don't run," begs Ron. Just as the cattle are a matter of feet away from us they stop as quickly as they started. "See," says Ron, "no problem" I have broken out in a sweat and my shoes are covered in - what I hope is - cow dung! If it isn't cows', it must be mine. I was terrified. Ron couldn't stop laughing.

Unfortunately for us our guidebook appears to be out of date. Our next instruction is to walk

The Corner Shop, Pluckley

along the road for 200 yards and look for a stile on our right and head across more fields until we reach the Black Horse, back at the village. We were unable to find any stile anywhere along the road. By continuing along this road, however, we did get back to the Black Horse.

If you have never been to Pluckley before, please go. Just to visit the pub. Forget that it was in The Darling Buds of May. Just visit it for what it is. A beautiful, old-fashioned historical public house, with one of the warmest welcomes both Ron and I have experienced for many years. It must have brought memories to Ron as he hesitated going up the front steps but once inside, Olivia and her staff made us feel so comfortable. Ron explained about his parents meeting in this very pub and Olivia explained what the pub would have looked like in the 1940's, walls knocked through, toilets moved etc. Ron was disappointed not to be able to purchase his usual pint of Harveys but made up for it by consuming two pints of Speckled Hen. "Not the same as 'arveys but a lovely pint all the same. Too good to 'urry." I asked if it would be ok to wander and was told that a number of historical facts could be found on the walls, along with some local artists' pictures from the area. I had noticed the shape of all of the windows in the village and found, hanging on a wall in the restaurant part of the pub, an explanation.

One of the wall pieces advises that Pluckley used to be called Pluchelei (from The Domesday book) and, in the 13th century its main industry was weaving. Brick making has also been carried out in the area. The name Dering is very prominent throughout the village. In fact, during the reign of Charles I, the squire of the village was Sir Edward Dering. There is a story that is told that a member of the Dering family escaped from Cromwell's men through an inverted 'U' shaped window. Sir Edward Cholmesly Dering, in the 1800's, altered all the windows in the village to the current shape.

There are a number of pictures around the walls including various ones from the making of the TV series. With an equal mixture of the old, with the new, with the very old, makes the atmosphere even more enjoyable. For £1 you can purchase, at the bar, a booklet about the 12 ghosts of Pluckley that is an interesting little read (ghost list at end of chapter). Olivia's invitation of calling in again with my family for a meal will, I'm sure, be taken up shortly. The menu looked inviting and the surroundings were very comfortable.

The Church of St Nicholas

No walk would be complete without visiting the church and the purchase of pies. This one was no exception. Leaving the Black Horse and bearing left heads you towards the church of St Nicholas. A formidable building that can be dated from around 1300s' although monks from Canterbury have recorded a church in Pluckley in 1090[39]. Within the church is a small chapel dedicated to the Dering family which contains many memorials to that name over many years. The churchyard is a little overgrown in some places but very tidy in others that suggests someone, at least, cares. Wandering around the church we were hoping to see a name that Ron would recognise but, unfortunately, no luck. A lady suggested we speak to the owner of the village stores who has lived in Pluckley all her life and may be of some help. She did suggest an address that she thought may be a relation to a Mr Gilbert but was not sure. I have suggested to Ron that we could look at Parish Records to establish who and where his mum worked. After the purchase of two very tasty chicken and mushroom pies, it was back to the car and head back to Sussex. Ron is fishing for his passport, just in case he needs it.

As we head back, Ron reflects on the day. I believe he managed to get something out of the experience and I hope I, in some small way, have helped him to achieve that.

---

[39] Leaflet, St. Nicholas' Church, Pluckley, "1000 years of history" collected from the church

Next week's walk, at this moment in time, is totally undecided. I hope Ron and I, when we meet on Monday, can make next week's walk just as enjoyable as this one.

Extracts from 'Haunted Pluckley' by Dennis Chambers[40]

Coach and Horses – From the many variations in the details given and routes taken, it could well be that Pluckley has more than one phantom coach.

Colonel of Parkwood – Hung himself from the branches of one of the trees that provides the home for his restless spirit

The Highwayman – There are a number of accounts of how the Highwayman met his death at a place called 'fright corner'.

The Miller – The owner of the mill, Richard Buss, had to close the mill down. During a violent storm in 1939 the mill was struck by lightening and burnt to the ground. One of the mills' previous millers is reported to have taken his own life and now his spirit is said to return.

The Monk – Said to have had a relationship with **The Tudor Lady**. The two ghosts walk the lanes together

The Red Lady – Wanders mournfully through the graveyard said to be searching for the body of her baby in an unmarked grave.

The Schoolmaster – Hung himself in Buss Lane and found by school children.

The Screaming Man – No reports of a visible ghost only the echoes of his last terrifying screams as he hurtled into the workings of the brickyard.

The Tudor Lady – See **The Monk**.

The Watercress Woman – A gypsy woman who used to sit and sell watercress from the bridge over Pinnock Stream. Used to drink gin and smoke a pipe. Her shawl got covered in splashes of gin and a spark from her pipe fell onto the fabric and set it alight. The flames engulfed her body – moments later she was dead.

The White Lady St Nicholas Church – Wife of Lord Dering who died at a tragically early age. Her ghost confines its appearance to the inside of the church.

The White Lady Surrenden Dering – Some say she is the same White Lady (above) but this time appears as a poltergeist at her former home, Surrenden Manor

---

[40] *Haunted Pluckley* written and published by Dennis Chambers 1984 (2002 edition)

WALK 16 - Ninfield

Wednesday 17th May 2006

On the Monday before this walk both Ron and I had a bit of a problem. A good friend had asked us if she could accompany us on one of our walks. We had no problem accommodating the request but we wanted to make it interesting for her. For this to happen we had to incorporate some history into the walk. Our friend had recently acquired a University degree in History. We didn't want to appear ignorant, should our friend ask us any questions about the history on the walk so we hit on the idea of doing some homework on The Battle of Hastings. I vaguely remember that William landed at Pevensey in 1066 and headed for Ninfield (then known as 'Niwnumenan Felda' – Newly Cleared Fields). So that we could get a feel for William we decided that we should find a circular walk around Ninfield, for Ron and me, for walk 16 and another walk around Battle and the 1066 battlefield to complete next week with our friend.

I hunted everywhere, the Library, the Internet and our borrowed books but the only walk I could find for the Ninfield area was, would you believe, a 'Wealden Walk' and how we distrust these walks. But it was all we had. So we swallowed our pride and went for it.

The weather forecast for this afternoon was rain. Ron said it wouldn't rain but there may be some very low cloud with a bit of heavy dew. "It'll make you feel wet but it ain't rain." I have my doubts. It was overcast and the clouds were looking decidedly grey when we parked the car in Church Lane, Ninfield. I will say little about our Wealden Walk[41] pamphlet other than a caution is printed on the front of this particular walk stating – 'This walk includes two

Our one and only sign?

crossings of the A271 road'. The map attached to this caution shows the A269?? I will say no more.

In the year 1,000 the Saxons, literally, cut Ninfield from the Wealden Forest and ended up with a population of about 50 people with no less than 6 lords owning different parts of the parish. Now the village is a thriving little community with many large houses nestling into the rural surroundings[42].

The start of our walk takes us down Church Lane, close to the beautiful church that we will call into on the return leg of our walk. But now we pass the school and bear left onto a narrow tarmac path, behind houses, heading towards a road. Here we find Ninfield Village Stores. Ron can't resist. He comes out with two chicken and mushroom pies. Homemade and he's happy. We cross the road and the Wealden Walk marker directs us into a private close of houses. At the end of the close is a dead end. No path, no marker just a dead end. "Good start," says Ron, "only been walking 'fer a few minutes 'an we don't know which direction 'ter go in." "Lets head back to the entrance to the close and see if there is another path somewhere," I suggest. Sure enough we found an overgrown path leading us to the A269/271(?). Our path here, as can be seen, is a little overgrown. We manage to fight our way through the brambles and nettles and eventually emerge into a small orchard. Compared with the orchard at Pluckley this

Overgrown footpath

[41] Part of a series of pamphlets obtainable from the offices of Wealden District Council, Crowborough
[42] Ibid

orchard was miniscule with only twenty or so trees but they are in blossom and it is a pretty scene.

Sprays Wood

Prior to us starting this walk we had a little chat with one of the locals who warned us that some dogs could be about in the Ingrams Farm area and sometimes they are left to run free. As we approach the farm you could hear the barking of dogs. Lots of them. But in true male bravado style we continued onwards only to find that the dogs are all in kennels and cannot get at us. The earliest record[43] of Ingrams Farm is 1264 when Robert and Andrew Ingeram owned it. In 1570 it was described as '*a mean thatched house with a kitchen, an orchard with garden and cartilage containing half an acre*'. Today it is still an impressive building.

We leave the farm area and walk towards Sprays Wood. It is about now that you start to hear the constant hum of the Transformer Station built deep into these woods. Pylons carrying high voltage electricity cables are all around as we

A carpet of bluebells

wander down the slopes towards the station. We bear right, into a clearing, just as a large fox runs across our path and into the next field. We stood and watched as the fox ran along the hedgerow until he went out of sight. Suddenly there was a loud noise from a pheasant and we assume the fox has caught tonight's supper. "Can you imagine mother fox when 'e gets 'ome. 'Not pheasant again' she'll say 'rabbit yesterday, pheasant day before, now pheasant again' poor bugger can't get it right."

We now bear right and head back into the woods. There used to be a chain of ponds that provided power to Potmans Forge ironworks that was nearly half a mile away. Most of the ponds have now dried up. The forge itself had a short life; built by William Waters around 1580, it is last heard of in 1637. It did, however, produce one unique piece of work that we will see at the end of this walk.

The beauty of this place is strange in some way because it is totally unspoilt. It must have looked like this so many years ago. It is peaceful. No sounds of motor vehicles, just the constant hum, hum, hum, of the transformers. After a while it starts to get at both Ron and me. You try to blot the sound out but it's impossible. It's like a

Rusty bark?

toothache, nagging all the time. But you then realise why it was put out here, in the middle of nowhere, so that its noise doesn't annoy people. The surroundings certainly make up for it. Bluebells are numerous throughout the woods and act as a wonderful, fragrant carpet.

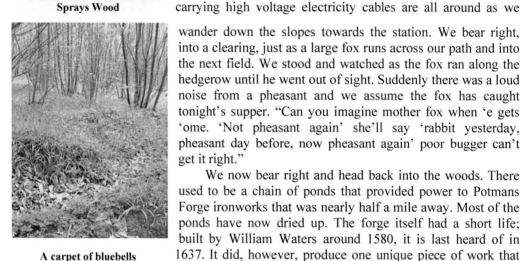

Where all the noise comes from

I now have a confession. With every walk we have completed, something has gone wrong, in some way. We had no map on one walk, no camera at all on another, dog bite; animal encounters are just a few of the things that have happened to us.

Another is that on every walk, where I have mentioned bluebells, I have taken a photo, but this is the first photograph of bluebells that has actually come out. I have had black

---

[43] Ibid

and white photos of bluebells or no photo at all. This photo, therefore, is the first. But in true tradition, I've lost my pen. I can't tell Ron, but everything from now is from memory.

We exit Sprays Wood and come face to face with the reason for the constant hum. The large Transforming Station nestles, in the lowland between Sprays and Reed Woods. "Don't seem to bother them sheep none," says Ron as numerous sheep wander about between the pylons oblivious to the noise and, thankfully, me and Ron.

We approach Reed Wood just as the low clouds produce the dew and I notice a tree that looks as if it's going rusty. "Any idea why that tree looks like that Ron?" I ask. Ron, being a true professional looks at the tree, rubs the bark with his hand, sniffs his hand, licks his hand lightly, steps back, looks at the tree again, turns to me and says "No idea, could be fungus," and walks off. For once I think Ron is lost for words and I'm amazed.

Leaving the wood we now make our way, across fields to a place called Catsfield Bridge. Here the owner has planted Christmas trees and sells them during December. There is a small stream, crossed by a bridge and the pathway is clearly marked. On the side of the path are lots of second-hand Staffordshire Blue paving bricks. When I worked for a building company these bricks were like gold dust, especially second-hand ones. I wonder if the owner is aware of the value.

We now cross a road and the public footpath takes us between buildings and up a farm entrance and into open fields. Previously I have mentioned the poor hard up

Worth how much as scrap?

farmers and fail to understand how they can leave items of farm machinery laying to rot. This farm was to be no different. "Look at all this gear just laying to rot," says Ron. "You'd think the farmer would let a museum 'ave it, or at least another farmer could use it 'fer spares" The photograph is of just one machine. I'm not sure what it did in its previous life but the farm had several of these machines just left to rot. The dew was continuing and Ron was right. It was making me feel wet. "Do you realise," said Ron suddenly, "we 'aint met a sole since we started this walk". He was right. We had walked over halfway round and not met a single person. "Remember walk we did at Pevensey, that was to do with Normans 'an that. Never met one then neither," continues Ron. "Could have something to do with the weather," I suggest, "if I remember we had a bit of dew that Wednesday as well." We head towards an area called Marpits, which used to be the industrial area of the parish. The disused quarries are still visible. A list of trades published in 1681 includes *one innkeeper and shoemaker, one shoemaker only, one sawyer and carpenter, one carpenter only, one sawyer only* and slightly more versatile, *one joyner, carpenter and fiddler.*[44]

We turn left onto a main road and walk through an area that, I think, has changed very little over time. At last we meet another person. A lady out walking her dog, and she looks drenched. "Just thought I'd pop out to give the dog a little walk and got caught in the downpour," she explains. "Hasn't rained," says Ron "just a bit o' dew that was." The lady is not sure of Ron and neither is the dog. "Been for a long walk, have we?" Ron asks the dog as he bends down and the dog backs off. "Only to the top of the road and back," explains the lady looking at us a little suspect now, "have you walked far?" she asks. "Only around Ninfield, we're heading off down this track now, towards the water tower and Standard Hill," I say trying to ease the woman's fears as to what she's met on this country road. "Why not carry along this road, it's quicker," she says as she tries to make her escape. "Can't do that," says Ron "would be cheatin'".

Cold, dark path to where?

[44] www.VillageNet.co.uk *Ninfield* viewed 15/05/2006

We descend the bank into a narrow path. "Dog didn't seem too friendly," says Ron. "Looked nervous, to me. Was ok if yer didn't bend down to it." "Yes Ron, perhaps it was you he was scared of." The path we now find ourselves on is dark, damp and slippery. Where the water has gone down the path it has eroded the soil around the tree roots and made the path a bit treacherous. It's pretty obvious that this is where the locals get rid of their rubbish. Plastic bags and bin liners are plentiful. When we exit the path, onto another road I turn right. Ron turns left. "Where are you going?" I ask. "Sign says turn left," is the reply. "Map says turn right". I show Ron the map. "Can't 'elp what map says. Sign on that tree says turn left." I went back to the tree and, sure enough, turn left is the indicator. We turn left and continue up the road. When we eventually reach the road junction the water tower is nowhere in sight. "We will have to turn right here and walk along the main road to the tower, " I tell Ron. "Used 'ter cut grass 'ere abouts," says Ron, "and the 'edge." "Is there anywhere that you didn't cut grass Ron?" I ask "Not many, loved me job I did," is the reply.

We pass the Water Tower, and cross the A271/269 and we are at Standard Hill. This is the spot where William the Conqueror is alleged to have raised his banner on arrival in England. On the whole, the Norman Conquest was not good for Ninfield. Parties of soldiers looted all

the villages in the area to feed themselves before the Battle of Hastings. Prior to the soldiers arrival Ninfield was valued at £6 and was worth £1 when they departed.

Our route now takes us to Moorhall, which was one of the original clearance sites and became a separate manor. By 1342, however, much of its wealth was gone "*a great part of cultivated land had been submerged*" (by the sea) and a further "*130 acres of land lay uncultivated on account of poverty*"[45].

Nessie, Ninfield style

Standard Hill

From the Hill to the Church

Our walk now takes us into more woodland as we head towards the church. Within this woodland it is obvious that someone has taken some time and been a little constructive and imaginative. A tree has fallen into a pond and been transformed into a 'Loch Ness Monster', which Ron found fascinating and little walkways across streams have been constructed. At the top of the climb towards the church Ron found, and used, a well-constructed seat, "How could you not use a beautiful seat like this, in the middle of these fantastic surroundings? Not a sound to be 'eard but birds on the wing, not a car to be seen. Tis great". He laid back and savoured the moment. From this point it is just a small walk, out of the woods into open land again.

It is now that you must let your mind wander and your imagination take over. Because it is at this point that William's camp was set up and his men prepared for the oncoming battle with Harold.

I have a very fertile imagination. No one can tell me that I did not hear the forging of metal nor smell an ox roast at this part of the walk. It was so real to me. The smell of leather, the sound of horses as they got excited with the prospect of battle. I could hear it all. The strange language spoken at the time, men laughing. It was there in front of me for just a few minutes. I can only say that it was a very strange experience.

---

[45] *Ninfield* viewed 15/05/2006 www.VillageNet.co.uk

Turning around from this field you are met with the view that William and his men must have had of the church, not with the wire fence, but with that small gap in the trees. The church itself is a wonderful place and dates back to around the eighth century. The churchyard of The Church of St Mary the Virgin is well-kept and is home to one of the oldest and largest Elm trees I have ever seen, or likely, to see again. It is believed to have seen the coming of the Normans. The bole gives the appearance of several trunks joined together, caused by the tree pushing out new shoots from the lower part of the bole. There is a story about the Ninfield yew that states that, if the trunk is viewed from the side nearest the church, the observer could make out the form of an angel in the tree. I tried but couldn't see it.

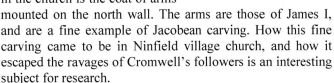

Inside the church is cold but welcoming with, as always, that smell which is so common with churches. In the 17th century a Minstrels Gallery was constructed at the west end of the church. It was closed and boarded up during restoration work in 1885 but was re-opened in 1923. When it was in use, it is recorded that a flute led the music, and later a harmonium. Now, of course, the Gallery is not used and the church organ has taken over. There is nothing on record to reveal the origin of the flags hanging either side of the Gallery but are thought to date from around the 1890s.

Formidable Yew Tree

Another fascinating feature in the church is the coat of arms mounted on the north wall. The arms are those of James I, and are a fine example of Jacobean carving. How this fine carving came to be in Ninfield village church, and how it escaped the ravages of Cromwell's followers is an interesting subject for research.

The mechanism for the clock, installed in 1897, can be viewed through the glass-panelled doors in front of the casing. The bell is a single survivor of a ring of three, but by 1864 the other two were sold to raise money. The current bell is thought to have been cast in 1395 (Richard II). It rings for services and strikes the hour.

Jacobean carving

The scenery, as with all the walks we have carried out, has had something special to do with that particular walk. All the walks have been different in some way. But this one has had just that little bit extra. Next week's walk will now be a little more interesting, knowing where

William was starting from, on his way to claim the English Crown.

By the way, earlier I mentioned Potmans Forge and the 'unique' piece of work that can still be seen. How many people, and I must admit that I am one, have driven through Ninfield and never noticed the stocks on the side of the road by the entrance to Church Lane. Not just a simple stocks but also doubled up as a whipping post. "Should 'ave them in use now, "comments Ron, "stop some 'o them 'ooligans that thinks its funny to.." "Yes Ron, lets leave it shall we?"

The local stocks

WALK 17 - Battle

Thursday 25th May 2006

It started in the year 1085. King William ('The Conqueror' from 1066) started the ball rolling with his Christmas Court at Gloucester. He asked for a survey to be carried out across the whole of England. Royal Commissioners were sent to every shire in the country with a long list of searching questions. The completed survey is what is now known as The Domesday Book. Unfortunately for King William he died in 1087, before his survey was completed, but I believe its effects continue to this day with the prospect of Identification Cards and 'big brother' watching over us.

I hadn't realised what could be gained by supplying a number to an individual, over the telephone, in an office miles away, until I had a problem with my National Insurance. As you will know my new employment started at the beginning of the month. I supplied my new employer with a P45 (statement of tax). The wages pleb at my previous place of employment had put the wrong NI number on the P45. It was only one number out, but that number could cost me plenty. For two years my NI contributions have been credited to another person. When I phoned the tax office and supplied the correct number to them, after some confirmation, they knew my name, address, post-code, employment status, employer, employer reference number, previous employer and reference number, tax office, personal tax code and from that they will be able to tell my marital status and if I had children and how much I earn in a year. Is this a form of big brother that King William has introduced and people are still opposing at the slightest mention of ID cards? Who knows? But on the 28th September 1066 William the Conqueror invaded England to stake his claim to the English throne. A claim that was upheld by the Pope. That now infamous battle, at Senlac Hill on the 14th October 1066, saw Harold killed and William was crowned King of England in Westminster Abbey the following Christmas Day.

Our walk this week is to look at the battlefield and tread on the same ground that William and Harold, with their troops, took on that day, 940 years ago. Lyn (she who has the degree in history from Sussex University) has asked to accompany us. As she is unable to be with us on Wednesdays, due to work commitments, you will have noticed that this walk has been carried out on a Thursday. Despite Ron's energetic efforts to encourage Lyn to wear a French Maids' outfit, she has arrived suitably attired, although I do have doubts about the trainers. "I've got another pair of shoes in the bag," explains Lyn as she climbs into the car, not only with a full plastic bag, but also her handbag. Must be a girlie thing? "I've got a present for you, Graham," she says. "Bribery will not work with me Lyn. You asked to come with us, so presents aren't going to ease the pain," I reply, as Lyn produces a bottle of brandy and a candle from her plastic bag. "It's not a bribe you silly s*d, you won them at last night's raffle" I didn't like to ask the significance of the candle but the brandy will certainly be appreciated. "Someone suggested I give you the basket of fruit but I said that you weren't an invalid and thought the brandy more appropriate." Offering my thanks, we head off towards Battle.

The weather forecast for today is dry at first with rain later. Ron's constant reminder that 'it doesn't rain on a Wednesday afternoon in Sussex' is no comfort on a very grey Thursday morning as we drive through Herstmonceux and Boreham Street. If you remember from other chapters something, at sometime, has to go wrong. Usually it happens halfway through the walk. But not this time. It happens before we even get to Battle. The road is closed. According to the police officer there had been 'a major incident' in Battle and all roads were closed. I was directed to another road but was advised, most assuredly, that access to Battle would not be possible for some time. "What's the contingency plan then?" asks Lyn. "We ain't got a plan, let alone a contingency," says Ron from the back seat. I pull over and consult the map from our guidebook, and suggest that rather than start in Battle, walk to Sedlescombe and then back to Battle we will head for Sedlescombe and start our walk from there. We all agree, so I head for Sedlescombe. The car park is behind the Queens Arms and is free. We park and get out. Lyn now has to remove some items from her handbag such as ciggies, lighter and mobile phone and asks if she can put the bag in the boot. "Why did you bring the handbag?" I ask. "Don't go anywhere without me handbag," says Lyn. So, why did she leave it in the boot of my car? Another girlie thing?

Walking towards the Queens Arms we suddenly realise that we have no idea how to pick up the walk, so I decided to ask a local. The lady we selected looked at our map and told us we should be starting in Battle. We explained that roads in and out of Battle were closed and she proceeded to tell us about how roads aren't meant to take the amount of traffic that now trundle through these villages etc. etc. She eventually directs us to a playground where our walk will be found. "It's very muddy along that path," she offers, looking at Lyn's trainers. "I've another pair back at the car," says Lyn as we make our way towards the playground.

Sedlescombe is a very pretty village with many houses dating back to the 16th century. There is an old water pump under a gabled roof shelter on the green that is dedicated to members of the Pratt family. We locate the playground after turning right by the garage. This is a let down. The grass is very long and in the process of being hacked down by a young man with mower. Mowing the grass would not be a term to use. "Can't believe it's grown so much," says the young man. "Only cut it three weeks ago." "You get it down by Sunday an' we'll bat first," jokes Ron. "Yea," says the youngster, plugging in his Walkman and starting the mower.

Overgrown footpath

From here we need to head down the side of the play area towards a field. The next few pictures will indicate how this walk has been neglected. You can just make out a vague pathway from the picture on

Lyn, determined not to drop her cake

the left. With seven days of light rain the grass, coming up to over knee height, got us soaked. We hadn't got through the first field and our trousers were wet through and because you couldn't make out any faults in the path slipping became increasingly easy. On more than one occasion Lyn was heard to swear as she lost her footing. Ron lightened the situation by producing, not pies, but three of the largest cakes I've seen. Mine did my cholesterol the power of good. All that icing and lemon filling has got to be top secret from the wife. She will go spare should she find out.

Climbing stile, note cake

We are directed towards a footbridge. From here we can hear running water. Lots of it, but because the whole area is so overgrown, we are unable to see where the water is coming from. It sounds like it may be a water mill but who knows.

Perhaps the owners were fed up with people looking and decided to hide behind the brambles and nettles instead. We now head across, what is described as 'rough ground' in our guidebook. So far we have seen nothing but rough ground. The simple act of climbing over a stile in soaking wet trousers and carrying a cake is not easy. We now meet a road and need to cross over and head for Beanford Farm. The first farm we arrive

A clear path for once

at has no name and looks brand new, and deserted. No cars in the double garage but horses are in the stables, but there's no one in sight.

It was me that noticed the large dog kennel first as we head up the drive towards the front door. "Let's go and ask directions," suggests Lyn. I'm not sure. The kennel looks empty. The dog must be out, somewhere. "Let's go back to the gate and take another look at the map," I offer. Without waiting I turn and head back. Luckily everyone follows. "If we had an Ordinance Survey map we could easily find our way," says Lyn. "I'm surprised you don't have one but perhaps it's a woman thing to be organised." "Ah, but daughter," replies Ron "you now understand why we takes longer to complete our walks than they says in them books. Would spoil it if we knew what we be doin'." We walk along the track away from the now barking dog and come to the gate where we find Beanford Farm, and another barking dog.

Ron thinks it's funny

We pass through a second gate and head down into a sunken path. Since starting this walk Lyn has sworn on a number of occasions due to either a misplaced foot or being hit by low branches. It is at this point in the walk that she tells us that she will kerb her language. It didn't last long. Her first slip on the mud produce "S?*t, I'm sorry, I didn't mean to say that." Peering through a fence Ron sees Bulls. "Lets 'ope we don't 'ave to go through this field, eh Graham." I'm not amused and frantically looking through our directions to find out our next route. When I find that we actually turn left onto a grassy ride I heave a sigh. We now follow a number of rides through Battle Great Wood.

We come across in the middle of nowhere, a seat, complete with footrest, dedicated to Ray Collier with Tara and Trubshaw. The seat was placed in such a way that if used you could see out across the countryside. The dedication on the seat is dated

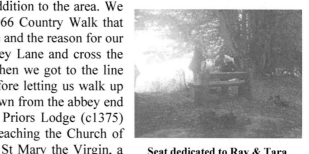
Seat dedicated to Ray & Tara

1927 to 2004 so is a relatively new addition to the area. We are now joining what is called the 1066 Country Walk that will take us towards the town of Battle and the reason for our walk. First we have to walk up Marley Lane and cross the railway line. The gates were down when we got to the line and seemed to stay down for ages before letting us walk up the hill into Battle. We arrive at the town from the abbey end and have to walk past houses called Priors Lodge (c1375) and Abbots Cottage (c1400) before reaching the Church of St Mary the Virgin, a magnificent structure

The Church of St Mary

on the opposite side of the road from the abbey. I am afraid that it is now that things become very disappointing. The walk to this point was, in itself, a bit of a let down. The pathways were unkempt and very overgrown. The usual footpath signs were not as abundant as other walks, and, as Ron said "You'd 'ave thought, bein' a 1066 walk an' it's 'istory they'd 'ave made some effort to keep it lookin' nice". But they hadn't. Now the church is locked and we can't get in. The church is said to include a Romanesque nave, a Norman font and rare 14th century paintings.

The abbey is just a short walk from the church and is a grand building, which can't be missed whichever way you arrive in the Town. Prior to the battle between Harold and William in 1066, William vowed that if God permitted him to win this battle he would build an abbey on the spot where he secured victory. As you know William did win, and this beautiful abbey was built. However, after the Dissolution of the Monasteries, Sir Anthony Browne, Henry VIII's Master of Horse, converted much of it into a

Battle Abbey

private house. (A case of being in the right place at the right time??) Today Battle Abbey is in the care of English Heritage and is an immensely popular tourist attraction. Unfortunately to be able to witness anything of the actual battle, the grounds, the battlefield etc., you must pay. Now, again, I find this quite sad. I understand that the upkeep of a place such as this must run into lots of cash but at the end of the day it is part of our heritage and should be subsidised, in some way, so that people can enjoy and appreciate our history and culture without having to put hands in their pockets. The picture of the front of the Abbey was taken at around 1 pm in the afternoon. You can see that it is not busy. I appreciate that it is a weekday and that the town has been closed for vehicular access for a couple of hours but I have seen this place heaving with people. For some reason the place is deserted. Why? The High Street is buzzing with people. There is to be a Medieval Pageant being prepared in the High Street. Banners and flags are everywhere yet the one place that should attract visitors had no one anywhere near it. Just a ways down from the Abbey they are building a modern new complex. I presume money gained from Joe Public has paid for it. But why is a new complex required. The Abbey has survived all these years without it. Surely the money could have been used on something else. I am so disappointed yet embarrassed to admit that I never thought that I would have to pay to see the Battlefield. "Lets walk down past the car park," says Ron, "I'll show yer the smallest cricket field in Sussex. Scored 68 last time I played 'ear, all in ones, fours and sixes. You couldn't run for twos or threes. Pitch was too small." Ron just stands and looks awhile. "If your going

to talk cricket," says Lyn "I'll just have a nicotine break," ciggie and lighter in hand. "That's ok," I say, "we'll head towards Mount Street." "I'm not smoking while we walk along a street," replies Lyn. "Why not?" I ask. "Something I don't do," is the reply, "never smoked in the street and I'm not going to start now." I said, "Isn't that strange, when my mum was alive she would only smoke in her own house, never outside or in someone else's house. She could go hours without a cigarette, but as soon as she stepped inside her own house she had to have a smoke. Must be another one of them girlie things?"

Ron remembers his own battles

From Mount Street we have to locate a bungalow called Little Twitten. Hawkeyed Lyn found it as we were leaving the car park. We are now on the Malfosse Walk, according to our

The path was impossible

guidebook. There are no signs to indicate this. In fact all markings have now disappeared and the book doesn't appear to make any sense but we eventually find a sign that directs us into another overgrown footpath. Having only just managed to dry out from the first part of the walk we now had this lot to get through. We head towards the woodlands in the distance, walk under the railway line and veer left following the woodland path. We now climb a number of stiles that are placed at the bottom of some very nice houses until we reach a footbridge. We are advised to use the right-hand bridge. We could only find one so assumed it to be the correct one. Another mistake. We end up at a Sewage Works with one path leading to the left and one leading to the right. "Which one do we go on?" asks Lyn. There is no mention, in our book, of a Sewage Works. "We've gone wrong, again, 'aven't we?" offers Ron. "We'll go left," I say, I had a 50/50 chance of being right. And I was wrong. It was leading along the railway line. I could hear trains. A strange thing happened at this point. Both Lyn and I could smell Brylcream. It was strong, and definitely Brylcream. But we couldn't find out where it was coming from. Ron thought we'd gone crazy, but it was definitely Brylcream. Very strange. Back to the Sewage Works. We now take the right-hand path. A lady is walking towards us. "I'll ask." She advises us to carry on up the path. When we get to a road we need to turn right. But that can't be the correct way because we should be heading for Sedlescombe. If we turned right it would lead us back to Battle. When we get to the road, Lyn wants us to turn right; I want us to turn left. "She said turn right," insists Lyn. "Yes Lyn, but she was wrong. Call it a man thing. I know we need to turn left and head for the woodland that will be on our right-hand side by the road." Lyn gives in; we turn left and walk up the road a short distance. A hole in the hedge, with an overgrown path leads us into the woodland. We still have no signs to indicate that we are going in the correct direction. There should have been a car park. How can you miss a car park? Easy, if you haven't got to it yet. We literally came across the car park by sheer luck. The instructions in the book now make no sense at all. The path we are directed down, by the side of a stream is impassable. Ron is in hysterics when Lyn sinks up to her shins in mud. He is crying. Lyn, for once, does not lose her self-control. She simply calls Ron a little bugger and drags her sodden trainers out of the mud. There is no way that we could walk along this part of the pathway. We double back, find the road and walk along it until we reach the A21. From here we cross the road and find the marker heading us across a field and back to Sedlescombe. Looking back across the road we could see the overgrown pathway that should have brought us to this point and it's obvious, from the picture, that it hadn't been used for some time.

Our walk in the field back to Sedlescombe was carried out in practically silence. When we reached the playground the grass cutting had come to a halt. The mower had broken down. "Won't get a game on Sunday then?" asks Ron. I don't think he got a reply

I will admit that I was very disappointed with this walk. As Ron had said no effort had

It was all so overgrown

been made to keep the walk open and I had looked forward to it since last Wednesday. The fact that it was now nearly three fifteen in the afternoon had made it a long walk and I was knackered.

To offset some of the disappointment of not being able to visit the battlefield we diverted slightly on the way home to let Lyn see the church, the stocks and the site of Williams' camp at Ninfield. I am pleased to say that the experience was the same for Lyn as for me. Just stop, look, listen and imagine. Lyn's expression, looking out across the fields to the camp, was a true picture and completed the walk for all of us.

I have found writing about this walk the most difficult so far. Throughout all the walks we have completed I have needed to take some form of notes. This one I couldn't find anything worthy of taking notes about. If it wasn't for the company of Ron and Lyn I would have turned back and gone home shortly after I started. Lyn's dainty language and Ron's anecdotes along the way have helped make something of the day. Both Lyn and Ron have thanked me for the day out but let's hope that next week will be more pleasurable and interesting.

WALK 18 – Northeye & Hooe

Wednesday 31ˢᵗ May 2006

Did you ever have friends, years ago, when you were at school that were known by a nickname? That nickname lasted throughout school and, forty years later you can remember the nickname but can't remember their real name. Two of my best friends throughout school were known as 'titch', because of his lack of height and 'fluff' because of his blonde fluffy hair. Ron knew someone by the name of 'dolly' at school, and it was only recently that he found out his name was Alan. Today, I am ashamed to say; I can't remember what my friends' real names are. But it can happen in a different way. Do you have a friend who is known by a nickname but you don't know what that friend's real name is?

On our usual Monday discussion a friend asked us if he could join us on today's walk. We know this person as Taff. We know he is ex forces (Queens Own Hussars), we know he is a musician, he drinks Harvey's bitter, and he's Welsh and lives in Hailsham. Yet we have no idea what his real name is. Why don't we ask him? I don't know. Perhaps we did, and he said his name was Taff. Who knows?

Taff joins Ron on the walk

Today Taff, Ron and me are off to Hooe, near Bexhill. The name Hooe means 'Spur of Land' in Saxon and describes the area exactly. Since Saxon times, the sea level has dropped and Hooe is now about two miles inland but the sea used to wash around Hooe, on both sides, up the Ashbourne valley.

The main income from the village was from the Salt works on the Pevensey levels and from farming. It is possible that the Normans passed through Hooe on the way to Standard Hill (Walk 16) in 1066. Hooe's nearness to the sea, and its remoteness, once made the area perfect for smuggling, and the landlord of the Red Lion Pub, James Blackman, was a member of the Groombridge Gang (1733-1749). The lime trees that stand outside the pub signify that this was a safe haven for smugglers. To the south of Hooe lies the site of the abandoned village of Northeye, which is on Hooe levels.

Today's walk is taken from a new book, found by Ron, titled East Sussex Walks by Ben Perkins and is compiled by The Argus[46]. The walk is on page 40 and is called 'Bumpy remains of a lost village'. From this book we are advised to use a detailed map, as some of the paths are difficult to follow, so an Ordinance Survey map will be used along with the directions from the book. Our first mission is to find the starting place, which is along a tiny lane, called Horse Walk, and links Wartling with Hooe. We start at what is described as a Car Park in the book, but is actually a lay-by? We climb a stile and walk along a raised grassy bank with the wide waterway of Wallers Haven on our right. Anyone who knows Taff will understand when I say he is a man of few words, he says little until you talk about something within his sphere, like music, and then you can't stop him. I have noticed that Taff is saying little. "I'm looking at the scenery," he says as we stroll down the riverbank towards a gate about 300 yards away. But that's it. Conversation over. Throughout the whole walk Taff observed a lot but said little. Once we reached the gate we turn left, cross the pasture to a barway. "What's a barway?" I ask. "No idea," replies Ron, "but we must find

Is this Waterlot Stream?

out soon cause we're about to fall into a dyke. Just in front of the dyke is a fenced off piece of land with tall grass growing in the centre. Since returning home I have looked up the word

---

[46] *East Sussex Walks* by Ben Perkins reprinted from The Evening Argus (Southern Publishing Company – October 1995) Page 40

'barway' and cannot find the word in any of my four dictionaries. At the dyke we turn right and walk for about half a mile along the edge of Waterlot Stream. Along here Ron points out yellow Iris growing in the bank. I explained to Ron that I have a number of Iris plants in my garden, brought or sent to my daughter from America. Mine were either a deep blue/purple, or a pure gold colour. "The usual colour is blue," he says, "and normally they have larger flowers than these. Must need splitting, I wonder 'ow deep water is." "Your not serious?" I ask. "Course not," is the reply, "just a shame we aren't on the other bank." We come across our usual livestock here and I notice that both Taff and Ron let me lead the way. "What happens if one of the cows ends up in the stream?" I ask, "there's no barrier or hedge, they could just slip in." "'Ave to call fire brigade to get 'em out," explains Ron. "Only people

A hazard for cattle?

with right gear to pick 'em up." I notice, in the same field some sheep, "look out Taff, sheep in the distance, control yourself." "Don't like to worry you Graham, but them's ain't sheep, them's rams," points out Ron.

Over a stile and we are now by the Lamb Inn just off the A259, Eastbourne to Hastings coast road. Anyone who knows this area will be aware at how difficult it can be to cross this road. Traffic seems endless and it's a mad dash to get to the other side. We now have to walk

No alligators this time

a few yards and find a stile and gate. The first gate we come to had no stile next to it and the gate is secured with the usual Sussex lock or bailer twine. Our ordinance map indicates that this is the way to go, as a deep dyke should lead us to a bridge. It is now that both Ron and I visualise the Normans, heading towards Standard Hill from their landing point. The whole are is flat and the sea must have submerged the point that we are now standing. It is difficult to imagine what it must have looked like over 900 years ago. Now it is a very pleasant area, you can see for miles and is just alive with wildlife with a maze of dykes lined with hawthorn.

The guidebook, at the start, tells us that some of the paths were non-existent and now is the time that our first problem occurred. We are advised to bear left over a reasonably new footbridge and go ahead to converge with a fence and a dyke on our right. The arrow on the post indicated this, but we were unable to pick up the path by the fence. We could see the dykes, obviously, but we needed to cross a deep ditch to get to them. We eventually decided that leaving the path and finding our own way to the dykes would be simpler.

Country views

"I would have thought your army training in orienteering would have come in handy for this walk, Taff, what with the problems we are going to have with paths." "Yeh, right, I didn't bring a compass." is the reply.

Still, we managed to find our way to the dykes eventually. As we walked past a hollow, that looked as if it was used for the animals to drink from, reminded me of the nature programme on the telly when a wildebeest went down for a drink and a crocodile leapt out of the water, grabbed the animal by the throat and drowned it. I remember, at the time, how it made me jump when it happened. "So we've got 'ter look out 'fer crocs now 'ave we?" asks Ron. In the distance are more cattle, this time with calf. "I wonder, if a cow messes with the wrong calf, she's known as a 'cowdephile'?" suggests Ron. All Taff said was "Yeh, right," with a grin from ear to ear. "I think we've got to make for that post over to our right," says Ron, peering through his binoculars, "looks like a sign on top of the post is a yeller' un." This is where we need to look out for a stile but couldn't find one. What we could find was a gateway, on our left, tied up with string with a barbed wire fence across the gate. Over and under we go. The view from here is amazing. Our instructions tell us that we should be on a clear grass track but the only similarity to the description is grass, acres of it. To our right is one of the reasons for this walk. The area we are now in is said to be the bumpy ground that is all that remains of the lost medieval village of Northeye. On a purely personal note, I wasn't impressed. To me it was a hill. It did nothing for me, I'm afraid.

Stunning views

Leaving the 'bumpy ground' we head for a farm track that will lead us back to the A259, at the top of the hill, before Little Common. The farm track is said to be half a mile long and has a couple of gates to get through. This is no problem. Suddenly, in front of us, flies a green woodpecker. I was stunned. I have never seen a woodpecker in the wild before and to actually see one in flight, in front of us, was amazing. Having a close look at the area the bird flew from we found a tree with a couple of holes in the trunk and can only assume this is

Woodpecker nest

where it came from. I had to apologise to Ron and Taff. I got really excited. Further up the lane we could hear a constant tap, tap, tapping on metal. Everyone knows my feelings on poor hard up farmers leaving machinery to rot in fields. Would you believe, we actually came across a farmer, who was working on some old machinery? Not only was the man wielding a sledgehammer but also he bore an uncanny resemblance to another of our friends, Phil Anderson. White hair, build and looks. It wasn't till we got up close we realised that it wasn't Phil. They say everyone has a double. The way he was hitting the machine, with the hammer, I couldn't make out if he was repairing it or smashing the thing to pieces. But with a cheery "Good morning, luvely ain't it?" from Ron we moved on to the top of the hill.

From here the view is even more stunning. At the top of the hill is a new Farm Shop. If

The view from the Farm Shop

you stop and look across to your right you get a stunning view of our coastline. You can make out the sea in the far distance. It really is breathtaking. To think I pass this spot every day, four times a day, and only on rainy or foggy days does it look any different.

Our instructions now tell us to take life in our hands again and cross the A259. We need to look for a public footpath sign to Hooe. To say this path was a little overgrown would be an understatement. Luckily for us, the rain which made the ground so wet on last week's walk, with Lyn, had held off and the overgrown weeds and nettles were dry. Because you couldn't see where you were putting your feet the going was slow. The path leads us around the perimeter fence of what used to be Northeye Prison[47] that closed, as a Prison, in October 1992 and is now used for other purposes. Walking round the outside I was amazed at the actual size of the place. From the outside it now looks like one of the old Hi-de-Hi campsites seen on TV. Ron believes the army is now using it but from our vantage points, along the

[47]Related by ex warder at Prison. Had to phone farmer to get his free roaming cattle out of the Prison grounds. Farmer told warder that if the Governor could keep his prisoners in, he'd keep cattle out.

perimeter, it certainly didn't have any evidence of that. Ron pointed out a badger sett by the wire, but I like to think it was someone escaping the holiday camp. Our guidebook now becomes even more confusing, not helped by the lack of marked pathways. It became a case of head were the nose points you and hope it bears some resemblance of the map.

One of our directions takes us down the edge of a field of wheat. The farmer had left a wide path for walkers to take. After a short distance Ron noticed, what at first looked like a tombstone. Carved on the face were the letters 'B B' and under this the number '25'. Any ideas on what it is can be sent to Ron, on a postcard. Unfortunately, we have no idea why it could have been placed at the edge of the field for or what it means.

No walk would be totally complete without a confrontation with animals. This was to be

A country headstone?

no exception. I don't like animals. Ron is ok with them. Taff is a tall guy, but he was also worried about the size, speed and temperament of the herd of bullocks that headed in our direction. Someone sitting back at the Kings Head, after the event, telling me 'they wont hurt you' and 'I've been round bullocks all me life, they just want to say hello' doesn't help, when you are confronted with, not just one but a large number of ½ ton animals hell bent on destroying you. That is what it felt like. Even big brave Taff was waving his arms and shouting 'shoo' when these animals got close. A couple of them were even snorting and pawing at the ground as they looked at us. They even tried to cut us off from getting to the next stile, which, in true cavalier fashion I was first over in one leap, closely followed by Taff then Ron who, again, is laughing hysterically. Why does Ron see my

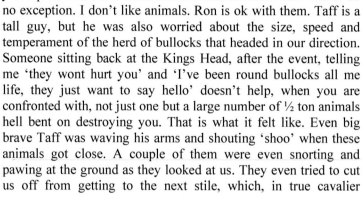

VERY frisky calves

fear as something to laugh at? Once out of the field of bullocks I, and Taff, are much happier and relax as we head across more fields.

I turned to Ron and said, "I thought the sign at the start of this part of our walk said a mile and a quarter, we've been walking for ages." "'Tis a country measure," replies Ron, "take no notice of what it says, just direction is all we need". We seem to be getting better directions on the stiles now although some of the directions take us through the middle of crop fields, which doesn't seem right. One of the things both Ron and I do on these walks is walk behind each other. Lyn noticed, last week, that should the front person come across an obstacle such as a hollow, a clump of mud, a low branch or a large pile of dung we call it out so that the person behind is aware. Taff, unfortunately is unaware of this little 'rule'. He climbs over a stile, with me behind him. He walks off into the field. I climb the stile, and once over the other side promptly fall into a hole. As I'm going down I try to think of what I should protect first. In a split second, as options race past, I decide to save my pencil. I crash down in the grass like a floundering whale. Ron is falling over the stile, laughing, and when I look up Taff is walking off in front of me totally oblivious to the events unwinding behind him. Luckily we managed to find the camera and guidebook without too much of a problem.

Our next direction is to walk down the side of a house, onto the driveway and towards the road that joins back to the A259. We should walk parallel to the power lines from here but can't see any. What we did see though was a 'charm' of goldfinches.

Field of wild flowers

I'd not heard of this expression before, come to think of it I'd not seen that many goldfinches at one time, but as we walked across a field covered with wild flowers a number of the birds took flight for a short time before realising we were no threat and returning to what ever goldfinches do.

We can't be sure, but from here we can only assume that the farmer didn't want walkers

Hooe Church

on his land. There were no 'Keep Out' posters, nothing that subtle, just the odd electric fence across a stile, or gate covered in barbed wire and an electric fence which could have caused us problems in reaching the main road into Hooe. But nothing could stop us. We were getting close to the car and the end of our walk.

All that was left to see was the village and church. Unfortunately the church is down a narrow lane, in the middle of nowhere and we do not get to see the village. "Only got a pub and some 'ouses," says Ron, "nothing else ter' see 'cepting the church." So we head down the lane.

The church itself, I'm afraid to say again, is another disappointment. Apart from the fact that the doors are locked so we are unable to gain entry the graveyard is unkempt with long grass and weeds. What is surprising, if you wander round reading the inscriptions on the tombstones, is how many young people are buried at this church. One headstone lists a family with the children all passing away in

Another unkempt churchyard

their early twenties. It makes you wonder why such a thing should happen. Ron is on a mission here. He is looking for a particular headstone but can't find it. He'll have to get some more information on it and come back some other time. One of the headstones I noticed was to a man and his wife who are described as 'loved, sadly missed and always in our thoughts'. The headstone is dated 2003 and I had to move all the weeds to read it??

From the church it is just a short walk back to the car and another walk is completed. Before getting to the car Ron

found what he thought to be Green Winged/Tipped Orchids growing wild on a grass bank. He'll have to look up the name. That's it for another week. Taff enjoyed himself and Ron was just Ron. The walk, for me was ok. I may go back and look at the pub, for purely historic reasons, of course.

WALK 19 - Brightling

Wednesday 8th June 2006

Monday's discussion was not about the walk at first, but me becoming a granddad again. My son, Anthony and his wife, Nicole presented us with a lovely granddaughter over the weekend. Megan arrived in the early hours of Friday morning and is a sister to Chloe. Both mother and baby are doing very well. I've started making a dolls house already.

After the customary beers, purely in the time-honoured tradition of wetting the baby's head, of course, our discussion turned to the forth-coming walk. We thought we'd have a little change this week and head for Brightling, home of John 'Mad Jack' Fuller. Our trusted book, 50 Walks in Sussex[48], has supplied us with this week's 5-mile circular stroll starting and finishing at the churchyard of St. Thomas à Becket.

For those unfamiliar with 'Mad Jack' I give a little of his history. He was born in 1757, the son of a Hampshire rector. He attended Eton and on his 20th birthday inherited the entire family fortune and its estates. At a very early age his future was secure. He came close to marriage in his 30's but his proposal was declined and he remained a bachelor for the rest of his life. He stood for Parliament on several occasions and eventually became the Honourable Member for East Sussex. He was forcibly removed from The House by the Sergeant at Arms and told to apologise for swearing at the Speaker of The House of Commons, which he refused to do. He also refused a peerage and was known to thunder down from London in a carriage with footmen armed to the teeth with pistols and drawn swords. He is said to have consumed three bottles of port a day and stake reckless, impossible wagers. It was hardly surprising he became known as 'Mad Jack'. With his 22 stone frame and loud, bellowing voice, Fuller often induced fear in the strongest of souls. A little more about 'Mad Jack' will come from the walk.

It must now be said that I believe my expectations of our walks must be a little too high. I have, recently, returned from walks and been a little disappointed by what I have seen. The company has been excellent and don't get me wrong; the scenery around all our walks has been stunning. Both Ron and I have expressed our admiration of the rural scenery throughout these chapters, but recently, I, personally have found something missing. I have been disappointed about the same thing in some of our previous walks to a point where it is starting to make me angry. But what can be done? After today's walk my daughter put this very question to me: "If you are so unhappy with what you see, what are you going to do about it?" I don't profess to know the answer. But something, surely, must be done. All will be clear as you read this chapter.

Familiar - overgrown path

Firstly you may notice that this walk was carried out on a Thursday (date at start of chapter). I had a problem with a little decorating job that had to be completed by Thursday morning and couldn't get it finished until Wednesday afternoon. We set off at 10 o'clock and head towards Brightling. Again it was one of those villages that I had heard of but was not aware of how to get there until I asked a work colleague. Arriving just about 10:30 we park the car, as instructed, by the church and head towards the kissing gate, which signals the start of the walk. We now meet three ladies, also out for a walk. "Which walk are you completing?" we are asked. "Brightling Folly Trail," I reply. "So

[48] *50 Walks in Sussex* – AA Publishing - Page 26

Steps leading up the Tower

are we," says one of the ladies, "but we don't know how far it is, do you?" "Our book says it is 5 miles," I offer. "But don't you foller us," says Ron, "'cause we gets lost and will do about 9 miles today." The trio try to ignore Ron. "Our instructions tell us to walk along a clear path from here, but we can't seem to see one," says one of the ladies. "We'll head down the right hand side of the field. When we get to the bottom we should see a stile," says I, and off we go. The three ladies head down the other side of the field. Guess who was right. We didn't catch up with them for a while. The view from the start of the walk is breathtaking, as always. You can see for miles. The fact that today was very hot and clear certainly helped. We approach a small path and are directed to turn right along the pathway. As you can see the pathway was up to its usual poor standard. Again, as in other walks recently, the weeds and nettles are so high it is impossible to see your footing. We are now heading towards the Tower, one of the 'Mad Jacks' folly's. One of his wagers was that he could see Bodiam Castle from Brightling. Of course that was impossible, so to win the wager he built a high tower. By standing at the top of the Tower you could, in fact, see the castle. He won his wager. Another story regarding the Tower is that after purchasing Bodiam Castle for £3,000 he could watch its restoration from his high vantage point. Which one is true I am unable to tell. Perhaps neither? The Tower, which dates back to the 1820's, is a formidable structure. It is within a small wooded area and the trees protect it from general view.

If the guidebook didn't tell us the location we would never have seen it. Some renovation work has been carried out and The British Gypsum Company has installed a new metal staircase. From the outside the structure seems very strong but once inside and climbing the stairs little blemishes can be seen

The pointing between the brickwork isn't good and birds have been able to build nests in the mortar. On reaching the top landing a metal ladder takes you to the very top. Because of the trees surrounding the Tower you are unable to see through 360 degrees and, I'm afraid to say, I could not see Bodiam Castle. Ron noticed that there was no plate on the wall of the Tower explaining what the Tower was or why it was built. It is assumed that you did your homework before starting the walk.

At the start of the chapter I described, briefly, the view on this walk. We are now standing in Brightling Park and some of the land is used for horses owned by Mrs Grissell. The picture on the right is just one of many I took whilst looking over the park. In the distance you can just make out Darwell Reservoir, the Tower is directly behind us.

From here we descend a slight slope, climb a stile and we are onto the road from Brightling to Dallington. Our guidebook then tells us to bear right for a few paces and turn left by some barns and

Horses graze peacefully

outbuildings. We presumed we had to turn left into Ox Farm. There didn't appear to be any signs. Our instructions tell us to cut between ponds and lakes and look for a cricket pitch. Just to mention the word 'cricket' gives Ron a buzz. "We're goin' right way fer pitch," exudes Ron, "tell yer a funny story when we get t'pitch." Two well-known cricketers, the Buss brothers who played for Sussex, apparently came from Brightling. "It seems a strange place for a cricket pitch, Ron, in the middle of nowhere," I comment. "Yes but tis peaceful. When we played 'ere, against Buss brothers, we 'ad tea and cake, during interval. All 'omemade, by the ladies of the village. Best tea 'an cake I ever 'ad," continues Ron, "when I used ter play I was openin' bat, but I'd been told that some mushrooms were growin' down the slope by the wood, so I put me self in at number 5. I 'ad some time ter spare so I went picking mushrooms. Only been down

The Rotunda Temple

there a while and there was one 'ell of an 'oller for me to get me self to the crease. Three bats were already out and I only 'ad two minutes to get to the crease. I ran up the 'ill, shot over the fence, ran out to the crease, with me mushrooms, and realised I 'ad n't got me bat." "How did the game go?" I ask. "Lost!" is the reply, "but mushrooms were good." It is now that we see the three ladies. They are on another path to us so perhaps they are lost now? Who knows?

From here you can see the Rotunda Temple, a circular domed building. Again stories have been told about this building. Built by 'Mad Jack' in Brightling Park, which, incidentally, was landscaped by 'Capability' Brown, it is said to have been used as a hide-out for smugglers or a store for contraband or it was built, and this is my personal favourite story, by 'Mad Jack' for gambling sessions or entertaining ladies.

We now turn left and join a footpath alongside some trees. Our guidebook tells us to look out for a house to our right. All we could see were trees. Tall ones. This became a big problem for us. We needed the house, so that we could find the cottage that had a stile next to it that would lead us back to the Brightling to Dallington road. No house, no cottage, no stile, no road. Just a very long track. We've managed it again and got ourselves lost. We can hear cars, so the road must be close. We come to an opening and see cars to our right and head up the field to reach the road. I had to take a break here and sat down on the stile and marvelled at the view. This picture is

Wonderful panoramic views

Overland conveyor belt

made up of four different pictures and, hopefully, gives the reader some idea of this beautiful scene. Even if we have no idea where we were. Our instructions tell us to turn right on the road. I tried to explain to Ron that if we'd come out too far down the road we would need to turn left to get back on track. I was persuaded to turn right and after a mile or so we came to a large farm called Coldharbour Farm Estates. A very helpful lady explained we were heading in the wrong direction and need to go back up the road about a mile and look for a sign for Darwell Hollow. Whilst I might have been tired I did feel smug. I'd actually got it right, we should have turned left. Now all we had to do was walk back. The mile turned out to be over a mile and three quarters, but who's counting. "Must 'ave been a country mile," explains Ron, "she was a country lass after all."

We are now heading into Darwell Wood along a clearly signposted track. "Shame the rest of the walk wasn't as clearly signposted," says Ron, "wonder where the three ladies are now?" "Probably back home, sitting down to a nice cuppa I shouldn't wonder. We've been doing this 2½-hour walk for nearly three hours and we're nowhere near the finish yet."

Before starting this walk I looked at an ordinance survey map of the area. Clearly marked on that map, and our guidebook are the words 'conveyor belt' with a thick ink line. Would you believe it but the last thing I expected to see was an actual conveyor belt? I was thinking of all sorts of technical things about tracts of land, irregularities in the soil structure etc. but it is an actual conveyor belt that linked Mountfield and Brightling gypsum mines and runs right through the middle of Darwell Wood.

We now need to follow the track to our left and then veer right to cross Darwell Stream. Picturing the reservoir as being an enormous expanse of water holding 15 million cubic feet of water I expected the stream to be just as big. What a disappointment. As you can see from the picture Ron was impressed as much as me. We must follow the track that will, eventually lead us to a lane, called Kent Lane. It is here that I take exception to our guidebook. At the beginning the book rates this as easy, with few, small, hills. I

Darwell Stream

have to say now that the walk up this track was far from easy and I warn anyone thinking of going on this track to take heed and view the difficulty rating as a little suspect. On reaching the top, I was knackered.

We turn left and walk along Kent Lane, back over the conveyor belt and towards the hamlet of Hollingrove. It was walking along this lane that we came across a deer wandering along in front of us. We must have scared it because it shot across the road and up a steep bank to our right, never to be seen again. But it was nice to see an animal like that in it's natural habitat. At Hollingrove we pass Glebe Cottage and are

Brightling Church

advised to take the stony path on our right. The only path we could find led to someone's garden. Again there are no signs to help. We walk up the road a little further before deciding to head back to Glebe Cottage. Just before the cottage a couple appear at their garage and Ron asks directions. We are told that the path is up the stony lane leading to the garden but before getting to the garden the path veers sharply to the left. We find the path without further problems and find ourselves heading back, past the Tower, to Brightling church.

Thinking about this, after the walk and whilst writing this, has made me angry. As I said earlier in the chapter, perhaps my expectations are too high. But I believe, very strongly, that our history and heritage must be protected at all costs. Reading the visitors book inside this church proves that not only local, British

'Mad Jacks' tomb

people visit our places of historical interest but so do people from overseas. What must they think when they see a churchyard as poorly maintained as Brightling. Wire fencing has been erected along both sides of the path to the church doorway. Whilst I respect that this may have been done to protect, in some way, the tombs within the yard no effort has been made to make the area look as if it has been or is cared for. Monuments are left to lie on the ground. Weeds abound, all round the church and I can only say what a very sorry sight the place looks. Why, oh why has it been left to get in this state? The sandstone pyramid mausoleum, 'Mad Jack's' final folly, is overgrown with weeds. This is the place where John Fuller is interred, it is said in an upright position, dressed for dinner, holding a bottle of claret and wearing a top hat, this is part of our history and, sadly, it is left in this state. I am gutted.

Which brings me back to the question my daughter asked –"If you are so unhappy about what you see, what are you going to do about it?" and, I am so ashamed to admit, I have no answer.

On our way home, due to the very hot weather, it was decided to break one of our rules. Call into a pub and have a long, cool drink. We headed for Rushlake Green and The Horse and Groom. My grandparents lived and died in this village. My mother went to the school here, the school now demolished and replaced by Osbourne House, a home for pensioners from the area. When I was at school in Hailsham I attended band practice here with The Warbleton & Buxted Brass Band, every Wednesday and Friday evening at the Dunn Village Hall. I first met my wife here. I have very fond memories of this wonderful place. The Flower Show, Tug 'o War competitions, Fun Fairs, Band concerts were all held on the Green every year. I remember my mother catching the number 95 bus from Hailsham, three times a week, to tend to her parents during their old age. All this came flooding back to me as we pulled up outside of the pub. "Not been 'ere for a year or two," says Ron. "Me neither, but the place is still popular, look at the cars in the car park." But when we go in the bars empty, apart from someone talking in the back of the pub. We wait; no one comes to serve us. We wait some more. "Excuse me!" calls Ron. We wait some more, still no response. We slam the door on the way out, just to let them know and headed for the Merrie Harriers in Cowbeech. Nice pint of orange juice and lemonade for me and Ron surprised me when he ordered, not his usual Harvey's, but he actually drank a pint of lager and lime. Perhaps people can change. Let's wait and see.

WALK 20 - Warbleton

Wednesday 14th June 2006

Monday we spoke of family. Readers are aware that Ron's mum and dad met at Pluckley (Walk 15). My parents met at East Grinstead when my father, injured in the aftermath of the war, was hospitalised at the Queen Victoria Hospital, where my mum was a nurse. My mum's parents, if you remember from Walk 19, lived for a long time in Rushlake Green. My earliest memory of my grandparents, Lilian (correct spelling) (nee Brook) and Thomas Churcher, is travelling with my mother, on the number 95 Southdown bus to Pleydells Cottages in Rushlake Green. Their home for a number of years before moving to Osborne House, built on

My Grandfather, Tom

the site of the old school. I can also remember the Village Fete. An annual event which always started with a cricket match. Because the Green was so small they had to devise a few rules. If the hit ball rolled onto the road around the Green, this was deemed a 'three'. If the ball hit the road, without touching the Green, this was a 'four' and if the ball flew over the houses it was a 'six'.

My grandfather was the first death that I had to deal with. He was born in 1891 and died in 1970. I was 19 years old and I was gutted and remember being told of his death as if it was yesterday. For some reason, I can't remember, I was not allowed to go to his funeral. At the time I loved my grandfather, yet no one would explain to me why he was to be buried in an unmarked grave, at Warbleton Church. The church I can understand. Both my grandparents worshipped at the church. My grandmother played the church organ at some time (perhaps that is where my phobia of

church organs originates?). Through constant questions to relatives about my grandfather, I have discovered so much about him. But everyone I asked has told me he was an ogre. My grandfather, the wife beater, the drunkard. I couldn't, and still can't, believe what I was hearing. But all the people I asked all said the same things about him. Most of his children (2 sons and 3 daughters) left home, in their mid-teens, just to get away from him. One of my grand fathers' last wishes to me was that, should I get married and have children of my own, he would like to see them christened at Warbleton Church. I never disclosed this to my wife until, whilst trying to get Michelle and Anthony christened in Hailsham and the

Christening font

vicar refused our request because we didn't worship at his church. The vicar at Warbleton was more considerate. I am pleased to say that we, due to these circumstances, managed to grant him his wish. Despite his reputation I found Granddad Tom a warm, considerate man who loved his large garden at Pleydells Cottages, always smelt of mints and was always ready to give advice.

Warbleton Church

My grandmother, Lilian, is buried with him, in the same, unmarked grave, at Warbleton Church

after her death in 1983 aged 89. Now she could be nasty, not violent but she had an evil tongue and was very manipulative, I'd witnessed it, but everyone only had good words to say about her at the funeral. Aren't relatives strange?

By pure coincidence, Ron also has memories of Warbleton Church. His brother was married there and he was best man. So, it was decided, Wednesday we would complete a circular pub walk, starting at Warbleton Church and ending up at The Warbill-in-Tun public house. The weather is turning hotter by the day so a shorter walk this week with a delightful pub lunch at the end.

We arrive at the church and are pleasantly surprised by how neat and tidy the churchyard is. The last time I was actually at this church was for my grandmothers' funeral but it felt like yesterday. Entering the church you are greeted with the customary cold chill and that familiar smell. The stain glass windows are really beautiful and are mainly 19th century. In the north aisle is the manorial pew, which is accessed by a flight of stairs. This pew was used by the owners of Stone House, Rushlake Green and has long been associated with the Roberts and Dunn families. Just below the raised pew is what is believed to be the

parish chest and is said to date from the 14th century. There are six bells in the bell-chamber at the top of the tower. The oldest bears the inscription 'Richard Phelps made me in 1724'. The others bear the dates 1826, 1864 and 1907 when the older bells were recast[49].

Hanging on the wall is a list of all the names of children who have been christened in the 13th century font near the south porch. I remember standing there when Michelle and Anthony were christened. The church is very beautiful and well-kept. It brought back so many memories to me. The site of my grandparent's grave,

Parish Chest

although unmarked, was easy to find and I stood for a few moments with just silent thoughts and some unanswered questions.

There is a sign in the church porch, which explains why part of the churchyard is not kept as nice as the other. It is simply being used as part of a nature conservation area and will be mown at the end of the summer period. It is in this area that we found a gentleman and his

two dogs, out for a stroll. One of his dogs ran towards us and the man assures us that the dog is harmless. Deaf but harmless. Ron does his usual and speaks to the dog as if it's human, asking all sorts of questions and only getting a tail wag and a lick as answers. Ron tells a story about a man called Roy Walters who used to tend the churchyard some 35 years ago. "'e was cutting the grass an' 'e thought 'e saw ground move," relates Ron, "tries to ignore it but it 'appens agin. Now 'e starts ter get worried. All of a sudden the ground moves an' up pops a mole. Poor ol' Roy nearly fainted on the spot, fair

More overgrowth!

scared 'im, it did." I must say that it made a change to start our walk with the church rather than at the end. Gives you a bit of a lift before you get going.

This week's walk is taken from 'Pub Walks in East Sussex' by Mike Power[50] and is walk number 37 in his book. From the rear of the church we are instructed to go over a stile and enter the field. The field drops away from us and we head for the bottom and a line of electricity cables. No visible signs have been seen and when we get to the bottom of the field the

The new and the old

pathway is not very clear. Our instructions tell us to follow the line of the electricity cables to our left. But that would mean walking across the middle of a field of wheat. We walked along the left-hand edge of the field hoping to find a bridge in the hedge at the other side of the field. No bridge. The hedge was vastly overgrown so, armed with my new thumb stick, kindly given to me by Des from the Kings Head; I attempt to get through the undergrowth. "There's

[49] *Look out for Our Church* compiled by Vernon Pearcy obtained from Church
[50] *Pub Walks in East Sussex* by Mike Power (Dorset : Power Publications) Sept 1994 Page 88

no bridge in here," I shout to Ron. "We'd better go back to other corner of field," suggest Ron as I clamber back into the field. We still can't find a bridge and look at the instructions in the book again. It clearly shows a bridge over a stream but our map doesn't show field boundaries. "Per'aps we need to walk into the next field an' we'll find it there," suggests Ron, "as long as we keep the church behind us, we must be going in the right direction". So off we go, into another field. The wheat is so tall, and because it had been raining for 24 hours before our walk, our legs were soaked within minutes. "You'd 'ave thought," muses Ron, "that with a pair 'o leggins' in me bag I'd put 'em on so I didn't get me legs wet. Too late now though, I'm bloody soaked." After two wayward directions we eventually find our bridge. A solid construction and a mixture of old with the new. The council are certainly hoping the new one

lasts as its made out of metal girders, railway sleepers, concrete and oak. A wonderful achievement of engineering science. The remainder of our path is very clear although not marked. Straight through the middle of the farmer's crop of wheat. Luckily the farmer has left the path unsown and it is easy to follow. Ron, always on the look out for the odd and hopefully financially gainful picks something up from the ground. "Look at that," he exclaims, holding up something black and round in his fingers, "looks like an old button, wonder where that came from?" "Looks like a solid lump of

A low down sign

liquorice to me," I reply turning away and heading towards a farm gate and the lane towards Vines Cross. All I heard was "no, it ain't liquorice," and I don't want to think what he did with it to make that decision.

We walk past a number of very large, very expensive houses. One of which had a five-door garage, large pond and geese visible from the road and a really fantastic house in the distance. You'd need a car to get from the garage to the house. How the other half live. It is over a mile along this road before we need to look at our directions again so we start to

reminisce about families and friends, in general. As said in our previous walks Phil always seems close to out thoughts when we are out in the middle of nowhere. We knew Phil had been about on last week's walk around Brightling because all the finger posts and letters had been painted white waiting for him to return to black up the letters. On this walk we noticed that the signs were a little bit lower to the ground. Knowing Phil's dread for heights we wondered if he's starting to place the signs at an easier level. How motorists are supposed to see them that low down I'm not sure. We must ask him next time we see him.

At the next junction we cross the road and head for field

Abandoned JCB

opposite. We still have not seen a sign indicating that we are on a public footpath so are unsure if we are even permitted to be on this land. As we had not met anyone since the churchyard to tell us otherwise we carry on. With all our walks we get lost. I'm sure it can't be my entire fault but I am starting to get a guilty conscience. I try to involve Ron in the decision making and, for once, when asked which way we go now, he produces the binoculars, points to a piece of wood in the distance and says, "that must be the bridge we're lookin' for, we'll go that way." We pass a gap in the hedge. The grass is, again, at waist height. There is a wood to our left-hand side. I look at our map to discover the wood should be on our right. When we eventually get to the 'bridge' we find it's a sign, which reads 'Private Woodland – no public right of way'. "Couldn't you read that through those binoculars?" I ask. But the whole thing just became funny to Ron. "Now you can understand how easy it is to go wrong when there're are no signs to help." I show Ron the map and explain that we are on the wrong side of the wood. We head back to the gap in the hedge and walk along the other side of the woodland and find a nice brand new footbridge, complete with public footpath sign, the first we've seen since the start of the walk. Unfortunately it was also to be the last. Our instructions tell us to follow the stream on our left and re-cross the stream at the next footbridge. We never found it and yes we managed to get miles out of our way. From the top of the hill we could see Warbleton Church in the far distance. Far, too far in the distance. The whole walk was only three miles long and the church must have been that far away from us now. Suddenly we could hear traffic and headed towards the sound. We came out at a place called Bathurst Farm. "Isn't Bathurst Farm in Rushlake Green?" I ask Ron. "Believe so," is the reply. "If that's where we are there's a turning up the road which will take us back to the Church." The finger post at this left-hand turn states that it is 1 mile to Warbleton Church. While we walk along this road Ron asks, "if your grandparents went to Warbleton Church every Sunday did they walk along this road?" "No, there used to be an old bus, pick them up in the Green, take them to church, wait for them and take them back after the service. I think it was an old Killick and Vincent bus."

The Warbill-in-Tun

Memories come flooding back again. The times I travelled on that old bus. We walk in silence as I remember, again, my grandparents and holidays with them in the cottage, outside toilets. Wonderful times, yet, who knows?

We pass a tumbledown farm and buildings around the Kingsley Hill area. "I wonder what this place will look like in 50 years, Ron?" I ask. "Won't be standing," is the reply. Yet in one of the tumbledown open barns is a JCB tractor that is turning orange with rust. "You'd 'ave thought 'e could 'ave sold that to do up 'is farm," comments Ron. Poor hard up farmers is all I can think of. Still there must be some reason for letting this farm fall apart?

It is but a short distance back to the church from here. We try to find where we should have emerged from our walk but all the signs tell us that the walk has been 'officially diverted'. Why we couldn't be told that in the middle of the walk I have no idea, but it would have helped. One thing I did notice, as we approach the Warbill-in-Tun, and the car, was another finger post. This one has a broken arm that we must tell Phil about. But what got me looking was on this post it tells us that it is 1½ mile to Rushlake Green yet the sign in Rushlake Green says it is only 1 mile to Warbleton?

From outside the Warbill-in-Tun the place looks a bit posh. Inside it is gorgeous. Having taken off our muddy boots as requested by a very polite sign outside the bar we are greeted with a "Good afternoon, gentlemen. Did you enjoy your walk?" I thought, how did he know we were out walking? As if he can read my mind he says, "I last saw you heading across the fields." I look towards the windows of the bar. There is no way he could see us from here. "What can I get you to drink, or would you prefer a table and a menu, we also do bar snacks if you would prefer." It is then that I realise that this was the gentleman out walking his dogs in the churchyard when we started this morning. Were we really out walking for that long?

Ron was happy; Harvey's bitter was on tap. My lager was ice cold and very refreshing. The food was filling and well prepared. Looking at the full menu I will be bringing the wife for a meal soon. The atmosphere, for a small pub, in the middle of some of the most beautiful countryside was exceptional. The staff were attentive but not obtrusive and the many customers they had whilst we were at the bar certainly seemed to enjoy their meals.

Next week it's Ron's turn to decide on the walk. This one, for me has opened many memories and I am pleased that my faith has been restored regarding the upkeep of churchyards. Again we missed the rain. We don't know how lucky we are.

WALK 21 – Weald & Vanguard Ways

Wednesday 21ˢᵗ June 2006

People can be helpful in many ways. Yet they can also be the opposite, without meaning to be. When Ron and I started these walks it was just the two of us with an old book to guide us, and our personal thoughts. Since Walk 1 we have become a little bit more, how you can say, technically minded. We still have the book and our thoughts but we also have Satellite Navigation to get us to the start of our walk, a digital camera, no less, for those all important pictures, a pair of stout walking boots each (Ron has two pairs) because we are walking further, pen and paper for note taking, bottles of iced mineral water for when it gets hot, a thumb stick (thanks again Des) to repel the unwanted attentions of animals, a pair of binoculars each, to be able to see things that are too far away for our old eyes to see normally

View from the start of this walk

View across the first field

and, of course, a couple of Ron's pies. So why is it being suggested, by many of our friends, that we now need to take a compass as well as all these things? So, we get lost. Not by far, and we always find our way back, eventually. All you have to do is head towards a church, towards traffic, towards a road and, without having to worry about if we are heading north, east, and south or west, we find our way back. It's not like we're crossing the Sahara or marching through a rain forest in some African jungle, where a compass would be a necessity. We are out for a walk in beautiful Sussex countryside. Even an ordinance survey map, to

Ron and me would be complicated; we could be down right dangerous with a compass as well. So it's not for us. We will follow nature's trail and end up where we end up, hopefully, a little wiser and with a funny story to tell.

A third party, this week, has selected our walk. One of our followers would like to join us on a walk around East Hoathly, her home village. Finding a walk was difficult but eventually I managed to find, through the wonders of the Internet, a walk of seven miles around East Hoathly. Regular readers will be aware that I have to be at work in the afternoons so we have been starting our walks slightly earlier, just in case the inevitable happens and I can't be late for work. As soon as we mention the start time of 10 o'clock our third party can't make it. On our Monday discussion a substitute has volunteered his company. Peter (Walk 7 and 8) has asked to be with us again (fool that he is). But a telephone call an hour before we set out tells us that Peter is confined to barracks. His wife has found him some jobs to do and he feels he should do as he's told. Bless. So it's just Ron, and me just at it was when we started.

Our walk is from The Argus website[51] and titled 'Weald Way and Vanguard Way'. It is suggested in the guide that the walk should take three hours and is described as 'Generally level field path walking, mostly well signed and defined'. We shall see.

We park the car in the free village car park, next to the church. As we walk around the perimeter wall of the church Ron is lost for words. The churchyard is waist high in weeds. "Used 'ter be like a bowlin' green when I came 'ere to mow grass on council land," says Ron. By the entrance to the churchyard is a sit on mower, "perhaps they are about to have the grass cut," I suggest, "lets complete the walk and come back to see what improvement there is."

---

[51] *www.theargus.co.uk/whatson/walks/eastsussex/areauckfieldheathfieldhailsham/* visited 18/06/2006

Our instructions guide us to Buttsfield Lane on the right-hand side of the main road. "This must 'ave been where the archers practised with bow an' arrer' in the old days," says Ron. A short way up the lane it divides and we fork left. We are now on the Weald Way. There is a yellow circular sign with two blue W's. The view at the end of the lane is peace and quiet. There is a tent pitched in the middle of the first field with a 'no parking' bollard by the entrance to the tent. We didn't disturb the occupants.

Abandoned vehicle

Whilst the weather today looked a bit bleak in the distance it was still pretty warm. Bottles of iced water were soon passed out along with the miniature pasties. Ron had bought supplies for our company but was gutted when he realised that he would have to eat them himself. Since our last walk, when I showed off my present from Des, a nice new thumb stick, Ron had been out in the local woods and cut himself one, and it was the exact size as mine. Again he had cut one for our company, which we left in the car. We cross two fields and at every stile we see the clearly marked Weald Way signs with arrows giving clear directions. Both Ron and I are impressed, so far. We eventually reach a lane where, again we see the clear sign for Weald Way. We cross the lane and enter a field opposite. Now I appreciate that we are out in the country and, every now and again, you will encounter that usual country smell. But, at the entry to this field, not only could you smell it you could taste it. It was awful and we couldn't get away fast enough but it seemed to follow us. It was ages before fresh air hit our nostrils and cleared that stinging feeling.

We are now heading towards Frith Farm, which is a large farm known for its pedigree Sussex bulls, which are big. As we approach the farm various implements, machinery and the like are left lying, to rot, in the fields. As I've said before, we can't understand why. I don't wish to repeat myself and will just let the photographs speak for them selves. I

Simply left to rust

would just say that these photographs were not taken at the same farm. The photo of the roller was taken further on in the walk, but the fact still remains regarding the habit of dump and forget.

Walking through Frith Farm was a very pleasant experience. It is obvious from our surroundings that animals are kept here but the place is kept neat and tidy with clear signs advising where you could and should not go. There was also a conservation area towards the end of the drive that contained wild flowers and a pond and

Conservation area, Frith Farm

looked really well maintained and was very pleasing to the eye. Both Ron and I stopped here for a while just to take in all the surroundings. Just to see this small conservation area is worth the walk of 7 miles on its own and is a credit to the landowner and the people who maintain it. At the end of the drive we turn left and head towards the village of Chiddingly. Regular readers will remember Walk 11. For those that are unaware this was the walk to Chiddingly that we got so lost on we didn't actually get to Chiddingly. On this walk, however, due to the very good signs found along our route, we have no trouble

Chiddingly Church

at all in finding the village, which still looks as it probably did years ago. Next to the church used to be the general stores, now converted into a private house, but it still keeps its shop

Enclosed path

frontage, complete with advertising boards. A real gem of a place. The Six Bells pub on the opposite corner to the shop is still, probably, the main attraction to this village. Unfortunately the church was being re-wired and closed to the public. Both Ron and I did manage a peek inside and it was full of scaffolding. We did manage to purchase the usual informative guide of the church and would you believe the very first line of the guide states that 'the spire is visible from every point of the compass'. "'Tis a shame, that," says Ron, "p'rhaps people are right. We'll need a compass after all." But it is true. When we walk away from the church, it doesn't matter which direction you go, you can see the spire for miles. The church is listed as being 15th century and was linked to a number of scattered settlements by an intricate system of footpaths and bridleways. The church guide is very informative and well worth its price. The churchyard, although small, is well maintained and the grass neatly cut.

We now leave the Weald Way and join the Vanguard Way, which starts by the telephone box opposite what was the general store. The path here is enclosed and leads us to a small field. Heading towards us is a man dressed in overalls and thick leather gloves. As he gets closer to us I can just make out the emblem EDF (new name for Seeboard) stitched on his overalls. "Hello, Ron," he says, "not working in Polegate any more, then?" "No," replies Ron, "semi retired, I am". "I wondered why I hadn't seen you for a while". I couldn't believe it. Here we are in the middle of nowhere talking to a man dressed in an EDF overall that knows Ron. It doesn't seem to matter where we go, someone knows him. It's amazing. But on reflection, what was the man in overalls, wearing thick leather gloves doing in the middle of a field in Chiddingly on a hot day in June?

Overgrown stile

Our signs have now changed to 'Public Footpath'. There is no indication that we are on the Vanguard Way. We are instructed to cross a number of fields, one being of manicured grass, used for turf cutting. This is where the earlier photo of the roller came from. At the edge of the field, just before a lane, is a stile and kissing gate. The plaque tells us that this stile and gate is maintained by d.e.f.r.a., which is part of the 'Countryside Stewardship Scheme'. From the state of the access they can't be in business any more. Once on the lane we turn right for a few yards before turning left along a drive towards Clarklye Farm and then right, over a stile through to a fenced path. So far the footpath signs are clear and both Ron and I are getting more impressed

More work for Phil

by the minute. We pass a paddock on our right and not a single horse can be seen. The horseboxes close to the path are all empty but a radio, attached to one of the doors, is happily playing away. Looking back along the path you can see that it is well maintained and the grass and hedge have been recently cut. Further along this path we come across a small lake complete with park bench. A really lovely setting. "Just the place to come 'fer some peace and quiet," says Ron. It really is idyllic. I notice a couple of ducks on the water. One is obviously fishing for food with its bum in the air. We stood, looking at this scene for some time. "That duck seems to be able to hold its breath for a long time, Ron" I say pointing to the bum in the middle of the pond. "You daft bugger," says Ron, "them's is decoys, them's ain't real ducks." I felt a complete idiot, but they were really lifelike and I swear the one on the bank moved.

`Further on from the pond we find ourselves walking alongside a caravan site, presumably used as holiday vans. Yet they all looked as if they should be mobile. They obviously hadn't moved for some time, as the grass was high around the wheels. Just looked odd? Our guidebook tells us that we should follow a fenced path from here and head for houses but the path actually takes us to a stile and another field. The public footpath signs have now disappeared and we are not sure what to do. We eventually decide to go into the field and follow the hedgerow on our right hand side. Good decision. This leads us to another fenced pathway where one of the owners has place their own public footpath sign. We are now walking through the area of Gray Wood that appears to be part of an old manor estate. Houses to our left and right are the sort that we would need a couple of very big lottery wins

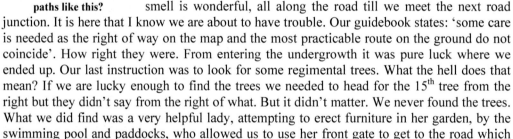

to be able to afford the door chimes. Way out of our price range. All Ron kept saying was "look 'ow the rich buggers live." At the end of this path we join a road and turn right.

We need to pass the first junction, signposted to Waldron and continue to the next. The signpost here should direct us towards Waldron, but as you can see we have found more work for Phil. The signpost has broken and is lying in the grass. From here we can hear running water and the map tells us that we should be crossing Scallow Bridge but we never actually found a stream or a bridge. What we did find was Honeysuckle growing in the hedgerow. "I've tried growing that in my garden for years," I tell Ron, "never had any joy yet you come out here and it grows wild without any trouble. Can we take a cutting?" I ask Ron the

How often have we seen paths like this?

gardener. "Come back later in the year, 'tis too early now". The smell is wonderful, all along the road till we meet the next road junction. It is here that I know we are about to have trouble. Our guidebook states: 'some care is needed as the right of way on the map and the most practicable route on the ground do not coincide'. How right they were. From entering the undergrowth it was pure luck where we ended up. Our last instruction was to look for some regimental trees. What the hell does that mean? If we are lucky enough to find the trees we needed to head for the 15th tree from the right but they didn't say from the right of what. But it didn't matter. We never found the trees. What we did find was a very helpful lady, attempting to erect furniture in her garden, by the swimming pool and paddocks, who allowed us to use her front gate to get to the road which

would lead us to East Hoathly. "It's about ¾ of a mile to the village," she tells us. We make our thank you's and I practically have to guide Ron by the arm to make sure he leaves the lady to build her furniture on her own. She was very pleasant. Just before we get to her front gate two of the largest dogs are heading towards us at speed. "Don't run!" are the last words I hear from Ron, as I hurtle towards the five bar gate. How Ron got there before me I will never know but he calmly talks to the beast that gets to us first whilst unlatching the gate ushering me out onto the road all in one movement. I was so grateful to get out without the arse of my trousers being ripped to shreds. "They won't 'urt 'yer," says Ron. Why do people always say that?

Yet more work

We discover that we are not actually too far out of our way. We've come out on the correct road but just one field up so no great problem. It's just a short walk, ¾ of a mile according to our nice lady, to East Hoathly. Unfortunately we couldn't check her instructions out because yet another signpost is broken, where is Phil when you need him?

It is just a short walk back to East Hoathly church from here and we are both looking forward to see if any improvement had been made to the condition of the churchyard since first seeing it, some four hours ago.

One of the churchyards best-known inhabitants is Thomas Turner. He was born in 1729 and died in 1793. During his life he wrote a diary[52], which has been published and is a wonderful chronicle of village life from 1754, when he started the diary, to 1765 when he stopped. It is fascinating reading, although sometimes a little difficult to understand. The entry for this day 250 years ago starts '*A very great tempest of thunder, lightning and rain, but in particular of lightning. It began about 12 o'clock in the morn and continued until near 2. This morn about 7.30 Mrs Porter was safely delivered of a girl...*'

He is buried, according to the church literature, at the rear of the church by the leper window. Unfortunately you will have to take the pamphlets words as truth because, bluntly, it could be anyone's tombstone.

I can say no more, about this churchyard, other than both Ron and myself could cry. What

Yet another unkempt graveyard

a disgrace. I have a 2 year old granddaughter who, given a toy push along mower could have made a better job than the person who had, presumably spent the last four hours trying to mow(?) this beautiful churchyard. We can understand preservation areas, but all this person had done was mow a few pathways clear and that was it! The grass and weeds would be taller than my two-year-old granddaughter. Haven't the vicars of these churches any pride at all? Obviously not!

We finish here. The walk was completed in practical silence. I don't know what to say except that it is obvious to me that seeing churchyards in my County of Sussex causes both Ron and me to get emotional. I will apologise for our sentimentality but history and the preservation of it is important to both of us. The more I write about the condition of these churchyards the more emotional I tend to become. In our future writings I will only write about the well-kept churchyards, the churchyards and vicars worthy of comment. The others will not be mentioned.

The two people who were to be with us today missed out on an enjoyable, and at the end, emotional walk. That is their loss. But it was a walk without a compass again. We made a slight detour from the written walk but we didn't get lost. Let's hope it's a turning point. Here's to next week.

[52] *The Diary of Thomas Turner 1754-1765* edited by David Vaisey Published by CTR Publishing, East Hoathly, ISBN 0-9524516-0-3

WALK 22 - Burwash

Wednesday 28th June 2006

Monday nights have changed for me. At this time of year Monday night is shove-halfpenny (pronounced shuv' 'ape 'knee) night. The Kings Head, South Road used to be league champions. Back then there used to be two leagues and we would travel far and wide for a league game. Games started at 8:30 in the evening and sometimes we had to leave The

Kings Head at 7 o'clock just to get to the away games on time, and sometimes it was not unknown for us to get back very late in the evening. I no longer play in the team where terms such as 'three in a bed', 'needs a tickle', 'cross board back spin', 'an easy lay' and 'playing the chalker' could be heard throughout each game. How Monday nights have changed. Now there is only six teams in the one league and the furthest the team travels is Horsebridge just 2 miles away. Ron still plays in the team so he has to be away some Monday evenings, during the league season, and we don't get to discuss Wednesdays walk, as we used to. It's sort of become my turn, your turn, that's where we'll go and at what time. At the home games we have a little more time to talk.

Heading towards Batemans

This week it's my turn to propose a walk. I have always enjoyed a good sponge cake so when I thumbed through our Sussex Walks book and found a walk for Kipling country I thought, why not; he 'makes exceedingly good cakes'. Seriously, though I am not a literary person. Some of Rudyard Kipling's work I do not understand. I appreciate his talent, the thousands of followers of his work can't all be wrong. But it is not my 'cup of tea'. Each to his own. A little bit like shove-halfpenny. You do or you don't.

So, this week's walk is around Burwash, (pronounced 'Burish' by the locals) the home of Rudyard Kipling since 1902 after his move from Rottingdean. It was here that Kipling wrote most of his famous works. The house, and the peace and tranquillity of the countryside inspired him over the years. Kipling loved gardening just as much as the house. He planted the Yew hedges to give him more privacy. He designed the beautiful rose garden after being awarded the

Batemans - the home of the Kipling family

Nobel Peace Prize for Literature in 1907.

The Watermill

Our walk starts from the public car park behind the Bear Inn. This can be easily missed if travelling from Heathfield, as it looks like part of the car park for the pub. It wasn't until we'd passed it and returned to the village that we noticed the sign. The walk commences in the left corner of the car park, behind the toilet block, and is clearly signed. After just a short walk through a fenced path you come to the first stile and we are greeted by the view, down into the valley, which will lead us to the road and on to Batemans. The signs here are clear and, after crossing three fields we arrive at the stile onto the road where we turn right. I am not sure what I expected, when we came round the corner of the road and faced Batemans. It was a lot bigger than I expected with the chimneystacks being a prominent feature. I had a picture in my own mind of a little country cottage with bay windows and a cottage garden. How wrong can you be? It's BIG!

We pass in front of the house and keep left and head for Park Farm. It is here that you see the watermill, built in the 1700's and restored by volunteers. It still grinds corn into flour but due to the current water shortage is only worked on Saturdays. Attached to the wheel is one of the earliest water-driven turbines, installed by Rudyard Kipling to generate electricity for the house. Behind the watermill is a large pond which helps feed the mill. In the water are a large number of carp, which Ron estimates to be in the 1 to 1½lb range. You could practically put your hand out and touch them. We stayed here for quite a while just soaking in the atmosphere. Batemans, and the watermill, are now owned by The National Trust and aren't open all year round and not open at all on Mondays and Tuesdays. As today was Wednesday we were surprised not to see anyone wandering around the grounds. The miller, resplendent in his white overalls, was ready and waiting to give his short tour and sell his wares but whilst we were there we saw no customers. We pass by here on the way back so perhaps, a little later in the day, we may see that trade has picked up.

We carry on towards Park Farm and Ron stops suddenly, "hear that?" he asks and before I can answer he continues "'tis a song thrush. Nothin' sounds nicer than a song thrush in full voice. 'An who taught 'im 'ter sing like that?" I haven't got chance to answer. "Even ol' Wibbs is bein' taught 'ter play that saxophone but no one teaches them birds 'ter sing like they do." Of course he's right but all I could say was "that bird's song sounds a lot nicer than Wibb's saxophone."

Feathered friend crosses the bridge

Passing over a wooden bridge Ron suddenly stops again. "For God's sake Ron, what now?" "Careful

Burwash views

where 'yer tread. Little baby wagtail 'bout to commit suicide if we scare 'im and 'e falls over the edge of the bridge into the water." Just in front of us is the smallest bird I've ever seen. As we slowly walk over the bridge the bird walks towards the edge. "Don't scare it!" insists Ron. "We'll walk over, one at a time, slowly" he says, "I'll go first." He creeps over to the other edge of the bridge and slowly walks over the bridge without looking at the bird. The bird doesn't move. "Right, now your turn," he whispers to me. I follow. Halfway across I can't resist taking a picture. I heard Ron tut but I needed that picture. When I slowly drew level with the bird for some reason, I do not know why; I looked away from the bird and looked at Ron. When I looked back the bird was gone! Whether he jumped, flew or ran I will never know. I rushed over to the edge of the bridge but I couldn't see him floating anywhere so I assume he's ok?

At the end of the track we pass through one gate and head towards another gate on our left. Again markings are very clear. We now head up the field slope keeping the trees to our right. It is the view from here that makes you realise how far away from the village of Burwash you have walked without realising it. We need to make our way towards a gate at the top of the field but stop short just to admire the view, and if I'm really honest, to get my breath back.

We are now instructed to look for a bridleway post. No problem. We follow the sign and pass through a small wood to a track. As with all our walks, things go wrong and it's here that all signs disappear. It's as if someone is saying 'we got you here now find your own way!' We are advised to 'bear left, then immediately right and follow the bridleway'. There is no sign for a bridleway but we have two grass tracks, one left the other straight ahead. We take the straight-ahead track and end up in a field of broad bean plants. Thousands of broad bean plants ".. an' not one bugger with black fly," comments Ron. We go back to the other track.

Leggets Wood

War Memorial

Our instructions tell us to pass a solitary cottage. We never saw one. Further on in the instructions I notice that we turn right onto a road. We can hear traffic so head for the sound. We still couldn't see the cottage, which should have set off alarm bells. But it didn't. We found a road and turned right. "I've given in to our friends," I try to explain to Ron, "I haven't bought a compass but I have bought an Ordinance Survey map of this area. Trouble is, I've left it at home. Still, look on the bright side. I'll be able to tell us where we went wrong on this walk when we get home." I don't think Ron was impressed. He was even less impressed when we pass the field of broad beans and , after walking about ½ an hour, we came across a signpost for Brightling and just round the corner we found ourselves standing outside Brightling Gypsum Mine (Walk 19). "Lets go back an' 'ead for that sign with 'footpath' on it," says Ron, "we can find our way back to Burwash from the other side of the wood." So back we go. We turn left, along a marked footpath into Leggets Wood. This turned out to be a maze of paths and cut through's and was a fascinating place to be in. We eventually found our familiar yellow signs, which made it so much easier to follow a route. The natural undergrowth through this wood was unbelievable and the way that little streams are formed and meander through the woodland is outstanding. The bright sunlight streaming into the woods gave it an eerie feeling. The path seemed to go on for ever and was crisscrossing tracks and bridleways in all directions. When we eventually reached a clearing, Burwash village and church was just a short distance away to our right so it was just a case of getting to the end of the wood. No problem. When we looked at our instructions and map again we had come out practically in the correct place. But with a slight detour.

Passing Batemans again it is obvious that there are more people about. The sound of people talking and laughing can be clearly heard. I read somewhere that Rudyard Kipling once bought a Rolls Royce motor car stating that it was the only car he could afford to run. Apparently, the actual car, complete with receipts for it's upkeep, are on show within the grounds of Batemans.

The actual village of Burwash is a delightful place. Very well-kept and wonderfully old. The village isn't mentioned in the Domesday Book but is thought to have been a small settlement in about 1090. The Church of St Bartholomew is a truly holy place. Walking in the church gave me that really strange feeling that I only find in few churches. Goosebumps up my arms, a lump to the throat. A very peaceful, tranquel and lovely place. The churchyard is a veritable credit to its parishioners and I must congratulate them on the overall appearance and presentation of their place of worship. Outside the church gate is a memorial to the brave men of Burwash who gave their lives during the wars. The monument, unveiled

Burwash Church

by Rudyard Kipling, (his only son is one of those commemorated), not only supplies the name of the deceased but also the person's regiment and the date that he fell. A true gem of a find to anyone tracing their ancestors as is a little sign within the church porch which advises that all the headstones within the churchyard have been transcribed and a look-up service is available should anyone require it.

"What time is it?" asks Ron. "Half past two, why?" I reply. "Any chance of a quick pint in one 'o them old pubs?" he asks. "We could go to the Rose and Crown in Ham Lane if you like." I know Ron likes his Harvey's and I noticed that the Rose and Crown was a Harvey's pub.

Throughout this walk in Burwash countryside we haven't met a sole. Human or animal. We walk into the pub in Ham Lane and a voice says, "Hello Ron, what are you doing in these parts?" I couldn't believe it, not again. The young lad behind the bar recognises Ron straight away. "Been fer a walk around these parts," explains Ron. "Not all the way from Hailsham?" the lad asks. Is there nowhere that we go where Ron is not known? There has to be somewhere. After a pint and a packet of crisps we head back to the car. Another walk completed.

I am told that some of the locals pronounce the name of this village Burish. I wonder why. I should think that little has changed since Rudyards day, apart from the amount of traffic. Rudyard lived at Batemans for 34 years and died in 1936. He once described it as 'a real house in which to settle down for keeps….a good and peaceable place.' Here's to next week. I can't wait.

Rudyard Kipling 1865-1936[53]
THE APPEAL

IF I HAVE GIVEN YOU DELIGHT
BY AUGHT THAT I HAVE DONE,
LET ME LIE QUIET IN THAT NIGHT
WHICH SHALL BE YOURS ANON:

AND FOR THE LITTLE, LITTLE SPAN
THE DEAD ARE BORNE IN MIND,
SEEK NOT TO QUESTION OTHER THAN
THE BOOKS I LEAVE BEHIND

Rudyard Kipling[54]

---

[53] Image obtained via www.google.co.uk using www.orwell.ru/people/kipling viewed 28/06/2006
[54] http://whitewolf.newcastle.edu.au/words/authors/K/KiplingRudyard/verse/p3/appeal.html viewed 28/06/2006

WALK 23 - Laughton

Wednesday 5th July 2006

World Cup 2006 fever has come to an end for England. Again we are not good enough. From the very start I have said that the only winner for England in this year's competition were the flags sellers. Let's hope they weren't made in Portugal. I am not being unpatriotic. I believe that today's English footballers are overpaid and not good enough and, at last, we will no longer have to suffer the smug Swedish idiot. Let's be honest, everyone I've spoken to

Local wood carving

could do a better job than him. Unfortunately I have little faith in the new manager of our National team. Let's hope I'm wrong.

This week's walk has been discussed over a number of days. Ron is unsure whether to go for a walk around Laughton, which has been mentioned before, or go for a pub walk around the Merrie Harriers in Cowbeech. The Laughton walk looked to be the winner until he noticed that the guidebook suggests it could be difficult to follow a route. With our sense of direction we could end up anywhere and we could be gone for days. Ron

was also worried that the book said the scenery at Laughton was uninteresting. So, on Monday evening, after a long discussion and a few pints we decided on Laughton. After all, it was going to be a challenge in more ways than one.

This week's walk is taken from the Argus, East Sussex Walks book[55]. An excerpt from the book reads, '..I would recommend it well shod and armed with a stout walking stick ….. the walk traverses a comparatively featureless landscape…..' Not very inspiring, to say the least. But we are not to be thwarted. Being well shod and armed with our thumb sticks (thanks again for mine Des) we set off.

The weather during the night and early morning had been horrendous. Thunder and lightning started at about 5 in the morning and the radio was warning of flash floods when I set off for work at 6. By the time we started our walk the rain had stopped (doesn't rain in Sussex on a Wednesday……..) but it was

All Saints Church

very humid and sticky. And the road we had to go down to park was closed.

Not a good start. But we are not to be thwarted. I find another parking place, right by the Roebuck Inn. Handy place for later perhaps, and we walk down the road towards the church.

All Saints Church is tucked away just past the Village Hall and cricket pitches and is a picture to behold. Laughton is mentioned in the Domesday Book as 'Leston' and over the years to the early 16th century has

Church interior

Path behind church

had various different spellings. The church was founded in 1229 and was administered by the canons of Michelham Priory. In the reign of Charles I the benefice of Laughton passed to Sir Thomas Pelham and then on to his successors. The Pelham name has remained connected to Laughton ever since. Again we purchased the leaflet about the churches history and it really is an

---

[55] *East Sussex Walks* by Ben Perkins Published from The Evening Argus 1995 Page 50

informative piece of writing. I must admit ignorance here. I had vaguely heard of something called the 'Pelham Buckle' and never understood what it meant. It appears to be a kind of signature used by the family to show off their work. Like a trademark. So many church towers were built, or rebuilt by the Pelham family, that they have become known as the Pelham Towers. Ashburnham, Chiddingly, Crowhurst, Dallington, East Hoathly Laughton, Ripe and Waldron churches all show the buckle on the arches of the tower's west doorways.

The footpath we are about to take, behind the church, runs past Glebe Pond, through ancient Blackshaw to Laughton Place. People, for centuries, have walked this very path and enjoyed the wild flowers. Until the late 1980's the sexton's hut stood at the entrance to the footpath. It makes you feel humble knowing that we were walking along the same pathway used in the 15th century.

For some reason, just seeing our current surroundings has given both Ron and me a lift. "Man that wrote this walk must 'ave walked it with 'is eyes shut," comments Ron. "It's a bit early in the walk to make judgement, Ron, lets see what the walk has to offer."

We walk to the end of the path and skirt around a field with the hedge to our right. You

Broken stile

can just make out the Downs in the distance. The sea mist practically obliterates the beautiful rolling South Downs but the views from here are still stunning. We are now instructed to turn left and head towards the distant Downs until we get to the corner and go through a swing gate and turn right. So far, so good. The signs seem to be clearly placed and easy to find. Although the pathways are not clearly defined we manage to keep on track. But..... our next instruction is a little vague. After 250 yards we need to veer right over a stile, cross a field and beyond a prominent oak in a scanty hedgerow, bear left to a footbridge and head across two pasture fields. Problem number one. We walked further than 250 yards but could not find a stile. Problem number two. There were a number of oak trees but none 'in a scanty hedgerow'. After much discussion and going back and forth we managed to find a footbridge. If you could call it that? How we got to it I have no idea. But the tower of Laughton Place could be seen in the distance so we must be on the right path. Our signs have also, mysteriously, reappeared. We are instructed to walk through the middle of this man's crop field. "Can't do that," says Ron, "we'll 'af ter walk round outside edge." It must have put on another mile to the

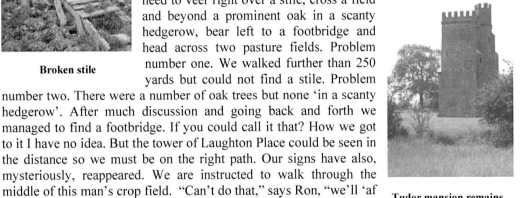

Tudor mansion remains

walk. The field was enormous. "How can the writer of this walk call this 'featureless landscape'?" I ask. "Just look at the scene from here." The sun has just started to come out. It

Feeding cattle

was around midday, getting hotter by the second and the sound of wildlife and the countryside was a joy to behold. I remember reading somewhere that if you stop in the countryside and listen very quietly, the countryside screams at you. Until today I didn't understand that. But now I know exactly what it means. Birds are singing. I can hear running water, horses, cattle, sheep, dogs barking in the distance, and not a single sound from a car or lorry. Wonderful. The tower is all that is left of the brick Tudor mansion built for the Pelham family in 1534. The lily-filled stream feeds, what used to be, the moat around the mansion.

We now cross two fields and head towards an isolated cottage which turns out to be two

Ron's fishing dream

quaint little cottages, one called Hole Cottage and the other has the number '197' on the door. The driveway is ¾ of a mile long. "Long way to walk for a pint Ron," I comment. "Afford ter live out 'ere you can 'ave it deliver'd," is the reply. As we walk along the drive an open field is on our right. The farmer has planted wheat and Ron can't get over how close to the drive he has managed to plant his crop. "Can't believe it," he says, "right up to the edge of the road. Not a wasted piece of land to be seen, marvellous." At the end of the drive we meet a lane where we turn right and after 100 yards go left through a gap in the hedge. We

still have our signs so we are ok. The book had said that the walk was very overgrown in places and was a difficult route but apart from the problem with the oak tree we had experienced very few problems at all and was becoming a bit confident in our abilities. The need for the ordinance survey map was also dismissed as a waste of money. We'd managed to get over halfway round this walk without technical aides so we are brimming with new found confidence. We pass a flint barn and, as instructed, head for the far right-hand corner of the next field where we '..should join the B2124'. Wrong. We could see the B2124. Men were working, laying tarmac, on the B2124. But there was no stile, gate, a hole in the hedge or any other way of getting to the B2124. "We've gone wrong," says Ron, "knew it couldn't last." "We can't be that far out. Look, " I say, "the map shows the road and that lay-by so we must be in the wrong field, that's all." I'm trying to be full of confidence, but our track record isn't that good. We walk back along the hedge and climb over a gate into the next field and there, thankfully in the right-hand corner, was the stile leading onto the B2124. Once onto the road

Lilly pond

we have to turn left and head for a 'roughly metalled drive'. Neither Ron nor I know what a metalled drive is but we found a tarmac drive leading to a farm. As we are walking up this drive I noticed the herd of cattle. Animals and me are not the best of friends but they are in a field and I notice that our next instruction is to carry straight on when the drive bears left. "Some 'o your mates up there, Graham," sniggers Ron. "As long as they stay up there I'll be happy." Don't be daft," he says, "lets go an' say hello." I was horrified. Realising there was a fence and a large gate between them, and me, what harm would it do to say hello to the nice moo cows? I kid you not when I say that as soon as this herd of wild animals took one look at me they stampeded towards us and skidded to a halt within inches of Ron. I am now standing directly behind Ron, well out of harms way. Ron puts his hand out, palm down, and this enormous animal sniffs up to it. Ron is making cooing noises and the animal licks his hand. "Tis the salt from yer sweat they like," says Ron, "try it, they won't 'urt yer." There's that saying again; they won't hurt you. Famous last words. But, a strange thing happened, which I felt, at the time, I had no control over. I found myself coming out from behind Ron's protection and actually put my hand out for the cow to lick. What made me do it I have no idea. But that cows tongue was rougher than any sandpaper I've used. We stayed with the animals for some time after that. I think it's the speed at which they come on to you that is scary, rather than the animal itself. I don't know. I can't analyse it. I'm just scared, basically. But I'm still not that confident that I'll be able to do that again. We'll have to wait and see.

We are now instructed to walk 'two thirds of a mile' along the grass track. Just as we start, and I'm still wiping the hand that was licked, we scare a deer in the bushes, which runs off across the field. It's strange that with all the traffic noise now prominent a deer gets scared of us and runs. We have now seen more deer in the last 23 weeks than I have seen in the whole of my 54 years. Just before we get to a gate Ron says, "Look at this," and heads through a hole in the hedge. On the other side of the hedge is a beautiful man-made lake, complete with lilies. "Can you imagine," says Ron, "sittin' out 'ere, fishin'. Test match on wireless. Crate 'o beer by yer seat with surroundin's like this. You'd think you'd 'ave died an' gone t'eaven." I must admit, I keep recalling the comments in the guidebook about featureless landscape and don't understand. The scene in front of us at this moment is inspiring, to say the very least. Ron is in a dream world all of his own. "Think 'ow big the fish must be in a lake that size. I'd like to 'ave a go at that." "Come on Ron, we've got a walk to finish, perhaps we can find out who owns it. A lake this good has to be private fishing," I manage to drag him away and we head back through the hedge and through the gate.

Here we turn right and walk parallel to the lake. Along a little grass track we come to

Blind folded horse racing?

some stables and paddocks. We are instructed to go over a stile onto a lane but again there is no stile but two iron gates lead us to a gravel drive past a paddock with a horse that appears to be blind folded. It isn't until you get closer that you realise that the horse can, in fact see, and that the 'coat and mask' are for the animals' protection. But it did look strange.

Our walk now takes us across another road and into a winding woodland path. We still haven't found any path that was overgrown or in poor condition and can only assume that since the writing of the guidebook someone has improved the walk in many ways. One of the instructions is to turn right by a fallen tree. Usually we can't find these landmarks for one reason or another but this one was easy to spot. Just in front of us is a large tree, listing at a funny angle and being held up by one of the largest thumb sticks we'd ever seen. Put ours to shame.

Just beyond this we exit the woodland onto the road, turn right and find ourselves within yards of the car.

We didn't get lost! We actually managed a walk that, according to the book, was going to be hard. We're chuffed with ourselves. A quick visit into the Roebuck and an ice cold drink completed the day.

Unfortunately our day ended on a bit of sad news. We heard this evening that one of our close friends at the Kings Head was found, by the Police, inside his house and rushed to Hurst Wood Park Hospital. At this point we know nothing more. Sean is a much-loved character in the Kings Head and I'm sure everyone hopes and prays that he makes a speedy recovery.

WALK 24 - Shipley

Wednesday 12th July 2006

Before Monday's meeting to discuss the next walk with Ron we learnt that Sean had lost his battle. I received a phone call from Bev on Friday 7th July to say that Sean had said goodbye at 11:20. I will never forget the way that Bev broke the news to me. What a beautiful way to pass on such tragic news on what would have been Sean's 51st birthday. Only the day before I was writing in a Birthday Card and a Get Well Soon Card. Sean was one of those characters that every public bar has. I've never heard Sean badmouth anyone, I have never heard of anyone who didn't like Sean. He had a way with words. He used to tell me that he was only a thick Irishman, but everyone would always be listening to what he had to say, 'one million percent'. His language could be colourful and Bev used to chide him about it. Everyone who knew him will miss him terribly. He was an everyday part of our lives. God bless you Sean, a day will not pass when you aren't far from our thoughts.

This week's walk is dedicated to Sean Snee (1955-2006).

Every week he would listen and laugh at our escapades. He rarely read a chapter but insisted we talk him through every walk. He was one of the first to utter the words 'they won't hurt you' whenever I mentioned animals. This week, I somehow feel, he will be with us.

I am on holiday from the School for a number of weeks, so we can travel a little further into Sussex for our weekly walk. Shipley is where we are heading this Wednesday. The home of Hilaire Belloc[56]. The same Hilaire Belloc who gave me the inspiration, to start this task. But first a little geography lesson is required. For those unaware of the fact, Shipley is located in West Sussex. We are not walking around the Shipley in Bradford, Derbyshire or Shropshire, but the Shipley located by the A272 just south of Horsham and east of Billingshurst. The windmill, at Shipley, has served as the fictional home of the hero of the BBC Television series 'Jonathan Creek'. A curly haired weirdo who solved crimes using magic?

In 1830 the population of Shipley was 1,100 with 113 families receiving relief and 46 paupers in the workhouse, which had a very bad reputation. One man received six weeks hard labour after bodily removing three of his grandchildren from the workhouse and giving the workhouse master a tongue lashing about the conditions. You may think that a rural farming village would be peaceful with no crime. Not so, as it was the home of the notorious "Shipley Gang", which terrorized the inhabitants in the 1800's. After a virtual reign of terror the gang

Boundary Gate

was captured and James Rapley, the leader, committed suicide in his prison cell. A new gang replaced the old one but confined their activities to poaching, which they carried out in an almost respectable manner. They had regular customers, and poached items would be tagged with the recipients address for faster dispatching.

Our walk, this week, is taken from the 'AA-50 Walks in Sussex[57]' and is Walk 31. It is described as 7 miles in length, very little gradient and should take a minimum of 3 hours to complete. We set off by car at 10 o'clock arriving, eventually, in Shipley at 11. We are advised that the Shipley Windmill, bought by Hilaire in 1906, is the tallest Windmill in Sussex. We can't see it? Is this an omen?

Our first instruction is to walk along the road, from the car park, until we reach a kissing gate on our right. We find the gate, pass through and follow the right-hand boundary hedge

---

[56] http://www.consolation.org.uk/belloc.html visited 12/07/2006
[57] *50 Walks in Sussex* – AA Publishing - Page 80

until we reach another gate leading us into Church Wood. We now follow a woodland path through the trees until we reach a stile and onto the road. Once over the road we follow another woodland path to a field. Across this path is a tall gate advising us that we are about to enter an area where animals roam free and all dogs must be kept on a lead. Once through the gate we are now in the very large estate belonging to Knepp Castle, which is described as 'a castellated sham' in our book. John Nash designed the 'castle' in 1809. It had to be rebuilt in the early 1900's after a fire. The time is now 11:15 in the morning and we hardly stop walking and don't leave the estate until 12:30. All the signs for the public footpath are in great condition and the route is very easy to follow. It's just the sheer expanse of the land that is really overpowering. To think someone has enough money to actually own all that we can see is astounding. It is obvious that we are not going to be able to get too close to the castle as the signs are steering us past the polo pitch (is it called a pitch?) but our quick photo towards the castle doesn't do it justice. The polo pitch (?) is to the right in the photo In fact you can't see anything at all. But believe us, it's BIG.

The Knepp Estate

We now head along the drive away from the castle and towards New Lodge. An apt if not a totally original name for a newly built mansion. The drive seems to go on forever. Ron is getting a little worried that he hasn't seen the windmill yet, "if it's so damn big why can't we see it?" he asks. All I could offer was that we were walking away from Shipley and it must be behind the trees. But it was little comfort for Ron.

We follow the drive as it runs along the side of Kneppmill Pond, which is a huge expanse of water on the left-hand side of the drive. "Can't see no pontoons or piers for fishin' from on that lake," comments Ron, "an its too bloody big 'ter call a pond!" We are still on Knepp Castle land and have been walking nearly an hour. Just round the next bend was the most beautiful sight of all. A small herd of wild deer were grazing in the field in front of us. All they did was look up and kept an eye on us as we passed by. They didn't seem that bothered we were there. We eventually arrive at the end of the drive. "Can you imagine, 'avin' to get

Kneppmill Pond

yer wheelie bin from the castle to the end of this drive, just ter see dustcart disappearing down the road. Butler 'ud be gutted," chuckles Ron. To our right you can just make out, in the distance, all that remains of the original Knepp Castle founded by William de Braose after the

Norman Conquest. It's taken us nearly forty minutes to reach the end of the drive and the main A24 road.

But crossing the A24 means you take your life in your hands. It is a very busy duel carriageway, which runs from Worthing to London. Once across to the other side we manage to find, very easily, a footpath sign and gate. We now have to cross various fields, cross small streams and head through woodland paths. What is so surprising for me is the ease at which we found the signs. What is so surprising for Ron is that we still can't see the Windmill! We are now heading towards West Grinstead. As far as we can make out, the only thing at West Grinstead is a beautiful church. Both of us are surprised at how many graves are within the churchyard and even more surprised to find a small plaque, which advised us that Hilaire Belloc was buried in this churchyard. Unfortunately the church was locked so we were not able to find out where his grave was within the churchyard. We wandered around for some time trying to locate it but without luck. The large tombstone in the picture is in sacred memory of Sara, widow of John Pollard who died in Brighton on 20th December 1855 aged 93. As far as I am aware she is no relation, but I will check the particulars, you never know.

Remains of Knepp Castle?

We now make for a kissing gate in the corner of the churchyard and follow the paved path south. Now I am beginning to get worried. All of a sudden the book starts to give directions by the compass point. We have no compass. "Don't need one neither," says Ron, "just look fer the sun. It's straight up. So that ways south," he says pointing towards the hedge in the distance. "How the hell did you work that out?" I ask. I am impressed. "Tis easy," explains Ron, "suns high in the sky 'cause it's around the middle of the day. It rises from the east an' sets in 't west. That way must be south," he continues, pointing in the direction we need

The Church at West Grinstead

to go, "not only that but I can see the only gateway in the 'edge over in that direction. Must be south, see, easy peasy." I am even more confused. We cross the River Adur by footbridge and follow the track to an area known as Butcher's Row. "Look at the state o'that footbridge,"

Still waters

says Ron, "bet no 'ealth 'an safety officer 'asn't looked at that fer a few years." "Probably not Ron but just imagine how many people have used it, over the years, to get to the church at West Grinstead." For the amount of houses within this area it really is astonishing how many people are buried in that churchyard. Why was Hilaire buried at West Grinstead and not Shipley, which, surely, would have been his parish church? The windmill is only next-door to it. As soon as I mention windmill Ron is off again jumping up and down looking over hedgerows trying to get a glimpse of the mill. Still no sight of the elusive windmill.

We follow the signs towards Rookcross Lane

without problems. We pass Rookcross Farm still following the clear signs. But it is now that our guidebook seems to go wrong. I say seems because it tells us to veer right just pass Rookcross Farm at a 'private drive' sign, and we have no sign. We walk on for some time knowing that the A24 is to our right and we should be heading towards the A24. But we aren't. We appear to be walking parallel to the road. We pass Rookcross Cottage. That's not mentioned in our book. We are just about to turn round and head back towards the farm when we think we see, in the distance, a sign. "Let's 'ead for that sign an' see what it says," suggest Ron. "If it's not the correct sign, we turn back, or we'll be a long way off course". Our luck, or was it skill, holds out and the sign is the one we are looking for. It is just a short walk now, across a field, over two stiles and we find ourselves back on the verge of the busy A24. Over the road, over a stile and along a path by the side of a bungalow and we find we are in the car park of The Crown Inn, in Dial Post. "Fancy a quick pint?" I ask. "Is the Pope Catholic?" is the reply and before I could turn round Ron was at the bar of a really nice old pub. We established that the person behind the bar was named Jason who, apparently, had a reputation to uphold because he was known as Super Stud? The only other person at the bar was a gentleman called Peter, who, once he established what we were about, proceeded to advise us of many of the local historical points of interest. His stories alone would fill a chapter and we are hoping that we may incorporate some of his stories in one of our future walks. Both made us feel really welcome and it was becoming increasingly difficult to want to get away.

Heading towards Dial Post

Funnily enough, Peter reminded both of us of Sean. He would talk to anybody just like Peter was now and would make it interesting. Ron's two pints of Firsty Ferret[58] went down well, as did my pint of ice-cold lager. It was really hot outside and we could have stayed a lot longer but I have a home to go to and we had been on this walk for three hours already.

We leave the pub and turn right. "Did you see that menu on the bar?" asks Ron, "they only 'ad liver 'an bacon casserole." Ron was drooling! "Yes Ron, and not a bad price either. Perhaps we should go back to all the pubs we visit, try a meal, and then write a book about that." You could see Ron thinking that over in his mind.

We turn left into Swallows Lane and as we leave the village we bear left and follow a straight lane towards New Barn Farm. After a long stroll through and between farm buildings we emerge at what appears to be a horse riding school. Young girls are practising over small jumps and a couple pass us, without speaking, as we head towards Pound Lane. Once getting to the lane and turning left we get our first glimpse of the windmill in the distance. We are advised to ignore the first public footpath sign and walk along the lane a little further until we reach a bridleway. We turn right here and walk along a sheltered path to the windmill. You can imagine, many years ago, people walking this track to get to church or heading backwards and forwards along the track to get flour for making bread. Suddenly, the track comes to an end and we find ourselves at the foot of the windmill. Walking around the apron is a man with a pole and hook pulling on one of the sails. "You want ter wait till the wind blows," shouts Ron, "you'll find they go round on their own." I thought the man was going to fall off laughing. "You could be right there," he manages to reply. "Least 'e as a sense o' 'umour," whispers Ron. While we watch it is obvious that the man is repairing something on the sail.

Wasted machinery?

[58] Firsty Ferret – locally (Horsham) brewed ale

He harnesses up and climbs one of the sails. Sadly the mill is only open on the 1st, 2nd and 3rd Sunday of the month so we are not able to get any closer than the base of the windmill but it certainly is a formidable structure.

Shipley Windmill

The walk is nearing completion. All that is left is to have a quick look at the church. To do this we have to pass the car. So rather than carry everything any further we decide to leave it all in the boot. As is not uncommon for Ron he finds a £1 coin sitting on the car park floor. Just round the corner, past a couple of pretty cottages is the church of St. Mary the Virgin. A reasonably kept churchyard, but certainly not the best, leads us to the door. Thankfully the door is unlocked and once inside the only word to describe it is tranquil. A real haven, beautifully kept and a pleasure to see.

We have come to the end of our 24th walk. This time with Sean who, I'm sure, led our way at times and ensured we could say, without fear of contradiction, we did not get lost!! If you have any doubts at all, ask Sean.

At the start I said that Sean would be missed. At times like this words fail to express our true feelings but, unfortunately, it is all we have. I am sure that both Ron and me are not the only ones who wish Sean's close relatives a safe journey back to their homes and that their brother will always be remembered, not just by us, but by everyone who knew him and loved him for what he was. A true and well respected friend.

Sean Snee 07/07/1955 - 07/07/2006

© Peter Thomas

These words are from us all; they are not only mine,
Sean will be sorely missed, and we mean 'big time'
We all have memories of Sean in our very own way.
But I'm a million percent certain, we lost a true friend today

© Ron Cousins

WALK 25 – Ashdown Forest

Wednesday 19th July 2006

Monday evening's meeting with Ron was a little sombre at times. As I write this, on Tuesday the 18th, I am about to get changed into traditional mourning clothes, as today is the day we say our final farewells to Sean. A lot of people are expected at the Crematorium at Langney, in Eastbourne, at a ¼ to 2, he was a very popular man.[59]

But our meeting did result in a decision on a walk for Wednesday. From our book – The AA 50 Walks in Sussex[60], we have decided on 'Pooh's Ashdown Forest'. Hopefully, it will give some light amusement at this sorry time and we must all realise that life does go on. To

brighten up the experience we will be accompanied by not one, but two friends. Both have been with us before. One, known for his silence, the other, known for her occasional colourful language. Lyn and Taff are looking forward to the experience of our seven-mile stroll through Pooh countryside. Taff informed me that he didn't realise there was an actual place associated with *Winnie the Pooh* and Lyn took some perverse delight in informing me that over 400 snakes had been released into the wild at Ashdown Forest just a few weeks prior to our walk.

Ashdown Forest represents the largest area of uncultivated land in the South East of England, covering about 20 square miles in East and

The familiar emblem   West Sussex. Ashdown was a royal forest for 300 years, established by John of Gaunt in 1372. Then it was a place of wild beauty and thick woodland, so dense in places that it used to require a dozen guides to lead travellers from one end to the other. After the Restoration of Charles II in 1660, large parts of the forest were enclosed and given to Royalist supporters.

Ashdown Forest is the real life setting for Winnie the Pooh and will rekindle many happy memories of AA Milne's wonderful stories. Our walk begins in a corner of Five Hundred Acre Wood – the 'Hundred Acre Wood' of AA Milne's stories. The return leg briefly follows a disused railway line before heading south across rolling countryside, passing close to Cotchford Farm, where AA Milne lived, and crossing Pooh Bridge, built in 1907 and restored in 1979. This landmark is where Milne portrays Winnie and Christopher Robin playing 'Pooh sticks'.

The temperature is expected to be in the 90's today. So I am not relying on Ron alone for water and nourishment but am taking my own supply. I also have sun cream and sun hat on board the car for the trip to Hartfield. I am well prepared for, what may be a long, very hot seven miles. Hopefully, some cool shade will be found through the forest.

I pull up at the Kings Head car park at 10 o'clock as arranged. Ron and Lyn are here but no Taff. As the temperature is so high both Ron and I have hats. Lyn doesn't. She says that she couldn't find one but she will be ok. We wait for Taff until 10 past 10 and decide we can't wait any longer. We found out later that he fell asleep reading a book and didn't wake up until ¼ to 11?

We just follow the path

Our first problem is finding the car park in Ashdown Forest. Our map pinpoints it as just off the B2026, on a small turning on the left, just before Hartfield. We must have passed it because we ended up in Hartfield. We thought we might start the walk at The Anchor in the

---

[59] Sean's family expected 40 mourners but 200+ of his friends turned up to say goodbye. The main chapel was packed with people standing and the remainder stood outside during the service.
[60] '50 Walks in Sussex' AA Publishers – Walk 21 – Page 56

village, which would be halfway round our planned walk. But, as I said to the others, having a pub halfway round could be very good for us, especially in today's mini heat wave. It was agreed to try and find the Pooh Car Park. So back along the B2026 we went. Tucked away in

Open views

the undergrowth was a small sign directing us down a narrow lane to our right. Just a short distance down this lane was the car park; a 'dirt clearing' would describe it better. We parked the car under some trees, gathered the rucksack full of bottled water, tins of coke, and sun cream and made a start.

Our instructions are very precise at the start. We are to follow the signpost for Pooh Bridge and take the third turning on the right that will lead us to a stile. For some reason, I do not know why, but at the start of our walks I tend to keep looking at the instructions in our book rather than to look where I'm going. Not a wise move when walking in a forest. A broken tree stump, about half the size as the post in the picture, placed itself in my way and sent me flying. Luckily I managed to stay upright but it

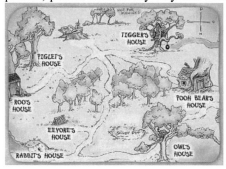
Typical Pooh map

sure scared the hell out of me. Both Lyn and Ron are now laughing hysterically. Lyn insisted on taking a photo of the offending stump and will probably use the evidence against me at some time. They are now trying to decide, should I have needed medical attention, how they would direct the paramedics to me while they went off to Pooh Bridge. It is at times like this that you find out who your true friends are. But I did see the funny side of it though. I must admit to having a chuckle.

We find the turning and the stile. Our directions now tell us to cross a number of tree-lined fields. Part of the path is diverted but the diversion is obvious, so we had no problems. We cross a driveway and enter a field that is obviously used for training horses. There are jumps in the middle of the field and all around the perimeter is a narrow track with sand as the base for the horses to run round[61].

We eventually arrive at the road where we turn left and need to find a house called 'The Paddocks'. Opposite this house is a turning on the right that leads us into Five Hundred Acre Wood – the One Hundred Acre Wood in AA Milne's stories. There is a real feeling of expectation between the three of us. The picture of the map, located from the Pooh web site bears absolutely no resemblance to the actual wood. We are told that various places on the map can be located but they are scattered all around the

Can you spot the tree trunk?

forest area and not just in one place. But walking through the wood was wonderful. You could see, and feel, where the inspiration for the stories comes from. What was very strange was that there were no bird songs within the wood. Lyn commented on it a number of times throughout the walk.

Emerging from the wood we reach Weald Way, part of another walk, which joins up with Forest Way. We pass a beautiful house called Kovac's Lodge on our left and walk along and up the hill, bear left onto a track which leads us to a path skirting a farm on The Buckhurst Estate. On our left-hand side is Buckhurst Manor House, which looks enormous from over the hedge, as we approach the outskirts of Buckhurst Farm. We turn right and head passed the

---

[61] We are informed by Lyn that the sand based track is used for riding horses on. It is to assist in rehabilitation after injury and strengthens the horses' legs.

farm cottages, which, on their own must be worth a lot of money. Every gate we pass has The Buckhurst Manor sign and it is obvious which gates you can and can't go through. The drive we are now on seems to go on forever. We come across a BT van parked on the side of the drive. A glimpse inside shows a man reading a newspaper. "Probably waiting for a call," suggests Ron, "shame to disturb him out here. Must be 'ell of a job on 'yer own."

Just passed here we locate the stile and path on the left that takes us across a field and towards a gate, which follows the High Weald Landscape Trail. It is here that we come to a bridge with a little stream running underneath. "I think we should practice Pooh sticks before we get to the real thing," suggest Lyn, picking up small twigs. "Pick a twig," she says, and offers both Ron and I three twigs for us to choose one from. What is it about Winnie the Pooh that makes people act this way? But both Ron and I acted like school kids, "my sticks better than yours," "your stick will sink before mine," are comments that spring to mind. "Come on children," commands Lyn, "after three. One, two, three." Three sticks drop into the water and we all race to the other side of the bridge to see whose stick appears first. And we do this because of some fictitious, honey loving bear that we read about nearly forty years ago?? Lyn's twig emerged first from under the bridge. Both Ron and mine didn't appear at all, we had failed Pooh sticks. Lyn was very gracious in her moment of triumph.

We now have to cross more fields as we head towards the village of Hartfield. We pass a farmhouse on our right. At the bottom of the garden is a 'Wendy House' and from this 'house' can be heard the cries of puppies. Not just barks but real cries. "Them dogs are in distress," says Ron, "look the 'house' their in 'as glass in windows. They must be cooking in this 'eat." "We can't do anything Ron, the door is open at the house, they must be able to hear the puppies," says Lyn. "Perhaps we could phone the RSPCA when we get to Hartfield," says Ron. I try to reason with him, "but we don't know the name of the farm or where it is, Ron, we can't tell the RSPCA anything other than we heard puppies barking. Lyn's right. We can't do anything." But Ron is very upset and keeps looking back as we walk away across the field. Just as we enter another field Lyn sees the herd of

Hartfield Church

deer. "Look, quick!" she whispers, "Over there," she points, "must be 15 or more." As soon as the deer see, hear, or smell us they run to the safety of cover in the hedge at the corner of the field. Three stay on the outskirts watching us but as soon as we move they're gone in a flash. To see animals out in the wild like that is amazing, and I have now seen deer on our last few walks.

It is just a short walk now until we arrive at the Church of St Mary the Virgin, a building of the 13th century although Hartfield is mentioned in the Domesday Book so it is reasonable to imagine that a wooden built church could have been in place as early as 1085. The sign on the ancient lych-gate states; 'Welcome, the church is open, please come in and be refreshed.' What a lovely church and yard it is and

Entrance into churchyard

is more than typical of what we have seen on our walks over the past 25 weeks. There are a number of entrances into the churchyard the most beautiful being by way of the Lych Gate Cottage, one of the oldest and smallest cottages in the area. Inside the church a wooden tripod shape covers the font, which in itself is a wonderful piece of suspended engineering. I thought the cover was fixed to the font until I brushed it and the whole top moved. There is a rope that is pulled to move the top from the font when in use. But it can only be millimetres above the stone font. All in all, a credit to the people of Hartfield.

The temperature is rising by the minute, Lyn is starting to look a funny colour, my offer to cover her with suntan lotion has been declined, on more than one occasion and she now informs us that a call of nature is required. What better reason do we need to visit a pub? Hartfield appears to have two pubs, The Hay Waggon, which had a no smoking sign on the door so we headed for The Anchor (Lyn also needed a nicotine fix!)

The Anchor

The bar we entered had a flagstone floor and oak beams holding up a low ceiling. Food was on offer (a little expensive we thought), The Harvey's was off (Ron's not amused) and the lager was something called Labbats (what ever that is) but the drinks were cold and refreshing. I wandered around the bar and found out that the building used to be known as Broome Place and was the home of gentry. A fireback bearing the date 1586, which was specially made for the house, is now in an American Museum. In 1777 the building became the Workhouse listing 54 inmates in 1821. Eventually, forty years later, in 1861, it was taken over by William Garrett for the 'purpose of selling beer.' Hanging from one of the walls is what looks like an old framed document, which reads:

Rules of this Tavern[62]
4d a night for a bed
2d a night for horse keeping
No more than five to sleep in a bed
No boots to be worn in bed
No Razor grinders or Tinkers taken in
No dogs allowed in the kitchen
Organ grinders to sleep in the washhouse
Lemuel Cox's Inn

Following the railway track

What was so wrong with Organ grinders? Whether it's original or not doesn't seem to matter. It just added to the atmosphere in some way.

Feeling suitably refreshed and with the thought of the real Pooh sticks to come we set off for the next part of our walk. Lyn has agreed to have sun oil put on her back so this is done before we cross the road and head for the path alongside the tennis courts, opposite The Anchor.

We cross a field and continue over the next stile to the Forest Way. Here we follow the old railway track bed. Our book advises us to continue until we reach a gate on our left. Up to now we have had no problems, so why should we get mislead now. The first gate we come across is padlocked with a no entry, no footpath, and no right of way sign. We then seem to walk forever before we come to another gate which simply has 'East Sussex County Council' stamped on the cross beam. Is this the gate we need? There are no other signs yet the line on our map indicates we should have turned left a long way back. Lyn makes the decision for us, pushes the gate open and walks through. We follow and walk across a field towards the shade of some trees in the corner. Into the next field and we come across a driveway. "We should be heading towards a road, according to the map," I offer, " but I'm not sure which way to head from here." "All drives lead to a road, 'ventually," says Ron. Again Lyn takes the lead and heads us towards a dead end. We turn round, without a word, and head back up the drive where we eventually find a gate that leads us onto a road. We now need to establish which road. I suggested that we turn left. Why, I don't know. But it seemed a good idea at the time. Everyone agreed so off we went, eventually coming out, after

---

[62] List obtained from unsigned paper hanging in bar of The Anchor, Hartfield

passing some very desirable houses, at a garage on a junction of two roads. "I'll go in and ask at the garage, you sit in the shade opposite," and both Lyn and Ron cross the road and sit by the bus shelter. Once inside the garage I ask for assistance. A man takes a lot of time, with my map, first trying to work out where his garage is on the map. I thought if he didn't know how could I, but I kept my mouth shut. He consulted his colleagues. Out of the corner of my eye I could see Ron and Lyn laughing. I had no idea what at. Eventually, all the members of staff advised me to forget the map and go down the lane opposite. Apparently that would lead us to Pooh Bridge. We probably wouldn't find many signs for Pooh Bridge down the road because the house owners would prefer the public not to go down there, so they remove any signs. I

thank them for their time and when I get out to Ron and Lyn, who are still giggling, Ron is leaning on a post with an arrow pointing down the lane to Pooh Bridge.

It isn't difficult to see why they don't like too many people down this drive, everyone is a mansion. At the end is a small sign directing us along the path to the bridge. Walking towards us is one of the few people we have met on the actual walk. He looked retired age, dressed immaculately and was striding out along the footpath. "Nice out today?" Ron greets him in his usual manner. "Is it? Apparently it is to become hotter," is the haughty reply as he passes without breaking stride or direction. "Supercilious p£*@k," whispers Lyn.

Ron's onto a winner?

Apart from the 'bugger' when she got hit by holly and the 'shit' when she got bitten on the leg by a horse fly this was the only real swear word she said throughout the whole seven miles. Both Ron and I were becoming impressed with her command of our native tongue. Obviously, neither Ron nor I understood the meaning of 'supercilious' so we just nodded in agreement and carried on. Education is a wonderful thing.

Eventually we reach Pooh Bridge. I am sure that I have read somewhere that the bridge is made of wood. But actually seeing it was a bit of a disappointment. The area could be anywhere. There is little indication on the bridge, or around the bridge that explains where you are or what you are about to do. It is the complete opposite of commercialism. There isn't even a picture of Winnie the Pooh or Christopher Robin. Just a sign requesting that you do not, under any circumstances, enter any fenced area looking for pooh sticks. The place is barren. The only way you could find a stick was to enter a fenced area or go for a paddle downstream. Should any reader wish to visit this area to play pooh sticks – take your own

The race is on

with you. As you can see from this picture Ron was hoping to be on a sure thing with the 'pooh stick' he managed to find. Eventually we managed to find three and performed the customary procedure. After a count of three. Sticks were dropped. We all rushed to the other side and modesty will not permit me to tell you whose stick came through first.

A long uphill stretch now led us back to the car park. The thought of having to bring young children down this hill to the bridge and then back up would make me think twice about going to Pooh Bridge. But at the end of the day we are all kids at heart and if my grandchildren wanted to play Pooh Sticks on the real Pooh Bridge I would go out of my way to get them there. Long, steep hill or not.

The book advises us that that walk should have taken 3 hours. It took us six. We did stop at the pub. We did have a little detour. The sunshine, at times, was very nearly unbearable but what could be better than a stroll, with good company, in wonderful Sussex countryside, even if I did find out later that a toy snake was going to be planted in front of me, just to see my reaction. All that, and being in Pooh country can't be beat. Or, perhaps next week we may have something different. Who knows?

WALK 26 – West Hoathly

Wednesday 26th July 2006

It's the 26th Walk and the 26th of July. We're halfway through our planned 52 walks. Coincidence with the number 26, or what? A few Monday's ago Ron thought, since we went back to Pluckley to where his parents met (Walk 15), it might be nice for me to go back to my roots. This Monday we got together and looked over some walks that would serve this purpose.

Me, Gran and Carol

Those who know me will be aware of my passion for Family History. Since the death of my sister, Carol, in 1996 I have endeavoured to find out as much as I could about 'my family'. Not just who they were, but what they did and where they came from. I would call round to my parent's house with a snippet of information or a name, for my mother to say "….. oh yes, they used to live at so and so" or "I remember them, didn't they emigrate to Australia in 1959?" Family photographs are great sources of information. Unfortunately my mothers' father (Walk 20) destroyed most of the mementoes of his life before he died in 1970 so I have little to follow on my mother's side of 'the family'. Luckily my parents had numerous photos to look back on and Family History is made a little easier on the father's side. The surname stays the same with each male child, so searching through old documents becomes easier. Unfortunately though, my father was not a good talker and kept a lot of things to himself. It wasn't until he realised how serious I was about our history that little memories started to come back, and, on some very few occasions he would actually let me drag the information out of him. Then both my parents passed away in 2005. Now I have no family to recall memories about my ancestors, apart from distant aunts and uncles who, for some reason, don't want to keep in touch with me. Over the years I have found out many things about 'my family' and about the places they lived. My fathers' parents, Stanley and Beatrice, lived in East Grinstead for all their married life. Beatrice's father and his brother were members of The Fire Service in East Grinstead. Beside my computer screen I have a picture of Beatrice with Carol and me, taken when we lived at 18 The Holt, when I was about five. My grandmother, Beatrice, didn't like my mum. My mum, Joan, wasn't good enough for her son, Kenneth. Beatrice did not attend my parents wedding. A saying comes to mind – 'You can pick your friends but you can't pick relations'. How true.

My parent's wedding photo

Edward & Sarah Pollard

My grandfather, Stanley Herbert Pollard (far right in wedding picture), was born 21st August 1902 in the village of West Hoathly. He was christened, in East Grinstead, when he was 37 years old. I have 'traced' ancestors back to John Pollard who was born, it is believed, in 1626 but I have been unable to establish where. My first actual connection to West Hoathly is Philip Pollard born in 1701 and died in 1766. Since then I have 'traced' 89 members of the Pollard 'clan' along with their wives/husbands and children. 'My family' now consists of over 300 names, and is still growing.

So, the walk this week is to be around West Hoathly, where some of my relations were active members of village life, all those years ago. My great, great grandfather, Edward Pollard was a hoop maker; his wife's name was Sarah, his brother George was a carpenter/coffin maker and their grand father, Philip, the shopkeeper. We take the walk from a book called 'Village Walks in West Sussex'[63]. It is a very small walk of only 3 miles but it is circular starting and finishing at the church just opposite the Cat Inn. Not only will we be able to take in a little history and West Sussex countryside but also a quick tipple in, what might have been, my ancestors 'local'.

The name 'Hoathly' means the heath or heather clearing. "West" was added to distinguish it from East Hoathly in East Sussex. The traditional pronunciation is "ly" to rhyme with "bye", but a rhyme with "mostly" is also common (although incorrectly!) used. The earliest documented reference to the village is an Anglo-Saxon charter of 765 AD when the King

West Hoathly Church

of the Hastings gave land to a monastery at South Malling. An area of the village known as Chiddinglye was used for the pasture of swine. Included, in this area is the "stone of the steam dwellers", which may be the famous rock called Great-Upon-Little which is now obscured completely by trees.[64]

Lyne has kindly offered to take a photograph of the halfway stage of our walks. She has agreed not to swear on one condition. She has noticed that I have started to use certain colourful phrases that should not be heard by ladies of the female persuasion and I have apologised and promised to obey her request. I collect my colleagues at 10 o'clock in the usual place. We head along the A22 towards East Grinstead and turn left just past the Llama Farm and drive through the forest to West Hoathly. If you have never visited this beautiful village it is not where you think it is. The

Parish Chest

county signs say you are in West Hoathly but to get to the village you must turn left just past the Cunning Fox Inn. This little lane will take you to the village of West Hoathly and its fantastic church, built on a hill. The graveyard slopes away from the church on what used to be a vineyard. The views from this terraced churchyard stretch out along the West Sussex countryside towards the South Downs. My Great Grandfather, James Pollard, his wife, Mary Ann along with a daughter, Ena have monuments at this church, along with other members of family whose tombs are impossible to read. The churchyard is well-kept and the church door is open. On the door, using hand-made nails is 'March 31 1626'.

Just inside the door on the left is what remains of The Parish Chest, carved from a solid oak.

Opposite the church is The Cat Inn. I have read somewhere that a felon tried to hide up the chimney whilst trying to evade

Fenced pond

[63] *Village Walks in West Sussex* by Douglas Lasseter (Newbury: Countryside Books) Page 92
[64] *The Story of a Forest Village West Hoathly* by Ursula Ridley Published by The Friends of the Priest House in limited number (100) 1971

capture by the local bobby. Unfortunately he was found, convicted and hung. They didn't mess about in those days.

Our walk starts opposite the Inn in North Lane. We pass Manor Cottage, on our left, where the path continues into dense bramble bushes. Lyn is glad she didn't wear her frock Ron is disappointed. The path leads us to a stile at a gate. We now need to follow the hedge on our right-hand side through some fields. Just into the first field we notice a newly fenced area. Within this area is a pond. Presumably man-made. Why it should be here or what it is used for I have no idea. Ron thinks it may be used for the watering of cattle or horses but it was impossible to see from where it was being fed. The open ground on our left gives great views across the Mid Sussex Weald to the South Downs. We approach a sign and now follow the track and get our first sight of the enormous California big trees at Chiddinglye. They really tower over the surrounding trees and you must be able to see

them for miles. Most of the fields to our right and left are planted with wheat and look as if they are preparing to harvest. Ron thinks that the field must be inhabited with hundreds of mice who are about to loose their homes. At the end of the drive we are advised that we need to use the gate or the stile. We are warned to ensure that the gate, if it is used, is closed behind us. When we get to the gate it is wide open and tied back. Through the gateway the track divides to the right. We are advised to go straight ahead. The signposts are very clear and easy to find. So far, so good. The track has now turned into a concrete lane and leads us to Chiddinglye Manor, a very imposing building, mostly hidden behind trees. Just past the Manor is a four-way junction. Again the signs are very clear so we can't blame them should anything go wrong. One, on the right, leads you to a place that sounded like a rehab centre for well-off druggies? For some reason Ron wanted to go and

Woodland by a ravine

have a look, but we pulled him back. One lane leads you to Chiddinglye Farm, which, apparently is farmed by a friend of Des, from the Kings Head. Another leads you to farm buildings. We are told to turn left and, when the track bears right, carry on towards a stile. For

a number of our walks we have not met or been pestered by animals, thank goodness. But as we approach the next field I can see young cattle, grazing. Sean's immortal words rang in my ears, 'Go on, they won't 'urt 'yer'. We crossed over this stile and the cattle didn't move. It must have been too hot for them, basking in the shade of the tree was no competition for the hot midday sun. The next stile couldn't come quick enough for me. "Don't run'" says Ron, "they're not following us." I didn't look to find out, but went straight for the stile. Once over and now safe from cattle we have to make for a large,

Path towards big trees

single redwood tree in the centre of the field. Once this was reached our book advises us to turn around to get a view back to the Manor house. Unfortunately all we could see was trees, not a house

in sight. From here the field narrowed into a corner where we are to find another stile leading us into a small wood. Once over the stile the path leads us to a footbridge, which turned out to be two railway sleepers over a dry ditch. We should then come across a 'squeeze gate' and another footbridge. We found neither. The fact that we didn't know what a 'squeeze gate' was meant that we could have missed it but all we come up against was another stile. From this stile we are advised to turn right at the way sign

California Tall Trees

onto a field path. We are now instructed, in a long drawn out fashion to walk around the outside edge of the field so that we 'end up at the opposite corner of the same field'. From here we go over a stile and immediately turn left. Again the signs are very clear. We are now in woodland and adjacent to a deep ghyll (ravine). The very steep slope of the ravine was to our right. The very narrow path takes you over a bridge and leads you through the woodland. I started to go to the left and up a steep slope when Lyn asked "Aren't we going to follow the path then?" "We are," is my reply, "the path goes up to the top and levels out by the school ahead." "But the path goes this way," she points at what could be described as a path. As the perfect gentlemen that Ron and me have become, we do not argue but follow in the direction that Lyn points. We didn't get very far before a tree, uprooted since the hurricane, is blocking our path. "Any suggestions?" asks Ron. "I think we should either return to the path I wanted to take earlier or we will have to climb this steep bank to get to the path I wanted to take earlier. What do you think?" I ask Lyn. She admits she was wrong so graciously. We climb the bank and proceed on the path I wanted to take earlier. (It so makes a change to be right for once.) We are now behind the play area for Philpots Manor School, which is an Independent Residential Special School, based on the principals of Rudolph Steiner(1861-1925). He

Steiner ponies

believed working along with the spiritual worlds enriches the life of the individual and the world. (Each to their own). The bridleway that we now find ourselves on is very clearly marked and the route is easy to follow through the buildings that make up parts of the school. We follow the track past some very hot, weary, fly infested horses that, presumably, are to enrich the life of the individuals that ride them. They looked a very sorry state when we saw them although they certainly looked well-fed. We pass what used to be Philpots Quarry. I say used to be but it was a hive of activity with men in hard hats working machinery etc. Unfortunately we couldn't get very close to the working because fences had been erected around the site with warning signs about entry to the public placed all along the fence. But it was obvious that some development was being carried out. Perhaps it is some extension to the school?

It is a short walk, along the lane and we are at the junction of Hook Lane and North Lane. Just before we get to the junction we, again, see deer running wild in the fields. That sight will never bore me.

Bowls is being played on the green as I explain that some of my family lived in the old cottages on our right-hand side. Opposite is The Priest House that is a timber framed hall house and was built in the 15 century. The gardens have been designed to be as close to the

The Priest House

original as possible. Entry to the House is £2.90 each and is only open during the summer months. But I have phoned and made an appointment and the custodian, who lives in the house, is willing to let you in at other times. Inside the place is unbelievable. Some of the documents have my families name on. My great grandfather used to light the gas lamps in the village. I found this out by looking at one of the diaries held at the Priest House. Should you feel the urge to look at your own family history places like The Priest House are always worth a visit.

Back at the car we deposit our sticks, and head for The Cat Inn. On this short walk Lyn asked me what it was like to be halfway through our plan of completing 52 walks in Sussex. I have to say that I have learnt a lot. My main reason for walking was to loose some weight but that's not happening. Both Ron and I have seen parts of Sussex, and a small part of Kent, that we didn't know existed. Each walk has, in some way, been different from all the others. But they have all been an education to me. At the start, I will admit, I was worn out. Wednesday would come round and I would not look forward to it. But I knew that Ron did look forward to these walks. By not going I would be letting Ron down and, at the end of the day, I would not be able to face you all in the Kings Head if I packed it in. So, I'm very pleased to say, I have learnt from our walks, I feel fitter because of the walks and look forward to the second half as much as I know Ron does.

Walking into the Cat Inn gave me a strange feeling. My ancestor's local. The photographs of the bar and Inn were taken many years ago, but I must say that very little has changed.

The Black Cat circa 1950 (old postcards)

Ron was more than happy, Harvey's bitter was on tap but he tried a local brew called Iron Horse. We sat and ordered a meal, which arrived, hot, looking very appetising, and, as is typical of all pub lunches, plenty of it. Ron treated us to our meals "as celebration of getting' 'alf way." It was delicious; Lyn couldn't finish hers so Ron helped her out by eating some of her chicken. "Bloody 'ell, it's 'ot!" exclaims Ron. He had only had a mouthful and the sweat was pouring out of him. "Probably the chillies," Lyn offers. But it didn't stop Ron from finishing it off.

A lovely time spent in a beautiful village. Although I have been to West Hoathly many times I had not been in the area we had just walked but had kept to the main road. The photo celebrates 26 weeks of outings and, would you believe, the last photo is the 26th photo from this walk. Perhaps I should try to work out how many miles we have walked in those 26 weeks. Perhaps it would be better if I didn't. But thanks Ron – it's been worth every second.

That was some meal

WALK 27 – Upper Beeding

Thursday 3rd August 2006

Has anyone any idea where Upper Beeding in Sussex is? I've heard of it but that's all. I haven't a clue where it is. Luckily, we have the modern wonders of Satellite Navigation (satnav.) to guide us, because Ron has found a walk that involves crossing Beeding Bridge. The bridge, over the River Adur, which was crossed by Charles II in October 1651, when he was defeated and on the run, to escape his enemies and flee to France.

Following the Battle of Worcester, where his army was soundly beaten, the young Charles fled across England, hotly pursued by Parliamentary forces, under the leadership of Oliver Cromwell.

CHARLES II
Founder of the Royal Society 1662
Old Ashmolean Series 50   Oxfoen

First he made his way north, intending to cross the River Severn into Wales where he could find a ship and sail to the continent. But the river was heavily guarded and Charles was forced to change his plans. He then travelled south, eventually reaching Charmouth on the Dorset coast. Again his plan to escape by boat fell through and, in a desperate attempt to avoid capture, he made his way along the South Coast. On route, to Shoreham, the King arrived in Bramber from the west; they were horrified to find Cromwell's men in the vicinity of the riverbank. Charles believed they had been sent to guard Beeding Bridge, which was his only means of reaching Shoreham, easily. Cautiously, he crossed the bridge and continued on his way undetected. Moments later the Royal party looked round to see a group of cavalry hotly pursuing them across country. Charles feared the worst, but as they reached him, the soldiers overtook the King and rode off into the distance. Fortunately, for Charles, they were pursuing someone else. At Shoreham King Charles found a ship that could take him to France. His journey through England lasted six weeks. In 1660, on his 30th birthday, and 2 years after the death of Cromwell, Charles returned to England to resume his role as King of England.

Back to the present day. Those who know Ron will be aware of his love for the gee gee's. You will also be aware that he has shares in some of our 'four legged friends'. One of those 'friends' is racing at Goodwood on Wednesday, so Ron will be at the meeting, to watch

Path from the Castle

Soviet Song perform[65]. Because of Ron's visit to the 'sacred turf' our walk, this week, will be carried out on Thursday and will actually be two walks combined into one and both are taken from our favourite book, '50 Walks in Sussex'[66]. The first, Walk 28 from the book, takes us around Bramber Castle and Beeding and is 2¾ miles and the second, Walk 29, takes us along the River Adur and Upper Beeding, which is also 2¾ miles. Giving us a walk of 5½ miles in total.

Wednesday was a beautiful day. Today, Thursday, it's raining. Shortly before I set off to pick Ron up the phone rings and I had the terrible thought that it might be Ron cancelling today's walk. But Ron asks if a young friend can accompany us. The friend who joins us today is Andrew, who is on holiday from his job as a schoolteacher at a Primary School in Eastbourne. He is six foot plus tall and looks as if he could have played rugby at University. A fit lad as well as educated.

I have actually looked at the map and found out that Beeding is near Steyning. Although I know the way I'm sure Ron appreciates 'Jane' on the Sat. Nat. and have her 'plugged in'

---

[65] Soviet Song came second in a 7 horse race, The Sussex Stakes.
[66] *50 Walks in Sussex* AA Publication Pages 74 and 77

when I pick Ron and Andrew up. Ron introduces 'Jane' to Andrew. "She's a clever lady," explains Ron, "but she does get angry if yer don't go in the direction she says. But don't you worry, Andrew, Graham 'an me know 'ow ter 'andle 'er." With that we set off towards Beeding.

Our instructions advise us to park in the free car park at Bramber Castle. Unfortunately I missed the turning and we had to turn round and head back to a small roundabout where it is very clearly signposted to Bramber Castle Car Park. So how did I miss it? We park the car; gather our things and head down the gravel drive, back towards the roundabout. Another car, a people carrier, is heading up the drive and, for some reason decides to slow to a stop before the car is at the top of the slope. Wheel spin is all that happens when the young lady, complete with young lady companion and many children, try to pull away again. She

Cygnets

goes nowhere. True gentlemen that we are, and Andrew is built like a brick s+*t house, one small shove and they're on the move again. With 'thank you's' ringing in our ears we start our walk.

At the end of the lane we turn right and head along a footpath. We head up through the trees and continue ahead to the next signpost. Down to our right-hand side, through the trees, we can see the River Adur. We carry on for some while until we reach a stile and another sign. This directs us across grassland with the river running to our right. A swan, with six cygnets, is in the river. The large female swan doesn't seem that bothered when her young start paddling towards me as I take a photo. The top of the water, as you can see, is covered with algae. Most of the river is covered in this green slime, until further on in the walk when the river is constantly on the move.

Slow moving river

We eventually arrive at a footbridge where the second walk joins the first. We need to turn sharp left here and follow the River Adur upstream. The water level is fairly low but this picture will give you some idea where the high water level actually is. It is still difficult to imagine barges and small ships heading up this river all those years ago. The river meanders along in front of us and we need to follow the riverbank and negotiate five stiles. At the end we should find a small wood and a signpost that will direct us 'south'. Whilst walking along the riverbank we see our usual 'friendly' wildlife. "We could be riding one of those soon, Ron," I say, pointing to the lovely horses in the distance. "Yes, thanks 'fer that, Mate." He replies. Andrew hasn't a clue what we're on about. "Next time you see the lager taking effect while me mouths open, for God sake, shut me up," I continue. "Don't you worry, next time yer gobs open that wide we'll put

Wild (?) horses

one o'them 'orses in it ter shut you up," says Ron who explains to Andrew, "Graham only asked Pip if she could arrange fer us to go trekking on a bloody 'orse on a Wednesday instead of 'avin a walk. 'An she only said yes. Now I've got to get on one as well. I only 'ope it's a small un, so's I can keep me feet on the ground." "You don't seem that happy about it Ron," remarks Andrew. All Ron would say was "silly sod." "I thought it might get me over my fear of animals, that's the only reason I asked," I say in my defence, but Ron was not looking forward to the adventure. In the light of day, I'm having second thoughts. Still it may do us both good. Something different for me to write about.

We keep the river to our left

We arrive at the fifth stile, there is no wood, and no sign. "I think your writer miscounted the number of stiles," says Andrew, " if you look in the distance there is a wooden sign at the next stile." Now I know my eyes aren't that good but I couldn't see a stile in the distance, let alone a sign. "We'll take yer word for it," says Ron and we head towards the 'sign', and I must admit, Andrew was right. We turn sharp right here and can see Lancing College's vast chapel against the skyline. At least we hope that's what it is, because our instructions tell us to head towards it. All along this part of the walk we follow a small stream that heads back towards Bramber and Upper Beeding. "Lovely place to hide a body, out here. You'd never find it, would you?" I ask. Ron suggests that you could throw a body into one of these streams and never see it again. "'Ave you seen Andrew, someone will ask us, tomorrow. We dropped him off at the pub after our walk, why, has he gone missing?" says Ron with his usual giggle. Andrew is not amused and decides to go off and find a place to relieve his anxiety. "I read somewhere," I say to Ron, "that celebrities are now scared to use a public toilet in case someone takes a photo of them with a mobile phone. Worried that there would be a picture of them in the tabloids." Andrew returns, mumbling something about needing a telephoto lens.

The famous bridge

We continue on and end up heading in the wrong direction. According to our map, such that it is, the Priory Church of St Peter should be on our left-hand side. It is on our right-hand side and far off in the distance. Both Ron and Andrew are certain that if we carry on, along this road, we will end up at Beeding. Just past some shops I spot an elderly gentleman, on crutches, and ask if we are on the right road to Beeding Bridge.

"Not sure what it's called," he says, "but if you turn right

Same bridge, different angle

at this roundabout there's a bridge up the road. Take you about ten to fifteen minutes." We thank him and follow his directions. It took slightly longer but we eventually found the very bridge, crossed by King Charles, all those years ago. As a moment in history, I found the sight a little disappointing. I'm not really sure what I expected but there was no atmosphere and nowhere did I see any notification about the event that lead to the King of England having to cross this bridge, under darkness on his way towards France and freedom. It was just a busy little street, with traffic heading in both directions. The pub, right by the bridge and aptly called The Bridge Inn, was totally different. It was 100% atmosphere. The walls and ceiling are covered in old wood workers tools and paraphernalia and is a

Dredging the ditch

veritable treasure trove of history. I sat, with my pint of coke (honest) whilst Ron and Andrew tried one of the five 'real ales' on draught, and just wondered about the tools and their uses. Another pint of Firsty Ferret later and it was time to complete the remainder of the walk. Just as we are getting ready to leave bar the gentleman on crutches appears in the pub. It had taken him all this time to get there and Ron greeted him like a long lost friend. What Ron said to him I have no idea but the old gent, jokingly, warned his wife about Ron? Perhaps they had met before.

We leave the pub, cross the bridge and immediately turn left, now following the River Adur downstream. The water is getting really low now. We come to a stile on our right and head across a field towards the main road. Just before the main road we are advised to turn right and follow a small stream until we reach a stile. Shortly along this unkempt pathway is a large machine being used for clearing the stream. It is a small JCB type of machine with a bucket on the front. The bucket has moving teeth, like a hedge trimmer. The bucket drops down the opposite bank, teeth chattering and cutting the overgrowth, goes under water, and emerges, teeth still chattering as it comes up the other side. He then drops the cuttings over the opposite bank, moves along and starts all over again. Neat or what?

Again our directions seem to go a little wrong. A stile should lead us to a driveway through some trees. But we seem to be walking in the wrong direction. It was sheer luck that Ron just happened to see a stile, which leads us to another stile that, eventually, put us onto the driveway. Ron will say otherwise. A young lady, Ron thought Dutch, actually asked us directions. If only she knew, but we did direct her on a northward course and along the River Adur. Let's hope she reached her destination.

Castle Hotel

At the end of the short drive we are back on the main road heading towards Bramber, which is another pretty village with character. I managed to steer both Andrew and Ron away from what must be one of the largest village pubs in existence. The floral decoration outside was stunning. Unfortunately the only other two shops we managed to see were an Indian Takeaway and a Chinese Takeaway. Now Ron really went into one! But there were a few really old houses here and well preserved. The village was very clean and tidy with next to no litter about. It is just a short walk from here to the Parish Church of St.

Parish Church

Nicholas. At the entrance to the path leading to the church is a sign that reads: 'Built in 1073 as the Castle Chapel and is the oldest Norman Church in Sussex.' "I dispute that," says Ron, "the oldest church is at Pevensey, built in 1068!" He then added that he would have to look it up to make sure. A note will be added when we have proof, either way.

The church, itself, is truly wonderful. I have a passion for churches but I have never mentioned that on arrival at any of the churches we have visited Ron will tell me that "this is the best" or "have you ever seen a better church than this" or "this is better than the last one". Today this church was, different. It was small, intimate, welcoming yet cold. To me this church was a village church with extras. It was bright, clean, evidently very old, and, evidently, used. The one thing that Ron was not pleased about was that the booklet about the church was only 20p. And they had sold out. He was gutted.

Just to the right of the altar is a small font. By this font I found a small, framed writing which I found touching. I have reproduced it below in the manner that I found it and hope that you feel that the words are everything they should be:

I think more of the place I was baptised,
than the Cathedral at Rheims where I was crowned.
For the dignity of a child of GOD, which was bestowed on me at baptism,
is greater than that of a ruler of a Kingdom.
The latter I will lose at death,
The other shall be my passport to everlasting GLORY
These words are attributed to Louis, King of France[67].

---

[67] Found framed and hanging on the wall inside the church

Another very pleasant walk comes to an end. All that is left of Bramber Castle is one very solid wall, on its own, standing 70 foot high and in the place where it was constructed around 1066. Sadly the castle was all but destroyed by the Roundheads during the Civil War. One other thing I found out about Beeding was that the time of the Norman Conquest this area was known as Sele, which is, apparently just another name for Beeding.

Let's hope Pip isn't ready with the horses for next week. I fancy a stroll around Goodwood, where Soviet Song made Ron a very happy man on Wednesday. I'll discuss it with Ron on Monday; I think he might agree.

All that remains of Bramber Castle

WALK 28 - Arundel

Wednesday 9th August 2006

Last Wednesday, after our walk around Beeding, I was confident that our walk, this week, would be around Goodwood. The place where Ron had seen Soviet Song, romp home, in second place in The Sussex Stakes. Then, for some reason things change. Something happens that makes you think again. Over the weekend we were given a new book, 'The Pathfinder Guide to Surrey and Sussex Walks'[68]. Thanks to Julie, who donated the book, I have had a change of plan. Thankfully, at our Monday meet, Ron is ok with my suggestion. It's not quite so far to travel but I honestly believe that it is one of the most beautiful areas in

Parish Church

Sussex. Built on the banks of the River Arun, Arundel has a Castle, church and a Catholic cathedral perched above a bend in the river. Although the castle was originally built by Roger de Montgomery, the then Earl of Arundel, in the 11th century it is mainly a 19th century reconstruction although the motte, an artificial mound, is said to date from 1068. Arundel Castle has been the seat of the Dukes of Norfolk and their ancestors for 850 years.

Nearby is the cathedral which was erected by the 15th Duke of Norfolk in the late 19th century after the Catholic church in England was allowed to organise itself into a diocese. I always assumed that if a town had a cathedral that town became a city. Arundel has a cathedral but is not a city. Yet Brighton has no

cathedral but is a city. I have since found out that it has something to do with Bishops and his diocese. Arundel is part of the Diocese of Brighton. But, surely, if you're a bishop, you have a cathedral, and if you have a cathedral you must have a bishop. Are you as confused as me now?

One other thing that Arundel is well-known for is its cricket. Unfortunately I have no love for the game. I find it uninteresting. I do not understand how, if Sussex score 600 runs and Kent score 200, just because it rains on the last day it's called 'a draw'. But each to their own. Every year a minibus is organised, from the Kings Head, and a trip to

Beautiful Interior

Arundel is made to watch Sussex play in a one-day game against County opposition. Much liquid refreshment is taken and, sometimes, a little cricket is actually watched. At the end of the day everybody enjoys themselves.

The Cathedral Spire

As I said this walk is from The Pathfinder book and is walk 19 on page 59. It describes the walk as seven miles in length, with slight inclines and should take us a minimum time of 3 hours to complete. Straight away I will make no excuse for the number of photographs in this chapter. The views are breathtaking, the scenery is stunning and throughout the walk we didn't stop being amazed at what we saw. So I took a photograph of practically everything I saw.

The walk starts in the Car Park (long stay!) in Mill Road. We haven't had to pay for a car park for some time but the fee of £5 was still a bit of a shock. We walk towards the town centre alongside of the River Arun, where it's possible to hire a small boat for £25 an hour. Into the High Street, we turn right and head up the hill towards the Parish Church of St Nicholas and

---

[68] *Surrey and Sussex Walks* a Pathfinder Guide Published by Jarrold Publishing 2004 – Page 59

the Cathedral Church of Our Lady and St Philip Howard. Inside the Parish Church taped music is being played which adds to the feeling of peace. A sign inside the church says that the cost of maintenance is £197 per day. Why is everything so expensive in Arundel? Around the walls of the Parish Church are wall paintings, believed to be from the 13th century depicting the seven deadly sins and the seven works of mercy. The pictures were used to illustrate the readings of the Bible. As most people were unable to read at this time it was a useful way to teach Christianity. Walking out of the church's, main door and looking right the

The Hiorne Tower

Cathedral can be seen through the trees. This very formidable and somewhat uninviting building is on the main road out of Arundel and overshadows many of the other buildings in the area. At the start, you will remember, that this walk was to take just over three hours. We hadn't covered a ½ a mile yet and we left the car over ¾ of an hour ago. If we were to complete this walk before it gets dark we decided to move on and not venture inside the cathedral.

The instruction from our book is to continue past the Cathedral and turn right opposite a Primary School. It is here that we enter Arundel Park. We pass through the great gates and bear right along the path with Hiorne Tower on our left. This Tower is one of the many follies built in Sussex. Frances Hiorne built it in 1787. Frances wanted to be commissioned to work on the restoration of Arundel Castle. But the 11th Duke of Norfolk, although assured that Frances was an architect of renown instructed him to build the tower as a test of his competence. Frances built the Tower, which is a tall triangular building with a rectangular turret in each corner. Although he made a great job of building the Tower he died soon after its completion and, therefore, didn't complete the work on the castle. Just in front of the Tower can be seen 'a gallop' which is were John Dunlop, the well-known Sussex racehorse trainer, exercises his horses prior to racing them at racecourses all

The Cousins machinery

over the world. Just past the 'gallop' Ron spots a piece of machinery bearing his name and insists that he now has proof that he has an ancestor with money (name on machine) and he was born to horse racing. The machine is used to level the 'gallop' prior to being used. We did see some horses at the other side of the Tower but they didn't use the 'gallop'.

From here we walk along a path, keeping the Tower on our left. It is obvious that we are climbing a slight gradient but it's not too bad. We are both amazed at how many dragonflies are flying in front of us. It is impossible to count the different breeds and their colours are really bright. Some were quite large. Will they sting you? Do they bite? All questions that I should have asked at the time and not thought about whilst writing this chapter.

View from exit of gallops

Our guidebook now advises us that from our path we pass through a gate and 'the track then begins a descent into a steep-sided dry valley'. What the book didn't say was that it is a **very** steep-sided valley with no fence to stop you from tipping over the edge. It also didn't warn you of the view from this vantage point. As we reached the valley I actually had to take a step back. It was one of those strange feelings that made you dizzy. The sheer drop seemed to encourage you to go near the edge yet you are aware of how stupid that would be. But, once I pulled myself together, the view is just so absolutely stunning. I have no idea how many miles you can see from up here. The view just goes on and on and on. Little did I know that there was more to come? From here we could see down into the valley, just make out the edges of Swanbourne Lake and our route was to take us along the track and down into the bottom of the valley. Working on the theory that what goes up must come down I wasn't looking forward to the other side of the valley. This thought was made even worse when, halfway down into the valley, we could see a couple walking up the slope

Looking down onto Swanbourne Lake

on the other side. They were just a speck in the distance, and the climb looked formidable. At the bottom of the valley we are instructed to cross over the track and head for a gate and a fence. I realise that we are not making the same climb as the couple seen earlier but our climb isn't so steep but it was a lot longer. In fact it was a hell of a lot longer. Both Ron and I had to make a couple of stops on the pretence of ensuring we were going the right way. Our book tells us that after ¼ of a mile we should arrive at 'Duke's Plantation'. I have to say that this was the longest ¼ of a mile I've walked. It was a time when you could see the wood (Duke's Plantation) but you didn't seem to be getting any closer to it.

Two ladies are walking towards us. "Can you tell us if we are on the Monarch Way?" asks one of the ladies. I couldn't breath so Ron tells the lady that we're not sure, "where are you 'eading?" he asks. "We're heading towards the river and we need to turn right to get to a pub for lunch." Ron points out that there is a lake at the bottom of the valley. We advise the ladies to walk the same way that we had come up because the path they were walking towards was very steep and that they would end up in the same place. While Ron is explaining this I look behind us and the view from up here is so worth the effort of the climb. Our guidebook says that on a clear day you can see the Isle of Wight from up here. Both Ron and I stop for a while. We just say nothing and marvel at the sight.

At the corner of Duke's Plantation we bear half right and head towards a chalk cliff, in the distance.

Some of the best views in the world?

From here the view is towards a little hamlet called South Stoke, which is surrounded on three sides by the River Arun. But before we get there we still have a lot of walking to do. We're only half way round the walk.

We now descend into another valley with a place called Duchess Lodge on our left. The slope is very steep and our thoughts went to the two ladies who must have walked up this slope a few minutes earlier. "An' we were worried about them going down the other side," remarks Ron, "'tis 'ard enough goin' down this 'ill, I wouldn't want ter do it t'other way." It really was steep and was beginning to tell on my legs when we reach a fence. From here we are instructed to turn left and follow the path into dense woodland. We are warned here that the path becomes steep (now they tell us) and dark. We need to walk along here until we reach a flint wall where we find a kissing gate that leads us back into Arundel Park. I didn't even realise we'd left it?

South Stoke Church

We now find ourselves on a bridle way with the River Arun on our left. It is now that we let our imagination run riot. This bridleway must have been here for hundreds of years. Whilst walking along the bridleway both Ron and I imagine that Highwaymen could have been active in this area. A posh gent, riding back from a lavish party, a little worse the wear, owing to the alcohol consumed, dozing off in the saddle, the horse knows the way home, purse bulging from wagers won. Late at night, at the very top of the slope, because the horse would be tired, out jumps a highwayman. I can picture it all but Ron tells me that in those days people wouldn't carry real money but would carry there own forged money made of brass. Should they get 'waylaid' they would hand over the brass money and the poor highwayman wouldn't be aware that he hadn't stolen the real thing. Doesn't seem fair does it?

We now reach the outskirts of South Stoke. A path along a field edge takes us towards the hamlet. At the road we turn left to head towards the church. Diversion signs are pointing us away from the hamlet due to bridge repairs but the church is before the bridge so have no trouble getting there. What a joy this little church is. There is no electricity at the church so all lighting is by candles. Even the organ, air pumped by two foot pedals, has candles strategically placed so that the organist can see the music. Our guidebook tells us that the place is dominated by a very large cast iron stove but it wasn't there, and the information brochure about the church doesn't mention it. What I did find, in the corner opposite the door was a book titled 'Reflections' by P.M. Dyson. In this book are photographs of the area with poems linking the photos. One, that caught my eye, because of our earlier thoughts, I reproduce here, hoping the author doesn't mind, is called 'Fate'.

> ***What cruel and tragic twist of fate***
> ***For these three men did lay in wait,***
> ***A mother's son, nephew and neighbour friend,***
> ***Their life of a few years did so tragically end,***
> ***Drowned in the Arun, in Eighteen thirty four,***
> ***On April 3rd, their life was no more,***
> ***In South Stoke graveyard in graves unknown***
> ***They lye in piece, but not alone,***
> ***Charles Chamberlain aged 20 William Gibbs 21***
> ***And Charles Morris just older by 5 years and one[69]***

The River Arun

From this beautiful setting we head back along the road towards the diversion signs and towards the River Arun. All we need to do now is wander along the riverbank heading towards Arundel. In the distance can be seen Arundel Castle but, because we are walking along the river bank, one minute we are heading towards the castle and the next we're heading away from it. We meet our usual animals, who for some reason, have to come over and say 'hello'. There is nothing nicer than walking along a riverbank on a beautiful summer afternoon, without a care in the world. Along the way Ron and I talk about the things we had seen. At the start of the walk, with the hills and valleys, we weren't sure if we should thank Julie for the book or whether we should never speak to her again. But I have to admit that for scenery, this walk is number one. The church at South Stoke is one of the quaintest churches I

---

[69] Reproduced from a hand written poem found in a binder, available to the public within the church

have ever seen. The organ brought back such fond memories of my grandmother, known to us all, even my children, as Nanny Loo Loo, (I never knew why) who used to own a very similar organ. When I was very young I used to sit between my grandmother's legs and pump the organ for her whilst she played hymns.

Inquisitive?

We stopped at The Black Rabbit, on the River Arun, for a pint. Very expensive but the place was heaving with people, eating a late afternoon meal. With boats coming up and down the river, couples doing what couples do on riverbanks it was a very nice end to the day. Our 3-hour walk had, in fact, taken us nearly 5 hours. But it was worth every minute.

Ron believes he has found our next project. "Do a boat up an' do river trips at £25 an hour, be a doddle. There's a boat laying on its side over there, just waitin' to be painted, look." I think we should finish this project before we start another one.

But that's the end of yet another walk. The drive to and from Arundel, along the A27, was horrendous but again we have both seen parts of Sussex we didn't know existed and it has been a real pleasure finding them. It's Ron's turn to decide where we walk next week and then I'm off on a short holiday in the Liverpool area. One other thing before I go. I weighed myself today and I'm actually starting to lose weight. Or has the wife 'fixed' the scales?

Just left to sink?

WALK 29 – Rye Harbour

Wednesday 16th August 2006

This Monday I was a little worried about Ron. I saw him on Sunday evening and he was a little worse for wear. He had been sampling some of the local brew for the best part of the day and by 8 o'clock in the evening it had taken some effect. He insisted that he would be ok for the usual Sunday Quiz at The Kings Head but his fellow contestants, usually happy to accommodate Ron in their team, because he could answer some of the questions, were a little reluctant, on this occasion, to welcome him with open arms. I left him discussing where he should sit with a couple of very young ladies who looked as if they were resigned to the fact

Cinque Ports Flag

that he would be in their team. Lucky old Ron!

I expected to catch up with Ron nursing a royal hangover on our usual Monday night discussion. Would you believe it, not only had he no hangover but he could also remember everything that happened on Sunday night? How does he do that? I'd have been laid up for days asking, "What happened?" But not Ron, he was as bright as a button and cheerily suggested that this week's walk could be at Rye. Just a small walk, this one, of only 4½ miles that looks as if it is mostly beach and nature reserve. Our guidebook advises us that the car park 'is spacious and free'. The word 'free' clinches it for me. So Rye it is.

On the way into Rye is a sign that calls it a Historic Town. Further into Rye is another

Welcome resting spots

The tide is out

sign that says it is a Cinque Port. If they don't know how can they expect the likes of us to understand? For some time I had no idea what a Cinque Port was. I have discovered that the words are Norman French for five ports and are only found in Sussex and Kent. The original five, established with a Royal Charter in 1155, were Hastings, New Romney, Hythe, Dover and Sandwich. These ports were to maintain ships ready for the Crown in case of need. The five Cinque Ports were supported by two ancient towns, Rye and Winchelsea whose councils have a long-standing tradition of maintaining defence contingents for the realm of England. Other Towns have since joined the 'federation', one being Pevensey. In return for becoming a cinque port the town received certain privileges, which paved the way for smugglers to go about their business with practical immunity because the authorities would turn a blind eye to ships and sailors from these ports. King Edward I, who granted the citizens of the Cinque Ports the right to bring into the country any goods without having to pay import duties, helped them immensely. The history lesson is over.

Our walk is taken from the book '50 Walks in Sussex'[70] and is the first walk in the book. It is also the furthest we will travel to the East of the County so an early start is needed. I am reliably informed it will take us an hour to get there, two hours plus, to complete the walk then an hour to get home, so our start time, today, is 10 o'clock. The drive is pleasant and the weather even nicer. One place we drive through is the village of Winchelsea. This is my dream retirement village. This is the one place I really could 'rest my hat'. I love it. The peace and

---

[70] *50 Walks in Sussex* AA Publication – Walk 1 - Page 8

tranquillity, the houses are old with character, traffic has to drive round the outside of the village, the church is 13th Century, and the scenery is a cross between rural Sussex with rural Kent.

I have never stopped at Rye, but always driven through it on the way to somewhere else. To my surprise, we have to turn right before we get to Rye to get to Rye Harbour. I thought they were the same place, but no. What is known as Rye Harbour is just over a mile away from the town and is a little community all to itself. With its own pub, its own shop and its own church. A mixture of the old with the new. We found the car park and headed for the Nature Reserve, which was to be the start of this week's walk. All along the path, as we head for the mouth of the River Rother, and the sea, are

WW II Pill box

chairs for you to sit on, facing the Nature Reserve, with little advice posters explaining what you may be able to see. Further along the walk is the inevitable pillboxes used as sea defences

The bird sanctuary

during the Second World War. These boxes can be seen throughout the walk in different states of disrepair. The one in the picture is the best of the bunch.

Even further along this path we eventually arrive at the mouth of the river and from here you can see the expanse of Camber Sands, the popular holiday resort. So where is everyone? The tide is out and you can see for miles along the beach and it's deserted. No windbreak, holidaymaker, or day-tripper, no one except us, on the sea wall looking across this vast expanse of sand.

We retrace our steps back to the path and turn left. On our right-hand side is the Reserve, fenced off with warning signs forbidding entry to the public. Every now and again, just up close to the wire, there is a small hut that you are able to go into for bird watching. Now each to their own, I say. But I likened bird watchers with train spotters. All anoraks and thermos

The road to RNLI Station

flasks. I can get about as excited at seeing the lesser spotted dragon bird as I can spotting the 9:45 from Victoria. Until today, that is. Because today I can now say that I have sat, and watched birds, in a hide. I have no idea what breed of bird I was looking at, out of the little slit in the front of the hide, but they were out on the rocks, just above the water, when as if they had received a secret signal, they all took to the air. Some barely made it but suddenly the air was black with birds in flight. All the birds headed towards, and over, the hide. A wonderful sight, that was over in seconds.

From the hide we walk along a long path towards a derelict building. The building, in the far distance, was once the boathouse for the Mary Stanford, a lifeboat manned by volunteers from Rye Harbour. The boat house has been deserted since a fatal day on the 15th November 1928[71] when the Rye Coastguard received the following message; *Steamer Alice of Riga – leaking – danger – drifting SW to W 8 miles from Dungeness – 04:30.* Within minutes the 17 strong crew of the Mary Stanford headed towards the boathouse. Because of the appalling weather it took three attempts to get the lifeboat into the sea. The time was now 06:45. They proceeded to row towards the *SS Alice*. At 06:12, over 30 minutes before the lifeboat was launched, the Ramsgate Coastguard Station received a message saying that the *SS Alice* was now ok and that her sailors had been rescued by the *Smyrna*. The Coastguard at Rye didn't receive that message until 06:50, which was too late for the Mary Stanford. Men

---

[71] Information from 'The Mary Stanford Disaster – The Story of a Lifeboat' by Geoff Hutchinson

rushed into the water with loudhailers trying to stop the boat. Two white Verey flares, the recognised recall signal, were fired. Facing out to sea, with a 15ft oar in their hands and sails set in a gale of wind, and with spray and teeming rain blowing into them it is small wonder that they never saw that all important recall signal.

RNLI Boat - The Mary Stanford - before these tragic events[70]

At midday on the 15th November the lifeboat was seen upside down. The bodies of the lifeboat crew were washed ashore at regular intervals over the next two hours. 15 bodies were recovered that day. It was not until three months after the funeral that lifeboat crewman Henry Cutting, was washed ashore at Eastbourne and taken to Rye Harbour for burial. The other body, John Head, the coxswain's son, was never recovered. No one on that lifeboat survived[72].

The deserted boat house

Walking around that boathouse gave you a very cold and strange feeling, and throughout the remainder of the walk the boathouse was always in sight. High on the beach, and no longer used. The boathouse is now surrounded in fencing to stop people getting inside. The seaward side of the boathouse has been bricked up but it is evident that flowers are left at the spot where the boat used to be launched and seventeen red poppies have been placed on the door. Other trinkets have been laid around the building, all evidence that on the 15th November 1928 a disaster took place that must have affected this little community immensely. Families were torn apart. Sons died with fathers, brothers died together. Each one was given a military funeral and they were buried as they worked, together, in the small churchyard at Rye Harbour. It is said to be one of the worst tragedies in the long and

Castle Water - a series of lakes

courageous history of the National Lifeboat Service.

Tearing ourselves away, but constantly looking back, we head towards the outskirts of Winchelsea where we turn right and now head inland. On our left-hand side are houses and on

---

[72] Image from 'The Mary Stanford Disaster – The Story of a Lifeboat' by Geoff Hutchinson

our right is some form of construction work. The fencing around this work leads us to another public footpath, which will turn us right again, and we will be walking parallel to the sea, back towards the Harbour.

Both Ron and I have seen some odd things during the past few weeks. We've even met some odd people, but one disgusting habit, which seems to be coming more and more apparent to both of us involves, I'm sorry to say, dog mess. It was very noticeable at this part of the walk. It is now becoming the 'done thing' that once little rover has performed his

natural duty, owners are required to collect it, in a plastic bag. All very hygienic and proper. But we have noticed that the requirement is not to take it home and dispose of it sensibly, but to hang it on the fence and leave it there, like some sort of trophy? My dog pooh is bigger than your dog pooh!! Now is that really necessary? (I was going to take a photo but thought it in bad taste.)

Throughout this walk the main theme is water. On our right, work is being done, presumably, to improve the sea defences. Although both Ron and I stood and watched for some time we could not understand what the JCB or the bulldozer were actually doing. The large mound of earth was already there and stretches the length of the shore. All that appeared to be happening was that the top layer of grass was being removed? On our left is what is called Castle Water. This immense water complex of lakes and ponds stretches the remainder of our walk, nearly two miles, and is a fisherman's paradise. All the water you can see is private and owned by various societies and tickets need to be purchased at enormous expense, and once the fish are caught you throw them back, so what's the point?

Derelict Machinery

Another thing that regular readers will be aware of, is my hate of the saying 'poor hard up farmers'. Over the last few walks I have resisted saying anything about abandoned machinery that could be turned into money. But this week I will let the pictures do the talking. All three of these pictures were taken within 100 yards of each other and I could have taken a lot more like it. Machinery just left to rust away. Tractors, trailers, JCB's, you name it and it was here. Yet it appeared to be a working farm. With buildings and useable tractors, trailers and the odd Range Rover parked up and running.

But I will get back to our walk. We are now back in the village of Rye Harbour. Our book advises us to look at the parish church, which is a little way down the main road to our left. The Church of the Holy Spirit is a bit of an unknown. The shape is strange. One end is rounded. Unfortunately we are unable to get in. A sign on the door suggests that if we need a key it can be found at 2 School Cottages. Unfortunately the hand written sign gives us no idea where 2 School Cottages are. The graveyard is in a very poor condition (another gripe of mine) but the memorial to the lost crew is a beauty to behold. At the top of the monument are engraved the words: 'We have done that which was our duty to do.' Below these words is a lifeboat crewman, in uniform, looking down. Each of the lost crewmen has his name, age and rank on a separate stone around a planted crucifix.

Church of the Holy Spirit

Both Ron and I were disappointed at not being able to get inside the church. On our return home I have tried looking on the Internet to find out what I can but have had no luck. So, unfortunately, it will have to remain one of those mysteries.

Our short walk back to the car is interrupted by a place called The Inkerman Arms. A delightful pub with, what would appear to be connections to the Crimean War? Our Landlord here believes that the name is derived from The Battle of Inkerman that took place on the 5th November 1854 when the French and the British troops got the better of the Russians. Ron's couple of pints of 1066 ale, another local brew, and a cool larger for me with a quick bite to eat eased the aches and pains I was now starting to feel.

This proved to be a very touching walk. I must apologise if I went on a bit about the disaster rather than the walk itself but I feel, on this occasion, the history of that tragic event brings things into perspective. What a difference a few minutes can make.

Next week I'm on my holidays, again. My wife and I are heading towards The Peak District. I'll let you know how we get on.

A Very Impressive Memorial

WALK 30 - Cuckfield

Wednesday 23rd August 2006

A change of plan was needed. As I am writing this I should be in Cheshire, Oswestry to be exact. I thought I had booked the hotel for Wednesday to Saturday. Four nights. What I have actually done is booked the hotel for Thursday to Saturday. Which means we come home on the Sunday. Four days. I knew there was a four in it somewhere. My error was pointed out to me by my wife over the weekend, so on Monday, I gave Ron the good news that we could, in fact, go for our usual walk on Wednesday. As it was my turn to make the decision I chose, what I thought would be, a relatively easy walk. My father-in-law Sam, God Bless Him, used to have a great saying which fits this decision – 'you're never right son and your wrong again!' I will explain.

View of Cuckfield Church

This week's walk is around Cuckfield, pronounced *Cookfield*. It comes from our favourite book, '50 Walks in Sussex'[73] and is described as 5 miles long. What I failed to see was that it was steep in places. In fact, it was very steep, in a lot of places. But my male ego would not show Ron that I was worried. But I was. As with most villages there is a name that is prominent, and Cuckfield is no different. It was the determination of the Sergison family not to allow the railway to run across their land that saved Cuckfield from becoming yet another commuter town. The line was diverted to the east and provided a link to Haywards Heath instead.

It had just started to rain when I collected Ron from the usual pick up point. 'Don't you worry," he insisted, "T'aint afternoon yet. It'll soon stop." Out drive to Cuckfield is completed within 45 minutes and we find ourselves at a free car park in Broad Street. We are required to walk through part of the village towards Church Street and the lych gate leading to the Parish Church. On the corner of Church Street Ron sees, what he thinks is a pie shop and is in like a rocket only to emerge with, not home-made produce but mass produced

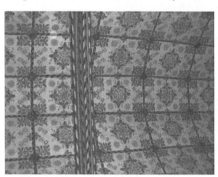

The impressive ceiling

fare. He is not amused and hands me a currant bun wrapped in plastic. "As soon as I saw them plastic bags I should 'ave come straight out. Waste o' money buying this rubbish." A question came to mind but I thought better of it. Would you believe it but the rain's stopped. "Told yer," says Ron

The lych gate led us into the churchyard of Holy Trinity Church, Cuckfield, which has to have one of the largest and best kept graveyards that we have seen, since the start of our walks. The church is dated around the 13th century and has a unique ceiling.[74] The original unpainted ceiling is dated from the 15th century and is believed to be the gift of Edward Neville, Lord Abergavenny, the grandson of John of Gaunt, who was writing from Cuckfield in 1464. The now decorated ceiling is the work of C E Kempe (1838-1907) and was painted between 1865 and 1866 at a cost of £215. Some restoration work on the ceiling, beams, bosses and angels was carried out in 2002 at a cost of £75,000.

---

[73] '50 Walks in Sussex' by Nick Channer-Published by AA Publishing-Walk 22-Page 59
[74] Information gathered from leaflet, Parish Church of Holy Trinity, Cuckfield. Originally produced for the celebration of the 900th anniversary of Cuckfield Church in 1992. Available from the Church

As you walk into the church lights automatically come on, triggered by breaking a beam of light from the rafters. It was really strange, being in a building, so terribly old (the 14th century Holy Water Stoops along with the font, are said to have been broken by Cromwell's men during the Civil War) alongside today's technology. But little things made this church

different. Everywhere there are little notes explaining what you are looking at. A printed guided tour is available for you to take as you wander round. And if you really had problems looking up at the high painted ceiling, large hand mirrors were supplied for you to look down into. We also met the Parish Vicar who really made us feel welcome and explained certain items that could be found around his church. And this is why our walks always take longer than suggested in the books. We stay at places like this church, for ages, simply admiring the beauty. Just outside the church door is a white painted, wooden memorial from the Sergison family to the memory of Sarah Tulet, servant for more than 50 years who died in

The broken font

'the 78th year of her age…March 9th 1840' But we need to get on.

From the churchyard we need to locate a kissing gate on the far side and turn left, heading towards Newbury Pond. "Look at the blackberries around here Ron," I say as the whole hedgerow is covered in the juicy fruit, "I didn't think they would be ready for picking until next month." Ron picked a blackberry, popped it in his mouth and simply said, "They're ready." "But we haven't got anything to put them in, Ron. We'll have to bring some plastic containers with us on next week's walk." "There's some sloe's in the 'edge as well, look. I'll try one o'them, just to see if they're ready." In it goes, and he pulls a funny face, "not ready just yet, give 'em another week or so. Bloody bitter they are now."

We pass Newbury Pond, a lovely, peaceful place and walk through even more blackberry and sloe infested paths. "We're

Newbury Pond

passing a lot of Blackberry an' apple pies," says Ron. "Not to mention all the bottles of sloe gin," I reply. "Don't forget the containers next week, we could make a fortune." After crossing the busy A272 and walking along more fruit infested paths we reach Copyhold Lane. Here we turn right and head along the lane. The scenery along this lane is incredible. Although the rain has stopped the clouds still look a bit menacing, but it has turned warm all of a sudden. After walking for some while we pass Lodge Farm and the lane swings to the left. We are advised to carry straight on at the public bridleway,

Bridleway

ignoring the path on our right. All is well. We walk ahead and follow a woodland path down to a lane. All along this path, to our left, is a fence that appears to run around the playing field of a large school. The litter on the left-hand side, by the fence is disgraceful. Empty bottles, cans, wrappers are discarded and left. Ron wants all kids to be made to clear up their rubbish and get 'some discipline'. I have to agree with him. The litter certainly spoilt, what is a very beautiful bit of countryside, and, because of the way it is manufactured, this litter will not just break down into the soil but could be picked up by animals unless, of course, Ron gets his wish.

It is now that instructions become vague. I'll be honest; the

Woodland Stream

instructions here are spot on. It's Ron and me who give each other doubts. Our instructions tell us to *cross a stream and bear right to join a footpath, quickly crossing a footbridge.*' This we did. "Aren't we 'eadin back in the direction we just came?" asks Ron. I look at the book. "The map doesn't show us heading back the way we came," I reply, "but you might be right. Let's head back to the river and have another look at the instructions." Back we go. Looking at the map it looks as if we should carry on in a straight line, once we crossed over the stream, but the instructions say *'bear right to join a footpath'*. "Let's carry straight on and see what lays ahead," I suggest. So off we go, in a straight line along the lane. "This can't be right," says Ron, "'tis a bridleway 'ere, not a footpath. Let's go back". So back we go. "If we follow the instructions and turn right here we may have to lead off in another direction at the end of the path," I offer as a suggestion. "Let's try it," agrees Ron. So we end up going the same way we went originally, but this time we kept going and, sure enough, at the top of the slope, we are directed away from the stream and into a field. Which proves something, does it not?

We continue along the fields' edge. The smell here is a bit overpowering. The farmer has recently spread fertiliser and I'm beginning to taste it. We have now started to try the blackberries and sloes, purely in the interest of quality control, of course. Ron points out the elderberries, "make some lovely wine with them," he says. "But Ron, how many plastic containers are we going to need? We won't be able to carry them all." In the distance we can hear a farmer cutting the hedge with a tractor and rotary blades. "If he carries on cutting this hedge there won't be any left to pick," says Ron. Shame to leave them to rot.

Footpath after the bridge

We leave the fruit and head along the lane. Ron looks to his right. "I don't believe it!" he exclaims, "We've been walkin' fer nearly two hours an Cuckfield Church is only two fields away!" In the distance you could see the church on the horizon

We continue to skirt farmland until we reach the A272 at Ansty. Here we turn right into Bolney Road and right again by St Johns Church into Deaks Lane. What can be said about Ansty? The pub looks delightful, big and colourful. The church is a small chapel. That's it. That's all I can say about Ansty.

The pub looked inviting, but we didn't go in, honest. The church wasn't inviting so we didn't bother, but carried on walking down Deaks Lane. "Has that fertiliser got into my clothes? I can still smell it," I ask. "Don't be daft," is the reply, "field over 'edge as been fertilised as well." "Thank god for that. I can just imagine what my wife would say if a came home smelling of fertiliser. That is after she'd thrown a bucket of water over me".

Strolling along the road we pass the cricket field. Ron doesn't say a word. Has he not played here? I thought. Just as I'm about to ask a lady pulls up and asked us if we could direct her to the cricket field. We must have sounded like locals as we directed her back down the road. "You can't miss it," says I. "We already have," she replies, "perhaps it's a woman thing?" and drives off. Just at the side of the road we noticed what could only be

Bird box with no box?

described as a bird box roof on a pole. We have no idea what it's purpose in life is but, surely, it has been put there for a reason, hasn't it?

After over a mile of sampling blackberries, sloes, elderberries and some fruit that Ron thought were called 'Bullust', I was beginning to feel queasy when we reached a house called The Wyllies. Here we turn right, go through a gate and head down the slope to the corner of the field., following the High Weald Landscape Trail. We now cross a stile and climb steeply through the woodland to reach a fence. After a while we reach a galvanised gate and stile. This is the edge of Cuckfield Park, where we need to cut between the trees and bracken and drop down to a footbridge. The pathway here is very overgrown. The blackberries are ok but the path isn't. We have walked many routes without signs and waded through thick overgrowth to reach villages. Perhaps the reason very few people walk these 'ways' is

Another overgrown path

because of the state of the walk and the lack of direction. This walk has taken us three hours so far and the only people we have met on the way are the lost lady of cricket field fame and the vicar at Cuckfield Church. Is there a budget for clearing public walkways? Who is responsible? Can they give us a job?

Our next instruction is to climb a steep bank to reach an iron-kissing gate. This one had me beat. I just had to stop; half way up I was shattered. Even Des's trusted thumb stick wouldn't get me up this slope in one go. Eventually the top is reached and just the other side of the gate Ron sees the first animal. The path runs alongside a metal fence. Under the tree I can see what looks, at first glance, like a large mound of earth. A cow is grazing by the mound. As we get closer I can see that the large mound, is in fact, more animals. Lying down as well as standing. "Lets walk round them," I plead. Ron says with a smile, "the path goes straight through where they're sitting."

"Yes Ron, but let's walk right round them," I'm practically begging. It is now that I noticed Ron's step quicken a little. "Don't run," says Ron, "but one on end is a bull. And a big bugger at that." I was first to the next gate. "Never seen a 'erd like that before," says Ron. "They were all black an' fluffy[75]." "That bull looked like a bison," I reply. "Must be some special breed," says Ron with a chuckle. "I've 'eard that if a bull is in a field with cows 'e won't 'urt yer," he says. "So why did we hurtle across that field so fast?" I ask as I'm still trying to get my breath back.

Walk through or round?

Just a short walk through the village and we're back at the car. Another lovely walk completed. Not too long, but the steep hill made it tiring all the same.

I'm off to Cheshire in the morning so we haven't stopped for, what is fast becoming, our customary liquid break. I need to get back and help the wife to pack, and I feel that Ron has accepted this although he has given me some strange looks as we walk passed three pubs.

Next week is another week closer to me returning to work. The last few weeks seemed to have flown by. Our next walk may be the last, for a while, where we travel some distance to the start. I'm hoping to pick some fruit during the walk but if I can't I'll have to arrange to take the wife with me next weekend. A walk with the wife, is this what my life is turning too?

---

[75] We are reliably informed by Des, back at The Kings Head, that the cattle are Aberdeen Angus

WALK 31 – Twineham & Wineham

Wednesday 30th August 2006

We had a great time in Cheshire. The lodge we stayed at was very comfortable and fairly central to the area we wished to visit. With the aid of Satellite Navigation we had no problems at all in getting around. Unfortunately getting back to Hailsham came all too quickly and Monday's meeting with Ron seemed to come even quicker.

"Fancy Twineham," says Ron. "Where the hells Twineham?" is my reply. "Very close to Wineham," says Ron, "they're two villages in West Sussex an' the book makes 'em look good, so I fancy Twineham and Wineham for Wednesday's walk." "If you can tell me, exactly, where they are I'll see if I can get us there," I offer. "They're somewhere near 'ickstead," Ron advises. "It's in this book 'ere, Village Walks in West Sussex[76]. Looks really lov'ly in the pictures and sounds a nice walk." I'm still not convinced, and the words 'lovely' and 'nice', used by Ron, have me a little worried. But it is Ron's request, so I can't argue. It will certainly be a new part of Sussex that neither of us has seen.

Twineham Church

As regular readers will be aware I try to do a little homework on a place before we start our walks. This one was no different. But all I could find out about Twineham was that it lies in the Adur Valley, the Church is early Tudor with a slate roof made from Horsham slate and it has a peal of 5 bells.[77] On the same web site, when I asked for information on Wineham, it listed three properties? Should I have taken this as a sign? All will unfold.

We arrived at the church car park at 10:45ish. Along Church Lane, Twineham we have passed a Primary School. Nothing else. "Seems a little small to have a school," I comment. "P'rhaps village is further down the road," offers Ron. When we come back to the car, after the walk, we'll take a look.

The book advises us that the walk is 4¼ miles in length. We start at Twineham Church, walk along the countryside, over the River Adur to Wineham, and return to Twineham via different countryside.

The current Church of St. Peter is 16th century[78] but the original is dated around the 1200-1300 (and would have been made of wood). The current church is one of the earliest brick-built churches in Sussex and looks odd, simply because of its construction. The earliest Rector recorded was Thomas de Swaffham in 1287 and one of its other oddities is that, just inside the gate looking towards the church, on the left, is a plot of land purchased by the Society of Friends (Quakers) in 1694 for the burial of 'their' people. Four stone pillars, one in each corner, mark the area and there is a monument in place that tells us that 56 burials have been recorded and the last was in 1732.

Church Interior

Every third year there is still a service held at the church where the Friends Society pays the Rector the 'peppercorn rent'.

---

[76] 'Village Walks in West Sussex, Douglas Lasseter-Published by Countryside Books, Walk 17, Page 79
[77] www.visitsussex.org - visited 29th August 2006
[78] Pamphlet obtained from Church

Leaving Twineham Church we turn right and walk along a path that leads us to a ramshackle gate. For some reason the stile here is quite high and is a little difficult to get over. We are now confronted with a three-way sign and advised to take the path leading to our left. Once we arrive at the opposite corner we again have to turn left heading towards some farm buildings. At this point I could let you have the name of the farm but what we saw as we walked between the farm buildings and down the lane just confirms what I have said about 'poor hard up farmers'. I have resisted any comments, for some time, but even Ron was amazed at the amount of machinery, just abandoned, and left to rot, at this farm. We just could not believe the amount in scrap value all of this machinery could be worth. But practically everywhere we looked, around the buildings, along the tracks and even in the

Collection of rubbish

hedges we found abandoned, rusty, machinery of some sort. There, I feel better now, got it off me chest, again.

We follow the track and come to a stream bridge and a two-way sign to turn right. The path here is non-existent but we manage to see what could be a stile, in the distance. "Needs a trim up," says Ron. "I still think we should approach the Councils and see if we can get a job. We could carry out running repairs to all the signs as well as cutting pathways while we're out writing this book." "We'd better hurry," I reply, "we're on walk 31 so we've only got a few weeks left." But it does make you wonder if we could offer our services at some time.

We now walk across fields whilst the River Adur meanders on our left, according to our map. We haven't actually seen it yet. We could make out, in the distance a large farm called Great Wapses Farm, which is surrounded by paddocks and horses. All very friendly. They come over to say hello and I'm pleased there is a large fence between us. Just past this paddock we are advised to take the bridleway towards Gratten Lane, leading to Wineham Lane. The West Sussex Council calls this part of the bridleway 10T. The sign, attached to the gate, also told us that the bridleway was closed to all people due to resurfacing work. "That can't be right. You can't just close a bridleway without a warning," exclaims Ron, "where do we go from 'ere?" he asks. There is a phone number on the notice but, would you believe it, the first time I leave my mobile phone at home has to be today. "It's disgustin'," says Ron, "they've not even the decency to tell us of a diversion!" Ron is not amused. "We need to head to our right," I think out loud, "lets head around this paddock and see if another path will lead us to Wineham Lane."

Great Wapses Horse

Off we go. Ron is still muttering obscenities about Council staff getting off their bums and coming out to see what problems they cause from their nice warm offices etc. etc. Ron is definitely not amused. There is no way that we can turn right here and head towards Wineham Lane. We go back to the gate. "Look," exclaims Ron, "you'd 'ave thought that if they didn't want us to go up the path they'd 'ave locked the bloody gate!" as he pushes the gate open. "Lets risk it," I say, "if we get stopped we'll just say 'what sign', after all, according to this sign, this part of the bridleway is only 2,000 metres long." But Ron wasn't sure. "Let's walk towards that farm an' ask someone if they know a diversion," he offers. So towards the farm we head. It wasn't as far as I thought but it was certainly big. Nothing but stable after stable, but no one in sight. Big cars in the driveway. Suddenly the guard dog has woken up and comes charging towards us, teeth bared and barking. With trusted thumb stick defending us, inches from sharp pointed teeth, I walk, backwards because I'm not prepared to turn my back on the beast. Ron didn't bat an eyelid, but strolled up the drive without a care in the world. Still no one came out to see what all the noise was. Heading towards us are three horses and riders. When they get close to us I ask, "Is this the right way for Wineham Lane? The bridleway to it is closed and this is the only other route we could find." "You can get to the Lane from here," one of the young ladies tells us, "but you are on private land and shouldn't really be walking here." I explained again about the bridleway and showed her our book to prove what we were doing. She then gave us directions but also warned us that some of the farmers at the end of the drive may 'get funny' about us walking on 'their drive' but just tell them that we had spoken to the girls at the stables and we should be ok. We thanked them and continued walking along the drive. The

The River Arun

inevitable question about girls in the saddle comes up again. We really must ask someone who would know about these things.

The drive goes on for ages. We pass other farms and buildings but no one approaches us about walking up 'their drive'. We are stopped and asked directions to some business park but we have no idea where we are let alone a park. We advise the driver of the stables with a nasty dog. A few minutes later he is heading in the same direction as us. We eventually reach a road and turn right, hoping that the village of Wineham is in this direction. We walk for what seems like miles when we come to Gratten Lane. There is a sign here that advises the bridleway is closed, which starts Ron off again. I steer him away from the sign and we come to a bridge over the River Arun, just before Fryland Lane. The picture shows the river moving down into a pool. What the picture doesn't show is

138

that, by the wall on the left, the water is being diverted past this pool, under the road and then continues on its course. In this pool are trout. Not very big trout, but they are easily seen. But they can't go anywhere. The next picture is over the other side of the road, where the actual river runs. As you can see it is full of weed and doesn't appear to be moving. There is no way that the fish would swim into that is there? Or am I just being sentimental? The fish can't swim back up river because of the fast flow over the rock, yet they can't swim along the

river's course either. Needless to say, both sides of the river are owned by fishing clubs. I shouldn't think the rough side would catch many, but who knows?

Our map, in the book, does say that it is not drawn to scale. How true that is. According to the map The Royal Oak pub is opposite the path leading down past Groveland Farm, our next route. But the instructions say that the pub is a 'few paces' past this Farm. In reality it was a lot of paces but it was well worth the time. What a beautiful 14th century pub[79] this is. No hot meals available apart from toasted sandwiches and their ploughman's lunch is something to die for. Trust us, we tried one. The atmosphere inside is olde worlde with extra. It is a living history of the area with artefacts hanging from the walls and ceilings. What is strange is that there are no pumps on the bar for pulling a pint. "Good afternoon, gentleman, what can I get you?" is the request

The Royal Oak

from the barman. "What beers do you do?" asks Ron, looking around and finding nothing that looks familiar. "We do a lovely Harvey's bitter," says the barman, "straight from the barrel." "That'll do me," says Ron, and off the barman goes, into another room and comes back with a foaming pint for Ron. I asked for an orange juice and the barman reeled off about eight different versions of orange juice for me to pick from. While we sat eating our ploughman's, the conversation at the bar was about perpetual motion. All above Ron and me. We sat quietly eating. Customers were in and out all the time. When you consider that this place is in the middle of nowhere the bar staff were kept busy. One customer came in asking if they took credit cards. The barman, very politely said, "I'm very sorry sir, but this pub is very old and our accounting machine is also old and only accepts cash." Both Ron and I nearly choked when the man then asked if the pub had a cash machine. Again the barman, very politely, and with an expressionless look, advised his customer that the nearest cash machine was 5 miles away.

Before we leave the pub I walk around looking at various things and one that I just had to write down is reproduced here because of the truth it tells.

---

[79] www.horshampub.co.uk/royaloak - viewed 30/08/2006

A good Landlord/lady of a public house
Should posses the dignity of a Bishop,
The smile of a film star
The elastic conscience of a Member of Parliament
The hope of a Company Promoter
The skin of a Rhinoceros
The patience of a Saint
The senility of George Robey[80]
The voice of a Sergeant Major
And if they can say 'time gentleman please' in a tone that combines regret, firmness, condolence and hope for the future, together with the suggestion that it hurts them more than it hurts you, they are set for success.

From the pub we walk back to Grovelands Farm and turn left. We head down a track towards Twineham Grange Farm that is now, largely an industrial site. Our book tells us to head for a three-way sign where a pylon stands in front of the industrial units. Unfortunately there are a number of pylons and the one we chose didn't have a three-way sign near it. We walk back through the industrial units and head for another pylon. Still no three-way sign. Reading further on we should pass some cottages on our left. Looking down one of the tracks we can see some cottages so head in that direction, hoping for the best. Sure enough we now come to a footbridge that crosses the River Adur. Once across the bridge we are instructed to turn left and head for another pylon. But the sign says turn right. The pylon is on the right and so is the gap in the hedge. Yet the book says turn left? Now, perhaps, you can understand, after today, why we get lost. It's not always our fault.

The car is just a couple of fields away as we come to the end of this walk. All in all, the entire walk was less than inspiring. Both Ron and I expected to be able to wander round a couple of quaint villages, but no. Wineham has few houses but a wonderful pub. Perhaps there is more and we didn't get to see it. We drove around Twineham but could find little else other than the church and the school that was, to say the least, a little disappointing.

Next week I'm back at work, transporting Hastings little darlings to school, and back. Our discussion, on Monday, will have to be around a shorter walk or less distance to travel to the walk. It's my decision. I'll have a good look at the books, before I decide.

---

[80] George Robey CBE, Born 1869, England's famous music hall artist, known as 'The Prime Minister of Mirth' – www.its-behind-you.com viewed 30/08/2006

WALK 32 – Old Heathfield

Wednesday 6th September 2006

As usual Ron and I met on Monday to discuss this week's walk. What wasn't usual was that I couldn't decide where to go. I start back at work on Wednesday after nine weeks off. I am conscious that I have to be in Eastbourne at 4.45 in the afternoon so our walk cannot be long distance or too far from home. I parted from Ron on Monday telling him that I will think about it during Tuesday and let him know where we were heading when I pick him up at 10.00 on Wednesday morning.

The Star Inn

My problem is that I am torn between two walks that I would like to do. One is a circular walk from the Star Inn at Old Heathfield and the other starts at Three Cups. Both walks sound attractive. Neither is far from home and both walks are not long distances. So why am I undecided? I have family ties around the Three Cups area. My grandmother, Lilian (Walk 20, Page 85) was born in the area and, although I love my family history, I have never been to see her birthplace. It's strange, but it is just something I've never been inclined to do. I wonder why? We could walk the Three Cups area at a later date and the Old Heathfield walk does sound interesting with its mixture of fields and woods, as well as its history. So after lots of thought and a certain amount of soul searching, Old Heathfield it is, my grandmother's birthplace has waited this long, another few weeks won't make too much difference.

Have you ever had your mind go blank? For some reason you can't remember something.

The view across our first field

I don't know why but I couldn't, for the life of me, remember how to get to Old Heathfield. Now is that stupid or what. I actually had to look at a map to find out how to get there. Of course, once you glance at the map you know exactly where it is and how to get to it. But, just to make sure, I asked Ron for directions when I picked him up at The Kings Head. He looked at me as if I was some sort of a moron when I asked but I just had to confirm the directions, in my own mind, just to make sure. Perhaps it's my age?

Our walk this week is a short 3 miles across farmland, through woods and along shaded paths fringed with wild flowers[81]. I have been up since 5.30 this morning so a short three miles, if there is such a thing, is all I can manage. We park the car in the car park of The Star Inn at Old Heathfield, originally built in 1348 to house the masons building All Saints Church. In 1388, with the consent of the church, the hostel became an alehouse known as The Starre. I am advised that it is a very popular inn and is visited by, not only local people, but by people prepared to travel from some distance to taste its fare. Perhaps we may get a taster later on?

First we are advised to leave the pub and walk down the lane at the front. We come to a stile, on our right, which leads us into a field. The views here, across the countryside, are astounding. Again the Sussex countryside has amazed us. We are only a short distance away from the hustle and bustle of today's hectic life and you get views like this. Unfortunately, the map reading went a bit askew here. We've only got into the first field and I can't make out which direction to go in. Our instructions tell us to walk down the field to a stile at the bottom. As you can see from the picture, the field drops away in a number of directions, and yes we picked the wrong direction. Reading on, our instructions are to go over the stile and

---

[81] 'Pub Walks in East Sussex' by Mike Power-Published by Power Publications, Dorset-Walk 26 Pge 62

cross the road. It was the third stile we found that had a road we could cross. "Got 'ere 'ventually," says Ron, "only been walkin' 'alf 'our an' we've crossed the first field."

Sometimes Ron's comments can hit the spot. But, after 31 weeks of floundering over maps, directions and vague instructions my skin is becoming hardened to everyones comments and we soldier on.

Our instructions now tell us to pass through a gate. The gate looked as if it had seen better days and Ron was seriously thinking of a quick repair job. But I managed to drag him away before he got out the bailer twine and penknife.

Gate in need of repair

We now follow a shaded path down between the fields before we come to a stile where we turn left. It is here where it's a bit like déjà vous. "Have we seen a path like this, before?" I ask. "Does look familiar," says Ron. "How many walks have we been on where we have to go through or down a path like this one?" I continue, and if you look back through the pages of this book I'm sure you'll see plenty of tree-lined, shady paths. "Could be any one of 31 walks," says Ron and they do all look the same.

The footpath has recently collapsed here so we are diverted down to the stream. On our left you can hear running water and when we went to investigate we found that the stream drops quite suddenly down, what looks like, a man-made wall. But the effect is very stunning as the water cascades down the steep slope. The path now leads us around a large lake. I always have to admire the way

Typical Bridleway

reflections are made in water and this is no different. With the trees overhanging the waters edge and the stillness of the water makes for a great picture. The actual lake appears to discourage fishermen as there are no little gaps in the trees to sit and fish. To get this photo I had to lean over a bush, point the camera and hope for the best. But all around this area is peace and quiet. Nothing moves, yet the sound of water from the stream behind us can be heard. Ron's dream of fishing, whilst listening to a Test Match on the radio and a crate of beer at his elbow is being renewed as we just stop and look. A truly unspoilt and tranquil place.

As we leave this place we head up a small slope and the footing

Reflections in the stream

starts to get a little slippery. I could feel myself going before it actually happened but my brain did nothing to stop me hitting the ground as my right foot decided it had had enough. Ron didn't bat an eyelid as I clamber back to an upright position. My left knee hurt like hell but my pride was hurt even more. Being a true macho male I said little out loud but continued up the slope as if nothing had happened. We are now on a concrete lane heading up towards a cottage. A very large AA lorry is heading towards us down the hill. We manage to get sufficiently off the road for the lorry to squeeze past us and round the bend. I turn to Ron and say, "I bet this is a fun place to live in the winter." "Yeh," is the reply, "but a great place to be in the summer."

We pass the cottage and maintain our direction, over a stile and into a field. Our instructions advise us to continue to a finger post,

Pheasant's graveyard?

but we didn't see one, so we continued ahead. We step over a small stream and enter another shaded path. One of the things we notice is that we can actually hear birds singing. It has been ages since we have walked along country paths and heard birds singing. Ron tells me they are

Jays, and have to accept what he says. I have no idea but it was really a pleasant sound. Our guidebook advises us that this path takes us through a bluebell wood. Obviously we are too late to see and smell the beautiful fragrance of bluebells but it is a very tranquil wood with mostly beech and coppiced chestnut trees. We continue along this path, climbing stiles and crossing tracks until we pass some very desirable residences, which must have cost real money, and we reach a road. On the opposite side of the road is a lane, Furnace Lane, and we are told to go up this lane until we reach a track, on our left. We find the track without problems and proceed to walk up towards a gate. It is here that the map and directions seem to vary from the facts.

We are instructed to go through a gate into the field on the left. We have a gate, but the field is in front of us, not on the left. We are advised to follow the path signs, but there wasn't one. The book says 'make your way down and across to the far corner, over the stream and onto a track ahead.' So, we head off towards, what we believe to be, the far corner. As we approach the hedge Ron says, "Look at all those young pheasant, through the 'edge there." He points towards the pheasants. "They look as if they're in some sort of cage," I can see wire fencing and what looks like lots of pheasants. I can also hear voices. We walk on and Ron suddenly gets touchy. "They call that sport?" he grumbles. "One minute they feed 'em an' the next they put a bullet in 'em! Make 'em nice an' plump with corn from yer 'and, let em loose

Path through bluebell wood

in a field and then scare the shit out of em' as they make 'em fly towards a load men with shotguns. That's not sport, it's murder!" Ron, again, is not happy on our walk.

A van is heading towards us across the field. My first thought was that Ron's outburst had been overheard, but we were, apparently, heading in the wrong direction. "Are you two gentlemen lost?" we are asked. I showed the man our map and explained what the instructions were, only to be told that we should be heading for the top of the field, not the bottom, and that our map was not correct. We thanked the man for pointing us in the right direction and headed back to where he had directed us. When we got there all the 'public footpath' signs were now white plastic with 'footpath' printed on them with a black arrow pointing the way? What happened to the official, council, signs I have no idea. Then Ron says a strange thing. He tells me that it was the gamekeeper's job to help prepare these pheasants. Perhaps I'm stupid but surely the term 'gamekeeper' implies that he 'keeps' game. I looked up the term in the dictionary and the word 'gamekeeper' is described as '*n.* A person employed to protect and maintain game birds and animals, especially on an estate or game preserve'[82] I have always known about pheasant shoots but obviously, and now stupidly, thought that they shot wild pheasants to keep the numbers under control. I had never realised that it was such an organised slaughter of birds, purely shot and killed for fun in the name of sport and maintained by the one person whose job it is to 'keep' game birds and animals. As we walk towards the hedge numerous young pheasants are running in front of us, so tame you could practically bend down and pick one up.

We are approaching the end of our walk and the pheasant episode has put a bit of a dampener on it. Ron is now quiet. As we approach the church and pub I'm hoping his spirit will be lifted. The view up the short lane looking towards the church is my idea of what an entrance to any village should look like.

Part of the church area is cordoned off because steeplejacks are working overhead but All Saints Church is one of those, oh so cold, churches that I love. Ron has found someone to talk too in the churchyard so; hopefully, it will take his mind off the pheasants. As I said, earlier, in the chapter the church dates from around the 13th century and a very good guidebook can

---

[82] Readers Digest, Universal Dictionary - Published by The Readers Digest Association Ltd 1987

be obtained from inside the church for £1 and worth every penny[83]. The guidebook is crammed with history and facts about this beautiful, old church.

Perfect approach to church

When Ron returns he has been chatting to an old cricket opponent. Unfortunately he can't remember his name and didn't think to ask, but they instantly recognised each other and chatted about old times. Apparently the graves that Ron's friend was attending spanned over 150 years of the gentleman's relations. Unfortunately, he will be the last to perform this task, as his only son has moved and now lives in Australia. The end of an era.

All that is left is a visit to the pub. We certainly saved the best for last on this walk. Although only small, in comparison to some of the other pubs we have frequented on these walks, it certainly makes up for in character. Ron surprised me yet again by foregoing his usual Harvey's bitter and had a pint of Whitstable Bay, yet another real ale. A very attractive, and attentive, young lady behind the bar asked us if we would be requiring something to eat. One bar is full of blackboards offering such fare as 'fresh anchovies, served with balsamic onions'; deep-fried Moray scampi and other such unknown delicacies. But I did manage to find some more basic meals that might have appealed to our taste, but I have to be terribly honest, both Ron and I thought it a bit pricey. Saying that though, every table in the bar had a 'Reserved' card on it so they can't be doing anything wrong can they?

But one touch that I did appreciate was that, on a bookshelf, was a four ring binder, which contained some historical facts, as well as copies of census returns from the East Sussex Records Office, of the pub[84]. One is dated 1636 when Noah Taylor and Ralph Stretill (possibly Streeter) described as unlicensed alehouse keepers, were each find 3s 4d (about 17 pence), for 'tippling without a licence' Not a lot of money at today's standards but back in 1636 it must have been a fortune. I could have stayed a lot longer just looking at that binder. But the pub is beginning to fill up with hungry diners and I needed to get home. Ron is now chatting to the diners about the benefits of drinking real ales as opposed to chemical rubbish. We thank the young lady behind the bar, who Ron wishes to take home, and head for the car.

A Rural collection box

Another different walk completed. It was a short three miles and the history at the pub made it for me, personally. Unfortunately Ron is still upset about the pheasants but I assume that is the way it is in the country. It's probably been going on for years and nothing we do will stop it. But perhaps another name for a game 'keeper' should be found.

---

[83] A Guide to the Parish Church of All Saints, Heathfield – by Barry Jackson (Vicar 1988-1997)
[84] Information gathered from an article within the binder contributed by Janet Pennington and dated October 1998, Sussex Inn Histories

WALK 33 - Alciston

Wednesday 13th September 2006

On Monday night our usual conversation, regarding Wednesday's walk, needed to consider the state of my car. It had just failed its MOT. At last, someone has found what I had been complaining about for a number of months, that I had problems with the brakes. It had already been to two garages, one being Caffyns in Eastbourne, because they are Daewoo dealers, and they couldn't find anything wrong. The MOT tester said that my brakes were dangerous. That was last Friday. I couldn't get it to a garage until tomorrow, Tuesday. So we decided to veer on the side of caution and go for a more local walk, just in case, and Ron fancied the four mile pub walk[85] around Alciston. Starting at the Rose Cottage Inn and returning sometime later.

A number of things have happened since our last walk. Apart from the car, which could cause a problem in the short term, I have been offered more hours at my place of work. This could cause a long-term problem because our walks are carried out on a Wednesday afternoon. Obviously the offer of more hours also means more money coming into the Pollard household, which can only be a good thing. My problem is that I have now got used to not having to work. But, as my lovely wife has pointed out, the cash flow is leaking in the wrong direction, and I really need to give the bank balance a bit of a boost. So, a little reluctantly, I have accepted the situation for what it is and agreed to the extra hours. Explaining this to Ron was easier than I thought it would be. As he says, we can always do shorter walks during term time and longer ones during holidays or we could change the walk day to a weekend. That settled, it was off to Alciston on Wednesday, another place I had never been to.

One of our drinking partners at The Kings Head, Rodney, used to work with pumps. Apparently, at Alciston, there is a pumping station that used to be infested with snakes. Rodney had to maintain this pump at regular intervals and was terrified of snakes. So much so that before he got to the door of the pump house he used to rattle the gates and make a terrible noise. He then, once he got to the door, used to bang his tool box on the door and fuss with the keys. Just to let the snakes know he was about. "But aren't snakes deaf?" I asked. "I don't know about that," replies Rodney, "but they sure as hell knew when I was coming. Once I found a bl*$dy great adder coiled up on the motor. Scared the s^!t out of me. Took me ages to get back in that room to sort that pump out." I make a mental note of what Rodney is telling me so that both Ron and I can avoid the area. "The road's a dead end, at Alciston, but it's a lovely village, you'll enjoy it."

One of the problems of this walk is that Ron has kept the guidebook we are to use so I haven't had chance to see what the walk involves. As you will know I do like to do a bit of homework on the village we are walking round. Unfortunately one of my other problems,

since last week's walk, is that my computer has, for some reason, decided not to function correctly and has been sent away, to be repaired. I am typing the first draft of this chapter on my laptop, which isn't connected to the Internet, so I am unable to find out anything about our walk. But I was soon to discover what was in store.

For anyone unsure of the area, to get to Alciston, you travel along the A27 towards Lewes, cross the roundabout at Drusillas and take the 2nd turning on the left. It is well marked. I have never been down this lane before and passed the Rose Cottage Inn before I realised. You can use the pub car park but be aware of where it is. We parked on the side of the road, in a small lay-by.

The bridleway before the downs

Alciston village is one of those places that time has forgotten. Old dwellings with thatched roofs line what is the main street. One

---

[85] Pub Walks in East Sussex by Mike Power, Power Publications Sep 1994, Page 6, Walk 1

of the things I notice, about the walk, is the comment by Mike Power that this walk is not arduous. He also describes the walk as 'downland'. "Means it's on the flat," says Ron. "But doesn't downland mean downs as in South Downs, those big hilly things we can see in the distance?" I ask. "Book says it's easy," says Ron, "trust me."

We pass the Rose Cottage on our left and walk down the road towards house number 53 where a track opposite leads us towards a field. The path is clearly marked so we have no trouble finding it. The gate is brand new as are the next few, as we head through the fields following our book's instructions. Considering how close we are to a main road the traffic noise is at a minimum. This gives a strange surreal feeling. We can see large juggernauts heading along the main road but are unable to hear them. We reach a lane and turn left. The views over to the South Downs are fabulous. "We seem to be getting close to the Downs Ron," I observe. "Yes," is the reply, "can you see that path running up to the top? That's a steep bugger." "Tell me we're not going up there," I plead. "Book says it ain't arduous," he

At the top of bridleway

replies, "we'll need t' turn off before we get that far," he assures me. We now turn right and head along a concrete lane towards a pottery. Ron is sampling the blackberries and sloes as we walk. "Enough 'ere to supply Tesco's," he says as he pops another fruit in. By now our reader may have noticed a lack of pictures. The camera has packed up again. All the pictures I have taken are no longer on the camera. Don't ask me why, but after 32 walks I must still be doing something wrong. Perhaps it's because my hands are big and the camera is so small. I must press buttons without realising I'm doing it. But trust me when I say that some of the pictures I have taken since we left the Rose Cottage Inn were stunning shots of this beautiful county of ours. The fact that they no longer exist is totally my fault.

Once we pass the pottery we continue in the same direction until we reach a turning onto a drive. The directions seem to show this drive as only a short distance away but, in fact, we walked across a few fields before finding the driveway. The weather has turned really hot.

Still climbing

The forecast was for showers and it did look a little overcast when we left the village, but now the skin had started to leak quite badly. And all the time I can see the South Downs looming over us. Is it the weather or the thought of having to negotiate the climb up the downs that makes my skin leak? We now pass some disused farm buildings and head along a track. Again we cross fields and I'm amazed at how many wild pheasant we see in these fields. "Now this is my idea of a pheasant shoot," I explain to Ron. "A couple of men, walking along the countryside, shooting at the 'wild game' they manage to find. Not sit back and wait for the poor birds to be shoed across the barrel of a gun." Ron doesn't comment. Our guidebook tells us to follow this track until we meet a bridleway as it rises gradually to a gate. (I've got the camera working again.) "As it rises gradually," I point out to Ron. It doesn't look that gradual to me. I read on a little and the instructions do say that we turn left '...to join a sunken track....'[86] so perhaps we will skirt the downs after all and Ron keeps assuring me that downlands means level or downhill. I'm not convinced. As we come out at the gate we are in a clearing. The photograph is evidence

You can see for miles

---

[86] Pub Walks in East Sussex by Mike Power, Power Publications Sep 1994, Page 7, Walk 1

of the view from the top of the 'bridleway as it rises gradually'. You could see for miles. But worse was to come. Our guidebook now advises us about the sunken track up the hillside and tells us to look back and admire the views. The track Ron jokingly spoke of earlier is the very same track we are about to climb. I read on a little further into our directions and notice the words Bo-Peep. Anyone who knows the area at all will recognise these words as being an area where they used to perform hill trials for cars. It is high up, and it is steep. Some cars didn't make it to the top; it was that much of a challenge. I look up this path and I don't know what to think. Ron is apologetic. He honestly thought that it wouldn't be hard work. And I have to say, should I have meet the author of our guidebook, at this precise moment, I would shove it where the sun doesn't shine. Please, please, please, if after reading our chapters you feel smitten by the Holy Spirit and wish to have a go yourselves do not believe everything that is said about this walk by Mike Power. It is very scenic. There are some great views but it is very arduous and it is very steep. Even the birds up here are carrying oxygen tanks and

Is it a woolly connection?

wearing breathing apparatus. Both Ron and I had to stop, on a number of occasions, just to sit and rest as we climbed to the top of the South Downs. Of course the views from up here are unbelievable. But so was the effort to get here. As the path levels out you pray that you have reached the summit just to go round a small bend to find the path takes you even higher. I was shattered when we reached the very top. I was so knackered that I didn't care what the view was like. I just wanted to let myself collapse and rest. If you are in any doubt about your ability to climb hills please do not attempt this walk. You may regret it. All the other walks

we have been on have warned us of any parts that could be difficult but this one tells you the opposite. Not only am I knackered but I'm angry as well.

Luckily Ron has brought along some liquid refreshment, only water, honest, but it went down really well as we sat at the top of the Downs contemplating the downhill stretch of the walk. I must admit that calling into the Rose Cottage Inn was appearing more and more attractive as the minutes past. With that thought in mind we started our descent.

We turn left and head along the South Downs Way until we reach Bo Peep Bostal. Why is it called that? What is a 'Bostal'? There are a large number of sheep up here. Bo Peep, sheep. Is that the connection? I have no idea. My usual sources, encyclopaedias and dictionaries do not list the word 'Bostal' and I can't get onto the Internet. Ron thinks it means 'the top, or

On the way down!

summit' but I have never heard of the word. Perhaps someone could advise as on its meaning or origin?

Downland farming

From Bo Peep Bostal (?) we turn left and head down the road, once used for hill trials. This road is as steep downhill as the path was uphill, so be warned. At one of the sharp left-hand bends is a gate on the right. We go through the gate and bear left as we head down the hill towards the village of Alciston. Again this path could be anyone of the paths Ron and I have walked down over the past 32 weeks. Yet each one has something different from the last. Ron noticed the lack of litter. "Too far fer the riff raff to come," is his comment. But the area is very unspoilt and incredibly clean. "Just think, people must have walked this path fer years, going ter church an that," says Ron. "Is there a church in Alciston?" I ask, "There isn't one on our map of the walk and I didn't see one when we walked past the pub. In fact the only thing I did notice was the thatched roofs on the cottages and the pub." "P'raps they walked to Berwick," offers Ron.

At the end of this path we arrive at a signpost pointing us in the direction of, would you believe, the ancient church? "That answers our question Ron," I say. "Let's hope it's open."

Before we get too far down the lane I notice, on our left, a field of cut hay. Not only has the hay been cut but it has also been made ready for storage. On some of our previous walks I have noticed that some bales of hay are round in shape. Some are the more traditional oblong shape. But this farmer was different. Half the field was tied in the oblong shape and the other half of the field was round. I assume that square is easier to store, so why have round. There must be a reason. Again, any insights from readers would be appreciated.

The lane leads us down past some very old properties and right opposite a house called 'Old Postman's Cottage' is one of the most idyllic places for a church I have ever seen. Nestling between Court House Farm, a large tithe barn and a 14th century dovecote and backing onto the South Downs is Alciston Church. A Norman church whose dedication is unknown. Vicars are listed from 1353 and its register is dated from 1575. Inside the church is a little strange in layout. The altar is at the very far end of the church and there is an area of about ten feet square which is tiled and has a cemented up archway on it's right-hand side. Unfortunately there were no church guides for us to purchase so we are unable to establish why the church should have this area left vacant. It also appears that there is no electricity within the church as candles hang from the ceiling beams in chandeliers. The organ has to be the smallest church organ in existence. All of this makes it an unusually atmospheric but quaint building.

Outside the church, and to the left, is what remains of the dovecote. The sign tells us that the original was built by the monks

Alciston Church

from Battle Abbey and now belongs to Firle Estate Settlement. Restoration work has been carried out with the aide of grants from Wealden District Council, East Sussex County Council as well from English Heritage. Again I have a question. Why did the monks, from Battle Abbey, come all the way out here, to Alciston, to build a dovecote? Why Alciston? Why a dovecote? I thought that the keeping and breeding of doves was for their beauty or something to do with peace. But on my return from this walk I asked a colleague from work if he knew of the reason for keeping doves. His reply surprised me. Apparently he visited a

The remains of the dovecote restored by local charities

place called Dunster Castle, which has one of the largest dovecotes in the country. When he asked his guide why doves were kept he was told that a dove was the quickest bird to grow from egg to adulthood. Once the bird reached adulthood it was killed and eaten. If a large dovecote were maintained there would always be a supply of food. Whether this is true I have no idea. But this walk has produced more questions than any other. For once, Ron is unable to answer all of my questions. This is another thing that has surprised me.

Not a particularly pleasant walk due to the climbs but, once rested the views at the top of the South Downs at Bo Peep Bostal were astounding. A walk that produced some surprises but I have more questions than answers.

A short walk from here and we are back at the car. We stow our bits and pieces in the boot and head for the Rose Cottage Inn. You have to realise that the road to this village is a dead end. There is no 'passing trade' for this pub. People visit the Rose Cottage Inn to eat and relax. They do not offer exotic food just good, old-fashioned pub grub. And it is packed. The bar area is only a few feet square and I fail to see how Ron's father played darts here 50 years ago because the place is wall to wall tables. All the tables, inside, are taken. The pub is full and the car park has people jockeying for places to park. We managed to find a table, in the shade, and dined on a 'mature cheddar ploughman's'. The lunch turned out to be the perfect end to a 'long' four miles.

WALK 34 – Three Cups

Wednesday 20th September 2006

I could be really nasty, after last week's walk, and suggest a difficult walk for Wednesday. It took me a few days to get over the climb to the top of Bo Peep Hill, thanks to Ron's 'it's on the level, trust me' walk. But, I'll be honest, my mouth started working before my brain got in gear, again, when I volunteered us to do an eight mile sponsored walk, for charity. Not only was it eight miles but it was also on a Sunday. Not only a Sunday but during the time that most people were either at church or, more importantly for me, having their Sunday dinner. The walk was completed on Sunday 17th September and I have written a few words about it for this journal that can be read in full sometime later.

For now I have chosen Punnetts Town for Wednesday. A six-mile stroll, across farmland where an area known as 'Cherry Clack' can be found. There used to be a Windmill here known as The Cherry Clack Mill[87]. The mill was originally built in Biddenden, Kent and was sometimes known as Three Throws Windmill. It was taken down in 1856 and moved, in pieces, to Punnetts Town. F. Neve and Son, the Heathfield millwrights, carried out the entire move and replaced an old post mill that was struck by lightning and burnt to the ground. The 'new' mill ceased working in 1927, when the sweeps and fan were taken down. Shortly after 1934 its owners Messrs. Dallaway Brothers, had the hooded cap removed along with all its machinery.

The name 'Cherry Clack' is thought to come from when the mill had spring-sweeps that closes with a distinct snap or 'clack' as they reach the lowest point of their arc of travel and come out of the wind. This very likely reminded folk of the little windmills so often set up in cherry trees to scare birds away from the fruit, which made a regular 'clacking' noise. That is where the name, 'Cherry Clack', is said to originate?

After finding out all this wonderful, informative facts regarding windmills and Cherry Clack I take a quick look at the book before picking Ron up on Wednesday only to find out we are going to Three Cups and not Punnetts Town. Never mind. I got the six miles right.

Track, opposite the pub

Before I start the chapter fully, you will be aware that I have had some technical problems with the digital camera. It is a Samsung Digimax 202. It has been repaired, along with my computer (another story). Although I am assured that the camera has been repaired I now find, just before the camera stops working, the picture it takes is slightly dark. You will notice, throughout this chapter, that a lot of the pictures are dark. I'm sorry. The camera will be on e-bay before the end of the day.

Parking at The Three Cups pub is no problem. It's just after 10 o'clock and they're not open yet. The large car park is

Animal damage

completely empty. Our more educated followers, the ones who know the area, have pointed out to me that this walk is hilly. When reading the route I missed the fact that we started at Three Cups[88] it's not surprising that I missed reading the hilly bits as well. But they were right. It was hilly but not in the way of last week and Bo Peep Hill. All will be revealed.

We set off northwards along a track, which leaves the road, opposite the Three Cups. After 250 yards other paths and tracks merge and we need to go half-right. The signs are clear

---

[87] Notes on Sussex Smock Mills, The Rev. Peter Hemming Pages 65 - 67, sussexmillsgroup.org.uk (viewed 18/09/2006)

[88] Argus, East Sussex Walks by Ben Perkins, Published by Southern Publishing 1995 Page 46

at this point. Just as we need to bear left, by an old rusty corrugated shed we notice a cider smell coming from the apples lying on the ground. The trees branches, above us are laden with apples. "I need some apples to make some wine with. But I think I need crab apples?" "They aren't crab apples," says Ron, "they're eatin' apples. I'll get some crab apples for yer

Bridge over river

wine making." I have noticed that it is difficult to get home-brew chemicals and equipment locally. Boots, the chemist, used to supply most of my needs some years ago, when I first brewed wine, but they've not stocked it for a number of years. I've looked around in a few towns but the most obvious place is the Internet. If I start now I might get some wine for early next year?

Our instructions tell us to cross over the next track and continue downhill and cross a bridge over the River Dudwell. Our map, for what it is, shows that on our right is Little Poundsford Farm. "Must 'ave somethin' te 'ide," says Ron, "or 'ees won the lottery.

Fence must 'ave cost a fortune." All the way along this path, it must be nearly a mile to the bottom, is a very nice wooden fence enclosing, what we assume to be, the farm. But every now and then it looks as if someone, or something, has tried to escape for there are holes in the fencing. Some of them look quite big holes. Because of our surroundings Ron wonders if it's deer but we really have no way of knowing.

The bridge we cross is relatively new but the river has been reduced to nothing more than a trickle. The riverbed is fairly wide so it gives some idea where the water level used to be but it is now just a shadow of its former self. In years gone by it must have been

Gravel path

extremely pretty and tranquil down here. The sounds of the water and the birds combine to give a pleasant picture.

Obviously, a downhill is usually followed by an uphill. This is no exception. But this uphill is, thankfully, gradual and the gravel underfoot helps. The path slowly becomes even more solid as we approach the top. The amount of hardcore and ballast used to make this path must have cost someone a fortune. But it made for an easy uphill walk.

At the top we reach a gate and through this gate we come to a drive. As with most of our walks once we get to the top of any incline we stop and admire the view. I didn't realise exactly how high up we were until we looked back, through the gap by a fence. We could see

The top of our climb

a fair distance and just managed to make out the Windmill at Punnetts Town that I mentioned at the start of the chapter. So my early research on the Internet wasn't wasted after all.

Our map shows a place, on the right-hand side called 'Luck Farm'. Our instructions are to turn right, just past this farm. You've guessed it. We couldn't find the farm. We found a place called 'Hunters Hill, on our right, not mentioned on our map, nor was 'Seaview Farm', on our left, as was 'Hunters Lodge' and a beautiful cottage called 'Greenore'. We are instructed at the top of the rise '..just as the road begins to drop downhill, turn right over

a stile'. The only stile we found was exactly opposite the gate to the cottage called 'Greenore'. So why didn't the author of the walk write that as an instruction? It would have made the walk so much easier.

Confusing sign

We are now advised to keep left of two fields, but there was only one? We did find a high perimeter fence where we turn right and join a lane. After a right turn and about 100 yards we arrive at a place called April Cottage. Here we turn left and cross the stile. After hunting for a while we manage to find another pathway that leads us onto a road. The sign here is a little confusing. We have arrived, at the sign, by the tree in the background of the photo. Our book tells us to turn left. The wooden finger sign tells us to go ahead. It isn't until you get to the other side of the sign that you see a little yellow arrow telling us the correct way to go. So why is the finger post pointing in the wrong direction. (If you follow the sign you start to walk into private property) and why isn't the yellow arrow, placed so that you can see it when you get to the junction? A walker's life can be so confusing at times. We walk along this road heading towards Burwash Common.

The Wheel Inn

Burwash Common has a strange little bit of history[89]. It is a village with an identity crisis. If you arrive at the village from Heathfield it is signposted Burwash Common. If you arrive at the village from Burwash it is signposted Burwash Weald. [90]It is made up of the two hamlets, but because they overlap the East Sussex County Council decided not to put up two additional signs to define the hamlets. In the 1830's people, from as far away as Portsmouth, have described The Wheel Inn, at Burwash as 'the roughest public house they had ever been in'. It is believed that the pub was once called the 'Catherine Wheel', after Catherine of Aragon, Henry VIII's first wife in 1509. That 'roughest' quote is certainly not true of today's Wheel Inn. Our welcome was extremely warm and the inside of the Inn is both comfortable and well-kept. Ron said his pint of Smild (brewed at Rother Valley) went down well, but not as good as his pint of Harvey's and I have, provisionally, booked a table for my birthday meal. Just inside the restaurant doorway is a copy of an article from the Sussex Advertiser dated 29th September 1788 which reads;

> *The smuggler who was shot by the Dragoon at Bexhill is living and thought to be in a fair way to recovery.*
> *A similar instance occurred last Wednesday at Burwash Wheel, nr Burwash. Mr. Pudsey, a Revenue Officer at Battle, seized 15 casks of foreign spirits and two or three horses and deposited them, for present convenience, in a stable belonging to the Burwash Wheel public house. But where the seizure had not been long, before the smugglers, from whom it was seized appeared to retake it, which they attempted by forcing open the stable door, in the presence of the officer, who, having expostulated with them in vain on the impropriety of their conduct, drew his pistol and shot one of the smugglers through the arm, after which he obtained the assistance of a peace officer and, thereby, secured the seizure.*

As we are leaving the pub a not too familiar sight greeted us. I believe it was our walk that took us to Dial Post that the first mention of 'Rambling Associations' was heard. Walking along the road is what I can only describe as a geriatric Boy Scout group. They each wore matching brown tailored shorts, matching socks and sweaters. All carried little blue knapsacks on their backs and were being lead by the aged tawny eagle, or whatever they are called, complete with map tied round his neck and a booming voice. Ron, being Ron, couldn't resist. From across the road, opposite the pub, he calls out a cheery greeting. "Good afternoon people, you go in ter that pub, there. You'll get a luv'ly welcome an' a luv'ly pint too!" What we didn't expect was for the leader of the group to tell his little followers "that really isn't on our agenda. But if you feel the need for some lemonade we may stay just a few moments.

---

[89] www.villagenet.co.uk/esussex-iron/villages/burwashweald.php - viewed 21/09/2006
[90] Picture taken from above web site 21/09/2006

Now, where was I before being rudely interrupted from across the road!" I had to hold Ron back from going over and giving the pompous arse a piece of his mind.

I manage to get Ron down Willingford Lane. He's still grumbling about pompous attitudes and Rambling Associations. "You're not thinking of joining a Rambling Association then Ron?" I ask. I can't print his reply! After a few yards we turn right onto a gravel driveway, which quickly becomes a narrow path descending into a wooded valley. It's steep. It's very steep. But at least it's downhill. "Remember," says Ron, "one down'hill means one up'ill." At the bottom of the valley we cross the River Dudwell again. Now the water is a golden brown colour. "That's because of the iron in the ground," explains Ron. Unfortunately the photograph isn't that good (a poor workman always blames his tools) but the colour of the water was a gorgeous golden brown. We stopped here for a while. The thought of the climb up the hill kept me planted for a few minutes, but eventually it had to be faced. It was worse than Bo Peep. Practically mountaineering.

Views after the long climb

Looking back, though, made up for the struggle of the climb. Once at the top we headed for a gap in the hedge and

Rusty Water?

down the centre of the next field. Very few markers are evident here and the advice of going down two thirds of the next field didn't make sense. The next stile and gate were right at the bottom. But from the top of this field, looking at the way we were heading made me want to turn and run. We were heading towards Dallington Forest. That's the great big dark green mass seen in the distance of the next photograph. You will also notice the first part is downhill again. I must admit that this part of the walk was not as difficult, or as strenuous as I expected. Yes we did have to walk to the bottom of this field and then up through the forest. The forest walk is about a mile long. Although some effort was needed we weren't in full sunlight and with the odd sip of water we managed to get to the end without difficulty. With water in mind you may have noticed, in all the photo's Ron always carries a plastic bag. It's a little bit like Compo, in Last of the Summer Wine, with his matchbox. Ron always carries a plastic bag. I'm scared to ask what's in it.

After our wander through the forest we are back on the track we started from, but heading towards the Three Cups instead of away from it. As this will be our last Wednesday walk for a while it is decided that a little liquid refreshment is called for. We need very little excuse, I know. But I am a little disappointed that Wednesdays will not be the same. We have decided to continue our walks so that our goal of one walk every week for a year can be achieved. The difference being that a few walks will not be on Wednesday. I just hope that on the other days it doesn't rain. Ron's old saying that it doesn't rain in Sussex on a Wednesday won't mean the same thing.

We are sitting in a country pub I haven't sat in before. Why is there always someone loud at the bar? He used to own a Porsche. He's just flown back from a business trip. It's the end of the month and his staff need paying but this month he won't need a bank overdraft. He's just increased his life insurance. This one man didn't stop talking, loudly, from the time we entered until the time we left. And as I am tucking into one of the best plates of ham, two eggs and chips I've eaten for some time I hear Ron exclaim, "I don't believe it! That bunch ov' toffee nosed walkers (I think he said walkers) 'ave just come up the path 'an are sittin' under the tree outside the pub!" He's rising to go and confront them. "Sit down, Ron," I plead, "your chips will get cold and your Harvey's will get warm." Gladly he saw reason and we finished off our meal with pleasant conversation.

I was hoping that Ron would give me a clue as to next week's walk. But he's making me wait until Monday. I'm beginning to dislike surprises.

WALK 35 - Lewes

Saturday 30th September 2006

You will see, from the heading, we have agreed to carry out walks on other days. This is mainly due to my change in work hours. Monday's meeting at The Kings Head discussed all alternatives and it was decided that during term time, I work at a school; walks would be carried out on different days, depending on the length of walk. During school holidays we would revert back to a longer walk on a weekday.

Some weeks ago we were introduced to a lady who has become a very close friend to one of our followers and, we're pleased to say, a pleasant addition to The Kings Head 'family'. Her name is Roz and she has been reading one or two of our chapters. At our meeting on Monday Ron mentioned a walk around Lewes. Roz appears to be a hive of information about

the history of Lewes. She mentions places, such as, 'Gallows Lane' and ancient ditches running under foundations as well as old churches and the Battle of Lewes. Both Ron and I are hooked. We asked Roz if she would like to accompany us on today's walk and show us some of the history of Lewes and she has agreed. Not only are we on a history lesson but also Roz has worked out the walk for us, so I won't need a book or map in front of me.

Another addition to our walks is a new camera. My birthday was during the week and my wife has given me a new digital camera. She's fed up with me throwing a tantrum every time my 'old' camera

Lewes Naval Prison sign

misbehaved and is hoping for a more peaceful time when I insert photos into the chapters. The following pages will, I hope, be successful.

Today is Saturday 30th September 2006. The rain has been falling all night. But the sun is now shining so, as I drive to the usual pick up point, I hope that it will stay dry for us today. It is one of those days when you can't make up your mind what to wear.

We get to Lewes and the sun is still shining. It's started to get warm so I leave the overcoat in the car. Roz produces an umbrella and Wellingtons from the boot. Perhaps she has some insider information about the weather. I decide to take a jacket, just in case.

We leave the car in North Street and turn left into Lancaster Street. Roz points out the plaque on the wall where the old Naval Prison used to stand. All that is left standing, since its demolition in 1963, is the wall. Further along the road is a row of terraced houses known as 'The Fosse' which is built over an old Roman ditch which is still accessible from the cellars of the houses. Next to these houses, after a very short walk, is the Church of St John sub Castro. Since I have started to delve into the realms of Family History the term 'sub Castro' has always been prominent in Lewes documents. I have always wondered what it meant and never had the nerve to ask. Once inside the church we are greeted by a gentleman who proceeds to offer us books and information about the church. When I asked Roz, on the way to Lewes, the meaning

St John sub Castro

of 'sub Castro' she was unsure of its origin. Roz asked our greeter who explained that the term was Latin. The word 'sub' means under, and the word 'Castro' means Castle. Obvious now, isn't it? Yet the booklet, purchased at the church[91], describes the name as 'St. John **in the** Castle'. Now it's not quite so obvious?

The 'Magnus' wall

The church is said to originate from the year 1000, 66 years before the Norman Conquest. Only a small part of the original church is still standing. In 1121 the church came into the possession of Lewes Priory, the Priory of St Pancras (the remains of which we will pass towards the end of the walk) During this period the Priory, as Patrons, held the right to appoint the Rectors and the first use of the title 'St John sub Castro' is found in a document of 1190, apparently to distinguish it from the Priory Church at Southover, also dedicated to St John the Baptist. Still not confused?

It was around the 12th or 13th centuries that a Danish prince named Magnus is said to have walled himself into a cell to pray. There are 15 inscribed stones set in the eastern wall which are thought to have originally surrounded the access to the cell (probably built on to the chancel) which reads *"There enters this cell a warrior of Denmark's royal race: Magnus his name mark of mighty lineage. Casting off his mightiness, he takes the lamb's mildness, and to gain everlasting life becomes a lowly anchorite[92]."* There have been various theories as to who Magnus was and why he should have given up arms and taken up a life of solitary prayer. But it remains a mystery.

It is recorded that in 1386 'William, parson of St John sub Castro' was arrested with others for stealing a chalice from Hamsey Church and for highway robbery. He later received the Kings pardon!

For all this history both Ron and I thought the inside of the church would be inspiring. Unfortunately this was not the case. The current church was constructed in 1839/40 and doesn't have that old church feel or old smell. It is very colourful with painted balconies with a strange square painted ceiling. In 1741 John Crofts, a lawyer of Lincolns Inn, donated a huge painting, which is hanging on the wall at the rear of the church, when he acquired the church's patronage.

Russian Monument

The churchyard is huge and reasonably well-kept. Within this area is a monument put up by the then Czar of Russia[93], Alexander II, in memory of the Finlanders (Finland was part of Russia at this time) who were taken prisoner during the Crimean War (1854-1856) and died while housed at the old Naval Prison that we passed earlier. The Soviet Embassy restored the monument in 1957 at the request of the 'Friends of Lewes.'

Pells Pool

As can be imagined, we spent some time at this church and we still had a fair distance to walk. Roz had written down the route for me to follow as we went along. At the top of the first page she has written 'approx 5½ to 6 miles'. We can't have gone more than ¾ of a mile at this stage. We needed to get on.

[91] Ten Centuries of History, The Story of St. John sub Castro Lewes, by Richard Field. First published as A Brief History of the Parish Church of St John sub Castro Lewes in 2000 revised 2006 with new title
[92] an-cho-rite *n.* A person who has retired into seclusion, usually for religious reasons; a hermit, a recluse – Universal Dictionary
[93] Leaflet – A Tour Round St John Sub Castro, The Churchyard Para 11

We leave the church and head down St John Hill towards 'Pells Pool'. Here you can imagine, in Victorian times, couples punting up and down this man-made lake or feeding the many ducks that swim here. Although the lake is man-made the water comes from a natural spring. To our right is what Roz tells us the largest outdoor swimming pool in the country that is fed by the same natural spring. It was padlocked so we couldn't get too close but the water didn't look that clean!

River Ouse

The sun is still shining but Roz has decided to change into wellies? Has she been tipped off about the weather? "No," she says, "but the path along the river bank may be wet and dirty. The wellies are a precaution." We enter a wooded area and the path leads us out onto the bank of the River Ouse. The area around here has obvious fond memories for Roz as she relates stories of her youth. Her childhood home is over to the left, as we walk, so she knows this area very well. Stories of swimming in the river, jumping in from a suspension bridge, no longer in place, all bring back some good times to Roz.

One of the stories she relates is about building rafts that would horrify parents of today. To our left runs the main railway line to London. Roz tells us that between her house and the line

Strange stile

is a small stream. Roz and her friends used to build a raft and test it out in the small stream. If it floated they would then carry it, dripping water, over the railway line, and head for the River Ouse, where they would spend the day. They would then carry the raft back over the railway line, still dripping water. They never once thought they were doing anything wrong!

We walk along the riverbank heading towards the chalk pit. The tide is on the turn and Ron gets excited when he sees large fish in the river. We cross one of the strangest stiles we've seen since the start of our walks. The river meanders to our right and all is still. We wander along this beautiful area until we bear left

St Peters, Offham

and go under the railway line into a field. "This area is called Landport Woods," explains Roz, "this path leads us to Offham." Apparently this village, if you're local, is pronounced Oaffham. Roz insisted she corrected my pronunciation. The path is typical of all the paths we have walked and will be recognised by you all. About the same width as a horse drawn cart, and uphill. I notice there is nothing on Roz's instructions about 'uphill' and point this out to Ron, quietly. Roz overhears my comments and tells us to wait until we reach Offham Hill "to see what a real hill is like." Both Ron and I hope it's not like Bo Peep. There can't be another hill like Bo Peep, can there??

When we arrive at Offham, St Peter's Church is closed, so we are unable to get in. What does seem strange is that there are no gravestones here. Where did they bury their dead? But the church does have one of the most picturesque entrances that I have seen where you have to duck under branches of a tree which overhang the pathway.

Outside of the church is the main road to Cuckfield. Suddenly I'm aware of where we are and now know the church as one that I used to pass on my way to Ditchling. "We have to cross the road here," says Roz, "and head up Offham Hill to get to the top of the chalk pit. From there you will see for miles. The views are fantastic." Offham Hill is a little steep. Not

Roz needs a rest

as bad as Bo-Peep but still steep. But the long climb is well worth the effort. The sun is still shining and the clear views across Lewes and the river are outstanding. You can literally see for miles. In the distance is the riverbank we walked on just a little while ago and it looks miles away. We stop at this plateau (Roz tells us that we still have a climb to make it to the very top) while Roz changes back out of her wellies into trainers. I must have lost a bit of weight because I haven't stopped sweating since the start of the climb. The thought of a further climb didn't help. Again once we reached the very top of the chalk pit the views were even better than previous. It was breathtaking. The clouds had started to form and although it was sunny a chilly wind had started to blow and the temperature was beginning to drop. "We walk along the top now and head towards 'The Gallops' and the site of the Battle of Lewes," says Roz as she heads off, on a mission.

With her umbrella in hand, suddenly Roz becomes a tour guide. For as far as we could see to our left and right is the site of the famous battle of 1264 fought between Henry III, who arrived in Lewes on the 11th May, and the baronial army led by Simon de Montford. The Kings garrison had been

We get to the top

reinforced with mounted soldiers led by Henry's son, Prince Edward, and now amounted to 10,000 troops, twice as many as the baronial forces. On the morning of 14th May the baronial forces drew up in battle formation on Offham Hill. Prince Edward quickly mustered his troops and marched straight towards the enemy. The King was left to gather the bulk of his army, who were demoralised, tired and poorly led, and followed on behind the Prince. The outcome of this battle was defeat for the King. The death toll is said to be 2,800 men, mostly Royal troops, some drowning trying to escape across the River Ouse. The King and his son were placed under 'house arrest' and de Montfort became the ruler of England. After less than a year of 'house arrest' Prince Edward escaped and raised another army in Wales. In 1265 he defeated de Montfort at Evesham. In a short, bloody battle de Montfort died, together with his son and 4,000 of his troops. Henry III was restored to his throne and reigned, unchallenged, for another seven years[94].

A familiar name in Lewes

We now head back into the Town of Lewes. Past Lewes Prison heading along the High Street. We pass The Pelham Arms where Roz has another story of a Christmas incident, which, she believes, got her barred from the pub. I have promised Roz not to give details of the events here but I may use them later if required? The Pelham family are a prominent people of the area. In 1356 Sir John Pelham, a local knight, with Sir Roger de la

The scene of the Battle of Lewes

---

[94]Walk 9 - Walks into History-Sussex by John Wilks, Published 2003 by Countryside Books

Warr (Bexhill?) captured Jean, King of France at the battle of Poitiers and, because of this, Sir John Pelham was presented with the Kings belt buckle as a badge of honour[95].

Further down the High Street and on our right we come to Keene Street. This Street is made from cobbled stone and brick and is very steep. This picture doesn't do it justice. It is here that King George IV, for a wager, drove a carriage and four horses down the street. How it was done I have no idea. I had a job to keep my footing, what it must have been like for a horse with shoes doesn't bear thinking about.

Keene Street

We now walk towards Priory Crescent and the Parish Church of St John the Baptist, Southover. This is a strange shaped church. You enter the church through the tower and turn left into the nave. From this doorway, straight ahead, is the chancel and altar. But to the right is a south aisle, which, if you sit at the front, you cannot see the altar. At the end of this south aisle and to the right is a small chapel known as Gundrada Chapel that was built in 1847[96]. This chapel houses the remains of William de Warenne and his first wife, Gundred (m.1070). These remains were found at the Cluniac[97] Priory during the building of the Brighton to Lewes Railway, which runs through the centre of the Priory.

William de Warenne[98] was the 1st Earl of Surrey and died in 1088. He was one of the aristocrats to fight at The Battle of Hastings and became a great landowner in England being awarded the Rape of Lewes as well as land in twelve other shires. Unfortunately, although our guide leaflet describes this chapel as an important part of our history, the chapel is currently being used as a storeroom. Roz was not impressed!!

The Warenne Chapel

We now proceed towards the Priory. We have to go down a road called Cockshut. I pronounced it as I read it. But, again, Roz corrects me. "Locals pronounce it Cockshoot," she informs us. "That can't be right," says Ron, "there ain't no double o t on t'end. So it must be shut. Cockshut." But Roz was adamant. So Cockshoot it is then.

All that remains here are a network of stone walls

The Priory remains

but you can get the real impression of what the overall size of the place was like back in the period when the Priory played an active part in the everyday life of the people of Lewes. Unfortunately, when we were looking round, the 14:25 train from Seaford (?) went through the middle of the remains, which gave the place a weird and surreal picture.

Anne of Cleves House

We now pass Anne of Cleves House[99], which is a timber framed house built in the 16th century as part of the divorce settlement from Henry VIII in 1541.

[95] www.villagenet.co.uk/sevensisters/villages/laughton.php - viewed 01/10/2006
[96] Leaflet – Parish Church of St John the Baptist, Southover – Printed by Barbican Press, Castle Ditch Lane, Lewes.
[97] Cluniac - order of Benedictine monks founded 910 in France – Universal Dictionary
[98] http://en.wikipedia.org/wiki/William_de_Warenne,_1st_Earl_of_Surrey visited 01/10/06
[99] http://www.sussexpast.co.uk/ - includes the photograph of the house

Shortly after is Lewes Railway Station and we head up towards the High Street, passing Pelham House. We cross the road into The Barbican, a walled area with the castle in view to our left. Lewes Castle is strange in itself having two mottes and a bailey. It was built by William de Warenne in 1087[100] and was originally called Bray Castle. As you walk through the Barbican Gate the castle remains can be seen on your left-hand side.

It is now just a short walk down to where we started, St John sub Castro and back to the car park. Of all the walks we have completed I have found this to be one of the best. I love history. This walk had all the history I could handle and some more. I have learnt so much today and both Ron and I can't thank Roz enough. Her enthusiasm for her subject really showed through and her knowledge of getting from point a to point b in Lewes is commendable. I have been through areas of Lewes I never knew existed and shown things that I never realised were there. Thank you so much for your time and the obvious trouble you went through. Not only the time it must have taken to plan and write the route but also passing on your knowledge of the area.

Next week it's my turn to decide on a walk. After today I'm not sure that I can find a walk to match this one. But, luckily for me, another birthday present that came my way, this one from my daughter, was a new book, titled 'Walks into History' Sussex[101]. With the new camera behaving beautifully, surely I can find somewhere to walk??

The famous Barbican

---

[100] http://en.wikipedia.org/wiki/Lewes_Castle viewed 01/10/06
[101] 'Walk into History, Sussex' by John Wilks Published by Countryside Books, Newbury, Cheshire

WALK 36 – Ewhurst Green

Saturday 7th October 2006

They say it is a woman prerogative to change her mind. But it can also happen to us males. On Monday when I met Ron at The Kings Head we were going to walk around Michelham Priory on Saturday. So how come, on Saturday, we are heading towards Ewhurst Green? I changed my mind at the last minute. I was sure that the Michelham Priory walk, starting at The Plough, walking for 5 miles and returning to The Plough for lunch was a nice

St James Church

way to spend a Saturday morning. Something changed my mind. The directions around Michelham, in the book, were a little vague. Some footpaths may be difficult to locate. As you will know both Ron and I have a poor sense of direction. Perhaps that is what persuaded me. But by the end of the evening, Ewhurst Green it was to be. It had clear instructions in our new book[102] and was completed in 3 miles. The walk not only included a castle, a 12th century church but also a 16th century pub. What more could we ask. All I need to do now is find out how to get to Ewhurst Green, yet another place I've never heard of.

Impressive Village Sign

We managed to find Ewhurst Green by heading for Bodiam Castle and looking out for street signposts. I had found a map that told me that Ewhurst Green was on the B2165 but then left the map at home. Typical. But we eventually found The White Dog Inn, Ewhurst Green, which is where we parked the car.

Our instructions tell us to turn right and walk along the road and pass the church. We could not pass the church without calling in and having a look. The churchyard of St James the Great is immaculately kept. As we walked towards the church door two motor mowers are in operation cutting the grass between the many monuments. Inside had that cold, old, welcoming feel, which has been missing in some of our visits to churches on recent walks. The aisle, towards the altar, is carpeted in red and looks and feels as if it is brand new. It gave

the impression that you had to remove your shoes before treading on it. I had read somewhere that there was a carved figure of a man blowing out his cheeks in the church but I was either mistaken or it had been removed because we couldn't locate it. I'll have to check my notes. A really good guide book[103] listing numerous facts relating to this beautiful church can be purchased just inside the doorway.

Church Interior

After leaving the church we pass the village sign and head down the road towards a house called 'The Old Library'. Just after the Great Fire of London, in 1666, the villagers of Ewhurst Green, then known as 'Yew Wood' collected the princely sum of seven shillings and eight pence (about 37p in today's money) for the relief of the poor of St Bartholomew for their losses sustained in the fire[104].

We arrive at 'The Old Library' and turn right through a

---

[102] Walks into History, Sussex by John Wilks, published by Countryside Books – Walk 11, page 73

[103] The Parish Church of St James The Great, Ewhurst by Gwen Jones & John Martin (Updated 2001) £3.00 from the church

[104] www.villagenet.co.uk/esussex-iron/villages/ewhurstgreen.php visited 06/10/2006

kissing gate. It is here that we get our first sighting of Bodiam Castle. A very majestic building that was completed in the year 1388. The founder of the castle was a Sussex knight, Sir Edward Dalyngrigge. He was born the son of minor landowning gentry near East Grinstead. He went to seek his fame and fortune, as a soldier in France during the early campaigns of the Hundred Years War. King Edward III rewarded his bravery, during this time, with a knighthood and he returned to England both famous and rich with plunder taken from the French. In 1377 he married Elizabeth Wardeaux, heiress to the manor at Bodiam.

The Hundred Years War saw sporadic campaigns by the English across the plains of

Where's the stile?

northern France and the French raided the southern coast of England. In 1372 the English had lost control of the Channel and the River Rother, which in those days was navigable as far inland as Bodiam, provided an inviting route into the heart of Sussex for French warships. In 1385 Sir Edward was given permission, by King Richard II, to fortify his manor house. Instead, Sir Edward decided to start from scratch and build a castle. The castle was never put to the test. By the time it was completed the English had regained control of the Channel and French raids ceased. Sir Edward made the castle his home until his death in 1395. His son John then took over residence.

As we walk down the field we pass, on our left, the recreation ground left to the Parish by Lieutenant A. Herdman, who was killed in the First World War. Young children are playing football, being coached by a supportive parent as mums and dads look on. At the bottom of the slope, just before some trees we turn left through a kissing gate. We then cross a stile ahead. Our instructions now tell us to turn half left. But if we do that we will be heading back, up the slope to where we started. Again we find an error in the instructions. The path is directing us right, not left. Which leads us to what should be a stile, next to a metal field gate. As you can see the stile no longer exists so we have to climb over the gate. "'Ere we go again," says Ron, "gets in 'ter the walk and things ain't what they're supposed 'ter be." For some reason I

The lucky ram

can't get my left leg over the gate whilst holding the camera, the thumb stick, the book, the note sheet and the pencil and the bottle of water all at the same time. Something has to go before I do. Just as my balance is going I throw the thumb stick, bottle of water, book and pad and manage to manoeuvre myself over the gate to hear Ron saying, "should complain 'ter the council, lazy bast&$ds, sitting in their

warm offices don't know what it's like ter be out 'ear in the real world!"

Wall to Wall sheep

We cross the next field, keeping the fence on our right until we reach the stile at the field bottom. To our left are fields of sheep. Wall to wall woollies. All with a blue mark on their backs. No other colour, just blue. For those who are unaware of what this blue mark signifies I will explain. The ram, (male) is fitted with a belt around his waist. On the belt is a coloured pad that is positioned on his belly. If more than one ram is being used, a different coloured pad will be on the belt. The ewes (females) are let into the same field as

Footbridge in corner

the ram (or rams). When the ram climbs onto the back of the ewe, to impregnate her, he will leave a coloured mark on her back. It is as simple as that. The farmer will now be able to know which ram has impregnated which ewe by the colour on the back of the ewe. From the photo it is difficult to see how many sheep there are but we can assure you that, as far as the eye can see, the fields are full of ewes. Each ewe has a blue mark. No other

Crossing the line

colour but blue, which means that one ram has 'serviced' every one of these ewes. Back at The Kings Head, Des informs us that one ram can 'service', on average, thirty ewes a day. Think of that guys. Thirty times a day, on average. I'm exhausted just thinking about it. But give the old ram credit. From the number of ewes in these fields he must have been going at it solidly for over two weeks. And what does he do at the end of it. No cigarette for him, just nibble away at some grass, waiting for the next batch to arrive.

We cross another field and turn right to go over a footbridge in the field corner. What seemed strange was that the footbridge looked brand new. Just a few yards away the stile had collapsed beyond repair yet here some work had been carried out to make a footbridge. We wonder why they didn't include the stile?

Bridge towards castle

Just in front of us, as described in our book, is a very large, unused barn. Again we have to cross another new footbridge and pass to the left of the barn. Ron has been collecting (or is it picking) mushrooms all along this walk. He has enough for a really nice breakfast when he gets home. You really can't beat fresh mushrooms, straight from the field. They have a totally different taste from mass produced fare obtained from supermarkets. If you haven't tried fresh mushrooms, give them a try you won't regret it. (Unless you don't like mushrooms, of course!) Shortly after the barn we have to cross a railway track via two stiles. "Track can't be used," says Ron, "look 'ow rusty the rails are." "But the book tells us to be careful and listen for trains," I reply, "and look up the

An impressive castle indeed

line, there's a level crossing gate that's about to be opened." Just as we are heading towards the River Rother four other walkers approach us going in the opposite direction. "Luv'ly mornin'," offers Ron in his usual cheery way. "That it is," says one of the gentlemen. "Where are you walkin' to?" asks Ron. "We're heading along the river towards Ewhurst Green," is the reply, "we've got this map from t'internet." They show Ron and me their map which turns out to be the exact route we are taking, but in reverse. "You get 'ter Ew'urst you must go an' see the church in the village. Wonderful place it is, an' well-kept too." I advised them that our

Train stopped at Bodiam Station

route had a mistake in it but if they follow the paths they should be ok and once over the railway line they will be able to see the church and head straight towards it. They thanked us for the assistance and headed on their way. "Nice people," says Ron. "Yes, I wonder if we will see them at the village when we get back."

We now head along the riverbank towards the road that will lead us to Bodiam Castle. The car park is quite full and I notice that a gatekeeper is taking money from people passing through. "You don't think we have to pay to walk round the castle, do you?" I ask Ron. "Didn't when I bought me son 'ere, but that was over 25 years ago." I check the book and it advises that an entrance fee is payable between February and the end of October. It is now that I notice a World War II pillbox just in front of the castle. What a strange thing to do. Wasn't the castle thought to be strong enough to resist the onslaught of Hitler?

Bodiam Station

Just as we are discussing the pro's and cons of bold sir knights and the requirements of a fall out shelter in the 1300's we hear the most pleasant noise in creation. A steam train. We turn round, and chugging away in the distance is an old steam railway engine, complete with carriages. Our minds are instantly made up. Both Ron and I are kids at heart. The sight and smell of a steam train will always win against a castle. I practically ran towards the railway line, along the road, heading away from the castle and towards a restored railway station of the 1950's era. The train, in the station was beautifully restored to its original colours and was a childish thrill to not only see the train but to be able to smell that distinctive smell of steam.

Read carefully

We stayed too long at the station, chatting to the stationmaster, and looking round his station, but there is nothing else in today's society that will bring back such fond memories, to both Ron and I, than the good old days of steam. Magnificent. Yet, on a visit to the Blue Bell Railway, when my children were a lot younger, they thought that steam trains were smelly, dirty, very noisy, as well as slow. The youth of today!

We take a last look at the castle and head up the road, past Bodiam Nurseries and we turn left along a private lane, coming to a stile and a couple of fields with new fencing surrounding the animals. Ron starts laughing at a sign on one of the fence posts. I wouldn't normally reproduce what he was laughing at but the opportunity couldn't be missed; so here it is. Obviously Mr Paine and his son are very proud of this boast.

We walk along a lane from here and turn left to head back to Ewhurst Green. We haven't met the people who were walking in the opposite direction so can only assume that they found the church ok. They didn't find the pub because we didn't see them when we popped in for a well-earned pint and a bar snack. Although the food was a little pricey it was hot, well presented and very edible. Ron has fallen in love with another barmaid who fluttered more than her eyelashes but I have always said that Ron was a bit of a smoothie!

A lovely walk, short but it had everything. Some of the memories that this walk brought back to me I will cherish forever.

WALK 37 – Rotherfield & Mayfield

Saturday 14th October 2006

I must just remind readers that I drive a minibus for Moira House Girls School and transport schoolgirls from the Hastings area to the school, in Eastbourne, and back home again. It was my birthday at the end of September. Two sisters, who use the school bus to and from Hastings, every day, are Halle and Ellen. For my birthday they brought me a couple of books on walks in Sussex. I was very touched by such a thoughtful gift. The discussion on Monday, with Ron, involved one of these books[105]. Mainly because we have never done this type of walk before. It is a ghost hunter's walk. Why anyone would want to 'hunt' a ghost I'm not sure but the thought of carrying out the walk in daylight hours is not so frightening for me. If it was at night, I would not be so happy.

Spooky nights[104]

I believe I am what is known as a sceptic when it comes to ghosts and spirits. I have not encountered the phenomenon and I am not sure that I actually believe in their existence. I hope I'm not going to be proved wrong on this walk. My wife talks to her departed father regularly and feels his presence often. I really do not have a problem with that. Since his sad departure I will admit that some strange things have happened in our house. Why does the clock, in our lounge, slow down or stop on his birthday? I have no answer. Since both my parents passed away last year I have neither heard, felt nor seen anything from them. Again I do not know why. Both Ron and our friend Rodney insist they have seen the ghost known locally as the 'grey lady' at Michelham Priory. My wife tells me that I am not receptive to these things. But how do you become receptive?

Our walk for Saturday is Walk No 8 in the book (Page 46) it is a total of seven miles and we start in Rotherfield, walk to Mayfield and then head back to Rotherfield. A very famous visitor to Mayfield, in the year 959, was a man who was dressed in a monks robe and carried

St Dunstan & the Devil[105]

The Kings Arms

a staff. What made him different from other passing holy men was that he pushed a cart on which were loaded tools of a blacksmith and he had enough cash on him to buy a plot of land just off the High Street. Some time later the villagers discovered that this man was Dunstan, Archbishop of Canterbury. He needed a place to get away from the pressures of high office and chose Mayfield to engage in his old trade so that he could do some good, honest work.

One day, whilst working at his forge, a very attractive young lady asked him to make some shoes for her horse. Dunstan agreed to make the shoes but was distracted by the young ladies beauty and attitude. Dunstan also thought it was strange that a beautiful and very friendly young lady should be travelling alone. It was then that Dunstan saw a cloven hoof poke out from the hem of her dress. The 'girl' was the Devil, come to tempt Dunstan from his vows of chastity. He immediately whipped out his red-hot tongs from the forge and grabbed the 'girl' by her nose. The girl promptly vanished to be replaced by the angry demon. Dunstan refused to let go and was dragged, by the Devil, into the High Street where the villagers watched the tug of

---

[105] 'Ghost Hunter Walks in Sussex' by Rupert Matthews, published by SB Publications in 2006
[106] Image obtained via www.google/images/cartoon ghost visited 11/10/06
[107] Image obtained from www.google/stdunstan/image 11/10/06

war. Eventually, the Devil escaped and vowed to take revenge on the villagers of Mayfield. Dunstan then forged sacred horseshoes for the villagers to place above their doors telling them that this would keep the devil away. Superstition or fact? Who knows?

Our walk starts opposite the Kings Arms, in the High Street at Rotherfield. We are told, from our guidebook, that this lovely old pub hit the headlines in the early 1950's when the ghost of a young girl was seen and heard running around upstairs.

The girl was more often heard than seen; her footsteps seemed to run along the corridor into one of the bedrooms. When she was seen, it was only briefly, so descriptions tend to be a little vague. She is about 9 and wears a dress that reaches to her knees, and not much more is said.

The downstairs area of the pub is said to have an invisible spirit that taps patrons on the shoulder. When they turn round, of course, there is nobody there. I make a mental note not to stop here on the way back.

Local fishing area

Our instructions[108] are to head along the High Street, along the road, towards some overhanging trees. We should have realised something was amiss when we read *'this short section of the route is along a fairly busy lane, so care needs to be taken of passing traffic.'* We found that this *'short section'* was well over a mile long, all uphill and *'the fairly busy lane'* was busier than the southbound carriageway of the A22. You had to take your life in your hands, with no footpath; we were both leaping in to gaps in the hedge every few yards. But some of the houses, along this stretch you would die for!

On our left is a house called Rotherhurst House. Here we turn left and go downhill for a change. Our book tells us to walk for a mile when we will find another turning on the left. It seemed like two miles? Every few yards along this road I had noticed that white boxes had been left, or thrown on the ground. They were all empty but were exactly the same? Why would anyone, in the middle of nowhere, leave these boxes on the side of the road, every few yards? We must have seen 15 or 20 of these boxes.

Unusual litter

Another thing that I had noticed was the number of different fungi that seemed to be growing along the roadside. When I asked Ron about this he told me "'tis 'cos of the poachers moon. They be gone in a couple o'days. Be back in the next full moon an' then gone ag'in." "Are they all edible?" I ask. "No they aint," is the reply, "but if animals like slugs 'ave eaten 'em they can't be that bad, can they? But don't try any, just in case," he warns me, "long way from 'ere ter the nearest 'ospital by foot." I want to ask him what a 'poachers moon' is, but decide to keep quite.

Fungus

After a mile (?) we find a turning on the left, which is called Argos Hill. We are told to ignore this turning and head for the next, just a few yards further along the road. At this junction is one of Phil's wooden finger posts. It's in need of some tender loving care but we both noticed that there are no mileages on the post. Have they been removed, have they been nicked for some ghostly purpose or has Phil just forgotten to put them on? Yet another unanswered question?

No mileages on posts

---

[108] *Ghost Hunter Walks in Sussex* by Rupert Matthews (Published by SB Publications, Seaford) Page12

We turn left at the next junction and follow the quiet winding lane. In our last walk I spoke of, and learnt a little about, the facts of life of our woolly farm animals. I spoke of

Picture 1

coloured pads worn by the ram, so that when he mounts the ewe a coloured dye would be left on its back. From Picture 1 how did she get the dye on the back of her head and isn't Picture 2 a bit of a hussy?

At the end of this lane we find we are on the busy main A267. We cross this road and get to a lane, which leads us, uphill, into Mayfield. Halfway up the hill is a seat, donated by the Parish to commemorate the completion of the bypass around this very old village. I can remember Mayfield before the bypass and it was a little hub of a place with shops all along the High Street and steps down to the road. A really quaint old town. Now, unfortunately, probably due to the bypass, all passing trade has gone and little is left of the hustle and bustle that I remember when visiting my aunt and uncle so many years ago. My last visit

Picture 2

to the church here was when I attended a double wedding of my cousins, which must be over 30 years ago. God how time flies.

The church is dedicated to Saint Dunstan and a wonderful history of the church can be

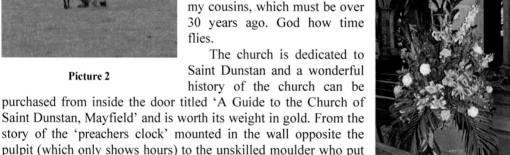

purchased from inside the door titled 'A Guide to the Church of Saint Dunstan, Mayfield' and is worth its weight in gold. From the story of the 'preachers clock' mounted in the wall opposite the pulpit (which only shows hours) to the unskilled moulder who put the number '7' and the letters 'N' and 'S' back to front on one of the three tomb slabs set in the nave floor are just two of the many facts found in this little gem of a booklet[109]. The church grounds are well-kept and the inside of the church is, as usual, a beauty to behold. Unfortunately, scaffolding has been erected for much needed repairs so I didn't take that many photographs. Also this was to be our first church on this walk. We also need to see the church at Rotherfield so I need to save space in the chapter for later on in the walk.

St Dunstan Church

We now leave Mayfield and retrace our steps back along to the busy A267, cross back over the road and head for a turning, on our right to Pages Farm. Our instructions tell us to head towards Pages Farm by *'taking this driveway to its far end.'*

To Pages Farm

What it fails to tell you is that the drive winds itself up a very step hill. Our guidebook also advises that the farm is on the left, by a pond, and the path continues straight ahead across open farmland towards a windmill. Halfway up the hill I have to stop. I'm shattered but both Ron and I use the rest time to collect chestnuts that have fallen from the trees. I've now got so many chestnuts in my pockets my trousers won't stay up. I must be loosing weight!

It isn't until you get to the farm and the drive turns into a bridleway that our book tells us that the path may be very wet and muddy and it may be advisable not to walk all the way up the drive but take an alternative route from the bottom of the hill. It is also at this

---

[109] A Guide to the Church of Saint Dunstan, Mayfield, Text by Jean Barnes, Pub 2003 Price £3

point that I notice a large sign warning that a guard dog is loose. Something big starts to bark. I'm through the gate like a rocket. Ron is close behind me. We still have an uphill bridleway to climb and the chestnuts are getting heavier. This bridleway seemed to go forever. Again I notice more different mushroom type fungi on the banks of the path. Some are really strange colours. Reds, pinks, greens and all look as if they had been eaten, at some time by animals. Yet there was one whole group of fungi that had not been touched. They are very small mushrooms and grow in clumps.

Fungi group

Eventually we arrive at the end of the bridleway and meet a lane. We are told to turn left here and '*follow the lane downhill to a T-junction.*' We turn left but the lane is uphill? Since starting our walks this must be the first where, after two hours of walking, we are still going uphill. At last the top of the hill is reached and it is a pleasant change to be going downhill towards one of the most picturesque cottages I have ever seen. Which started us thinking of winning the lottery. Owning one of these beautiful places must cost a few quid

If only I won the Lottery

but would you want to live out here? The insurance alone must cost a fortune and whilst the surroundings are very peaceful and you would be close to nature, the thought of being away and the house left unoccupied would scare the hell out of me. There are no neighbours to keep an eye on the place. There is no such thing as the local bobby (policeman). I really don't think I would like to live in the countryside but I am very grateful that we are able to walk and admire what others have acquired knowing that it is their responsibility and not mine.

It is now that everything went wrong. We are told to look for a place called Holme Park on our left. We didn't see it. We were told to turn right up Sherriff's Lane. We never saw Sherriff's Lane. We are told to head towards Town Row. You guessed it. Never found it. And why you may ask. I'll tell you. We turned left too soon and found ourselves walking, not towards Rotherfield, but on the lane that emerges at Argos Hill (Page 359)! We are now 4 miles off route and all we can do is retrace our steps back along the road and into Rotherfield.

The walk back to the village is carried out in practically silence. I can't believe I would make a stupid mistake like that. Ron doesn't seem to mind yet he gives a little giggle every now and then. I can imagine what he's laughing at.

Tree at St Denys Church

Rotherfield[110] was a royal estate and is mentioned in the last will and testament of King Alfred in 899AD. It is mentioned again in about 1015 in the will of the third son of King Edgar when the lands were to be given to the Nuns Minster of St Mary's, in Winchester, together with one silver crucifix, value £5, a lot of money in those days. St Denys' was a Frenchman who became the first Bishop of Paris. On the orders of the Roman Emperor he was tortured and beheaded for refusing to offer sacrifices in the Temple of Mercury. Legend has it that his decapitated corpse was taken north where the Abbey of St Denys' was founded. Back at Rotherfield (then known as Ridrefeld) Duke Bertoald, the Duke of the South Saxons, was taken ill and went to France to seek a cure. He visited the Abbey of

---

[110] A Guide to St Denys' Church, Rotherfield, East Sussex – Leaflet – Printed by St Denys' Printing Service. Available from the church.

St Denys' and in a few days, by the mercy of God, he was completely cured. As a thank-offering he built a church on his estate in Ridrefeld in the year 792AD.

Within the current churchyard of St Denys' must be one of the oldest trees in existence. Said to be over 1,500 years old and still surviving even though it is practically hollow. Another peculiarity (?) of the church is that the pews at the back rise slightly above the other pews, giving the effect of sitting in a theatre. Again the grounds are well-kept and it was a pleasure to carry out a walk and find that both churches were open for us to see. Unfortunately, the lights at St Denys' Church had been vandalised and the place was a little dark. But this didn't detract from what is a very beautiful, atmospheric church. Again a guide to the church is available.

500 yards past the church is the Middle House Hotel. This was the hostelry where Queen Elizabeth I stayed when she visited in the 1570's. The ghost here dates from around the 1770's. The landlord at that time had a wife, whom he found most inconsiderate when his mistress came calling. On the evenings when his girlfriend was due to visit for some illicit lovemaking, the landlord would drug his wife's dinner so that she would collapse into unconsciousness. One evening, however, he made a mistake in the dosage and the wife woke up whilst her husband was in the throes of passion. Picking up an iron bar she smashed in his head, then fled.

The wife was never seen again, at least not in mortal form. It was not long, however, before she began to return to the Middle House and nearby areas in ghostly form. Dressed in a long grey dress and carrying the fatal iron bar.

We have come to the end of a slightly different walk than usual. Although it was originally to be seven miles I think, due to a wrong turning, we covered almost twelve miles. But all in all it was very pleasant. Thankfully we saw no ghosts; sadly we didn't have time to drink any spirits.

St Denys Church

Next week we may be back to a normal type of walk, who knows? I have a couple of villages that I would like to visit, one is a village said to contain more thatched cottages than any other village in the country. But I'll have to decide on which walk it will be on Monday.

WALK 38 - Balcombe

Saturday 21st October 2006

Things have been going a little strange at The Kings Head since the start of our walks, over nine months ago. The atmosphere has changed and it is very noticeable how many 'locals' do not now use the pub. I have my theories but here and now is not the place to air my views. Suffice to say that our landlady has decided that the time has come to cover the pumps for the last time and is leaving her trade for pastures new at the end of this month. I don't know why but I wasn't surprised to hear that Ron would not be using The Kings Head until the new tenants arrived. So this Monday's meeting is to be carried out at a new venue, The Grenadier. Yes, it is another pub in Hailsham. It's still a Harvey house so Ron will still be able to have is regular pints of Harvey's best bitter.

Last week's walk finished with me thinking of going to Amberley, or Climping. These walks were discussed in our usual manner. We thought about the pros and cons of both walks, including length in miles and gradients in feet. After much discussion and in depth analyses we have decided to walk in Balcombe[111], famous for its railway viaduct, which we will see just over halfway round this 7½-mile walk. My usual look on the Internet found nothing on Balcombe, so I was a little apprehensive when I picked Ron up on a wet Saturday morning.

St Marys Church

Also waiting for me, outside the Kings Head was Marian. Now Marian used to be in a profession that I have a real problem with. Marian used to be a taxi driver in Hailsham. I am not prejudiced when I say that I do not like taxi drivers who are women, because I dislike all taxi drivers. They have their own set of rules when it comes to stopping on roundabouts, across your driveway, on double yellow lines, on pavements or hogging any available centimetre of space in the High Street, although they have their own reserved spaces to park, called taxi ranks. What makes it worse is that our local constabulary will always turn a blind eye to anything illegal that these drivers do. Yet have you tried to park on a taxi rank in the town? They are some of the most abusive drivers around. Yet they seem to be above the law. I will now climb down from my soapbox. Marian has seen the light and left this obnoxious trade!

Has he left his hat & coat?

On the way to Balcombe it started to rain again. It started to rain very hard. The sky looked black with rain clouds yet Ron is still his jovial self explaining to both Marian and I that it is a clearing up shower and that it will stop raining when we get to Balcombe. And it did. How does he do that?

The first place we visit is the church. This was a hive of industry with people mowing the grass, edging the pathways and cleaning. The welcome we received was very warm and we had no end of advice from the locals on where to go and what to see. One lady even offered us tea and biscuits while we waited for the weather to improve. What caught my eye was the hat and coat hanging over the stone cross. Perhaps the interred was about to take a stroll and had some insider information about the weather? But the Parish Church of St Mary, Balcombe is a

---

[111] Walks into History, Sussex by John Wilks Walk 16 – Page 104

beautiful, large structure. From the outside it doesn't look that big but it is like a Tardis. Once inside it looks and feels very impressive. From the booklet purchased in the church[112] I discovered that a church had stood on this spot since the year 1090, when records show that the church was given to the Priory of St Pancras at Lewes. The present church was classified

in 1987 as Grade 1 (the highest listing) because of its special historic and architectural interest. A nice touch that I haven't seen in other churches is a remembrance book, kept under glass, opened on today's date. Just as we were leaving we were presented with a small pocket diary each, "just something to remember us by," said the lady.

Leaving the church we head towards the village of Balcombe. We pass the Half Moon pub on our left. The pub is dated 1735[113] and both Ron and Marian gave it long glances as we walked past. "Don't worry, we'll be able to call in on the way back," I inform them, "the pub is on the return leg." Both seemed happier at the thought.

We pass the village stores and turn right along a tarmac drive.

Wherever Ron goes, his carrier is always with him

At the end of the drive is a kissing gate, which we pass through, and head down the left side of the field. I mentioned the rain. It had been very heavy, not only during the night but for most of the journey to Balcombe. Marian is wearing trainers. One of our previous companions wore trainers and regretted it. It really must be a 'girlie thing'. As we slip and slide down the field Marian is now regretting the trainers, "Knew I should have brought me wellies," she says just as her mobile phone rings. Apparently bringing a mobile phone

Wet fields

was the most important thing on her mind yet keeping her feet dry and ensuring she didn't fall over in the mud wasn't. It is definitely a 'girlie thing'.

One of the habits that Ron and I have, whilst walking, is to inform the person behind you of any hazards ahead. If anyone hears us shout 'Cow', 'Horse', or 'Elephant' it simply means that there is a mound of manure in line with our path. 'Low branch', 'deep mud', 'animals' are also used as warnings. I am leading down this field and call 'Cow' as a warning to both Ron and Marian following behind. Ron either didn't hear me or wasn't following my lead. There is a yell from behind me

Boardwalks

followed by a squelching sound and Ron is up to his ankles in cow dung. Marian is laughing at the

Beautiful reflections

sight of Ron trying to get the dung off his boots. "Do you know where the word s.h.i.t. comes from?" asks Marian between giggles. "Apparently animal excrement used to be loaded into a ships hold and then transported overseas." "Why would they want to do that?" I ask. "No idea," says Marian, "but when it arrived at distant ports, due to humidity below decks,

---

[112] The Parish Church of St. Mary, Balcombe. Printed by The Throgmorton Agency, Buttlesland Street, London -Price £1
[113] www.travelpublishing.co.uk/CountryPubsSussex/chapter3/CPS31092.htm visited 22/10/2006

the manure was useless. They decided that if the manure was to be stored higher in the hold the heat would not affect it. So to ensure this was carried out they used to stamp the container with the letters S.H.I.T. which means Store High In Transit." Is this a Marian Gem or just bull s(tore) h(igh) i(n) t(ransit)?

Walking down this field we are entering Balcombe Park, formerly the grounds of Highley Manor and laid out in the 14th century as a deer park by the Duke of Norfolk. Highley Manor

is now demolished but the large Georgian house on our left is Balcombe House, formerly the village rectory.

We continue down the field to reach a kissing gate leading into woods. The instructions now advise us to take various paths that lead us to the bank of Balcombe Reservoir. All the paths are well signposted so we have no problems at all. Slipping on the mud is a problem for Marian and her trainers. I must give Marian credit. She slipped on more than one occasion. Once I heard Ron say "I'll give yer 9 point 9 fer that pirouette Marian. You'd 'ave got a ten but yer left one foot on the ground." But not once did she swear or loose control.

Despite the rural impression of Balcombe Reservoir it was actually man-made as a fishing lake for Highley Manor. Regular readers will be aware of my love for the water. Especially taking photographs of

Marian's most important phone calls

reflections. Our very first walk was around Arlington Reservoir and I was hoping to make some comparison

between Arlington, Balcombe and Ardingly with photographs to show the difference. The immediate difference between Arlington and Balcombe is size. Balcombe is a lot smaller yet, somehow, this adds to the beauty of the place. Again, searching the Internet for information about Balcombe Reservoir revealed nothing except the type of fish that can be caught there.

Deadly fungi??

We now follow the bank of the Reservoir to a kissing gate and more fields. Again Marian has to answer her mobile whilst trying to keep her feet dry. On our last walk I mentioned the different types of fungi found growing in the fields and along high banks. This walk was no different except that most of the fungi on this walk hadn't been eaten which would suggest

that it should be left well alone. One such fungus was brown in colour with white spots but the different colours and shapes are a credit to what nature can produce. In one field Ron managed to find some mushrooms that he recognised and it seems that his breakfast for Sunday morning is sorted out.

Leaving Balcombe Reservoir behind us we now head towards Ardingly Reservoir. After a few more fields we come to a road and we turn left. After a few yards we cross the head of Ardingly Reservoir and turn right through a gate. This is the main entrance to Ardingly Reservoir. We now descend a path and follow the lakeside shore for 1½ miles. The Reservoir is enormous and is no comparison to Arlington or Balcombe. It is a hive of natural beauty and the size of the overall area is outstanding. The Reservoir was created in 1978 when a dam was constructed to flood 78 hectares of land. The water collected here is used to top up the River Ouse in times of drought. From the pictures it can be seen that the water level is quite low in comparison to the height of the bank. This is another difference with Arlington Reservoir, which was relatively full at the time

Balcombe Reservoir

of our walk. I hope the pictures on this page reflect, not only the physical size of this place but also the natural beauty. This has to be one of the most picturesque places in Sussex.

I tried to find out how big 78 hectares is. I am informed by Des[114] that there are 3½ acres to 1 hectare and each acre measures 70 by 70 yards. One acre equals 4,900 sq yards (70*70). So one hectare measures 17,158 sq yards (4,900*3.5). If this calculation is correct that means that 78 hectares equals 1,337,700 sq yards (17,158*78). Is that big or is that BIG? I wonder how many gallons of water that is.

Wood carving

After 1½ miles we cross the lake at a causeway. At the far end of this causeway we turn right and resume our walk along the lakeside path for a further mile until we reach the dam and the visitors centre with its much-needed toilets. As we approach the visitors' centre I notice a wooden carving on the bend that made me look twice. A very large creature had been carved out of wood that looked ominously at you as you pass.

We now climb a short bank and follow the path through a number of fields, heading towards Balcombe Viaduct. It has now started to rain. Despite Ron's promise and the offer for Marian to beat him about the head with her thumb stick if it should rain, the heavens opened. At least Marian had packed a coat in her bright mauve haversack and really looks the part as we walk alongside the River Ouse. Unfortunately the rain made the pathways even more sodden and keeping dry feet and an upright position become a bit more of a problem. But Marian remained cheery throughout the walk which seemed to me to be getting longer than the 7½ miles that it was supposed to be.

Marian feels the rain

Balcombe Viaduct was an essential link in the London to Brighton Railway. The viaduct was designed in 1842 by John Urpeth Rastrick, a largely self-taught civil engineer. The 37 brick arches carried the track 1,475 feet across the valley, 80 feet up at the highest point. The viaduct was the most ambitious piece of railway engineering in Sussex and also one of the longest viaducts in England. Caen limestone was imported to face the brickwork, and architect David Moccata was employed to add aesthetic touches such as the classical balustrade and the mock Grecian pagodas on each end. A very impressive construction indeed but as Ron said "I'm glad I wasn't first train ter go over it!"

Balcombe Viaduct

Someone's got wet feet?

Our walk is now coming to an end. Or that's what Ron and Marian think. I've got the map and it still looks as if we have another 3 miles to go before we can rest with a welcome pint at the Half Moon. Since our early downpour the rain has stopped and it's getting warm again. Underfoot, as we make our way through fields and along lanes, is still difficult and it's beginning to get tiring as we slog it out up steep hills but Ron is still all smiles. Field follows field and lanes look longer. We have to walk back over the very busy railway line and follow an enclosed path up a hill

---

[114] Des Pelling, Kings Head

towards more fields. On the way up this hill I notice, again, yet more fungi growing next to the track. All were pure white, growing in a small clump. It's amazing how many different varieties there are.

We pass the bottom of what looks like a rock formation but a tree seems to be growing in the face. "If you look carefully," says Marian, "you can see a baby holding on to the trunk, halfway up. Do you see it?" We finally reach the recreation ground at Balcombe where the local teams are battling it out in a local derby. "Can't see any potential internationals out there," says Ron as the ball bounces between player and goalkeeper. "Maybe not," I reply "but at least they're not play acting or swearing and spitting at the referee." "No, they learn that sort o'thing when they start earnin' money!"

The footpath from the recreation ground along a road called 'Jobes' takes us out and in front of The Half Moon. Marian looks physically shattered and reckons a hot bath and four days sleep should make her feel better. I must admit that the walk did seem to be longer than 7½ miles but we have said that before about other walks. We started out at 11 o'clock and the time is now 3.45 so we had been walking some time.

Next week's walk is arranged already. My wife sees that as a reason for me not to go out on Monday night. But an offer of horse riding had been made to both Ron and me, during my half term holiday from the school, so I'll have to go out to finalise the details. Well, that's my excuse.

Strange rock formation

WALK 39 - Cowbeech

Thursday 26th October 2006

We are now ¾'s of the way through our year of walks. We have reached a bit of a milestone for both Ron and me and, possibly, a need to celebrate? The weather has started to take a turn for the worse. It seems to rain more days than not. The ground is getting boggy, the air cold and the walks are becoming more and more difficult to write about. I'm a bit down and need something to give me a lift. The Kings Head isn't the same without Ron sat at

the bar. Whilst he now drinks at other pubs I can't bring myself to do that. The Kings Head is 'my local' and has been for more years than I can remember. I don't feel comfortable anywhere else and I don't think Ron does either. Our new landlord and landlady take over next week so I am hoping that things may revert back to the way they were.

The Merrie Harriers

Although both Ron and I met at the Grenadier on Monday the walk for Thursday was already worked out. A few weeks ago Ron mentioned to one of his customers,

Audrey, that I enjoyed building model boats. Audrey's husband also enjoyed model making and had brought a boat, as a kit, but sadly he passed away before he had chance to start it. Audrey asked Ron to pass the kit to me, for which I am very grateful. Audrey would not accept anything for the kit so it was decided that we would invite her on one of our walks (payment or punishment?). It was agreed that the walk would be short and that at the end I would buy Audrey dinner, as a thank you for the boat. Luckily, Audrey accepted our invitation and asked if we could dine at The Merrie Harriers, Cowbeech, as her daughter worked there. A table was booked for 1.30 on Thursday. Lyn was also invited as official photographer, to record the celebrations, and the pub walk has been found in our book[115]; so its all systems go.

Audrey insisted not to break tradition and found her way to The Kings Head pick-up point for 10 o'clock. The approximate distance of this walk is only 4½ miles and should take us about two hours. Parking is no problem. The pub isn't open when we arrive so there were plenty of spaces right outside.

Two posers?

We leave the car and turn right heading towards Shaw's Garage. I can remember when this place actually sold petrol and cars. It is now more of an

agricultural outlet and has got rid of the pumps. There are always lots of cars on what used to be the forecourt but I'm never sure who or why they're always there. They can't all work for Shaw's yet they can't always be that busy with customers that the forecourt is full up.

Our instructions are to turn right where a finger post points to Warbleton. Part of the way down this lane should be a turning on the left that is the official 'right of way'. Unfortunately the path was not passable when our book was written and to be honest we never saw the turning. What we did see was some real Sussex cattle. I had seen

Sussex Bull

---
[115] Pub Walks in East Sussex by Mike Power-Published by Power Publications Walk 11, Page 29

pictures of these large beasts but had never seen one close up. Today was a first for me. They are really big. Not just the bull but also the cows seem enormous too. We walked only a few feet away from them and they showed absolutely no fear. They just stood and stared at us, truly magnificent animals.

More Cousins machinery

We continued down the lane until, just before the waterworks, and on a bend, we found the alternative route in our guidebook that would take us up the drive towards Blackbird Farm. Pheasants can be heard along this lane, which prompted Ron to ask our lady companions if they knew how to stop pheasants making a noise. "Make a sound like a shotgun," he says, "that soon shuts the buggers up!" The driveway towards the farm is a little steep. Lyn reminds me that there is no indication that hills needed to be climbed

Farm driveway

in our guidebook. It is now that I realise that all girlie things cannot be pointed at our female companions. Both are wearing suitable attire, not trainers, and Lyn has actually foregone her handbag. She still has her mobile phone and 'ciggies' but she has them in her pocket. Audrey is used to walking with her dogs so is well prepared for all eventualities, including a 'mac. Halfway up the drive Ron notices a piece of machinery, sporting his name and poses next to it. The plastic bag has now become his trademark. The drive rises gradually and we meet a tarred drive. We walk past the farm and its barking Labradors and eventually reach a lane.

Immediately on our left are some steps leading up to a gate. We climb the steps and enter the field and bear left, heading for a gate in the far boundary. The view from the top of this field is tremendous and again we wonder at the beauty of this county we call home. At the end of the field we go through a gate and into the bluebell wood. As it's been raining over the past few days the path is very slippery in places and care is needed to make sure that your footing is sure. Audrey seems to be amused about our warning calls for water, muddy, horse and slippery as we wind our way through this beautiful setting.

Bluebell Wood

Demolished stile

As with many of our walks, from our guidebooks, the instructions aren't and can't be what is written. This is one of the reasons we encourage company on our walks, just to prove that Ron and me aren't so thick and others can see the errors in our directions. For now, at the far end of the bluebell wood, we are confronted with a ploughed field. Our guidebook tells us to '*bear slightly right up the rise to a stile, cross into a field and head up to the top keeping close to the field boundary on the right.*'[116] The sign on the gate tells us to turn left or walk across the middle of the ploughed field. If we bear right we, again will have to walk across a ploughed field. I also notice at this point that, without exception, everyone has gone very quiet. It's obvious who is going to have to make the decision and who is going to be blamed should I make a wrong decision. So we turn left and head around the edge of the ploughed field. I thought I'd read somewhere

---

[116] *Pub Walks in East Sussex* by Mike Power (Dorset, Power Publications) Page 29

that if a farmer made a public right of way impassable he had to restore the public right of way within a certain time. I'll have to check that out, but in the mean time, after walking all

Beautiful countryside view

around the field, it was obvious why we couldn't see the stile. It had been demolished. But at least I'd made the right decision and we are back on route.

We now wander through a couple of fields and up through another small wooded area until we reached a lane. Would you believe we actually came out next to Shaw's Garage and are now about 750 yards away from where we started? Up and over the stile and onto the lane now heading towards a lovely large cottage called 'Inchmerry Cottage'. Just past here Ron noticed a gate,

Audrey, as ladylike as ever

heading into fields with a ladies undergarment stretched from one post to the other. "Must have blown off someone's washing line," says Audrey. "She must 'a been a big girl," replies Ron, "wouldn't want to meet 'er on a dark night, walkin' back from the 'arriers".

Just past Inchmerry Cottage is a small track, on the left, leading to a stile. We climb the stile into the field and need to bear half-right and head for a number of stiles. All these stiles have been replaced by a gate, which makes it so much easier to go through rather than over. Although, it must be said, that both our female companions managed the many stiles with the utmost femininity and grace. Once inside the field you are able to see for some considerable miles to the north of the county. Although this field had a large and somewhat frisky horse, running free our previous day's lesson with Teresa[117] has me brimming with confidence and, although he trotted very close, and in front of me, I was not afraid. Scared perhaps but at least I didn't show it.

We now exit the fields and join a lane, which if we continued, would lead us into Herstmonceux. But we turn left into the entrance of Greenway Fruit Farm. Here, again, I have a problem with the guidebook because it says that the public footpath leads us to 'Studdings Lane'. Yet, many years ago, when I was the postie in the area, the lane was called Studdens Lane, and not Studdings. But Audrey points to the stone marker and it does say Studdings. Now I'm even more confused.

Greenway Fruit Farm

Our instructions tell us to pass through the orchard and follow the track. I was amazed at how large this fruit farm is. I used to deliver the mail to the farmhouse but never ventured into this part of the property. Again, because of the rain, the track was very muddy and care had to be taken. But it reminded me very much of our walk in Pluckley with the exception that it appeared that many of the apples in this orchard had been left to rot on the ground. Ron, of course, made many

---

[117] See 'Walk Extra' chapter at back of book dated 24/10/2006

comments about 'waste of money', 'disgustin' ter just leave 'em ter rot', 'too lazy to pick em up' etc. etc. Over three quarters of the way through the orchard I noticed, what I thought to be an apple called 'Braeburn'. None had been picked and all the trees were swelling with fruit. A

few had fallen to the ground and I picked one, bit into it and it was a very beautifully tasting Braeburn. "Do you realise that's stealing," says Lyn. "I'd call it quality control," I replied. "You could get done for that," she continues. "I picked it up from the ground," I counter. "I saw you pick it from the tree," she accuses. Now that's the sort of friend you need as a character reference. Drop you in the s£&t for the fun of it. Then, to cap it all, all three of my accusing friends go into great detail on how they used to go scrumping, on a regular basis, when they were youngsters. I call that double standards but Lyn made me feel so guilty that I couldn't finish the apple and dropped it after a couple of mouthfuls.

At the end of the orchard is a gate that leads us into a very pretty woodland path. As soon as I mention that we have to cross

Pooh sticks again

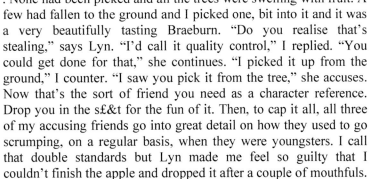

two bridges all three say 'Pooh sticks'. What is it about bridges and the need to play Pooh sticks? But off they ran, like schoolkids, rummaging about for a suitable stick to drop in the water. You wouldn't believe the cheating that went on, just to get his stick under the bridge first.

We now approach what I know as Studdens Lane and I am surprised at how open and clear the area is. When I delivered mail here it was overgrown, damp and the old farmhouse at this end of the lane was very much in need of some restoration work. Obviously the current owners of Old Studdens Farm had done a lot of clearance

Llamas

and renovation work that I hardly recognised the place. The walk up the lane to an area known as Trolliloes brought back very fond memories of my postman days including the strange animals that are kept at Studdens Farm. And at the end of the lane is the old sign that does read, Studdens Lane.

At the end of the lane we turn left and walk along the road for about half a mile and we are back at The Merrie Harriers. The walk has taken under two hours and brought back fond memories for me. We are all now ready for a meal, and although we are early the staff at the pub have our table laid out for us.

The Merrie Harriers dates from about 1624[118] and is a Grade II listed building. The menu is served 7 days a week, and although, in my opinion, pricey the food is both delicious and very well presented, but it would have been nice to have a little more on the plate. I can thoroughly

Just had to take a photo

recommend the chicken with brie followed by any one of their gorgeous desserts. Our hostesses were discretely attentive and we managed to relax and unwind in pleasant surroundings. On the way home Lyn relaxes that much she nearly falls asleep. Something to do with food and wine, she says.

The clocks go back this weekend, which I believe, means that it gets darker, earlier. I will have to bear that in mind when we decide on the walk for next week. I've had a week off from the school because of half term holidays but I'm back to normal next Monday. I'm leaning towards a walk around Fletching. It seemed a pleasant village when we passed through it to get somewhere. Now where were we heading?

---

[118] http://merrieharriers.co.uk/about_the_pub.htm

WALK 40 - Fletching

Saturday 4th November 2006

Monday was the last day for Bev (our landlady) to be serving behind the bar of The Kings Head. A few people have come to say goodbye so it was slightly busier than normal for a Monday night. Ron and Rodney have decided to call in.

As I suggested at the end of our last walk I fancy Fletching. We passed through Fletching on our way to Horsted Keynes. My only personal memory of Fletching is that a famous comedian of the 1950's and 60's, the late Jimmy Edwards, owned property there. When I played trombone for a band we performed at the St Etienne Theatre at East Grinstead with Jimmy Edwards and another comedian of that time, Cyril Fletcher. Little did I realise that Fletching would be associated with some of our other walks until I, as usual, did a little research before our walk takes place.

The late J. Edwards[117]

On the 13th May 1264, just before the Battle of Lewes Simon de Montfort stopped at Fletching to celebrate mass and for the Bishop of Worcester (?) to bless his troops. In 1450 the great rebellion of Jack Cade (a future walk??) affected Fletching when Peter Denot, a Glover by trade, and others from the village took part in the uprising, but were subsequently pardoned. Within the church at Fletching is a brass of Sir Walter Dalyngrigge and his wife dated around 1380, one of Sir Walters sons, Sir Edward, was responsible for building the last great medieval castle at Bodiam. [119]

Something that tops all of these facts and dates from our past is the 4th of November 1972 at 2 pm. The date and time my true love became my wife. Within the past 34 years we have had our problems but we are still together, and our feelings for each other are still as strong, if not stronger, than ever. With today's attitudes towards marriage that may sound old-fashioned but I made a promise to my wife, on that day, at that time, and I am proud to say that I have kept that promise although at times, as I said, it's not always been plain sailing. But who else would let their husband go for a walk, with a mate, on their wedding anniversary? I have a lot to thank my wife for. I only hope she enjoys the very expensive restaurant I'm taking her to this evening, for letting me go on the walk!

The walk around Fletching is taken from The Argus 'East Sussex Walks'[120] by Ben Perkins and can be found on page 26. It is described as *'a five mile walk in the upper Ouse valley, linking Piltdown and Fletching.'* We start the walk in Piltdown; head towards Sharpsbridge, up to Fletching and return to Piltdown via the Piltdown Golf Course, so it's the usual pick up, at 10 o'clock from the Kings Head, on a bright but frosty morning. Marian enjoyed her last walk so much that she is also waiting, with Ron, for me at the Kings Head.

It is just a short drive to Piltdown and the subject of conversation centres around pyrotechnics. (Firework displays to you and me!) Ron is amazed at the cost of some of these rockets that will only last a few seconds. "Let's not light this one," he chuckles, "it cost nearly forty quid, we can save it fer next year. People must 'ave something loose ter spend that sort of money on fireworks." I can remember, when I was in the band, marching at East Hoathly, Lewes, Newick and Herstmonceaux bonfire processions and they were good fun. But as the years went on it started to become frightening as some idiots threw fireworks into the processions. Unfortunately, as with all things, it only takes a minority to spoil it for everyone.

---

[119] www.villagenet.co.uk/ashdownforest/villages/fletching.php - visited 1st November 2006.
[120] The Argus 'East Sussex Walks' by Ben Perkins Page 26

When we arrive at Piltdown we park near a pond. Again I have to say that I have driven through this small village many times and never realised that this pond existed. But it is a beautiful setting and the reflections on the water are very clear.

Piltdown Pond and its wonderful reflection

We head along what is described as '*a quiet, reasonably traffic-free lane*'[121] for almost a mile until we reach a place called Little Sharps on our left. Here we turn right, over a stile and find that the way is marked as 'The Fletching Millenium Trail'. It is this trail that we are to follow. Our next instructions are a little strange, because, again, we are instructed to walk across the middle of a field. I was always taught to walk around the outside edge of fields,

We keep to the outside

something about the 'country code'. The same as making sure that all the gates are closed behind you, all that sort of thing. Yet our instruction, not for the first time, tells us to ignore the country code. But old habits die hard. This particular field had been recently ploughed so we walked around the outside until we reached the next stile. Our next instruction advises us to maintain the same direction across the next field until we meet a hedge, with the grounds of Barkham Manor on our right. We are following the hedge around Barkham Manor when Ron notices, through a gap in the hedge, a very large pond with a couple of swans, with young, and some ornamental ducks. "I bet them ducks quack with a plum in their throat," comments Ron. "What does that sound like, then Ron?" asks Marian, and for the next few minutes Ron gives his impression of a posh duck while Marian nearly wets herself laughing. We pass Barkham Manor and head for a line of trees that are used to shelter a small vineyard. In the distance we can hear the high-pitched whistle of a steam train. For some reason I thought the trains must be on the Lavender Line but we are reliably informed by a couple we met at this point that it was, in fact, trains on the Bluebell Line that we could hear.

In the next field are a number of what look like large light bulbs in the ground. They stretch across the field in two very straight rows. "It looks like a landing strip," says Marian. "But

Backpacking Marian

---

[121] The Argus 'East Sussex Walks' by Ben Perkins Page 26

it's a bit bumpy for light aircraft," I offer. "Prob'ly used fer some o'them microwave planes," says Ron. Again Marian is in hysterics. All sorts of comments are now being said, including low flying dinners, ready made landing strips and 'do they land in six seconds ding?' "Did you 'ear about Irishman 'oo bought a microwave bed?" asks Ron, "thought 'e could get eight 'ours sleep in four seconds." I'm sure it was the sight of our first climb that brought them back to their senses.

We are now to head for the church steeple that can be seen in the distance, which meant walking down one field and up the other side. It didn't look that far but it seemed to take ages

Church steeple in the distance

with both Marian and me taking the Mickey out of Ron and his microwave planes. As we approach the recreation ground, in front of the church, Ron tells us that he played cricket and football here (surprise, surprise) for Hailsham. The story he relates is that he once hit a ball for six and it landed in the churchyard. He was then made to go and fetch the ball. I couldn't understand why he would be made to do that until I saw exactly how far he had hit the ball. It must have taken a fair time to walk around the field, down the lane to the church, find the ball and walk back again. "How come you hit the ball that far?" I ask. "Middled it!" is the reply. "Walked up the wicket and middled it a beauty," he continues. As you know my understanding of the game of cricket is limited, but he could have been speaking a foreign language, but I didn't show my ignorance by asking any questions about 'walking up a wicket' and 'middling it'. At the end of the recreation ground is a locked five bar gate with a very overgrown hedge hiding the stile next to it. Both Ron and I wade through the hedge and climb the stile, Marian scales the gate. When we look back at what we had just done we all notice, at the same time, the very large hole between the gate and the fence that would have been much easier to use.

Familiar sign for Ron

Unseen gap

We turn left here and head towards the village of Fletching and its very dominant parish church of St Andrew & St Mary the Virgin. Before we reach the church, on the right-hand side, is a wooden structure that I had passed on many occasions but didn't stop to find out what it was. It actually houses a very old water pump and is not, as Ron thought, a place of correction for ladies wearing French maids outfits, nor a Victorian bus shelter. There is no indication on exactly how old the place is except a plaque explains that it was refurbished by village donations in February 1974. Marian thinks they ought to have another 'whip round' soon.

Not a Victorian Bus Shelter

As always both Ron and I purchase the booklets that are available from every church we go into. This church was no different. Although extremely informative I found no explanation as to why the church is dedicated to St Andrew and St Mary the Virgin. But the booklet[122] is extremely interesting giving facts about Simon de Montfort and his time at the

---

[122] 'A Description of the Parish Church of St. Andrew & St. Mary the Virgin' -£1.50 – available from the church

church prior to the Battle of Lewes and his knights who were slain in that battle being returned to Fletching and buried, with full armour, within the church. There is also a reference and a large monument to the Dalyngrygge family. We also saw, within the south transept, a full size monument to Richard Leche and his wife Charitye. Richard was High Sheriff of Sussex and Surrey who died in 1596. His widow married the 2nd Earl of Nottingham. The marriage was not a happy one and, whilst still alive, Charitye had her effigy placed alongside her first husband so that she may be associated with a loving first husband rather than her second. There is also a brass monument to Peter Denot, Jack Cade Rebellion, which dates from 1450.

The tomb of Richard and Charitye

It is obvious, from the number of people working within the church grounds (I counted ten) that the church is the centre of this village's life and I would like to thank the people we met there for their warmth and hospitality. Even very young children were seen to be raking the grass around the tombstones of which there are many. Our book tells us to walk into the village of Fletching, with its wooden framed houses and raised footpaths, but then tells us to turn right into the churchyard. But we've passed the church to get into the village? We turn right into a car park but we are unable to get to the churchyard from here. So back we go, to the church, turn into the churchyard and make our way through the gravestones to a kissing gate at the far end of the churchyard. This church has the most enormous churchyard. And is very well-kept by the parishioners. The photograph, on the right, shows the church steeple, mostly hidden by the trees, and was taken at the far end of the churchyard. I am trying to give some perspective to size. It wasn't until I placed the photograph in this chapter that I noticed the name on the gravestone in the foreground is that of 'Arthur Herbert Pollard' who died, suddenly, on January 29th 1953. Perhaps I have Fletching ancestors?

Deceiving size

We are told that there should be a sign indicating the start of paths to Piltdown, Ruttingham and Mallingdown. But we didn't see one. But the four grain silos we need to pass are easily found as we head for the distant stile. We had noticed that the stiles on this walk varied to the ones we were used to. We all had problems getting over them simply because of the design. They didn't lend themselves to the usual combination of right leg following left. They were made of metal, so maintenance was kept to a minimum, but the footplates were positioned strangely. It's very difficult to describe the problems these stiles gave us on paper, but they were just difficult to get over.

Unusual stile

Again our instructions tell us to walk across the middle of a field. This one had an electric fence with a warning in front of us so, again, we headed around the field and the electric fence, until we saw yet more walkers walking through the middle and decided to do the same. It was about now that Marian appeared to be having a problem with her new walking boots and decided that her comfort might be improved if she took her socks off.

After walking along another couple of fields we eventually arrive at Mallingdown Farm. It is strange but we have been

A change of footwear

Always look where you're going Marian

carrying out these walks for 40 weeks now but I still feel uncomfortable walking through, what seem to be, private grounds. This walk was no different. We walk past the front door of the farmhouse and head along their drive. All the time I am waiting for someone to ask us what the hell we are doing on his or her land. At the end of the drive we turn right, onto a grassy path that winds through bracken for about 500 yards, where we meet a drive that takes us to the busy A272. We turn right here and follow the road for about 250 yards and turn left, heading up a drive signed 'Private driveway' to a house called Cogans. Shortly before the house we turn left and find ourselves on Piltdown Golf Course, just by the 16th tee. I have played golf on this course and I am led to believe that it is one of the only golf courses where the bunkers are filled with heather and not sand. It is also a little bit posh here. You cannot enter the clubhouse unless you wear a tie. But it is a beautiful course and extremely well-kept and a credit to the ground staff.

As regulars are aware, whoever is at the front always warns those behind of any obstacles or slipping hazards. I promise I did call out 'low branch' but it appears that Marian didn't hear me. Also regulars will be aware of my fear of animals. To get back to the car we had to pass through a small paddock that contained these black rams. I'm petrified and get through the paddock without touching the ground whilst Marian and Ron kept a very watchful eye on the

Black Rams

rams as they headed towards us, at speed. Thankfully a wave of the thumb stick and some Anglo Saxon language from both Ron and Marian kept the animals at bay.

It is just a short walk back to the car from the golf course and another walk is completed. Unfortunately, due to pre-arranged commitments, I am not sure when or where next week's walk will be. As usual though, our Monday evening meeting will be decision time. But at least it will be in what is fast becoming our old and familiar local.

WALK 41 - Wadhurst

Sunday 12th November 2006

I'd really like to go to The International Model Boat Show. It's on for three days; Friday, Saturday and Sunday 10th to 12th November, and it's at Leamington Spa in Warwickshire. I'm working Friday. I have now been diagnosed as diabetic so I have to attend a diabetic clinic and that's on Friday as well. Saturday has been lined up for Christmas shopping, all day in Brighton with my wife and daughter. So I've told the wife we will go to The Boat Show on Sunday. "But when will you do your walk with Ron?" she asks. We can't walk in the week during term time because of work unless it's a short, local one. So I decided to meet Ron on

Monday and approach the subject of not doing a walk this week. I even went to our local, on Monday evening, without the books so he couldn't choose a walk. But I couldn't do it. Our weekly walk has now become part of so many people's lives. People ask to accompany us, others suggest areas to walk and some just need to read the next chapter. If we don't walk how will I tell everyone? So I told Ron I'd forgotten the books and will have to meet again on Tuesday. All I've got to do now is tell the wife that I've got to go up the pub again on Tuesday evening, we're not going to Leamington Spa and I'm going for a walk with Ron on

The Greyhound

Sunday. Can anyone tell me how I got into this mess?

At our discussions, on where we walk, something takes our fancy for various reasons. It could be due to personal memories, or fleeting travels through a village, or our own personal ties with family or just historical interest. But Tuesday's decision was one of coincidence. A friend was telling us about where he was working just as Ron opened the book on Pub Walks in East Sussex[123]. Our friend was working in Wadhurst. The book opened at a pub walk starting in Wadhurst. So our walk, this week, starts at the village of Wadhurst, where at Cockmounts Farm on December 8th 1863[124] (some believe it to be the 20th December[125]) saw the last great bare-fisted prize fight in England. The fight, between an Englishman, Thomas King (The Fighting Sailor) and an American, John C. Heenan (The Benicia Boy) lasted a gruelling 36 rounds (Wikipedia states the fight only lasted 24 rounds???) with Tom King being the eventual winner to become heavyweight champion. As a lot of uncertainty about the fight can be found on the Internet I will say no more about it? Another item I found was that on the 20th January 1956 a Royal Air Force Meteor jet aircraft crashed into the High Street in Wadhurst, killing the pilot and his navigator as well as two members of the public. An enquiry revealed that the plane was 120 miles from base when the limit was 60 and that the pilot, Flying Officer Leonard Stoat, lost control after circling the village where his parents ran

a newspaper shop. Several of the villages' shops were destroyed in the accident and when new shops were built local people objected to them because they were 'not in keeping with the surrounding shops.' Having seen the old, as well as the 'new', I have to agree with the villagers[126].

Today is Remembrance Sunday (sometimes known as 'Poppy Day') and I am aware that Ron likes to get to the War Memorial, in Hailsham, and give thanks to those who died in wars so that we could live freely. The service is normally at 11.00 in the morning so we leave home at 08.00 on a cold

The famous poppy

[123] 'Pub Walks in East Sussex' by Mike Power, Power Publications, Ferndown, Dorset
[124] http://www.villagenet.co.uk/esussex-iron/villages/wadhurst.php visited 9/11/06
[125] http://en.wikipedia.org/wiki/Thomas_King_(boxer) visited 9/11/06
[126] http://newsvote.bbc.co.uk/mpapps/pagetools/print visited 13/11/06

Sunday and head towards Wadhurst. The walk is 'Walk 36' in 'Pub Walks in East Sussex' by Mike Power[127] and is described as a little short of 5 miles. We should make it round the walk and be back by 11.00 o'clock providing things go ok.

Not my favourite animal

We park opposite 'The Greyhound', which dates back to the 1700's, and we head straight for the church. Ron is unaware that I want him to 'rush' the walk and I am so pleased to see, and hear, that a service is in progress as we walk up the path towards the church door. That means we will have to come back to the church but can get on with the walk straight away. Opposite The Greyhound is a lane called Blacksmiths Lane. We head down the lane. The houses down this lane are not what is expected with the name Blacksmith. The buildings are known as Granary House and Granary Cottages, so where's Forge Cottage, Anvil House and Blacksmith Copse?

We continue down Blacksmiths Lane until we reach a sharp left-hand bend. Here we continue straight ahead onto a gravel driveway leading to a farm. All the fields, on our left, are full of sheep. "If I come back, after death, I want to be a ram in this area," says Ron, "just look at the amount of fun yer could 'ave." "Only if you get to wear the blue pad," I reply, "most of the sheep have been covered by the ram wearing the blue pad." "Knowin' my luck I'd get the red bugger," chuckles Ron. Further along, past the farm buildings, we come across a hop field. "How do you know its hops?" I ask. "'Cause the poles are too high fer grape vines

Hop field

an' the poles are too thick," replies Ron. Yet there didn't seem to have any plants at the bottom of the poles. Are hops annual or do they have to be replaced every year? I didn't think to ask. We pass through a number of gates and over stiles before we reach a stile that is dog friendly. "Seems strange ter 'ave a dog friendly stile all the way out 'ere," says Ron, "Must 'ave ter carry the dog over all the other stiles." When we look closer there is a plaque on the stile with a dedication, which read; '*Erected by High Weald Walkers in memory of a dear friend and fellow walker Eric Baldock 1926 – 2005. A gentle countryman.*' "Bugger me!" exclaims Ron; "I used ter work with someone called Eric Baldock, when I was on the Council. Wonder if it's 'im. Poor ol' Eric. Still, 'tis a nice way ter be remembered."

Erected for a dear friend

As we walk on we can hear the distinct sound of running water. I tell Ron that we should be able to see Bewl Reservoir at the bottom of this path. Our guidebook tells us that, although the path is a little muddy it is a very attractive with views across the water. But we seemed to be walking for some time before any water came into view.

"Reservoir level looks a bit low," comments Ron as he looks to our right, pointing out a stagnant pond. "It's also moved," I reply, "according to the book it should be on our left as we walk along this path. It was some time before the Reservoir came into view and it turned out to be a bit of a shock. On our walks at Arlington and Ardingly the Reservoirs there were reasonably full, but here was exactly the opposite. I had read that when the Reservoir was first built, between 1973

This can't be the reservoir

---

[127] *Pub Walks in East Sussex* by Mike Power (Dorset, Power Publications) Page 86

184

and 1975 it took a total of 31, 300 million litres of water to fill it. As we looked out across the vast expanse of land it looked as if the Reservoir is only half full. We had also noticed, on the way to the Reservoir, that a number of ditches seemed to be blocked with fallen debris and whilst the water in all of these ditches was running towards the blockage it could not get to the Reservoir. If we are so short of water why aren't these ditches cleared to allow more water to reach the Reservoirs?

From where this photo was taken it seems that the water should be lapping round our feet but the level hasn't been that high for some time. Fortunately the wildlife don't seem to be that bothered as there were plenty of birds around the edge of the water, yet it was obvious that there should, at this time of year, be a lot more water in the Reservoir. Could

Low water levels

clearing the ditches have an effect? I don't know, but surely it's worth a try.

We eventually reach a finger post that directs us inland. One of the things this guidebook doesn't tell us is that there are hills. The walk up this path is very steep and, because of the damp has become very slippery. It was a struggle to keep your footing and I was pretty breathless when we reached the top. Once at the top we join a drive and head towards a lane, which leads us back to Wadhurst. We can see the church in the distance but it looks miles

away.

Along the lane we meet three joggers who look as if they could be in some fancy dress competition with the cyclists from previous walks. Day glow colours and black lycra. The two girls were wearing much the same. Also along this lane we found a Health and Safety Inspectors nightmare. Two machines, one wood shredder and one wood saw, up to their axles in shavings and open to the elements, were simply left, in a deep hollow, by the side of the lane. Both the machines looked like death traps.

I take a crafty look at my watch to see that it is 10.30. Ron has complained a couple of times that we're not hanging about on this walk but I'm sure he isn't aware of why. Just as we cross the last field I can hear the church bells ringing in the distance. That sound still sends a tingle down my spine every time I hear it. "Can yer 'ere drums as well as bells?" asks Ron. I tell Ron why I am hurrying this walk, so that we can get to the memorial, in Wadhurst, so that we can still pay our

Health & Safety at its worst

respects to the fallen men of our armed forces. Just as we reach the road the procession, complete with pipe band, is marching past us, towards the church. Although only a small procession it was very nice to see. Not just the standards on display but also the children, girl guides, brownies, scouts and cubs all paying their respects to something they will only read about in books, hopefully. What we did find strange was that the church service started at 10.45. The procession had marched from the War Memorial to the church. Neither Ron nor I went into the church at this time but wandered along to the memorial. There was us, and one other couple. "I suppose it's because it isn't the 11th of

Bandsmen

the 11th that the people of Wadhurst will not honour the dead with two minutes silence at 11 o'clock," I offer. "Seems strange bein' ere like this though," replies Ron, and it did. At 11 o'clock Ron, me and the other young couple stood in front of the Memorial, with heads bowed and remained silent for two minutes. The memorial gives all the names of the men lost during the two world wars. During 1914 and 1919 Wadhurst lost a total of 114 men. That many men in a village the size of Wadhurst must have affected every family. Probably with more than one loss in a family.

We did wait for the service to finish before entering the church of St Peter and St Paul. It is one of those churches that make me sit and think. There aren't many that do that, but every now and again I just have to stop, sit and reflect. In today's world of uncertainty and doubt it is nice to feel a warm something in a house of God.

A walk with something different. Monday is my turn to choose the walk for next Saturday. Ron said that we only had another eleven to do but I would rather think of it as 41 completed.

Children join the procession

We leave you with what today is all about.

186

WALK 42 – Upper Dicker

Saturday 18th November 2006

Last week's walk was completed in record time, and the write up was also completed quickly. The chapter was in Ron's hands by 7.30 Sunday evening. The very same evening that the walk was completed. Hopefully I will not have to do that again. I felt that, although the walk was a little different, with the Remembrance Parade, it was all too rushed. No time to think or see. The visit inside the church seemed too short. Although we bought the pamphlet, giving the history of Wadhurst Parish Church, I didn't have time to digest its contents. I will take this opportunity to apologies to the people of Wadhurst for not stopping longer.

This week's walk was discussed on Monday, as usual. By Tuesday I had changed my mind and decided on somewhere else only to return to my original decision on the day of the walk. Why the indecision? I don't know. But it's like, when was the last time you went and sat on the beach. I live just a few miles away from some of the best beaches in England yet I can't remember when I spent time, with my family, just relaxing by the sea. The same goes for Michelham Priory. One of our local historical attractions, which is only a mile from my home. But I can count the number of times I've been there on one hand. What I can remember is that it is very historical and the moat around the priory held some big fish. That's it. But hopefully, today, I will learn some more about the area as our walk is taken from the book 'Walks into History – Sussex' by John Wilks[128].

Catherine of Aragon

During the Middle Ages the Church was the richest landowner in England after the King. Unfortunately the church tended to use its spiritual power to protect its outside interests and neglected its pastoral duties. During the reign of Henry VIII an increasing need to reform the Church coincided with the King's political needs, with disastrous results for religious houses such as Michelham Priory.

Henry, then married to Catherine of Aragon, needed a son and heir so that his right to the throne would be undisputed. After many years of marriage, Catherine had given Henry only one living child, a daughter Mary and it was doubted that a woman would be strong enough to rule. In 1527, with no prospect of a son, Henry decided to divorce Catherine so that he could marry the younger Ann Boleyn, who held out the prospect of producing a male child. Unfortunately for the King, the Pope rejected Henry's ingenious arguments as to why his marriage to Catherine was illegal and refused to grant a divorce. Henry started to put pressure on the Church in England and after very nearly five years the Pope resisted until, in 1533, the Pope excommunicated Henry. The King responded by declaring himself Head of the Church in England and the break from Rome was complete. Over the next five years the land and wealth of the Church was subject to widespread confiscation, and in the process known as the Dissolution of the Monasteries most religious houses were closed, their buildings demolished and their monks turned out to fend for themselves.

Ron keen to get started

Saturday sees the end of a week of bitterly cold winds, frosty mornings and constant showers. But today is cold but very bright. The sun is out and the day looks good. Ron is his cheery self when we set off for the village of Upper Dicker and the start of our 4-mile stroll around the Priory and the surrounding woods. Over the years a private school has practically taken over what was once, a proud Sussex village. Ron can remember playing cricket here, in the good old days, and obtaining his best ever score, 113 not out against Uckfield. An

---

[128] *Walks into History – Sussex* by John Wilks (Berkshire – Countryside Books) 2003 Page 84

achievement of which Ron is justly proud. But everywhere you look, around the village, is now influenced by the private school. The school now owns most of the land around the village. Although they have put it to good use by making football, rugby and cricket pitches as well as riding stables Ron is not impressed. "Surely, Ron, that's a good thing?" I suggest. "'Tis till yer want to make up a village team. Can't make a team up of village folk now. 'Ave ter use youngsters from school. Surprised they 'aven't asked to change the name of the village." We walk down towards the Village Store in silence.

A Priory Fishpond

To the right of a house is a path leading out onto a stile. We cross a small field and arrive at the edge of one of the school playing fields. "Got the best of everythin'," says Ron, "monies no object when it comes to this place. Even got nettin' attached to goals even when they ain't bein' used. Never 'ad that in my day. Just a couple 'o sticks out the ground fer posts, that's all we 'ad at my school." We get across the playing area as quickly as possible but it is evident that horses play a big part in the life around this school. Every inch of ground is cordoned off as paddocks with horses roaming around freely.

We now head towards a farm, which is said to have replaced the farm belonging to the priory after the Dissolution. The priory owned all the land we are to walk on throughout this walk. Dovecotes were used to supply the monks with meat. Although our guidebook states that there are still dovecotes in the grounds I never saw one until we got inside the priory itself. One of the feudal rights enjoyed by the priory was that its doves were free to feed on the grain of the local peasantry, whilst heavy punishments were imposed upon any peasant who killed one of the priory's doves. We now cross over a small stream, which served a dual function: it fed the moat that protected the priory, and also the fishponds that provided the monks with fish.

We now follow a track until we reach a gate leading us into the woods. Here is a clear path that we are instructed to follow for ⅓ of a mile. Like we know what ⅓ of a mile is? But at the end is a gate that leads us into another field and it is clearly

Track, leading towards woods

marked. Whilst walking through the wood yet more evidence of the hurricane of 1987 and the amount of damage that it caused is very clear. At one point the area looked like a tree 'graveyard'. All around us was uprooted, dead trees. It

Tree lined path

must have been frightening to be in these woods during that hurricane. Another thing, whilst walking through this wood that really got Ron going was the sound of gunshots. Not just the odd one but continued volleys. There must have been a shoot in progress because you could also hear the beaters as they walked through the woods to our left. Then, suddenly, we hear the sound of guns going off. "Poor buggers, don't stand a chance," says Ron. "Spend all summer bein' fed in the wild then get chased and scared senseless before bein' shot by the very same people been feedin' 'em." Again Ron is not amused. Perhaps this particular walk wasn't such a good idea after all?

1987 hurricane damage

We go through the gate at the end of the wood and make for a stile in the opposite corner. Here we turn right into a lane that is so beautiful in its autumn colours with the sun shining through the trees. As we walk along this track we are now close to what has become a popular place for children, 'Knockhatch Adventure Park'. To our left we can hear children screaming and laughing as they slide down the various poles and try to complete the assault course. I haven't been to the park myself but various people have spoken very highly of the activities that children can get involved with. "Never 'ad nothin' like that in my day," says Ron. "Nor me, Ron, but at least it gives the youngsters somewhere to let off some steam." "When we 'ad our 'olidays," reminisces Ron, "my ol' mum an' dad used 'ter take me an me sister campin' fer one week an' then we used 'ter go an' see me mums family in Bradford fer a week. Always went 'ter place near 'aystin's. Me dad used 'ter bait up our fishin' rods an' leave lines in river overnight. Used 'ter sleep in a barn with them chickens. Go back 'ter river in the

mornin' get the trout and cook it over a log fire with bacon an' eggs an' a pot 'o tea. Bloody marvellous it was". "It sounds very nice Ron," is my reply. "Never 'ad nothin' like that 'venture park in my day. We made our own amusements." It was about now that we arrived at the road and, as I was not sure of the direction to go, left it to Ron to guide us through the next stage of the walk.

We cross the road and turn sharp right. On our left-hand side is Arlington Stadium, the home of Eastbourne Eagles Speedway Team. On a personal note I am not a follower of Speedway. But each to their own. This track has been here for more years than I can remember. In fact it was the first place that I found that I did not like the sight of blood. Anyone who knew my father will be aware of his involvement with the St. Johns Ambulance Association. During any event held at Arlington Stadium a St Johns Ambulance presence had to be evident. No St Johns Ambulance attendance meant no racing. As well as Speedway the track is also used for Stock Car Racing. It

Events carried out at the Arlington Stadium

was at one of these meetings, when I was a cadet in the St Johns that my realisation about blood came into being. As always happens in Stock Car Racing there was an accident on the first bend. Apparently accidents on the first bend are mandatory, as all hell breaks loose at the start of every race. This accident looked bad. I can remember seeing a driver climbing out of his burning stock car. But as he tried to dodge other cars to get to the centre 'safe area' he was hit by another car and ended flying in the air. By the time my father and me got to the driver he had received a very nasty injury to the head when he lost his helmet, blood was very visible at the back of his head. That's all I can tell you. I woke up in the same 'safe area' that

the driver was making for and have never been to another race.

My dreams are interrupted with Ron telling me that the area we are about to walk through used to be a popular area for, how do I describe them, men with a different sexual requirement than myself. "Used to be awful, along 'ere," says Ron, "but it's a lot better now that the Police have regular patrols in the area." The book describes the bridleway as '*often muddy*' and because of the amount of rain over the last seven days I would say that today it was very muddy. Just as we are trying to wade through the mud

Feed time

and water a gentleman, who I will only describe as Irish with a lisp (but both Ron and I had our doubts to his masculinity) advised us that we should walk further into the woods and follow a well trodden path which wasn't so muddy. Personally, I was happy to do as we were told, just to get away from the man but Ron was happy to have a little chat.

At the end of the path we reach a road and turn left. This road leads us to The Old Oak Inn. Before we reach the Inn we get to a driveway leading into Primrose Farm where we turn right. Although the pathway isn't signed we are advised to go through the farm buildings, to the right and follow the lane. As we walk down the lane the views are spectacular. Although

Do we cross this field?

most of the area is flat it's just the abundance of colour that takes your breath away. Unfortunately the signs at the entrance to Primrose Farm were not the only signs to be missing. Our instructions seem to have both Ron and me confused as to which direction we should be heading. All of a sudden the temperature has dropped, the wind has got up and it has started to rain. To top it all my sense of direction is rubbish and I haven't a clue which way to go. "If we 'ead along this field edge in that direction we will end up on the road to the priory," says Ron, like it's that obvious. "Lead on, Ron," I say and within a short distance cars can be seen parked. "Told yer," says Ron.

We turn left and it is obvious that 'something' is happening at the priory. A sign declares that a Christmas Fayre is being held and the place is heaving with cars. I recognise Ben, husband of Teresa (Horse riding) who is directing cars away from the priory because the parking area is full. Not the time for photographs of the priory. "Come back when were closed," suggests Ben, "I'll take you round and you can get as many pictures as you want." We make arrangements to meet up on a later date and head up the driveway. Just as we reach the priory we are met

Got him at last!

by Russell, another friend who invites us into the grounds, as his guest. We wander around the fayre for a while looking at craft stalls and wonder at the skill that go into making some of the items on sale. Ron was shocked to find that thumb sticks were selling for £9.99 each and was sure that he could corner the market. But one item did catch my eye as a photographic opportunity and couldn't resist it. The picture was taken when Ron was trying to get out of the stocks. His problem was made even more distressing because he wouldn't let go of his carrier bag.

From here it was a small walk back to the car. Again, we had to cross more land owned by the school, which proved difficult because they had, again, made the field into paddocks. Climbing over or ducking under fences was the only way to get to the car.

The only thing left to see was the church. I had visited this church before and wasn't impressed. From the outside it is a magnificent building but inside it looses any character it had with the emulsion walls and ceilings. It is a warm, plain hall and has very little character. I apologies to its parishioners but, I'm afraid it did nothing for me. When Ron saw the inside he just turned round and left. "That's no church," is all he said.

Upper Dicker Church

Next week it is the turn of Ron to choose our walk. We are approaching the end of our year. But I'm sure we have a few miles to go yet.

WALK 43 - Winchelsea

Saturday 25th November 2006

We are now heading towards the completion of our task. After this walk we are down to single figures. It doesn't seem possible that we have completed 42 walks. I have learnt so much from Ron and being with him throughout these weeks I am unsure how I'm going to cope without our weekly stroll. We have already discussed a couple of options and I can assure you that at least one walk from the next nine will be a surprise. Again, I don't understand why, but I have opened my mouth before the brains engaged and talked both Ron and me into something a little silly. Photographs are to be taken to prove my stupidity and Ron is hoping that it will be a lesson learnt, and I'll keep my mouth shut in future.

It looks like rain on the way

Monday's chat about this weeks walk was, as always, carried out at our local. I'm very pleased to say the new landlord and landlady seem to be doing very well. Some of the old regulars have returned to the fold and it's nice to see them all chatting about old times. Thinking of old times probably prompted Ron to choose Winchelsea for our next walk. I can remember, many years ago, playing in a band at Winchelsea and confided in Ron, on one of our walks, that this would be the one place I would love to retire to. It is a beautiful town steeped in history. The original town was known as Old Winchelsea and was a Saxon fishing port on a small island off the coast, 1 mile south east of Winchelsea. A report compiled for Henry III describes Old Winchelsea as having 700 houses, 2 churches and over 50 Inns or Taverns. Implying a population of over 4,000. During the 100 Years War Old Winchelsea supplied 21 ships and 596 men for the King. Unfortunately, during the late 1280s' a great storm destroyed the town completely and the survivors moved to the current site. [129]

During the 14 century the French attacked the town, on many occasions, which is why its population dwindled down to only a few hundred people. In 1348 the Black Death also took its toll on the town and a mass grave, known to the locals as 'Plague Pit', is located just to the south of the Town. [130]

John Wesley (one of the founders of The Methodist Church) preached his last outdoor sermon at Winchelsea on the 7th October 1790 when he was 87 years old, and well-known comedian and goon, Spike Milligan, is buried at Winchelsea Church.

The Church of St Thomas

History lesson over, this walk is taken from page 92 of 'Pub Walks in East Sussex' by Mike Power[131] and is described as 4½ miles with *'the going mostly good underfoot'.* As we are now approaching completion of our year of walks, we are into the winter and the weather is none to pleasant, we have decided to go it alone for the remainder of the walks, apart from one where it will be a little silly and festive (?). The weather forecast for today was awful. Gail force winds, torrential rain and hail were promised for this morning. The picture of the Winchelsea town sign, with the very grey sky, gives a

---

[129] www.villagenet.co.uk/rotherlevels/villages/winchelsea.php visited 22/11/06
[130] http://Winchelsea.east-sussex.co.uk/ visited 22/11/06
[131] *Pub Walks in East Sussex* by Mike Power (Dorset – Power Publications) Page 92

good indication of what we were heading for, as we pulled up at Winchelsea, outside the pub, The New Inn.

Our first call was made to the church of St Thomas the Martyr. Everyone will know by now that I have this thing with churches. I take them or leave them, love or hate but every now and again I get to a 'sit down and think' church. The church at Winchelsea is definitely a 'sit down and think' church. It is beautiful. It is large and it is just fantastically old with more history than I ever thought possible in one place, and one of the very best churches we have had the opportunity to visit during our 43 weeks. I could have stayed all day.

Some may remember Walk 29, when I recounted the tragic deaths of the complete Lifeboat Crew of the Mary Stanford on the 15th November 1928. Within this church is the most remarkable stained glass window, named 'The Lifeboat Memorial'[132], which commemorates the heroism of that crew. A very detailed book, giving not only the history of this wonderful church, but also a tour of things to look out for, can be purchased at the price of £2.50 and is worth a whole lot more. Go and see it, if you like churches, you will love this one.

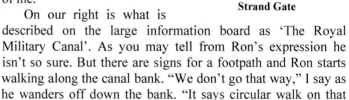

History leaps from the walls

After Ron had to drag me away from the church we head down the road towards Winchelsea Beach. To get there we have to pass through Strand Gate, one of the very ancient city gates that still stands today. Once through the gate we head down the road further until we meet a junction and turn right. Just a few yards down this

road we turn right along a road signed to Winchelsea Beach. The road here is very busy and I would like to take the opportunity to thank the driver who, whilst I consulted my map, came up behind us and tooted his horn. It scared the s*+t out of me.

On our right is what is described on the large information board as 'The Royal Military Canal'. As you may tell from Ron's expression he isn't so sure. But there are signs for a footpath and Ron starts walking along the canal bank. "We don't go that way," I say as he wanders off down the bank. "It says circular walk on that post," he replies. "So it might," I answer, " but it isn't the circular walk we're doing." "Then they shouldn't put sign there. Just confuses people, that does," he grumbles as he heads back towards me.

Strand Gate

At the Royal Military Canal

We eventually found our path, on a bend in the road. This would be a short cut, across grass towards another road. Again memories of Walk 29 come flooding back to us. I will just mention two words - dog pooh. If you are unsure of what I mean, then a revisit to Walk 29 is needed. Because along this short path must be the dog toilet for the whole of Winchelsea. Whereas in Rye they collected it, put it in bags and hung it from a fence, the dog owners of Winchelsea just leave it on the ground for you to tread in. Apart from one enterprising dog owner who put it in a plastic bag and then hid it behind the 'bus stop' sign.

What do we do with do-do?

[132] The Story of Winchelsea Church by Malcolm Saville purchased from the church £2.50

The promised high winds have now reached us and it's getting difficult to keep our balance as we walk along the road heading towards a pub called 'The Ship'. "Seems popular price fer a roast dinner, £6.95," says Ron. Nearly every pub we've passed today seems to do 'a roast' for £6.95. "Couldn't upset locals out ere," comments Ron, "be out 'o business within a fortnight. Only got four 'ouses an' a bus shelter close by." The turning needed, into Willow Lane, is on our left. Bearing in mind that our entire walk has been on pavements, apart from

The vastness of the area is breathtaking

the short cut on grass, neither of us is really prepared for the next hour. As you can see the countryside from here is very open. The wind is now approaching 'gale force' plus and spatters of rain can be felt. There isn't a shelter in sight. We reach Morlais Ridge and enter another path that will lead us to a gravelled area and another path towards the beach. Trudging across the gravel, with the wind in our faces was a struggle but we eventually managed to get to the bottom of the sea defences. In front of us is some steps, which we

climb, to get what is described in our book as '..glorious views across the beach.'[133] It was as if someone was waiting for us to get to the top of these steps. Did it rain, or did it rain? Thoughts of going back to walking on Wednesdays came flooding to mind. Luckily both Ron and I had brought coats with us but the rain and hail was so strong it wasn't long before the wet started to seep through.

Our instructions are to walk along this path for nearly a mile. Whilst looking out to sea was very exhilarating we were getting soaked to the skin. At one

Shingle path

point the hail became painful and we had to stop at the bottom of some steps and turn our backs to the wind. Ron decided he needed a closer look at the sea and went down the beach. "I'm surprised not ter see some o' them surf boarders out on the water," shouts Ron. "When we get back on the defences," I say, " you'll see some sail boarders getting ready to go out there." "You're not serious?" Ron asks, but when we returned to the top of

Deserted beach

---

[133] *Pub Walks in East Sussex* by Mike Power (Dorset – Power Publications) Page 92

193

the wall, in the distance, were two men preparing to go sailing in this weather. "Must be some sort o' loonies. And prats like that will spect the life boat people ter 'elp 'em out if they gets into trouble."

Another thing that I've noticed, as we battle the elements to find a stile on our right, is how much litter there is along this path. Whilst the strong winds may have some bearing as to why the path has so much litter but it does seem excessive. The rain is still coming down straight when I hear Ron say, "Silly bugger," as he stops walking. "Just remembered, I've got leggins' in me bag." "It's too late to put them on now," I shout, "you're already soaked." But Ron is not to be deterred; he promptly sits on the ground, and pulls on the leggings. Now if anyone has

A heavy sea breeze

worn leggings in the rain and not had wellies to go under the leggings you will know that the water runs off the leggings and ends up in your shoes. Now Ron has a soaking wet coat, the

Litter strewn path

rain has gone through to his jumper, he has soaking wet trousers, covered by plastic leggings and, after walking a few yards in the pouring rain, he has soaking wet feet as well. I'm just soaked, but if the rain does stop I'm hoping that the wind will dry my clothes before we get back to the car.

As we approach our stile on the right the rain starts to ease up although the wind is still very strong. Unfortunately our Guidebook has become a rain sodden clump of paper but I can make out that we now have to walk along what is known as Pett Level, following the line of the ditch on our left. Obviously, due to the rain, the pathway is just a muddy and wet trail but it is easily followed. In the distance are group of walkers heading towards us. The fields we are walking through, heading towards a concrete bridge, are full of sheep. Again, Ron is comparing colours on their backs and is happy to report that the blue ram has been busy again although we did notice a couple of sheep with red markings on the sides? Each field has a hedge and each hedge has a large gate, because of the rain we have to paddle

It's stopped raining

to it before you can open and close it. Our fellow walkers pass us with a cheery "Good afternoon," Ron wants to stop and chat but it is clear that the leader of the group wants to keep her followers on the move. When we get to the next gate it is very obvious that they had left the gate open, and Ron is incensed. "You could always chase back after them, if you like Ron. I'll wait for you here." I offer in the hope that he will calm down. But of course Ron is right. Each of these fields contained sheep. "Farmer been tryin' ter keep

Gate left open!!!!

sheep apart by puttin' some in each field. Then yer get morons leavin' the gate open. Not surprisin' the farmers don't want yer walkin' on their land."

We finally arrive at the concrete bridge and head up the field towards a stile and the driveway, where we turn right. Shortly after getting on the drive we pass under another of the gates, New Gate where it is said that troops from France, gained entry in 1359 and ransacked the town. It is believed that they were permitted to enter the town by someone from inside Winchelsea. All the townsfolk had

Wooden footbridge

made for the church as soon as they were aware of what was happening. Many villagers, men, women and children were killed within the church grounds. The marauding army also despoiled the church and raped some young women. The dead were buried in the churchyard, which had to be enlarged. But it must be remembered that only ten years before, the population had been much reduced by the Black Death.

At the end of this driveway we turn right and walk along the main road and back to The New Inn. I take a last longing look at the church, opposite the pub and another walk is completed. We are both wet through. Ron is struggling to get out of his leggings and the only one that doesn't seem that bothered with the weather is the duck, seen at Morlais Ridge, early in the walk.

Next week I hope the weather will be a little kinder to us. But as we approach winter I think that we are to have more days like today before we finish our quest. Nine to go, and counting.

Making the most of the rain?

WALK 44 - Buxted

Saturday, 2nd December 2006

Between Walk 43 and 44 both Ron and I, accompanied by Lyn, have completed a spell of 'ice-skating' (See Walk Extra). No damage has been done to any bodily functions so sitting down to discuss the location of this walk was not a problem.

Regulars will know that in my younger days I played various instruments in a village band. I met my wife, whilst playing cornet at the Eastbourne Carnival, with the Warbleton and Buxted Brass Band over thirty years ago and I own a very interesting book 'The History of a Village Band 1896 – 1996'[134] which was published by the then secretary, Trevor Jarvis, to commemorate the bands 100th birthday. In 1896 the band was formed as a contest band called The Warbleton Brass and Reed Band. Although quite successful on the contest circuit the band numbers started to dwindle and in the early 1950's amalgamated with Buxted Band

to become what it is today, a small village band seen at Flower shows and village events. This picture was taken in 1969, at Horsted Keynes Railway Station, the home of The Bluebell Railway. The extremely attractive and leggy young lady in the front row was to become my wife in 1972. One of my better decisions. (I'm the good-looking one with glasses, standing between Emelia and Tony, the drummer)

So, in keeping with interests I thought, as we had walked around Warbleton a few weeks ago it was now the turn of Buxted. I am afraid to say that this was not one of my better decisions.

Playing on the Bluebell Line

The weather has not improved since last week. The clouds overhead, when I picked Ron up, were decidedly grey and rain soaked. Our drive to Buxted was diverted due to a road accident on the A22 before Uckfield so we arrived via Heathfield. I have to say now that there are one or two things that get to me. One of these is having to pay to park your car in a railway car park. If I can avoid it, I will. So on arrival at Buxted the last place I wanted to park was at the station. "But it's only £2 fer the day," says Ron.

No Entry?

"So it may be," I reply, "but it's the principal." So we parked a little further into the village, in Framfield Road, for free. It is now spitting with rain as we head off down Framfield Road,

following the instructions from the leaflet, Route 6 Buxted Walk, obtained from the East Sussex County Council[135].

If anyone has ever been to Buxted you will have noticed the lack of a village centre. There are very few shops. There is a pub and a restaurant and, of course, a railway station. But that's it. The church is in Buxted Park, which isn't in the boundary of the village. To me, the place gives you that 'your not wanted' feel. The gate, in the picture is a good example of what, I believe, Buxted people seem to be saying to us outsiders. We have never seen so much barbed wire on a gate. With two padlocks as well as the wire we get the message, and move on. It's still spitting with rain.

We turn right, onto a road signposted Framfield. After a short distance we turn right onto a signposted footpath. I will say now that

Signed footpath

---

[134] *History of a Village Band 1896-1996* by Judith Kinnison Bourke Published by The Band
[135] www.eastsussex.co.uk/walks/heathfieldhailsham viewed 01/12/06

this route has to be one of the best-signed walks we have been on. Every turn and stile has a sign from Wealden or East Sussex that makes our walk a bit more enjoyable. It's started to rain harder.

We follow the field edge along very muddy paths and reach, what is described in our leaflet as a 'squeeze stile'. This is the first time that I had heard of this type of stile and was intrigued to find out what it was like. Again I was a little disappointed as it wouldn't be the first time, in this walk, that we come across a stile that it is easier to walk round than get over or through.

The paths are easy to follow, not just because of the signs, but it is obviously well used.

Under the Railway Line

It's really raining now as we follow the path leading us under the railway line. Luckily concrete slabs have been laid so that we can get through this small tunnel without difficulty. Just beyond the railway line the path drops slightly as we head towards Tickerage Stream, which supplies Heavers Mill in Framfield. The area we are now in has been designated as an area of outstanding beauty and we have to admit, despite the torrential rain, it is a really beautiful and peaceful area, just to stand, look and admire.

We follow the waterside path for just a short distance and cross the well-made footbridge and continue along a path with deer fencing on our right. "I wonder why it's called 'deer fencing'?" I stupidly ask Ron. "Probably 'cause it's expensive," is Ron's reply. Stupid questions always get stupid replies, especially when you're with Ron.

It has been some weeks since our last glimpse of wild deer and whilst we can hear gunshots in the distance, just to our left we see two young deer heading up the bank and, hopefully, not in the direction of the guns.

At the next gate we can see clearly the ground that is Buxted Park. The next gateway takes us into the Park as we head towards the Buxted Park Hotel. As I said all the way markers are very clear. The rain has got even heavier now and

Deer fencing

has started to get through my coat. We continue over the River Uck, the cause of the famous floods in Uckfield in the year 1974[136], and I have never seen so much water on the move. The power must be astounding. We pass the ornamental lakes of the hotel, as the rain gets even heavier. The reflections in the water cause me to stop and take a few photographs. I really am fascinated with water yet petrified of it at the same time. I have

My fascination for water

never been able to swim yet I'm happy to stand up to my armpits in water on a beach or in a swimming pool. As long as I can feel the bottom I'm ok. As soon as that feeling is gone, I panic. And I mean panic.

After passing the lakes we now descend another path towards a footbridge and boardwalk towards Views Wood. Now is decision time. Our instructions tell us that we can walk round Views Wood, which will add 1 mile to the walk, or we could turn right here and head towards the church. We are both soaked and it is still raining. Our instruction leaflet is fast becoming a pulpy mess. I'm cold. Although the walk is being

Wooden Walkway

enjoyable the weather certainly isn't. A decision was easy. We turned right and headed towards the church.

---

[136] The Sussex Weather Book, by Ogley, Currie and Davison - Froglets Publications, Westerham, Kent 1991- Page 110

Buxted church is an impressive building. It is not what I would describe as a 'sit down and think' church but it does have a certain something. It is big. It is well-kept and obviously the congregation look after the building which has stood on this site since1250 and was dedicated to God and in honour of Margaret Queen of Scotland (1045-1093), the wife of Malcolm the King.[137]

I can clearly remember marching, with the Warbleton and Buxted Band up the driveway, towards the church, on Remembrance Day playing 'Old Comrades' and 'Sussex by the Sea' followed by the standards of The Royal British Legion and members of many of the Buxted Societies. On the memorial to the fallen during the wars is the name W M Pollard. Unfortunately, it appears that he is no relation to me.

Within the church can be purchased various booklets and cards and I couldn't resist the book 'A Short History of Buxted' by Rosemary Alexander[138] which is a fascinating read about the village and its people and is a must have book if you are into local history.

Leaving the church we now walk along the long drive and turn right, heading back towards the railway station. Thankfully the signs throughout the walk were a lot better than the one in this picture

I have to say that this was not one of our better walks. Yes, the signs along the route

Buxted Church

helped immensely. The torrential rain didn't help at all. The scenery, although pleasant and enjoyable in places, especially around the stream, was not, in my mind, exceptional. The fact that the rain only stopped once we got to the church made conversation between Ron and me a little limited which, I believe, reflects in the way that this chapter is written. I suppose that one poor walk out of forty four isn't a bad average. The weather can play a significant part in what we do or say. I hope that next week's walk, chosen by Ron, will be a little more inspirational

And this points to where??

---

[137] Parish Church of St Margaret, Buxted – Leaflet by Canon Greville Cooke, M.A.,F.S.A. price 50p
[138] *A Short History of Buxted* by Rosemary Alexander (Tonbridge Wells, Opax Ltd) 1996

WALK 45 – East Dean

Saturday 9th December 2006

Christmas is getting ever closer. The girls on my minibus have persuaded me to dress up as Santa for the last run at the end of this term. I finish work at mid-day on the 13th December 2006 and don't return until the 8th January 2007. A nice break, during which time I am hoping to put these meanderings into some form of sense, with the view of contacting a publisher. Who knows, 'this time next year……………………'

For now, it's back to reality. Monday, as usual, Ron and I met at The Kings Head. Over the past few weeks Ron has mentioned a walk that he has wanted to do for some time but we haven't got round to it. So it was no surprise when,

again, he mentioned East Dean as being the place for this week's walk. This time I pinned him down and persuaded him not to change his mind. So East Dean it is. The walk is taken from the book 'Pub Walks in East Sussex' written by Mike Power[139]. I will say now that very little of the walk actually bears any resemblance to the walk from the book except that we start and finish at The Tiger Inn, East Dean. The bit in between is not the same as the book at all. We didn't get lost. We didn't find the start of the walk at all, so we just followed our

The Tiger Inn

noses. Or at least, the advice of a well-meaning gentleman, who came to our rescue when we looked confused whilst trying to decide in which direction to take. (Does that sound familiar?)

The morning is bright but very cold. My neighbour woke me at 6 o'clock this morning when he was scraping his windscreen free of ice. I am not feeling too good either. My throat feels like the bottom of a parrot's cage and my head feels as though a whole corps of drummers have been practicing all night. I haven't had a cold for years but I feel as if one is on its way. I'm sure a couple of aspirin will ease my aches and pains.

The drive to The Tiger is spent chatting about the possibilities of a publisher for the book. When we both

Across the Green

spoke to Lyn last night [Friday] she was very excited because she has found a publisher who may be interested. Instead of getting the manuscript ready over the Christmas holidays (three weeks), My proof reader/agent, Lyn, had given me until Monday night (three days). These agents can be so demanding!!

We arrive at East Dean and find the free car park. It is a short walk along the driveway until we reach a small village green, where we find The Tiger Inn. From here we turn right and walk up the hill towards a lane. Once at the lane we are to turn left along the lane, and then turn right and cross, diagonally left, a field. This is the point that confused both Ron and me. The gentleman who spoke to us said that we should head for Friston Church and the walk continues through the churchyard. But

From the top of the Hill

the book didn't say anything about a church. And to reach the church we would have to

---

[139] _Pub Walks in East Sussex_ by Mike Power (Dorset, Power Publications) Page 34

199

walk straight across, and up, the field, not diagonally. I have to say that it was a very 'steep up', but Ron said that he had always wanted to visit Friston Church but had never got round

St Mary the Virgin Church

to it. "A bit like Upper Dicker Church," I reminded him. "There can't be another church that boring," he says as he starts striding up the hill towards Friston Church. "But our directions say we should head diagonally left," I remind him. "If we do that we don't see the church," is the reply and he's gone. From the top of the hill we looked back and you can't see the village of East Dean yet we only left the car park a few minutes ago. Another thing I left in the car was my coat. Although it was reasonably warm down in the hollow, up here, in the open, it was getting decidedly cold. With my wife's words ringing in my ears about being stupid going out if you don't feel well and don't come home expecting any sympathy we head for the church without another word.

The Church of St Mary the Virgin at Friston is one of those places that I have spoken of many times in these pages. So much so, that I will not go on about it now. But the church does have one wonderful peculiarity. A Tapsell Gate. With all the walks we have completed this is the first one where this type of gate has been installed, yet some information, obtained from the church[140] describes the gate as 'peculiar to the churchyards of Sussex'. It is, basically, a five bar gate which pivots in the centre. The ease that this gate opens is a credit to the person who constructed it. Further research into the gate[141] advises that this gate was used to prevent cattle breaking into the Churchyard. It was designed and built by a carpenter, believed to be John Tapsell a widower from Mountfield during the 1700's. Although, when open, the gap was not big enough for large animals to get through, it was big enough for the bearers of coffins. It

A Tapsell Gate

The village pond

is a simple design but most ingenious. "'ave you noticed," asks Ron, "that since we started to slag people off fer the way they kept their churchyards everyone o'them 'as been real tidy?" I have to agree with him. Over the past few walks the churchyards have been a credit to the parishioners. Perhaps someone above has read some of my words?

Just outside the Church is a large village pond with strict instructions telling us not to remove any items from the water? Again my fascination with reflections encouraged me to take this photograph before heading away from Friston Church, along a path towards a place called Crowlink.

I keep checking the book, just to see if I can recognise any landmarks described but nothing looks familiar. In fact there is lots of nothing.

Of course that's not strictly true. The surroundings here, as you head towards the cliffs is very exhilarating. Bloody cold, at this time of year, but a truly open, and

Admiring the view

[140] Tapsell Gates by Rosalind Hodge, March 2002 price 15p
[141] http://www.villagenet.co.uk/reference/tapsellgate.html visited 9/12/06

green, expanse of land. Even the animals up on this part of Sussex must have thermal covering, and the views, across to the open sea are mind blowing. I must admit to taking one or two photographs whilst up on the top of these cliffs. As we walk towards the edge, but obviously not too close, the views seemed to get better and better. The bleakness and the wind that blows up here can be represented with the trees practically horizontal but if you forget how cold and bleak it is and just admire the coastline words cannot describe what you can see. I have seen picture postcards with these views but never seen them in real life. They certainly take your breath away.

Close to the cliff edge

We walk along the cliff edge for some time, admiring the sea views and watching the fishing boats out at sea. A fellow walker points out a ship that has obviously had troubles and has landed on the gravel below the cliffs. Which reminded me of the story associated with these cliffs involving a wrecker and smuggler known as James Dippery who lived in the village and made a small fortune in the early 1800's This area of the coastline was treacherous for sailors and many ships were driven ashore onto the rocks and the village often enjoyed the benefits of the sailors bad luck. This area then became perfect for smugglers and wreckers. Many ships were deliberately wrecked by fake lights being hung from the cliffs so that unsuspecting sailors thought they were near Eastbourne or Newhaven. James Dippery was arrested by the Customs and Excise and sent for trial, where in return for his freedom, he informed on his colleagues

We turn inland

who were deported to Australia. He retained his fortune and retired a very rich man[142]. "An' who say's crime don't pay?" asks Ron.

"According to the map I think we should turn inland now," I suggest to Ron. In the distance, to our left, is a track running up hill. We'll 'ead up that track an' look at what we can see," offers Ron. My only hope is that we can see East Dean. But no, once at the top of the hill all we could see was a shed with a red roof, far off into the distance. "Hang on, Ron," I say, "I seem to remember something about a shed in the walk book." I hastily find the right page and there, as clear as day, we are advised to walk towards '. *the building with a red roof and follow the path back to the village.*' [143]

With little said and much haste we head for the little brick building with a red roof. Just as we near the building, to our left, over the rise, we can see East Dean. The village was granted a licence to hold a weekly market and annual fair by King Henry III. East Dean is closely tied to the Bardoff family, who took over Birling Manor in 1257, when William married Juliana Gurney and gained the Manor as part of her dowry. Hugh Bardoff, a son of William and Juliana took part in a revolt against King Henry IV and was killed. The King seized the lands from the family in 1406 due to Hugh's treason. Later the King granted the lands back to the Bardolfs, unfortunately, another Lord William fought for the Lancastrians against King Edward IV and lost. The lands were forfeited again, and the family never held power in the area again.

The walk down towards the village takes us through some woodland until we, again, reach civilisation. Ron

Walking down towards the village

[142] http://www.villagenet.co.uk/sevensister/villages/eastdean.php visited 8/12/06
[143] *Pub Walks in East Sussex* by Mike Power (Dorset, Power Publications) Page 34

never ceases to amaze me with the people he 'knows'. Sometimes he gets it wrong. Today he is convinced he knows the gentleman who is tending his allotment, but, as it turns out, the man who he thinks he knows isn't the man he thought he was. (Now that statement has to be Sussex). Unfortunately the gentleman does know of two associates of Ron, both keen gardeners, who not only used to show their produce from their own allotments at local shows but also judged at many horticultural events. Peter and Brian Johnson. "Was a real shame," says the man, "Both died a couple of weeks ago," he continues, "One got took ill on the

Woodland path

Friday and was dead by Monday and the brother died on the following Wednesday. Had a double burial in the church." Ron is, obviously shaken. We walk to the church, hoping to locate his old friends' gravesites in silence. Both were easy to find, next to each other, as brothers should be. I felt so sorry for Ron and found myself wandering around the churchyard looking at headstones, while he spent a few minute with his thoughts. One of the headstones was to a sailor, aged nineteen at the time of his death, aboard H.M.S. Ocean Sunlight. The wonderful thing about the Internet is the information that you can find in seconds. Ocean Sunlight was a 131 tonne Drifter built in 1929 that struck a mine off the coast at Newhaven on the 13th June 1940 with the loss of nine lives. What's more, two of her sister ships, Ocean Lassie and Ocean Retriever were also destroyed by mines in our own waters[144]. But what really got to me were the number of ships in total destroyed between 1939 and 1945.

(If you have access to the Internet look at this wonderful website http://www.naval-history.net/WW2BritishLossesbyName3.htm you will be amazed at the number of ships listed.)

It is now that I heard the church organ start playing. People who know me will realise what that sound does to me, but I am determined to overcome this reaction, by facing it, head on. Both Ron and I enter the Parish Church of St Simon and St Jude to hear the player say, "this is the warmest church in Sussex". And she was right. But the place had atmosphere and old world charm. It wasn't a 'sit down' church until an organist and a pianist played in harmony. It was beautiful, not precisely in time with each other but nevertheless it sounded good. I sat. I had control and, I'm very pleased to say, I was ok.

From this church, passing through another Tapsell Gate we head for The Tiger Inn. After our walk, some shocks, and facing our demons, I thought a drink was called for. I order a lager, Ron, being Ron, asks for a pint of Admans Explorer even though his favourite tipple, Harvey's Bitter, is available. My lager was cool and refreshing; Ron's Explorer was dark and cloudy. "Bet 'e doesn't sell much o' this in a week," comments Ron, "not a patch on 'arvey's. 'Ope it ain't 'eadin' fer Kings 'ead." But when you stop and think, it's December and we're outside supping ale in glorious sunshine in the most beautiful surroundings imaginable. The Tiger at East Dean is not on a main road yet people are arriving from every direction to sit, eat and drink in this pub. The menu looked appetising and not too pricey and what we saw of the food looked plenty and nourishing. You can't get a better advertisement than that.

Tomorrow is my wife's birthday. I have to try and get six chapters printed along with the other requirements of our pushy agent before Monday evening. It's also my choice of walk for next week so I will have to do a balancing act to ensure my good lady isn't left out. Wish me luck. I'll need it.

---

[144] http://www.naval-history.net/WW2BritishLossesbyName3.htm viewed 09/12/2006

WALK 46 - Ringmer

Wednesday 13th December 2006

I have one or two problems with this week's walk. It is my turn to choose where we are to go. Originally, as you are all aware, we used to walk on a Wednesday. When I started to work full-time we moved to Saturday or Sunday during term time. I will now explain my problem. Saturday I have to work. A group of girls from school are flying in to Stanstead Airport and I have to meet the flight and drive them back to Eastbourne. So we can't walk on Saturday. My granddaughter is performing in her first nativity play at The Pavilion, in Hailsham on Sunday. So we can't walk on Sunday. Thursday my car is booked into the garage to have the brakes

checked out, again, and it's my son's birthday. I promised to take my wife on the final Christmas shopping trip on Friday, so both of these days are spoken for. When Ron and I meet up, on Monday, not only have I no idea where we are going I also have no idea when. On top of that Lyn, bless her, has delivered part of a fancy dress costume I stupidly said I would wear, on a walk, due to be completed in the week before Christmas. Which is next week, Walk 47. And it will be Ron's turn to choose where I will be seen. Yo Ho Ho!!!!!!!!!!!!

But let's get back to this week's walk. The school I work for breaks up for Christmas on Wednesday 13th December. I have to dress up, again, as Father Christmas. If I'm lucky I may get some time on Wednesday afternoon because school finishes at 12 o'clock. By the time I get back from Hastings and changed out of

Dressed as you know who

Santa's outfit it should be 1 o'clock and that may give us chance to do a small walk before it gets dark. I've managed to get six chapters printed, proof read and delivered to Lyn, our 'agent' so I don't have that to worry about. I just need to find a short, close to the area, walk for Wednesday and then get in touch with Ron to let him know what time I will pick him up. Piece of cake, isn't it?

But, by Tuesday afternoon, I think I may have found something[145]. A pub walk, naturally. Its only 1½ miles, so should be very comfortable. At Ringmer, that's pretty local and the start is at The Cock. Sorry, that should be, The Cock Inn. So, Wednesday afternoon it is. Now all I have to do is get in touch with Ron. I wonder where he'll be this Tuesday evening. I eventually caught up with him at The Hailsham Club, or Top Club, as it is known. Also there was our new landlady, Helen, to support The Kings Head shove-halfpenny team in one of the local competitions. Helen approached me and asked if Ron and I would let Darren, her husband and landlord of The

The Cock Inn

Kings Head, accompany us on one of our walks. "It would give him a break from standing behind the bar and get him out for some fresh air, for a change," she said. Always willing to keep on good terms with our alcoholic suppliers, we couldn't refuse. "He could take the dog as well", she suggests, "Give Laikaa bit of a run." Again my mind seems to work in the wrong direction. When we first met Laika I thought her name was 'Likeher'. Strange name for a dog but who am I to judge? They obviously saw the dog and 'liked her', hence the name. But no, that is not the reason at all; Laika is named after the first dog to be sent into space, connected to a life-support machine, by the Russians aboard Sputnik 2 on November 3rd 1957. She was also known as 'Kudryavka'. 'Laika' means 'barker' in Russian and 'Kudryavka' means 'Little Curly'. The 1,120-lb. Sputnik 2 was outfitted with scientific gauges, life-

---

[145] Walk 29 from Pub Walks in East Sussex by Mike Power

support systems, and padded walls, but was not designed for recovery. Laika was supported inside the satellite by a harness that allowed some movement and access to food and water. Electrodes transmitted vital signs including heartbeat, blood pressure and breathing rate The American press nicknamed the dog Muttnik. She captured the hearts of people around the world as the batteries that operated her life-support system ran down and the capsule air ran out. Life slipped away from Laika a few days into her journey. Later, Sputnik 2 fell into the atmosphere and burned on April 14, 1958. Laika is remembered on a plaque at the Moscow research centre where she was trained. [146]

The original Laika

The main problem, I discovered when suggesting this walk to Ron, was finding out exactly where The Cock was. (Innuendo again, I'm sorry!) I know Ringmer reasonably well and can't remember seeing it when I last passed through on the way to Lewes. So it's not on the main road. We asked a number of people but not one person could say, exactly, where it was. Ron thought he knew when he said it was nearer Barcombe than Ringmer. The book said it was on the A26 heading towards Uckfield but surely the A26 doesn't run through Ringmer.

I didn't get to pick Ron and Darren up until 2.30. My run to Hastings took longer than anticipated. When I pulled up, still not having much idea how to find The Cock, I was surprised to see Pip, not my son's dog, but a female acquaintance of Ron and me, who frequents our local, heading towards my car. "She knows exactly where The Cock is," says Ron with the biggest grin I've seen on him for some time. So, instead of just Ron and me heading towards Ringmer it became a little expedition party with Ron, me, Pip, Darren and, of course, Laika.

Doing what dogs do do !

Ringmer has been in the news for the past few days. A very large fire and explosion at a fireworks factory tragically caused two fatalities from the Fire and Emergency Department who were sent to extinguish the flames. Only a few days after this tragic loss of life an inquest was officially opened and immediately adjourned until after the cause of the tragedy had been established. People may remember Walk 24, which was dedicated to our old friend Sean who, tragically died on the 7th of July this year. Yet his inquest was held on the 12th December, five months after his death. It seems a long time to wait.

To find The Cock was a little confusing. We passed the turning before I realised it and had to detour round some country lanes, but we got there in the end. The walk, itself is only 1½ miles so it would be the shortest walk we have completed. I wasn't that sure what to expect and wondered what I would see to write about but I hope these few pages will be as amusing as the actual walk turned out to be.

Open fields

Dogs can be really strange animals. They seem to be able to operate their bowels at will. I have had many embarrassing moments with my sons' dogs when they decide to stop for a call of nature. Of course they aren't children, they don't understand "go to the loo before we go out" because the toilet is their main reason for going out. Laika was no exception. She squatted just as she got out of the car and we hadn't been ten yards into the first field when the call of nature called again. And it called out loud. Darren needed two plastic bags. A few yards further into the walk Darren needed another plastic bag. "I've only brought five with us. I hope she doesn't want

[146] http://www.spacetoday.org/Astronauts/Animals/Dogs.html visited 13/12/06

to go again," says Darren. Ron is out of control. He's suggested all sorts of things that could be done with the full up plastic bags but modesty and legal issues will not permit me to write exactly what he said.

Our walk continues across a couple of fields until we come to some farm buildings and a lane. Here we turn left. Our instructions are to proceed along the lane for nearly half a mile. "We should have brought a ball for Laika to chase," I suggest to Darren. "She doesn't like balls," says Darren, "she prefers plastic bottles or large tree branches." Darren managed to find a tree branch lying by the side of the road and Laika happily walked down the middle of the road with her tree in her mouth.

Laika walks stick

We are now in a place called Upper Wellingham, which is simply a small hamlet with some very nice, very expensive houses lying back off the road. The temperature seems to have dropped by some degrees and the wind is now getting stronger. My original thought that Pip and Darren had overdone the clothes disappeared as I started to feel the cold. "Should 'ave put som' in' a bit warmer on," says Ron. But I pointed out that it was a rush to get to the pub for 2.30. I had to wear what I'm wearing now or it was going to have to be the Father Christmas outfit. I think Pip liked the idea of Santa, or did I misread the look and sly smile?

After a while we find the turning on our left, opposite Wellingham House, which will lead us across fields and back to The Cock Inn. Standing in the field, just to the left of the stile is one of my favourite animals (?) "If he starts heading towards us," says Pip "I'll beat you to the next stile!" "I bet yer, Graham gets to it first," says Ron. "Lets hope we don't have to find out," I say as we step it out across the field, keeping an eye on the big black beastie behind us. But we

True Sussex Cattle?

didn't have to worry. He didn't budge. Just stood there and watched us. But it did have some effect on one of us. As we got to the other side of the field Ron decided that the combination of the cold, the walk and the animal was too much and shot behind the hedge.

Two more fields later and we are back on the road heading towards The Cock Inn and the end of this short, but enjoyable stroll through pleasant surroundings and with very good company. Laika has decided that enough is enough with the stick; if dad wants to throw it again he can go and fetch it.

As we are walking along the road it is just starting to get dark. "Perhaps we should have bought a torch with

Ron, doing what Ron does?

us," suggests Pip. "You won't need a torch," says Ron, "not with three strong brave men to protect yer. And Laika of course. Thinking of brave men," he continues, "'ave you decided what fairy costume to wear next week?" he asks me with that silly smile of his. I have to be honest. I've had one or two problems with the costume. The skirt I have, thanks to Lyn's friend. (Do I mean thanks?) It's the under garments that worry me. "I don't know what to wear on the top bits either." "What you need is a leotard," offers Pip. "In this weather I'm going to need something a bit warmer than a leotard. If it's this cold it'll make me nipples stand out." "Nothing wrong in that," says Pip. "If I was to ask, would you wear something that made your bits stick

The light is disappearing

out?" I ask Pip and as quick as a flash Ron says, "If she says yes ter that I can fill a coach with a load o' mates, all with buckets of ice. Love ter see it, they would." I said to Pip, "You should always be careful what you say in front of Ron, look at the messes I've got us into just by not thinking. He may keep you up to that now." But all Pip would say was, "We'll see," and I thought it best to drop the subject.

Back at the car Ron asks if we can visit the church at Ringmer. It's on the way home so neither of us objects.

Unfortunately the church is locked. We are told by one of the parishioners at the church that this is due to vandalism. But the outside of the building is impressive and the churchyard, which extends to the other side of the road, is very well-kept. The Church of St Mary the Virgin has very little documentation about what went on within the church[147]. Most of its history is about the building itself. It is believed that a church has stood on the current site for over 1,000 years and although we were unable to gain access to the church, the wonderful web site, listed in the footnote, gives you all, and I really mean all, the information you could want. Including a list of the people interred in the churchyard and a list of Vicars that starts with Richard in 1233. If you have access to the Internet, go see.

So that's the end of walk 46. As you will now be aware the next walk is just before the Christmas festivities. It will be carried out in fancy dress and my costume is to be the fairy from the Christmas tree. Joining Ron and me is to be Lyn, to take photographs and Audrey who was also talked into braving the elements. Sadly, for me, I will not be able to make Monday's meeting at The Kings Head due to a prior arrangement. So I am leaving the decision to Ron and Lyn as to where this embarrassing episode in my life will be. Please be gentle with me.

Ringmer Church at dusk

---

[147] http://www.ringmerchurch.org.uk/ visited 14/12/06

WALK 47 - Pett

Thursday 21st December 2006

As I was not present at Monday's meeting I had little input into this week's walk. However, back at walk 39, I stupidly made the suggestion, within earshot of everyone, that on the week before Christmas it would be a good idea to complete the walk in fancy dress. Walk 47 is the walk before Christmas. Apparently I agreed to dress as the fairy from the tree. Others on this walk are Lyn, who, at the time of writing the first part of this chapter, refuses to disclose what she is wearing, Ron, who has no idea what he will be wearing and Audrey who I haven't seen since walk 39 but Ron assures me that she is aware of what is about to happen on this walk.

Pett Church

Before the actual walk I have discovered that my colleagues, for the walk at least, have been very good to me and decided on a circular 4½-mile stroll around Pett[148]. This was Lyn's suggestion and when I asked why she simply said, "because I have no idea where it is and nobody will recognise me!" That's a good enough reason for me as well. Apparently, though, a trip to two of our favourite hostelries in Hailsham has also been planned.

My costume will consist of numerous layers of thermal underwear, dyed pink to represent my perfect skin tones, knitted leg warmers, to protect my beautifully structured calves, and walking boots to ensure that my toes are completely protected should I be required to do a pirouette. Due to the expected cold weather I will also be wearing a hat to keep in place my coiffure hairstyle and wings will also be worn as an obligatory accessory. A fairy wand replaces my usual thumb stick. Now doesn't that conjure up a serene picture? I'm sure that, within the following pages, a photograph of me, taken by Lyn, as that beautiful fairy will shock and alarm you all.

Looking back to the last time Ron and I were in the area (Walk 43) it didn't stop raining. Then we were at Winchelsea, just a few miles up the road from Pett. The church at Pett is relatively modern, being built in 1860 at a cost of £2,000. Its most noteworthy features are its tall, octagonal belfry and spire, and the large gargoyles that peer down from it[149]. Unfortunately for us, and luckily for the people of Pett, we didn't stop to look round this monument.

The Battle of Beachy Head

Whether this is coincidence, or there is some other reason for the town being called Pett, in 1679 a third rate, 70 gun, ship was built for the Royal Navy by a master shipwright named Phineas Pett II. The ship was built at Chatham. After a battle, just off Beachy Head on 10th July 1690, between the French, British and Dutch fleets the "Anne" was beached at Pett and burnt by her captain[150].

The battle was fought between an Anglo Dutch fleet under the Earl of Torrington with 56 vessels of which 22 Dutch vessels were under the control of Cornelis Evertsen. Vice Admiral Sir Ralph Delavall commanded the 12-ship strong rear, against a French fleet consisting of seventy ships of the line and five frigates in ten kilometre lines with the largest in the middle.

Although the French won, they failed to exploit their victory over the damaged opponent to deal a decisive blow to Anglo-Dutch sea power. Torrington, meanwhile, was court-

---

[148] The Argus, East Sussex Walks by Ben Perkins Page 38
[149] http://www.villagenet.co.uk/rotherlevels/villages/pett.php visited 17/12/06
[150] http://www.battleships-cruisers.co.uk/sailship.htm visited 17/12/06

marshalled for failing to support the Dutch and retreating but arguing that his action prevented an invasion, was acquitted[151].

Am I really going out like this?

Today is Thursday. The big day has arrived. The weather is very cold and foggy. Heathrow, Gatwick and Stansted Airports have grounded all their planes. Visibility in these places is down to a hundred metres or less. And I've only just realised that I haven't made my star. So it's out to the garage to knock something up. "Don't forget to clean the oven before you go on your walk," says the wife just before nine o'clock. I'm due to meet my walking partners in an hour and I have to get changed. Lyn phones, "Have you seen the weather this morning," she asks, "what have you let us in for?" "It's a little cool," I say, "it'll be ok. Just dress up warm."

The star is made, the oven is clean and I manage to get changed in time. My daughter insists on getting a photo before I set off "just in case you get locked up over Christmas."

At The Kings Head I am met by Ron, dressed as one of 'Santa's little helpers' and Lyn and Audrey, both dressed as 'Mother Christmas'. After a quick photo shoot we prepare for the off. One of the things I have been asked about this walk was 'why?'. My only answer was 'why not?' Before we got to the car a number of vehicles passed us and tooted. We waived at the cars but the one vehicle that really made it all worthwhile was an invalid carrying bus. The look on those people, as they passed and waived made the following suffering worthwhile. And we did suffer. Or, at least, I did!

Happy group photo

As I said earlier, Lyn had no idea where Pett was. As we drove through Hastings she realised that it wasn't just round the corner from Hailsham. She also hadn't realised it was a bit of a climb. The names Cliff End and Fairlight Cove meant nothing to Lyn. "I didn't read the instructions I just thought no one would recognise me," she says as we, eventually, pull up outside Pett church.

We actually started this walk twice. The first time I realised that I had left the camera in the boot of the car, so had to go back. Luckily it wasn't too far. Unfortunately I left my gloves in the boot, as well, but didn't realise until well over half-way into the walk. And it got cold.

View across the valley

The walk starts up steps and through a kissing gate just to the left of the church. The sign is very clear and we had no trouble finding the gate. Once through the gate we head down a few fields keeping the hedge to our left. The view across this valley, looking towards Fairlight, would be stunning if the weather was a little warmer, but it is freezing cold. Parts of my anatomy have started to shrivel in the cold and the thermal underwear is starting to feel uncomfortable. We've only gone a few yards and I was quickly realising the error of my ways and was promising myself that I would not suggest anything this stupid again!

It isn't until you climb over a number of stiles that you realise how exhausting getting your leg over can be.

Ron gives a helping hand

Throughout this walk Audrey and Lyn tried to keep count of the number of stiles we had to

---

[151] http://en.wikipedia.org/wiki/Battle_of_Beachy_Head_(1690) visited 17/12/06

get over but gave up after an hour. It just seemed to be stile after stile for ages. Field led into field and stile followed stile as we head towards New Barn Farm, before turning left onto Rosemary Lane. Again, although only a lane, the traffic along this small stretch of countryside all tooted and waived to us. "'ope nothin' goes missin' from round 'ere," says Ron, "we look a bit obvious walkin' along these fields. Be easy ter give a description." "But

Lyn finds the mud

can you imagine", says Audrey, "the look on the policeman's face when they tell him it was a fairy, two mother Christmases and an elf?" "They'd be breathalysed before they thought to catch us," offers Lyn. But its still getting cold and parts of me have now disappeared without trace. "Are you ok?" Lyn asks me, "You look very cold." "I'm not too bad," I lie, "I'll soon warm up when we start climbing that hill to the top of Cliff End."

As Rosemary Lane turns sharply right we find a path, on the left, up steps and over another stile. We now need to head towards some farm buildings, seen in the distance. To the right of the buildings is yet another stile. Over this and we then turn right and walk along the driveway, away from Marsham Farm. We find the double gate on the left that we need to go through but cannot see the 'widely spaced fences' that we need to walk past. A car pulls up behind us. "Can I help you?" asks the lady driver. "I think we have the right place," I say as I walk towards the car, battling to keep my wings from the top of my head "but our book says that there should be a fence running along this field." "I had that fence removed months ago. What are you doing on my land dressed that way?" she asks. We explain about our walk and she advises us that through the double gate is the right way, "but be careful as it is very muddy, there are lots of foxholes and badger setts when you head towards the road and will you please shut the gates behind you. Dressed the way you are you may scare the horses so be careful." "Merry Christmas to you ma'am," says Ron as she drives off down her drive. "You may scare the horses," imitates Lyn as she skips into the field. "It'll take something a bit bigger than us to scare any of these horses. Have you seen the size of them? They only raised their heads, took a quick look at us and carried on as if we weren't here."

Badger setts

Heading towards the cliffs

We walk on down the slope, past the foxholes and badger setts and joined a road, where we turn left. We now need to find a stream with a turning just after it on the right. We should then climb the steps and another stile. We are now on National Trust land heading towards Fairlight and the cliffs. The path winds through trees and scrub until we reach a small cottage. There used to be three cottages here but due to the erosion of the cliff two of the cottages fell into the sea leaving just the one, teetering on the very edge. The view behind us is brilliant even though the fog still overshadows the distant view. Without thinking I approach the edge of the cliff and a small gust of wind pushes me even closer to the edge. What I forgot was the wings strapped to my back.

"Overweight Fairy Plummets into Fairlight Cove," says Lyn. You can see the headlines in the papers. "Two Mother Christmases and Santa's little helper can't save fairy. Now get away from the edge while I answer my mobile." I love Lyn when she gets assertive. We walk

The view from the top

along this well trodden path for just over a mile before it becomes a lot narrower and leads us

behind some very nice, but expensive, houses. One old gentleman must have thought he'd had one two many brandies. He called his grandson to confirm what he was seeing. But with a cheery Merry Christmas we made our way to a small road and turned left.

We now had to find yet another stile, on the right, and head diagonally across a field heading to the right of a red tile hung bungalow. This we found without any problem. But this is where our real problems started. Until now we had managed to follow the instructions in the book without difficulty. All that was about to change.

Half-way across the field we see a large sheep. The sheep appears to be by itself until we notice a couple of lambs running

Path behind houses

about. "It's a bit late in the year for lambs, isn't it?" I ask anyone who's listening. "If she's got lambs she might not be very friendly," says Lyn. That's enough for me. I'm all for leaving the field now but Ron's soothing words, "she wont 'urt yer, just don't show 'er yer scared," reminds me of so many other walks we've completed. The sheep, with lambs runs off to the other side of the field and we pass, thankfully, without conflict. And now it all goes terribly wrong.

The instructions don't make sense. We are told to turn left over a stream and head up the slope, towards a stile. But we end up in a wood. There's no mention of a wood in our guidebook. Through the end of the wood we come to a stile.

Sheep with lamb??

Crossing over the stile we can see the steeple of Pett church to our right. "That church steeple should be on our left-hand side," I advise the others whilst looking at our map. "We must've had to turn right by the stream and not left," offers Lyn. "Lets go back," says Audrey, "and

follow the stream a bit further. We should be able to see the steeple from the stream." Ron just giggles as we head back, through the wood and to the stream. At the start of this chapter I mentioned pirouettes. When walking through this wood the first time, I called out 'hole', to warn my fellow walkers, behind me, of the danger whilst I promptly fell into another hole I didn't see. On the way back, remembering the hole, I advised them of slippery mud, only to slip myself, practically performing a double salco and obtaining 9.5 on the scoreboard. Ron is now in hysterics. "Now yer knows why I always walk be'ind 'im. I'd miss out on the laughs if I were in front."

We eventually get back to the stream and follow its path along the edge of a couple of fields until we can see the steeple

Ron looking intelligent?

again. The guidebook is still telling us to turn left but I suggest that we head straight for the church. There are no signs to let us know which way to go. At least if we head for the church we know we are going in the right direction. So it was agreed to head for the church rather than fathom out the rest of the instructions.

All the time around the walk I have had one or two problems with my outfit. The long johns, although thermal, certainly were not warm. I should have listened to Lyn's advice and worn a pair of my wife's tights because I may have saved what was now left of my

Making an adjustment

personal bits. But with the combination of skirt, underwear and long johns it was keeping them up that caused me problems. Everything kept moving and I found myself making a grab for bits as the walk progressed. But we all managed to the end even if it did mean a slight detour.

Our intention, when this walk was completed, was to visit The Grenadier and The Kings Head but time was not on our side. We managed to get back to The Kings Head where we were treated to hot food, thank you Helen and Darren. The open fire was made to good use as I tried to thaw out some bits that I'd thought I would never see again. We didn't manage to get to The Grenadier for which we apologies should anyone have been expecting us. But perhaps on our next walk...............

My fellow walkers will be pleased to know that I have promised myself that I will not offer any more suggestions on what we should or should not do on the remainder of our walks. This one has taught me a valuable lesson.

All that remains is for Ron and me, along with all our walking companions, to wish one and all of our readers a very Merry Christmas and a prosperous New Year.

Back at The Kings Head, parts of me needed a warm up!

WALK 48 - Slindon

Wednesday 27th December 2006

Monday was Christmas Day so Ron and I didn't meet at The Kings Head to discuss this week's walk. This is the second Christmas without my parents and I still miss them terribly. At this time of year the most important people, to me, are my family and the traditional things we do to celebrate Christmas. Thankfully my wife, Emelia, and my son and daughter also feel that this is the time of year we spend together. So it is a round of parties, at different locations, with good food, ample to drink and a few games thrown in that eases my thoughts of the ones who are no longer with us.

Finding time to look at walks is limited so I'm a bit relieved, on Tuesday morning, when my wife and daughter assist me to find a walk that will give us some history, some beautiful Sussex countryside but will not be too tiring after the festivities of the previous night. After much discussion and reasoning it was decided on Slindon in West Sussex[152].

I know nothing of this village but, as usual, scouring the Internet to come up with information about the place we are about to walk I found reference to Hilaire Belloc[153] and I couldn't wait to make our visit.

In walk 24 (Page 102) I state that Shipley was the home of Hilaire, but for three years 1903 to 1906 Hilaire lived, with his wife, Elodie, and four children at Bleak House, Slindon. Their fifth child, Peter, was born there in 1904. But over the following years tragedy was not too far away. In 1914, Hilaire's beloved wife died. A few years later, in 1918, his eldest son, Louise was killed on active service with the Royal Flying Corps. Hilaire's mother died, at The Grange, Slindon in 1924 and his second son, Peter, was killed in action in 1941 with the Royal Marines. In 1942 Hilaire suffered a slight stroke, which left him senile.

Hilaire Belloc

On the 16th July 1953 Hilaire passed away, in a Nursing Home, in Guildford, after a fall and, as I wrote in Walk 24, his remains are interred at West Grinstead Church[154].

Today is Wednesday. I'm due to pick Ron up at ten. There may be others waiting to go on the walk. The fact that we said we would continue on our own, till the end, doesn't seem to be working out as expected. When I arrive outside the pub I can see steam, or smoke, coming from under the bonnet of the car. When I lift the bonnet, oil is dripping down the side of the engine, onto the exhaust pipe. "That doesn't look too healthy," says Pip, one of our co-walkers for the day. "I'll have to shoot the car to the garage to find out what the problem is," I say to Ron and Pip, "I'll only be a few minutes." Darren has emerged from the bar, "do you want to wait inside?" he asks and Ron has gone before the last word has left his lips. "I'll be back shortly." I tell Pip and head for the garage.

The mechanic tells me that the rocker cover gasket has gone. It's not safe to drive and he could fit me in on 2nd January providing he can get the part. It's decision time. If I race back home, I could borrow my wife's car, and get back to the pub. With only Ron and Pip coming on the walk we could fit into my wife's Metro. Or, I could go back to the pub and call it all off. No, that

Slindon Church

---

[152] 'Village Walks in West Sussex' by Douglas Lasseter – Walk 7 – Page 34
[153] Walk 24 (Page 102) and Forward
[154] http://www.consolation.org.uk/belloc.html visited 26/12/2006

means I've let everyone down. So I race home, take everything out of my car, put it in the

Slindon Post Office

wife's, promise her I'll look after her prize possession and head back to the pub only to find that not only is Ron and Pip coming on the walk but so is Helen (our new landlady) and Laika. There is no way we will all fit into the Metro. So Helen and Darren offer the use of their car for the trip to Slindon. What could I say?

Slindon is mentioned in the Domesday Book when it was then known as 'Eslindone' and from watching the scenery pass us by, as I sit as a passenger, I should think that the last 100 years or so has not affected the village. It is one of the most picturesque places I have seen. The Post Office, only open on the odd day during the week, is a picture postcard of a place, with it's thatched roof and olde worlde charm is just begging to be made into a jigsaw puzzle. But our first stop, as usual, is the Church of St. Mary, which is possibly on the same site as the one mentioned in the Domesday Book.

Anthony St Leger

HMCS Athabaskan

One of the churches many claims to fame is that in the year 1228 Archbishop Langton died at The Manor and a plaque, commemorating the event, can be seen on a pillar by the north door[155]. Whilst wandering around the church, both Pip and I noticed plaques commemorating the name Izard. One of the Izard clan served in the Navy aboard HMS Sheffield. My father-in-law also served aboard a ship of this name, which is what caught my eye at first. But what we didn't understand was that a Lieutenant Izard served aboard HMCS Athabaskan. Neither Pip nor I could work out what HMCS stood for. I have since discovered that the ship belonged to Her Majesties Canadian Navy and she was an air defence destroyer[156]. The wonders of the Internet.

Another unusual monument found inside the church is that of Anthony St Leger Esq. of Binstead who died in 1539. He requested, in his will, that he be interred in Slindon and his effigy is believed to be the only one in existence, in Sussex, made of wood.

A very attractive, well-kept church and churchyard, worthy of more time than we, unfortunately, had. We had six miles to cover before the end of today.

It is now that I must offer my apologies to both Pip and Helen. Before embarking on this walk they both advised me that 'they don't do hills'. I think someone may have advised them that some of our past walks were not on level ground. I honestly thought that this one was. The book describes it as 'circular, around old Slindon, before striking out on tracks and wooded paths into beautiful countryside'. There was no mention of hills, but of course, I haven't been right too many times and I was wrong again. I am so very, very sorry.

To continue with the walk, we leave the church and head down Church Hill (the name of the road should have given me a clue about hills??) On our left we see a well-kept Victorian summerhouse, an old railway carriage, with a thatched roof. With Dyers Lane on our left, The Grange (the last home of Madame Belloc (Hilaire's mother)) is on the right. Just beyond this impressive house is the charming village pond, complete with nesting ducks.

Victorian summer house

---

[155] The Church of St Mary, Slindon, Leaflet purchased at Church
[156] http://www.navy.forces.gc.ca/Athabaskan/home/index_e.asp visited 28/12/2006

Our instructions are to continue into Church Road, pass the village stores, all of which remains is the shop front, and bear left into School Hill (another clue??) It is here that used to stand The Newburgh Arms but we were advised by a lady at the church that the owners of the pub had a dispute with some of the villagers and they sold the pub, converted it into a house and painted it bright mauve. "A village with no pub," gasps Ron, "should never 'appen!" Never mind that it was an ugly eyesore in the middle of a beautiful village.

The Grange

We move on, into Top Road, past the Post Office coming to the junction of Mill Lane. Next on the left is Bleak House, the home of Hilaire for a short time. Looking at it you can understand where the name comes from. It certainly looks pretty bleak. A few of the windows had been bricked up, presumably to save money during the 'window tax' era, but you would have thought that the current owners would have opened them up.

We have now completed a circuit of the old village and found the experience fascinating and steeped in history. We now head out into the countryside by walking up Mill Lane towards a way-sign that leads us onto a wide track. The instructions then say '..as you reach its high point the views begin to open up' and I still thought it was on the level? On our right is Dale Park but we have to descend the track and look for a three-way way sign where we need to walk ahead until we reach another way-sign that reads 'bridle road to Bignor'. Please remember that whilst we are walking, I am reading the next instructions. Sometimes I read too far ahead of where we are. This is one of those occasions.

Bleak House

The next five or six instructions involve one-way, two-way or three-way way signs. And I'm confused but Laika seemed to be enjoying the freedom. I have to admit that female logic and intuition saved the day. Both Pip and Helen managed to make sense of the instructions and led us in the right direction. That was, until we hit the wood. Again we are to look for way signs. We found none. We did find yet more hills but no way signs. So we walked through the wood. One of the things we did see, in the wood, was catkins. "Blimey," says Ron, "its a bit early ter see catkins out, ain't it? They shouldn't be 'ere till the spring. Just goes ter prove, don't it?" But what it goes to prove I have no idea. But catkins were to be seen in Nore Wood two days after Christmas. We walked for what seemed like hours but was probably not that long until we eventually found a way sign that had been demolished and lying on the ground, broken. I had

View over Dale Park

The Samuel Rofey folly

Laika having fun

no idea but again, Pip and Helen came to the rescue. They placed the way sign, with the bridleway arrow pointing at the path, which was obviously the only bridleway. From the position of the now upright sign we could establish the path that excludes cyclists (from our instructions) and found that we needed to turn left, along the path that had been paved with chalk. Oh so easy isn't it?

Unfortunately, the path we were now on brought us out on the wrong side of Nore Folly. But it mattered not. At least we were in the right area. For some unknown reason this Folly was built by Samuel Rofey in 1814 for the Countess Newburgh (Could she have been something to do with the now closed pub??)

Trying to miss the puddles

We pass the Folly with views of the Channel to our right. And head back, along various tracks to the village. At least the trip back is mostly downhill. Although both Pip and Helen still keep giving me funny looks I think they enjoyed the afternoon as much as Ron and I did.

One of these tracks led us past, what Helen described as, a seal emerging from a tree and the more you look at the picture the more it looks real.

For most of the walk along the countryside we managed to stay reasonably clean but our instruction book did advise us that it gets a bit muddy towards the end of the walk. You will see, from the picture that Pip appears to be the only one who was worried about keeping Darren's carpets clean in his car. Even Laika went paddling. But it was a lovely walk, even with all the ups and downs. Would you believe that the very last part of the walk, getting back to the car there was a hill to be climbed?

Thanks for your company Pip, Helen and, of course, Laika. We are all sure that Laika will spend the next few hours fast asleep. After all, she has walked a lot further than all of us.

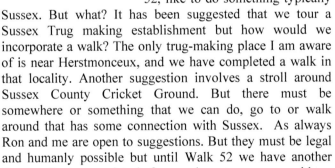

The Last Hill?

We are now fast approaching our last walk and would, for walk 52, like to do something typically Sussex. But what? It has been suggested that we tour a Sussex Trug making establishment but how would we incorporate a walk? The only trug-making place I am aware of is near Herstmonceux, and we have completed a walk in that locality. Another suggestion involves a stroll around Sussex County Cricket Ground. But there must be somewhere or something that we can do, go to or walk around that has some connection with Sussex. As always Ron and me are open to suggestions. But they must be legal and humanly possible but until Walk 52 we have another three walks to complete before we have to come up with an idea.

Beautiful Sussex path

A spooky vision?

WALK 49 - Waldron

Wednesday 3rd January 2007

This week's walk is set as a challenge. I believe that money has been wagered and bets are, as I write this, being placed on how far Ron and I get, following the instructions in the book, before we get lost. A trio of our female followers, I can't call them groupies, or can I (?) have wagered a pint of Harvey's Best Bitter against a glass of Archers that, at some point, we will get lost. As we seem to get 'geographically misplaced' on a number of our walks I can't understand why Ron is so sure that this time we will find our way with ease. "I've got ev'ry confidence in Graham getin' us round," he says, "It'll be the best pint ov Harvey's I've 'ad when I gets it, on Friday." I'm under no pressure at all, and when I see the directions of the walk chosen by Helen, Pip and Sophie I offer to buy them all a glass of Archers and Ron his pint of Best. I just wish I were as confident as Ron because we are to walk a relatively new circular walk from the village of Waldron, out to the village of Blackboys and back with instructions that are vague to say the very least.

But first, a little history on Waldron. In Saxon times the village was known as Walda, meaning wooded ground. The name was later changed to Walderne. In 1412 Sir William de Walderne, from the local manor, became Lord Mayor of London.

The village was visited by Cromwell's troops around 1650 and it is said that the troops rolled the font down the hill. The actual font has been restored to the church and is believed to be one of only three great round Saxon fonts to be found in Sussex.

The Blackboys Inn

The churchyard contains many memorials to the Fuller Family, the iron masters from nearby Heathfield and Brightling. One of the vicars of the Parish referred whimsically to the churchyard as 'Fullers Earth'.

During the mid 1800's the area produced a large volume of hops, but this stopped when the price of Sussex hops plummeted and Kent took over the main production[157].

As I said, our walk also takes us into Blackboys, a small village that is believed to get its name from the colour of the Charcoal burners when they emerged from the woods. However, others say the name means Black Wood, from the soot deposited in the woods by the charcoal.

The Blackboys Inn was founded in the late1300's and was known as a coaching establishment. It was, originally, a farmhouse but was converted to an alehouse to service the

Waldron Church

needs of workers at the local iron foundries. The Inn is reputed to be haunted by the ghost of Anne Starr, who died in childbirth in an upstairs bedroom[158].

Our walk is taken, this week, from the book 'Argus East Sussex Walks'[159]. It is described as '...a superb but poorly publicised network of new paths licensed for public use under the Countryside Stewardship Scheme'. A wonderfully grand introduction to a 5-mile, circular, walk.

We are to be accompanied today by Andrew, a college student studying I.T. at Eastbourne College. "I've been studyin' 'it' fer a long time," comments Ron. "Still

---

[157] http://villagenet.co.uk/sevensisters/villages/waldron.php visited 01/01/2007
[158] Around Heathfield in Old Photographs collected by Alan Gillet and Barry K Russell ISBN 0-86299-714-3
[159] The Argus East Sussex Walks by Ben Perkins – Page 48

don't understand 'it'. But, 'specs I never will." Andrew is nearly through part of his course and hopes, when he completes, in about two years time, that his qualifications will get him into University.

Today is Wednesday and it's raining. But, as always, when we pull up outside Waldron Church, the rain stops. How does he do that? My last memory of this church was a number of years ago when I was a fledging genealogist and looking for relatives graves (I found no connections!) and found that the graveyard went on and on for what seemed like acres. It actually stretched into some wooded areas where trees had uprooted the

A round font??

stones. The last time I was here I was unable to get inside the church but I'm pleased that today the church was open for us all to have a look round. Again the very informative leaflet[160], not only with information about the church but also about the village can be purchased and is well worth the £1. It is a minefield of information,

Our first stile

including some, perhaps not so Christian, comments regarding what was at first thought to be one of only three round fonts to be found in Sussex. You will see from the picture that the actual font currently used by the church is, in fact, far from round. But you will have to go and purchase the book to find out what happened to the round font. It's a wonderful story.

We need to walk through part of the graveyard to reach a stile leading into a field to the left of the church. The path here is well worn so we have little problems in tracing our way across two fields where we find a stile along the right-hand edge. "If we carry on like this that pint's as good as mine!" chuckles Ron. We now need to head towards a gate and once through there should be a grassy path continuing through newly planted woodland. As you can see from these pictures the going was very muddy and, as we pass through the gate, I manage to perform a double salco with 2½ twists and landed on the

Muddy paths

camera. Both Ron and Andrew give me a maximum score of 10 for artistic impression but only 9.5 for difficulty and it hurts. The first thing I do is check that the camera is ok. Thankfully I've done no damage to that but my ribs are, already, starting to hurt.

The newly planted woodland didn't look that new and when

Newly planted woodland

we looked at the book it was published in 1995 so it wasn't surprising to see the trees so tall. The reason that this walk was chosen by our three female friends was that they assumed the instructions would not be very good. In fact some of

Easily found gaps

the instructions advise us to look for gaps in hedges. But we all have to agree that, so far, the walk is very clearly marked and we have no trouble finding our way. We

---

[160] Waldron Parish Church and its Surroundings, by Frank M. McBain - £1 from the church

have one or two problems standing upright and I've even seen Ron and Andrew slide about in the mud.

Another easy to find path

We now follow this woodland path for about ¼ of a mile until we see another sign telling us to turn right. After just a few yards we then turn left and head along a winding path through older woodland. Alongside this path is a little stream, which runs down the hill and out of the woodland. Here is our first instruction that tells us to look for a gap in the hedge, into the next field. And we found it. Ron is getting really confident now of being able to drink his pint on Friday. Again our instructions advise us of being in some difficulty when it tells us that the next path may be obliterated by the farmer. But, as can be seen from the picture the path was easily located. We had more problems walking across the open, muddy, field than anything else. Ron is becoming impossible to be with. And every time I laugh it hurts.

At the top of the field we find the farmer has diverted the path, and the diversion leads us to the right of a house and we join a lane. Here we turn left, walk just a few yards, go right, over a stile and head, downhill between the banks. On our right, as we go over the stile, is a chicken run, full of chicken, obviously, and one very proud cockerel. "Used ter 'ave a cockerel like 'im," says Ron, "Cor 'e was a randy bugger. Use ter wait outside the 'en 'utch in the mornin' just waitin' fer them chickens ter come out. The first one out, 'e'd 'ave 'er. You could see the chickens in the 'utch pushin' and a shovin' the others ter make sure they weren't the first one out. Used ter makes me laugh. Funny though I can't remember what breed o' cockerel 'e was." I am in hysterics, and agony. We have to stop while I pull myself together and stop my ribs from hurting. If anyone knows the breed can you please remind Ron?

Light Sussex cockerel

No problems again

Our instructions, again, ask us to look for a hole in the hedge and I have to say that, again, it was found with ease. We are then advised to keep to the right-hand side of the field before going right again through a wide gap. This is too easy. Why didn't I wager a pint of amber nectar as well? I was beginning to feel left out. Ron is now thinking of putting a stick in his pint of Harvey's, leaving it the freezer and taking it as a lolly on our next walk. God help us!

We now join another lane and turn left. Our instructions now tell us to go right, after 100 yards, under some wrapped barbed wire and follow the

Into Beechy Road

edge of the woodland. We didn't find the wire but a clearly marked stile lead us to the edge of the woodland. After a short distance the wood edge turned right and we needed to go half-left and head for a gate. This took us out, onto Beechy Road, which we needed to follow until we came to Bushberry Lane. Our instructions told us that the way would be signposted to Eason's Green but we never saw the sign. Again thoughts of our old friend Phil come to mind and the amount of work we have found him over the past months.

The one sign we did see, Bushberry Lane, was falling apart and had a finger completely missing.

Turn right into Bushberry

We follow this Lane until we reach a place called Old Pear Tree Barn. Believe me when I say that this is no barn. It is enormous and been converted into a very desirable residence. "Another place that don't vote Labour!" comments Ron.

Just past the 'barn' we turn right over a stile. Again this wide pathway is very clearly marked and my fears about this walk have all but disappeared. All of us had noticed a lady walking a dog behind us. Always staying a few yards back and never getting any closer. "P'raps she thinks we're casin' the joint," offers Ron. "It must seem strange, three blokes walking across fields and stopping every now and again to take photos'," says Andrew, and to be honest I've never thought of it like that but, to some people, our actions must look a bit suspicious.

The pathway widens in places and, towards the end, is lined with a row of grand oak trees. After about half a mile of this path we meet another lane and turn left. As with the rest of this walk the signs are very clear and easily seen.

Path lined with old oaks

We follow this lane for just over a quarter of a mile. "Do you realise," says Ron, "that with all the lanes we've been on we ain't seen one car yet." But along this short stretch of road we counted four but didn't see another one until we got back to Waldron.

We are now at Blackboys and have to turn right, through a gate, with a Woodland Trust notice on it. It was here that I thought our luck had run out. For some reason the farmer had diverted the walk away from the signed path. But he had diverted the path with loads of signs, which explained that he had sheep in season and didn't want people disturbing or frightening his animals with dogs. The signs again were very clear and easy to follow. Sorry girls but it is beginning to look as if we might make it all the way without getting lost!

Christmas Trees

We eventually arrive at a concrete drive where we turn left and then immediately right just short of Dower House Farm. We continue between fences skirting to the right of some pheasant rearing pens. Knowing how Ron feels about this type of farming both Andrew and I keep him occupied by talking about the enormous Christmas trees to our right when we eventually reach a gate. It is very muddy here and Andrews's trainers, yes

Up the bank and over the stile

trainers, are looking a bit worse for wear. We walk through a licensed bridleway, which divides left, and right. We bear right and emerge at another clearly marked stile by a gate. We now need to head for the tree in the distance, which also

We head for a distant tree

had a waysign attached to it. We now follow a path through more woodland until we meet another lane and turn right. The next stile is on our left and we find it up a steep bank. "Should be able ter see church from up 'ere," says Ron, "eat yer 'eart out, girls, I knew Graham could do it."

It is just along a short woodland trail that we come out at the Recreation Ground at Waldron. Ron says the inevitable, "used ter play cricket 'ere. Got run out I did. 'it the ball real 'ard, I did, an' it went straight fer the slope. Should 'ave been four runs. But would yer credit it? The damn ball stopped, halfway up the bank, the fielder waited for it ter roll back towards 'im and 'e threw it at the stumps an' I was given out." You can always rely on Ron for a story of some sort. The walks wouldn't be the same without one of his "I used ter.....

Another walk completed and I must admit that it was a lot more enjoyable than I thought it was going to be, apart, of course, from the damage done to my ego as well as my now, very painful ribs.

Next week I will try to find a walk where there is every possibility that I might remain on my two feet or spend a little time seated. Does that give you a clue on what to expect??

Waldron Village Centre

WALK 50 - Bosham

Saturday 13th January 2007

My intention, for this week's walk, was something a little different. I had seen a walk in one of our many books that started in one town, and, after a few miles ended in another. The return journey, back to the car, was by train. A nice change from the regular, I thought, and, as I said, a little different. I checked train times and found that the hourly service would fit in ideally with our plans. I checked the walk; it was 5¾ miles across farmland, through woods and along country lanes. No problem. I then enquired about tickets. "Three pounds forty," said the British Rail ticket office. "But we're only on the train for three minutes," I protest, " The train leaves Etchingam at 13:30 and arrives at Robertsbridge at 13:33 and it costs £3.40. For two people that works out at £2.27 a minute. On top of that I have to pay for the privilege of parking my car at the station. And British Rail wants to encourage us to use the train service."

The murder of Sir Thomas

So we're going to walk round Bosham, instead. I am led to this venue for a number of reasons. The place is a hive of history, dating back to King Aethelred (known as 'the Unready') who died in 1016 and also, King Cnut (known to us as King Canute who tried to hold back the tide[161]). He eventually became King of England, Denmark, Norway and Sweden and was the most important man in Europe, second only to the Holy Roman Emperor. The walk is also described as '.flat, easy underfoot and route finding is simple.' To be honest my ribs, injured when I fell, last week, are still very tender, so easy and flat are what I'm looking for.

Our walk for this week is 5¾ miles long and at the far west of the county. It is taken from 'Walks into History – Sussex'[162] by John Wilks and can be found on page 39, Walk 6 of this book. As well as King Cnut, Bosham was also the home of Herbert (circa 1120-1190), who, in about 1162, joined the household of St Thomas Becket (Archbishop of Canterbury) and later became St Thomas's leading advisor and biographer. Herbert's account of St Thomas's life and his death on 29th December 1170 can be found in the book Historia Thomae[163], which is still being used in Universities today, to teach students about our history.

Whilst I have been finding out these interesting facts Ron has had a really bad week.

Bosham Craft Centre

England not only lost the Ashes series disgracefully, but the Australians rubbed our noses in the dirt. Apparently it's the first time in lots of years that we've been whitewashed at test cricket. To top this David Beckham, the footballer, has reputedly been sold by Real Madrid to an American Soccer Club and will now earn £70,000 per day. You can imagine Ron's thoughts on these subjects. Thankfully, when I pick him up at 10.00 o'clock he's not in a bad mood, even though it has started to rain. "Don't you worry," he says, "yer won't get soaked on a Saturday, not in Sussex." How he does it I have no idea.

But, again, when he gets in the car it starts to rain. When we get to Bosham it stops. We complete the walk in the dry. He gets back in the car, it starts to rain again.

It isn't until we get to Bosham that I realise that I have been here before. A friend of our son let us borrow his caravan at Selsey for a long weekend. We visited Bosham during that

[161] Picture from - http://www.nashfordpublishing.co.uk/monarchs/images/canute_tide_drawing.jpg visited 07/01/06

[162] *Walks into History – Sussex* by John Wilks page 39,

[163] *Harold : Rex* by John Pollock (Bosham, Penny Royal Publications) 1996

weekend. I loved the place then and I just knew that today was going to make an even bigger impression.

The Holy Trinity Church at Bosham is a must see place. It is truly a sit down church. The history inside this place is phenomenal. It has everything that any church should have plus

some more. One of its many fascinating memorials is that of King Canute's daughter who reputedly drowned in the Mill Stream, just behind the Church, when she was eight years old, in the early part of the 11th century. The memorial reads[164] –

Memorial

To the Glory of God
and in the memory of
a daughter of King Canute
who died early in the 11th century
aged about 8 years
whose remains lie enclosed in a
stone coffin beneath this spot.

Some people may be aware that King Harold II (he who fought William in 1066 at Hastings) came, originally, from Bosham. And it is believed that Harold's remains lie very close to those of King Canute's daughter[165].

From the church we head out towards the shoreline first passing the river where, it is said, King Canute's daughter drowned. The photograph was taken on the 13th January and daffodils are in full bloom??

It is here, on the tidal mud flats, that King Canute tried to hold back the tide. Some believe that the attempt was foolhardy, to say the least, but

The river where Canutes daughter died?

High tide marks on the walls

others now say that Canute wasn't as daft as first thought and that his bizarre actions were to prove to his people that even their great king had limitations to his powers.

This whole area is tidal yet people leave their cars parked on the road around the edge of the mud flats even though signs are clearly displayed, warning of the dangers.

We follow the road along the shoreline passing the Anchor Bleu Inn. "Cor look at that,"

says Ron, "bet it looks a picture in the summer with a high tide an' the water lapping at the wall. Must be a little gold mine fer the owners." We continue around the mud flats, occasionally looking back towards Bosham village and the church. I must admit that when I was here with my wife during that summer we missed so much by not walking round. The scenery and the views are stunning.

We now approach a whitewashed building, at the head of the estuary, which used to be the National School, built in 1834. Here we turn sharp left into 'The Drive' and then, after a few yards, and just past a bungalow, turn right along an enclosed footpath which will, eventually, take us across open fields. Whilst the rain is

View across Bosham harbour

---

[164] Transcribed from tomb within Holy Trinity Church, Bosham
[165] Harold: Rex by John Pollock published by Penny Royal Publications ISBN 1-900851-00-8

holding off the wind is now getting stronger, and colder, by the minute. We arrive at a lane, which we cross and continue ahead towards a house. Our instructions tell us not to bear left, with the track, but continue ahead, past the house and head for the corner of the field. Signposts are easy to find and are clearly marked. Whilst we were walking across these fields I happened to mention to Ron that my wife, on our visit to Bosham, brought lots of pearl beads from the craft centre, seen at the start of the walk. I think she used them when she was

Path through middle of field

making Christening Gowns. "Another thing yer don't see any more," says Ron, "button tins. I can remember me ol' mum sayin' she'd 'ave ter get button tin out every time me dad lost a button on 'is shirt. An' she al'ays found one ter match. Yer don't see that no more. Funny, though, saw a lady at 'ailsham market on Friday brought a whole tub o' buttons. Yer don't see that very often."

Straight tree-lined path

Past the house and through a gap in the hedge takes us out onto the road. Our instructions tell us to cross this road and continue ahead, through the middle of a field. This path eventually takes us to an enclosed path, which is a perfectly straight, tree-lined path of about ¼ of a mile. There aren't many places on any of our walks where both Ron and I have stopped and just looked. But at the end of this path, in a ploughed field, we stopped, listened and admired the view. Unfortunately the weather for this time of year doesn't do justice to the picture but in the summer this walk would be a joy to see. I've promised myself that, of all the walks we have completed, this is one that I must come back to in the summer.

We stop to admire the view

"And when it's 'igh tide," comments Ron, "we can sit at that pub an' 'ave a meal. Be lovely that would." For some unknown reason we start talking about the television series 'Vicar of Dibley', which has to be one of my favourite comedies of all time. There was an hour-long programme on the television, a few evenings ago, about how it was made and that was really funny. "You must be able to get the series on video," I say to Ron, "perhaps I'll have to see if I can find it."

Deer in the far distance

As we walk along the path, heading for the estuary, on our left, in the distance, we see three deer. They can just be seen, in the picture. Throughout our walks we are always on the lookout for these wonderful animals. Today, for once, luck was on our side. Because we are so far away from us they just stopped and looked at us, but didn't move. Another thing that is visible from here, although still some way away is Chichester Cathedral. Another place that is well worth a visit, if you ever get in the area. This is a truly magnificent building which you are able to walk round and discover so much about our history. It was free when I was there but I have noticed, with some cathedrals I've visited, a charge is now being made, which, I think, is a bit of a shame because, if you have a large family, it must put people off.

Chichester Cathedral

A well-fed stray?

As we walk around the head of the estuary, at low tide, it is amazing how much wildlife you can see and hear. The number of different birds that can be seen, either in flight or on the pools, are too many to count. At one point, I headed to the edge of the estuary wall, to take a photograph, and scared a kingfisher into flight. That is the first kingfisher I have ever seen. The trip here, just to see that bird, was worth everything to me. Gladly Ron saw it as well and he confirmed what I had seen. I, personally could have stayed just here for the rest of the day, but, of course, that's not possible. So we continue around the edge of the estuary. We are met by a dog, which appeared from nowhere and disappeared just as quick. No owner could be seen and we could see

Hanging dog pooh

for miles. One of the downsides with this part of the walk is that you have to mind your footing. It is obvious that the walk is used by a considerable number of dogs that brings the usual problems. Again we found one enterprising person who, after clearing it up threw it into the hedge. Perhaps they moved from Winchelsea? Apart from this it didn't spoil the views that can be found along the walk. From the edge of the estuary the walk also takes us through the reed beds, complete with railway sleeper bridges to enable you to get over the many little estuary rivers. Whilst writing this chapter I have come across the usual problem. I have too many photographs and am finding it very difficult to fit them all in. It's not the first time that I've had this problem but this time it seems worse. Perhaps that could be my next project, a pictorial book at the Sussex Countryside. I like the sound of that. Which leads me onto the next photograph. As we leave the estuary we arrive at the village of Fishbourne by a pond with the most attractive thatched cottage behind in a setting from the Victorian era. Both Ron and I were amazed at the tranquillity of this little scene. There were no cars in sight yet, just a few yards away, was the main road. We, eventually, walk up the lane and turn left into the main road.

Ron looks back

Picture postcard material

The Roman Palace at Fishbourne was discovered by accident during the digging of a water main in 1960[166]. It is believed that the site developed from a military base at the time of the Roman invasion in AD43 to a sumptuous palace by the end of the 1st century. Unfortunately, our instructions tell us to pass the road that leads to the Palace so we didn't get chance to have a look. Perhaps when we come back, in the summer?? What we did see was a cycle shop on the main road with loads of cycles outside. "Look at that, " says Ron, "a midwife's tricycle. That's another thing yer don't see."

Memories or what?

Just past the cycle shop we come to a pub called The Black Boy. Ron is gutted to find that the pub is deserted

---

[166] http://www.sussexpast.co.uk/property/site.php?site_id=11 visited 14/01/07

and looks as if it has been for some time. Here we turn left into Old Park Lane and head back towards Bosham. Where the road turns sharp left we continue, in a straight line, along yet another remarkably straight tree-lined path for a ¼ of a mile. It must be the influence of the Romans that have made these roads and tracks so straight. It's along this path that we see row after row of greenhouses full to the brim with plants and shrubs. "Must be the most borin' job in the world," says Ron, "prickin' out plants. An' look at 'ow many there is, in just one o' them 'ouses. Pity the poor bugger 'as ter prick out that lot." We continue along this path until we reach a road and turn left, passing Taylor Lane and School Lane. As we approach the Berkeley Arms we turn left again into an enclosed footpath, which leads us back to the mud flats at Bosham and the car park, where we left the car just four hours ago.

This was a great walk and one of the many walks that I must do again. But next time it must be a lot warmer and, hopefully, include a meal at the Anchor Bleu.

Next week's walk is Ron's last choice in our year of walks. I hope it is a wise one. The one thing I am sure of is that it will include some great scenery. We really don't know how lucky we are until we get out and see for ourselves what a beautiful county we live in.

A last look over the harbour

WALK 51 – Ripe & Chalvington

Saturday 20th January 2007

Monday's meeting took place, as it has done over the past year, at The Kings Head, South Road. Every Monday, since Ron and I started our walks, a decision is made on which area will benefit from our presence. It was Ron's choice this week and, for various reasons, he couldn't decide where we were to go. He had a couple of ideas but needed a little more time to think out his options. This hasn't happened before. I appreciated that this would be the last walk that Ron would be choosing but what was he planning? I was getting a little worried.

During this week the weather had been horrendous. Sussex was struck by storms with very heavy rain and gusts of wind reaching a reported 100 mph. We are told that Sussex bore the brunt of this storm yet, tragically, it was other parts of the country where 13 lives were lost. Unlike the violent storm in Sussex in October 1987, which occurred at night, this one continued during daylight hours and swept over most of the Country. Within Sussex a large numbers of trees were uprooted, large lorries were blown over which resulted in many blocked roads. Power cables were blown down and could not be repaired for some days. When we actually completed the walk on Saturday some 4,000 + homes, in the north of England, were still without electricity and would not be reconnected until, at the earliest, Monday morning.

The Lamb

I eventually caught up with Ron on Thursday night. He had made a decision. We are to walk from Ripe to Chalvington and back to Ripe. Depending on the weather it would be a 9-mile hike, which would include Michelham Priory or a 2½-mile circular stroll and a meal at The Lamb. I'm, obviously, hoping for the shorter distance.

Saturday morning and the wind is still blowing and the rain is persistent. I pick Ron up from the usual place and the rain stops. The drive to Ripe is short and discussion is limited.

England have lost a cricket match against the Australians, again, The Kings Head, South Road is becoming a busy little pub again and Ron can't wait to have a look at two churches he didn't know existed.

We decide to park close to The Lamb and make our way straight to Ripe church. Although we walk past the church, on the return part of the walk, we thought we would be 'muddied up' by then and wouldn't be able to go inside, with dirty boots. "It'll add another mile ter the walk," says Ron, "'cause we 'ave ter walk back ter The Lamb ter start the walk."

St John the Baptist Church

The actual 2½-mile walk is Route 35, published by East Sussex County Council's Rights of Way Team[167]. You can download all of their walks by visiting www.eastsussex.gov.uk and going to the walk section or you can pick up the leaflets from various places including libraries, tourist information centres and council offices.

The St John the Baptist church at Ripe is not mentioned in the Domesday Book. The first record of the church is in 1291 when it was taxed by Pope Nicholas IV and is also recorded in the Tax Roll of 1341. However, the Parish of Ripe is mentioned but in its more unusual name of Achiltone, nine portions of land are noted. Earl Herold owned much of the land until

---

[167] www.eastsussex.gov.uk/walks viewed 13/01/2007

October 1066 when he was killed at the Battle of Hastings. The church then came into the ownership of the Lewes Priory until 1539 when Henry VIII dissolved the monasteries[168].

A picturesque setting

From the church we walked back to The Lamb where we pick up the walk and head out, along a drive towards the countryside. Our instructions are to head along a gravel drive until we come to an enclosed path between two drives. It is obvious, from the debris lying in the path that the recent high winds have taken some of the dead wood from the trees. We follow the path through a gate and across a track until we reach a footbridge at the side of the road. The footbridge overlooks a small, brick built, bridge with two arches. Whether the two arches were to allow more or less water to flow or whether two arches made the bridge stronger we aren't too sure but the speed that the water was flowing was incredible. It was only this morning that we heard that the local water authority had lifted it's hosepipe ban. With the amount of water that had fallen out of the sky over the last few days lifting the ban was expected. Lets hope that the authorities can

Path by The Lamb

now keep the water we have without too much of it being lost through leakage in the underground pipes.

Once onto the road we are advised to turn sharp left, cross a small sleeper bridge and head, over a stile into a field. To our left is a small sewage works that has been discretely hidden by trees. The only reason we knew it was there was because it was shown on our map, otherwise we wouldn't have seen it. The views from this field are across open land to the South Downs and we think that the grass, seen very green in the photograph, is cut and used as turf. We cross this field and then bear right towards the field corner where we find a double stile and then follow the path towards a gate. Through this gate and along a little further we come to Langtye Lane where we turn left and walk along this quiet lane for about ½ a mile. We need to look for a bridleway on our left.

The massive Downs

Two-span bridge

Throughout all of our walks Ron has been a hive of information for me. With his sudden stops to look at, and point me towards, foxes, deer, skylarks and the odd kite I have been fascinated at how quickly, and precisely, he sees things. So I wasn't surprised when, suddenly, he stops me and points, but what I was surprised at was when he said, "look at that," pointing to the side of the road with his thumb stick, "'tis a pornographic book." He prods it with his stick. "Tis not a book at all, but a video thingie." "It's a DVD," I offer as Ron picks it up.

Fly tipping?

Langtye Lane

"The things people throw away," says Ron. "Perhaps we could have a competition an' use the video as a prize," he says. "What sort of questions are you going to set for someone to win a porn video?" I ask. Ron's got that silly grin on his face,

---

[168] Parish Church at Ripe, Leaflet purchased at the church

227

"I don't want to know," I quickly say, "but seeing as you haven't got a DVD player Ron, let alone a TV, I'd better take it home with me. Just for safe keeping, of course," and stuff it in my coat pocket as we walk on.

Approaching Church Farm

We came to a gap in the hedge but decided that this was not the bridleway we were looking for. A little further on we found the bridleway sign and turned left into a field. Along the lane, before the bridleway, both Ron and I had noticed rubbish dumped in the hedge. I believe it's called 'fly tipping' (?) but what we found, when we turned onto the bridleway, was rubbish just piled into a corner. Why do people have to do this to our beautiful countryside? Not only is it an eyesore but also it can attract vermin, which, in turn, can harbour disease.

We are now heading towards Church Farm, Chalvington and the wooden spire of the church, which, it is believed, is dedicated to Thomas ä Becket[169] can be seen above the farm

buildings. Looking to our left we can also see the spire of Ripe church. Both churches are less than a mile apart. We walk through the farmyard and come to the church, immediately on our left.

Chalvington church, like the church at Ripe, is first recalled, in writing, in 1291. Its turret is made of wood and used to lean, at a slight angle, after the storm of 1987. But, thanks to fund raising together with generous grants, repairs were undertaken in 1991/92. When the bell frame in the turret was removed for repair a sole from a child's shoe was discovered dating from the time the bells were originally hung, and when the tower was added to the church.

To enter the churchyard you pass through a metal gate, which is dedicated to the fallen men of the parish during the two great wars.

Chalvington Church gate

A few days before this walk one of our 'followers' told us about a headstone that we should look out for. A young man had died after being kicked by a horse. The stone was easy to find, right by the path leading to the door. The memorial reads[170]:

In Memory of
JOB, SON OF
BENJAMIN & ELIZABETH GUY
WHO DEPARTED THIS LIFE
BY A KICK FROM A HORSE
17TH APRIL 1878
AGED 8 YEARS 2 WEEKS

Tombstone

Thankfully the church was open to the public because inside this small church is, as always, that smell. I have to say that this church is not only what I call a 'sit down' church but a church that I would happily attend. It has an atmosphere that I haven't felt for some time. I must be honest and say that I sat, and prayed. I have not been affected in this way for many years. I felt humble and can confess to shedding a tear. People who know me will realise that I am not a religious person but standing inside this little church made me feel strange. Perhaps 'strange' is not the right word but I certainly felt 'something'.

Leaving the church we are met by a lady, "What a lov'ly church," says Ron, "an' thank you fer keepin' it open." "Yes," she replies, "we are very lucky. I'm just going in to turn the heating on for tomorrow's Sunday's service." "We noticed that each pew has an electric heater running along its back. That must make the place warm and cosy during the winter." "It does," she replies to me, "but it takes a long time to get the temperature up. That's why I have to switch it on, on Saturday. Have you signed the visitors' book?" "We certainly 'ave,"

---

[169] Parish Church at Chalvington, Leaflet purchased at the church
[170] Transcribed from tombstone inside churchyard at Chalvington

says Ron, " a very lov'ly couple o' villages, Chalvington and Ripe, an' I can remember playin' cricket at the Yew Tree." Ron then produces a score sheet from the very match, played on the 9th August 1970 against Laughton which shows Ron 'going in' at number 6, and scoring 56 not out. I have to say I'm impressed, even if the person completing the sheet can't spell or add up correctly?

Church interior

A little story that Ron related was that J. Brett (number 11 on the score card) was 74 years old when this game was played. Ron contacted the Cricket Association to see if he was the oldest cricketer in Sussex. But there was a man of 78 still playing village cricket. Mr Brett was known as 'pecker' because he always stood at the crease tapping his bat on the ground. When he sadly passed away his last wish was that his ashes should be scattered on the wicket. His son, standing at the crease, opened the urn, containing his departed dad's ashes. Just as he tipped the urn a sudden gust of wind took the ashes and covered his son, from head to toe. The only thing his son could say was "dad always had to have the last laugh."

We leave the church at the other end of the churchyard by way of another gate. This one is dedicated to Sub-Lt Trevor Bayley R.N. who was lost on HMS Martin on 10th November 1942 aged 21. We now head across more fields, with Ripe church in front of us. I will admit to looking back at Chalvington Church as we walk away and I still have strange feelings for that beautiful church.

The field we now cross is being used for turf. Machines are left by the church wall,

Rear gates

waiting for operators on Monday morning. The open surroundings and peacefulness just hits you. I am finding it very difficult to explain my true feelings in words. So I will stop now.

We had a meal at The Lamb Inn. Before we started this walk we were told that the place was very expensive and full of 'hooray henries'. But we did not experience that at all. Julian and Claire made us feel very welcome. The log fire was burning and the olde worlde charm of the place has to be seen to be believed. The meal – well, Ron couldn't finish his because it was too much, "must 'ave

been over a pound o' liver on that plate an' the gravy was beautiful." What finished Ron was the large plate of vegetables that came with his liver and bacon. My lasagne was very tasty and I was beginning to struggle with my meal, which included four large slices of garlic bread as well as a side salad. The price – very reasonable and the surroundings were a delight. Both Ron and I would recommend The Lamb Inn at Ripe to anyone.

We have now come to the point where I am looking at books and maps for our last walk. In a way it is a sad

Back to Ripe Church

time for both of us. I will admit that part of me is glad that it is coming to an end. My weekends will be mine again and I will not have to sit in front of a computer screen writing, and re-writing, and re-wording these pages. Yet it is something we have been doing for a year, and, of course, I will miss the walks, the scenery, the little jokes and finding out things about Sussex that I didn't know. Only last week, one of our original followers read one of our walks and admitted that I had told him something that he didn't know about Sussex. Just that one person saying that to me has made the last 51 weeks worth every effort.

I will meet Ron, on Monday, and discuss our last walk. I am still looking for something 'typically' Sussex. I have some ideas, but I'm still undecided.

By the way, does anyone want to buy a DVD?

WALK 52 – Woods Corner

Saturday 27th January 2007

For once I am unable to decide where to go for our last walk. I have been looking for something typically Sussex. But what, and where? I have considered Goodwood the home of horse racing in Sussex. But I've noticed that Ron hasn't been doing too well, with the gee gee's. I've thought about Hove, the home of Sussex Cricket, but cricket isn't one of Ron's favourite topics at the moment. My wife came up with the idea of a walk around Harvey's Brewery when chatting about my dilemma. Now that seemed a very good idea. Ron always drinks Harvey's[171] and Harvey's have been brewing in Sussex since 1794[172]. It was John Harvey (1784-1862) who established The Bridge Warf Brewery at its present site, on the River Ouse overlooking Cliffe Bridge, Lewes. Perhaps some tasting could be arranged? But

Ron's place of worship - Harvey's Brewery

little problems seemed to be in the way. We needed to complete our walk on Saturday, which may mean extra staff (?) and Health and Safety issues would not permit Ron and me to be let loose with all that alcohol. Despite the valiant efforts of both Helen and Lyn (thanks for trying) it was not to be. I did receive a phone call from Harvey's apologising for not being able to help us out.

So, on Monday evening, I was still not sure where to go. Not only did I need 'something Sussex' but I also needed it to be meaningful. A visit to the place where Sussex trugs are made has also been suggested. Good idea but...... Through the week I resorted to the Internet.

I typed in 'oldest', 'newest', 'strangest' and 'typical Sussex' into the search engine but didn't come out with any interesting places to go that we hadn't already walked. The majority of 'hits' involved Brighton University but, undaunted, I continued my search until eventually; I'd had enough, and went back to my old books. After all, they had served me well over the last 51 walks. There must be somewhere we could spend a few hours.

Some may remember my disappointment with The Battle of Hastings walk (Walk 17). Apart from the town of Battle being closed because of some criminal activity and having to complete the walk starting at Sedlescombe, I wasn't pleased with not getting close to where the action was in 1066. However, a book given to me by my daughter[173] has another walk, which does take in the area of this famous battle, so I am tempted to revisit the area. And who, in the whole country, doesn't associate the Battle of Hastings with Sussex?

Battle Church - Closed

But after much deliberation and thought I have decided that we will visit Dallington. Woods Corner to be exact. Why did I make this decision? To be honest I was getting desperate. It was Thursday and I still hadn't decided. It was to be our last walk and the last walk in a book we had used over the past 51 weeks[174] was Dallington. So the last walk in that book would also be the last walk in mine. It seemed a bit ironic and it appealed to my sense of humour. And, like I said, I was desperate.

The Swan Inn at Woods Corner is one of the oldest pubs in Sussex [1300's] and is located just outside Dallington, Nr Heathfield. The villagers strongly believe that a Dallington man

---

[171] Picture from http://www.allaboutsussex.co.uk/default.asp?id=picturegallery79 visited 23/01/07

[172] http://www.harveys.org.uk/lay200yearsa.htm visited 23/01/07

[173] Walks into History - Sussex

[174] Pub Walks in East Sussex by Mike Power

fought alongside General George Custer at his infamous Last Stand against the Sioux Indian at The Battle of the Little Big Horn[175] in 1876.

Dallington was also the home of war hero, the late Captain 'Mac' (real name George Douglas Machin) who was a camouflage expert and served his country as a balloon observer during World War 1 and was awarded the DFC (Distinguished Flying Cross). Later in life he gained fame as a cartoonist for his work on the soldiers' newspaper 'Blighty' His output was prolific and his signature, 'Mac', appeared on drawings in scores of publications.

The Swan Inn

The church at Dallington appears to have been dedicated twice. Once to St. Giles, and once, to St Margaret. The parishioners know the church as St Giles but the little pamphlet purchased at the church is a little confusing. The spire is a rarity in Sussex as it is tiled with stone.

And, finally, at precisely 1.55pm on September 28th 1940 a young pilot, Flying Officer Peter Guerin Crofts, bailed out of his aeroplane (a Hurricane) before it crashed at Earls Down. The young officer landed at South View Farm, Dallington, but died from his wounds. His mother had a memorial cross erected on the exact spot where he fell.

Now that must be enough history for everyone?

The walk is described, in our instructions, as '...pretty...fairly good underfoot but can be a bit muddy during wet weather'. [176]It also gives the distance as 3 miles.

You will not be surprised when I tell you that fancy dress is to be worn. 'Fancy Dress' is not a fair description. Some time ago it was suggested that we should dress in Sussex Smocks. My wife, bless, has gone to enormous lengths to make both Ron and I a smock each. So it is with this clothing that Ron and I meet at the usual place to commence our final walk. To my surprise some of our followers are at The Kings Head, to see us off and take photographs. Lyn is to be our official picture taker and

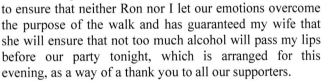
We set off in our smocks

to ensure that neither Ron nor I let our emotions overcome the purpose of the walk and has guaranteed my wife that she will ensure that not too much alcohol will pass my lips before our party tonight, which is arranged for this evening, as a way of a thank you to all our supporters.

Ron's not too sure

The drive to Woods Corner only took a few minutes and the parking space, down the lane opposite The Swan was no problem to find.

We walk down the lane and head towards the entrance to Deep Park Wood, which is on our right. We were a little confused here because there is also a recycling yard on the right but beady-eyed Lyn noticed the sign leading us to the track, which was more than 'bit muddy'. Lyn was heard to utter four expletives within the first 100 yards and the going was a little difficult as we pass a small pond.

Wading through the mud

All along this uphill and downhill path was hard work. Where horses used the path they had churned up the mud and made the path much more difficult to keep your footing. But we

[175] http://villagenet.co.uk/esussex-iron/villages/dallington.php visited 25/01/07
[176] *Pub Walks in East Sussex* by Mike Power (Dorset, Power Publications) Page 96

The exit of Deer Park Wood

Road to Burwash

Felled wood?

battled on seeing, the funny side of one of us falling base over apex and sliding back down to the bottom of the hill. But you could rest assured that Ron wouldn't let go of his carrier bag!

From what felt like miles, but was probably only a few yards, we turn left, onto another track. Here we meet a couple out walking their dogs. I'm sure that, seeing the way Ron and I were dressed, they must have thought something. But it didn't help when Lyn said, "Don't worry, your safe all the time I'm with them. I'm just taking them for a short walk as part of my helping in the community scheme." For some reason they appeared to be reassured by Lyn's comments and asked us where we were heading. When I showed him the map he gave us some advice on which way to head but assured us that it was longer than 3 miles.

We eventually emerge from the wood and meet a lane where we turn right and then left, along the signposted to Burwash. On our left should be '*a recently felled bluebell wood*', according to our instructions. But as you can see it must have grown again since our instruction book was printed.

After 100 paces, Lyn said it was actually 118, but whose counting (?), we again turn left and follow the lane until we reach a signpost directing us left, across a field. Over the past few days this area was not so lucky as Hailsham, with the weather. Although today is mild it is still evident that snow has fallen up on these hills. Yet, as I say, it is surprisingly warm. You could definitely think that it is later in the year. Whilst it is warm it is still very wet and muddy through our next set of pathways.

We follow the signs across the field towards a stile. Once across the stile we immediately turn right and follow a twisting path through woodland until we reach a concrete driveway. Lyn actually got stuck in the mud along this stretch but, although photographs have been taken and they are in my possession for later use, I will spare her blushes. I will admit that her language, on this occasion was perfect.

Wet and muddy

The signs along this walk are easily found and the walk is, obviously, well-used, so finding our way about was not difficult. The only problem we did encounter was the mud. Oh, and a few hills, which were steep in places but are not mentioned in our instruction book.

The concrete drive descends to a wooden bridge over a stream, and not for the first time on our walks, Lyn and Ron insist on playing Pooh sticks. This picture shows Ron racing across the bridge so that he could see his stick arrive at the other side first. He didn't gloat, much. But we heard about his victory for the next few minutes. Ron always throws a coin into the water when we come to any bridge on our walks and this one was no different. "Did you make a wish?" asks Lyn, "O' course," is his usual reply whenever I ask the same question and, again, today was no different.

Pooh sticks again

We continue along the drive and come to a lane. We cross the lane and head for the path opposite, skirting past a house with the gorgeous smell of home cooking. This path leads us into another field were we follow the edge of a wood. We walk along the edge of this wood until we reach yet another track which eventually brings you us onto the road by a very large house, called Brooklands, were we turn left and head towards Dallington village.

A photo opportunity

Here is the first mention of a steady climb. But I'm sure Lyn will tell that it was anything but steady. It was steep. At the top of the hill is Dallington Church. I'm not sure what to say here. I really do not wish to upset the parishioners of this church but there is something missing. That old smell is there, it's cold just like a church should be but............ Lyn thought that the place was unloved. And, strangely, there may be some truth in that statement. It looked as if the church wasn't used. There wasn't evidence that people actually attended. There were no hymn numbers on display by the pulpit, no bible on the rostrum. Yet the place had that simple, basic beauty. The stain glass windows are fantastic. But there is nothing else. I'm, afraid it did nothing for me at all. Which is a shame, because it just shouldn't be like that, should it? When you read the leaflet[177] purchased at the church you discover how the church is steeped in history, with wonderful

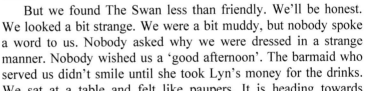
Stained glass

facts and historical references but I am very sorry, parishioners of Dallington, I was left feeling nothing.

It is but a short walk along the path and out onto the road that will lead us to The Swan and, hopefully, some refreshment. We arrive at The Swan Inn with yet more disappointment. I left my lights on the car and the battery is flat. Luckily I parked on one of the not mentioned hills so managed to roll it down and got it started. But not before we had sampled the hospitality of The Swan.

But we found The Swan less than friendly. We'll be honest. We looked a bit strange. We were a bit muddy, but nobody spoke a word to us. Nobody asked why we were dressed in a strange manner. Nobody wished us a 'good afternoon'. The barmaid who served us didn't smile until she took Lyn's money for the drinks. We sat at a table and felt like paupers. It is heading towards February and Christmas lights are still up, apart from one garland, which had been rolled up and placed in the clear plastic wrapper, but left switched on (?) flashing on and off. The food, whilst we saw nobody eating, must have been excellent because asking the prices that were displayed on the boards the portions must have been the size of your average banquet. The same meal, eaten by Ron at The Lamb at Ripe, was three times as expensive in this place. Needless to say we drank up and left and headed straight for The Kings Head.

The reception we got here, ok it is our local, was amazing. Even people we had never seen in the bar before had time for a chat and a laugh. And that is the way that it should be.

Sadly, we have come to the end of our walks. We have walked, on average, 6 miles every week throughout this year. Some have been a lot longer, mainly because we got lost; some have been shorter, for the very same reason. But, if you use an average of 6 miles each walk, Ron and I have both completed over 310 miles. Not bad since it was only supposed to be two mates going for a walk.

Whilst I am writing these last few words I can remember, earlier today, as we walk along the road, up yet another hill, heading towards The Swan Inn, Lyn asks, "When we get to the crossroads, is it 'Left or Right, Ron?'" So now you all know why the book is called what it is. Because we have no idea, until we get there!

---

[177] Dallington Church by W Hewett, leaflet purchased at the church

WALK EXTRA

There are times, sometimes more often than I would like, that the mouth engages before the brain has chance to get in gear. This is common when, on a Monday night, I have tended to let the amber nectar flow a little too readily. It is always when I don't have to drive. I have a wonderful daughter, Michelle, who takes me to and collects me from The Kings Head on Monday and Friday nights when I'm not working. It's heaven, but sometimes I let my mouth go and suggest that Ron and I do something out of the ordinary. In a way I blame Ron as much as myself. He never stops me. So, the following are just a few of the 'other walks' I have talked us both in to.

Sponsored Walk

Guide dogs are wonderful animals. They cost a lot to buy and even more to train, but the work they perform is outstanding. A lot of the money raised to purchase these dogs is by donations from members of the public. A local charity that has been going for years is 'The Milk and Ale Club'. First founded by milkmen in Hailsham who liked a drink and frequented The Grenadier. They decided to raise money for this worthy cause by various means. One of

Photo call before the start

the ways is a sponsored walk. Here enters Ron and me. Of course we will take part. It's on a Sunday, no problem. It's only eight miles, that's a doddle. My son and daughter-in-law have been very busy over the last week so I volunteered our services to take Tess and Pip for our eight-mile walk. We all meet up at the pub, signed in, and received a complimentary pint from the landlord and a printed card to carry with us, before we head off. Ron, Lyn and me keep together. We are advised that marshals will be on route to ensure 'fair play' and to sign our cards (People actually cheat when doing this??).

The whole walk, to Polegate and back, is carried out along the 'Cuckoo Trail', which is described in some of our other walks, so I will not be repeating any descriptions. Suffice to say that the company and conversation were pleasant and we met the marshals along the route, had our cards signed and we reached the pub, in Polegate, in good time. The dogs loved it.

After a short rest, we completed the return journey, arriving back at The Grenadier for another complimentary pint and a burger. I must say that the landlord at The Grenadier was very generous and made us feel extremely welcome, even though Ron and me are not regulars to his pub. Each walker was then presented with a certificate of achievement as well as a medal to prove to anyone that the deed was done. The three of us managed to raise over £400 towards this well-loved cause, bringing the total collected by 'The Milk and Ale Club', for this year, to over £5,000. Which, we are told, is only enough to buy and train one guide dog.

A welcome half way stop

To date, 'The Milk and Ale Club', have raised £111,000 (One hundred and eleven thousand pounds!!) to purchase and train over one hundred and five (yes that's 105) dogs. A truly outstanding achievement that Ron and I had great pleasure being part of. Perhaps we should make it a regular thing. We'll have to see if we will be invited to take part next year.[178]

---

[178] Pictures for guide dog walk taken and supplied by Ben. (Teresa's husband – see next chapter)

Horse Riding

Regulars will be aware of my fear of most animals. So how did we volunteer for horse riding? I'm not sure how it actually came about until one of our horsy friends told me that she was trying to arrange a riding session for both Ron and me. How could this be happening? I

I'm not built to be a jockey!

am terrified of horses. Especially big ones. As time went on our friend was finding it more and more difficult to get someone to agree to let two total strangers, and novices, ride their prize stallions. Can you blame them? Problems became bigger problems and our friend was having so much difficulty in arranging this that we told her not to worry herself any more about it. I thought that Ron and me were in the clear when along comes Lyn whose daughter, Teresa, just happens to work in a stables. She has worked with horses since she was sixteen so knows what she's talking about. God, how unlucky can we be? It's all arranged. On Tuesday 24th October at 12.15 we are to be at St Francis Farm Stables, Bexhill-on-Sea. Ron is threatening to lynch me if I don't keep my mouth shut in future and Lyn tells us that her

daughter has lined up an ex-race horse, which is old, but very big. I can't sleep at night and Ron has now stopped talking to me.

The morning of the 24th arrives far to quickly. "Have some breakfast before you go," suggests the wife. I decline the offer of a fry-up. My stomach is already performing somersaults and the butterflies are having a gangbang. I felt awful. My first thought was to phone and cancel. But people were expecting us to do this. There was no way out. Put on a brave face, swallow your pride and go for it. After all, what is the worse that could happen? No don't think about that!!

I met Ron and Lyn outside The Kings Head, as arranged. Lyn is as bubbly as ever. Ron looks how I feel. Awful. Of course I'm not worried, I tell them both. It'll be a piece of cake. The journey to the stables is completed in near silence. Unfortunately it is very easy to find. But when I pull up no-one is here to meet us. "We could always just go home," I suggest. Pretend it didn't happen. But Lyn insists that we find Teresa in the stables. But first we have to negotiate the wild geese. "Best guard dogs to 'ave on any farm, are them geese," says Ron. All we've got to do is get past them. "Just don't let 'em see yer scared," he prompts. As if that's the easiest thing in the world, right now.

In the stables we meet Teresa. She's busy doing what people in stables do at this time of day and apologises for not being ready. Another opportunity to back out stares me in the face, but she then tells me that she'll only be a minute and she'll be off to get 'Beaver', who is to be our horse, who is in a field doing what horses

Ron thought covering his eyes might help or is it just a pose?

do? Before she goes to collect 'Beaver' she tells us that he's 20 years old, just over 15 hands high (1 hand = 4 inches which makes Beaver just over 5 foot tall?) and a little darling. Both Ron and I look at Lyn.

When he arrived 'Beaver' looked every part of a plodder. I was so relieved to see him for what he was. A gentle, lovely animal. We made a fuss of him in his stable while Teresa prepared him for what was about to come. Teresa then kitted me out with the obligatory hardhat, explained safety issues, asked me if I'd ever ridden before and explained all that was about to happen. We walked around the yard in a large circle whilst Teresa talked to both

Safe, and back on terra firma

'Beaver' and me. Although the first impression, when you get on a horse, is that you will fall off because everything feels loose, I began to grow in confidence. Teresa explained how to steer 'Beaver' in the direction I wanted him to go and how to stop and start him. How to praise him, when he did well, and how to treat him as we rotated around the course, in circles, or in figure of eight. I had a great time. Teresa didn't expect too much of me or 'Beaver' and I must thank her for quashing some, but not all, of my fears of horses.

Seeing that I didn't have to go over jumps or gallop at high speeds seemed to give Ron the confidence to 'have a go' too. The same format was carried out with Ron, Teresa and 'Beaver' and I'm sure Ron enjoyed it as much as I did. Back in his stable, 'Beaver' was made a fuss of again and both Ron and I gave him a carrot to eat before he was let back into the field he came from.

Both Ron and I would like to thank Teresa for her understanding, patience, and knowledge in telling us about 'Beaver' and the many things discussed about horses, including freeze branding and micro chips as well as arranging for Ron and me to take part in this little 'lesson'. As for Lyn, she has a lot to answer for in winding us up about the size and masculinity of the horse. For that alone we will get our own back. Sometime.

Ice Skating

Every year, just before Christmas, Hailsham holds, what is known as, 'Cracker Night'.

The dynamic trio

The High Street is closed to all traffic from the middle of the afternoon, and the shopkeepers stay open until late in the evening. The evenings that I have attended, over the past few years have included street stalls and minstrels and have been well attended by not only Hailsham residents but also people from nearby villages and towns. All in all, everyone has a good time. This year, a few days before 'Cracker Night', they have decided to erect, if that's the right word, an artificial ice rink. The evening I was informed of this fact prompted me to offer Ron and me to 'have a go'.

"Don't be bloody stupid," says Ron, "I aven't been on ice skates fer over thirty years." "The last time I skated was when there was a rink at Hastings. Underground, on the seafront it was. My children must have been around ten years old so that would have been twenty years ago," I reply, "it'll be interesting to see if we can still do it." "Probably break somethin' more like," says Ron, but I noticed it didn't take too much persuasion. Lyn also offered to come along for support. Our original plan was do this in the evening, but that meant losing valuable drinking time so I changed the time to 2 o'clock in the afternoon, before the children come out of school, less people to poke fun at us.

Ron has been moaning about the skating for a number of days prior to the day of the skating and I was a little surprised to see that he had turned up. What made it worse was that I was a little late getting to the 'rink' and Ron must have thought that I had chickened out. The look on his face when he saw me was a picture to behold.

The 'ice rink' turned out to be some hard, white, plastic squares, laid on the ground with a barrier around the outside to stop you from heading down the High Street. I first noticed the St Johns Ambulance people in attendance and prayed a short prayer that they would not be needed. The price for this experiment in stupidity was £5. My first thought was that it was excessive, but we are informed that if we retain our tickets we can go back later. "Don't be stupid," comments Ron, "you don't think I'll be comin' back to do this again, do yer?"

Ron tries speed skating

We each paid our £5 and were supplied with skates. Now I can remember, back to my skating days in Hastings, that the skates should be done up reasonably tight, so that the foot didn't move in the boot and that both ankles were supported. You couldn't do that with these boots. They were too stiff and new and even after going on and off the 'ice' to try and tighten them it was impossible. Rose, a friend of Lyn's from darts was seconded to take photos of the event and within half an hour had taken over thirty pictures of what is now known to be Robin (not Ron) Cousins and Torville and Dean. However, modesty will not let me reveal what Lyn was making a grab for in our pirouette.

At the end, Ron and Lyn really enjoyed it and wanted to return later. I found the experience a little difficult. The thought of falling and breaking something was always in the back of my mind. Unfortunately, or luckily, for me I had to return to work so wouldn't be having a re-run on the 'rink'.

As you can see, from the pictures, the 'rink' was a little empty at 2 o'clock. Ron did go past it later in the afternoon and it was packed with skaters of all ages. Perhaps, next year it will be a bit bigger. If there is to be an event next year?

What have you got hold of, Lyn?

Finally?????

A whole year of walks, covering different areas of Sussex, has been completed. We also touched on other places but, in the main, Sussex is the place.

During this time we have been asked, by many people, which of the walks we enjoyed the most. Ron will say that he enjoyed them all. But all for different reasons. "Each one 'as been different," he says, "different scenery, different 'istory with different people ter chat too." But along the way I will admit to one or two favourites and one or two I really didn't enjoy. I found going to West Hoathly, my ancestors' birthplace, both fascinating and sentimental. The beautiful village of Slindon, with its connection to Hilaire Belloc, was a delightful walk. The tour of Lewes, with our knowledgeable guide Roz, was the complete historical tour. The memories and thoughts for Ron when we visited Pluckley in Kent, where Ron's mum and dad met, all those years ago, will always be with me. Playing 'Pooh sticks' in Ashdown Forest. Wadhurst on Remembrance Sunday, the visit to Chalvington church will always bring back fond memories. Unfortunately the walk around Berwick I found less than pleasing and I, personally, was not impressed with Firle. The soaking we got at Winchelsea didn't help us along what could have been a pleasing stroll. One of the things I would have enjoyed was completing a walk in the snow. Unfortunately this couldn't happen. But, I must admit that the majority of walks we have completed were interesting and enjoyable and both Ron and I hope that recounting our findings along our way have been amusing to you all as well as being a little informative. As I have always said, while someone reads the draft copy of the walk, if that person smiles, at some stage whilst reading the chapter, I'm happy. And I am pleased to say that I have witnessed some smiles during the year.

Obviously Ron and I have only touched on a few of the walks around Sussex. But we hope that you have enjoyed us, enjoying them.

One thing I must mention is the guidebooks we have used throughout our walks. The instructions from these are, without doubt, very explicit. What was disappointing for us was the poorly kept signs and paths along some, but not all, of our routes. The standing joke throughout the year was that we could get lost or 'geographically misplaced' very easily. But some of our walking companions can vouch for us that the signs and paths along our way have not been clearly marked. In some cases the signs are non-existent. Perhaps this could be our next project, working for the local councils mending signposts?

I have managed to obtain, via the Internet, a copy of a plan, by East Sussex Council, which lists improvement ideas and suggestions for our footpaths and bridleways. Should the council achieve half of what they propose, it must be an improvement.

What to do now? We really don't know. The first thing is to try, very hard, to get these pages published. If you are reading this, in book form with a front cover, we have accomplished one of our aims.

Right from the start I wanted to lose some weight and I have lost over a stone during the year. So this is another accomplishment. I have learnt a lot about my home county. Not just from Ron but from so many sources, by simply looking and listening. Towards the end of the year it was not easy to continue. At times, I have found it very difficult, not only completing the walk but also writing about it. But the encouragement from so many of our friends has made this all worthwhile.

To say I'm not sorry that it has come to an end would, in many ways, be far from the truth. Yes, I will miss meeting up with Ron. I will miss, very much, the banter at The Kings Head, when each of the walks has been completed. But more than this I will miss the discovery of a new, currently unknown fact about this beautiful county of Sussex that both Ron and I are so pleased to call home. So am I really sorry that it has come to an end? Of course I am. But, perhaps, this isn't the end. Who knows?